June '86

To Roz and Russ
Scott and Robin —

Thanks so much for being some of my best fans, ... well for buying this book retail, and a ... price yet! (Next time, I'll get it for you wholesale!!!) It's also great to share some time with all of you — my family, and I really look forward to our reunions."

I hope you enjoy this book, and that your holiday table is always laden with delectable Jewish (and low fat!) dishes.

"B'tayavon"!

Gloria —

Other books by Gloria Kaufer Greene
(with Nancy Baggett and Ruth Glick)

Don't Tell 'Em It's Good for 'Em
Eat Your Vegetables!

THE
JEWISH HOLIDAY
COOKBOOK

THE
JEWISH HOLIDAY
COOKBOOK

An International Collection
of Recipes and Customs

GLORIA KAUFER GREENE

Times BOOKS

Some of the recipes contained in this book previously appeared in modified form in the *Baltimore Jewish Times*.

Library of Congress Cataloging in Publication Data

Greene, Gloria Kaufer, 1950–
The Jewish holiday cookbook.

Includes index.
1. Cookery, Jewish.   2. Fasts and feasts—Judaism.
I. Title.
TX724.K392   1985   641.59'2'924   85-40437
ISBN 0-8129-1224-1

Coordinating Editor: Rosalyn T. Badalamenti

Designed by Janis Capone

Illustrations by Linda Tunney

Manufactured in the United States of America

9   8   7   6   5   4   3   2

First Edition

To my husband, Geoff, for being a sounding board when I felt insecure, for enduring many months of utterly eclectic meals, for cleaning dishes and doing laundry, for baby-sitting above and beyond the call of duty, and—most of all—for constantly encouraging and supporting me every step of the way, from the conception of this book until its completion and publication.

To my sons, Dylan and Trevor, for their lavish praise and hearty appetites whenever I tested a recipe, and for their wonderful patience at those times that this book just had to come first.

To my parents, Hindy and Irv Kaufer, for lovingly passing down to me the Jewish culinary heritage that they inherited from their own parents and grandparents. May the chain continue unbroken for generations to come . . .

ACKNOWLEDGMENTS

Several people have given of themselves in one way or another to help make this book a reality.

For encouraging me to write hundreds of innovative cooking columns that eventually became the inspiration for this book, I would like to thank Charles A. ("Chuck") Buerger, publisher of the *Baltimore Jewish Times,* Gary Rosenblatt, editor, and, in particular, Barbara Pash, local news/style editor, as well as many readers of the *Baltimore Jewish Times.*

In addition, I want to thank those wonderful acquaintances and relatives who talked with me for hours, and generously shared with me some of their most cherished possessions—their family histories and their heirloom recipes.

Sharon Cantor Gordon told me about her husband Michael's upbringing in Cuba, and about the tasty dishes her late mother-in-law, Regina Gordon, used to prepare for the family.

Denise Saville Zandman, native of Wales and citizen of Israel, and her sabra husband, Dov Zandman, helped me with many Hebrew food terms, and described in detail the Israeli celebration of many Jewish holidays. They also introduced me to two excellent Jewish cooks—Denise's mother, Pauline Rubens Saville of Wales, and Dov's mother, Liora Ben-Chaim Zandman, originally from Libya.

Kibbutzniks Jill Cohen Schein and David Schein, Americans who made aliyah to Israel, told me about meals in the kibbutz dining room, where Jill has worked as manager.

Rabbi Joshua Toledano, spiritual leader of Congregation Mikveh Israel in Philadelphia, the city's oldest synagogue and its only Sephardic one still in existence, and executive director of the American Sephardi

Federation, spent many hours describing his youth in Morocco and also Sephardic holiday customs in general.

Both Ralph Ohayon and Ginette Rosilio Spier told me about their Jewish upbringings in Morocco, as did Danielle El-Maleh Mosse, who also lived in Algeria and France.

Ida Revah Dana, her husband Leon, son Silvio, and daughter-in-law Dulcie Drazin Dana, enlightened me on the delights of Turkish-Jewish food, and treated me to many wonderful dishes in their homes. They also paved the way for my visit (during a trip to Istanbul) with the warm and memorable Salfati family, who taught me about Turkish-Jewish cuisine *in situ*.

Rachel Muallem Gabes and her son, Marc Muallem, shared details of Jewish life in Iraq and Iran. Bellah Ini, her daughter-in-law Willma Bross Iny, and son, Tzadok Iny, let me in on more secrets of Iraqi-Jewish cuisine.

Judith and Morris Erger recalled for me their early lives in Czechoslovakia, where they once owned a delicatessen, and taught me some of the delicious Ashkenazic cuisine they first learned there.

I discovered much about Syrian-Jewish culinary culture and tasted many fantastic examples of it at the New Jersey home of Ginger Kassin, where I also spoke with Rachelle Cohen, Shelly Djmal, Poopa Dweck, Sarine Kattan, Nina Shamah, and Jackie Esses.

Sandra Waldman Kahane and her sister-in-law, Ida Kahane, told me about Jewish holidays and food in their native Colombia, South America, and in their new home, Israel.

Lily Livne also described Israeli customs and cuisine, as well as that of her birthplace, Egypt.

Rianne Melmed, from Capetown, South Africa, gave me fascinating information about South African-Jewish food, as well as a few hints on Scottish-Jewish cookery, which she learned from her mother-in-law, Ethel Melmed.

Leia Derera taught me about delectable Romanian-Jewish specialties.

Rupla Eshai, a friend of years past, introduced me to some Pakistani-Indian delights.

Kathy Van Echo offered many insights into the baking of all types of bread.

My mother, Helene ("Hindy") Kaplan Kaufer, not only taught me several of the recipes that appear in this book, but also told me wonderful family stories, especially those about her late maternal grandparents,

Rose and Harry Levine. My father, Irving Kaufer, reminded me of the culinary prowess of my late grandfather, Joseph Kaufer.

My paternal aunt, Hannah Kaufer Hafetz, and my cousin, Lynda Kaufer Newirth, filled me in with details of family history and recipes.

My cousin, Debra Saidman Egber, and her husband, Mitchell Egber, patiently taste-tested many of my recipes in their early stages, and offered helpful criticism.

Other people gave me help with this book that had little to do with food, but was essential in its own right.

My sisters, Terri Kaufer Mayers and Pamela Kaufer, shared with me wonderful, nostalgic remembrances of our childhood holiday celebrations.

Whenever I needed expert assistance on Yiddish wording, my mother-in-law, Freda Michaelson Greene Cantor, and her husband, Samuel Cantor, were always helpful.

Donna Ellis, food editor for Patuxent Publishing Corporation, carefully proofread the first draft of the manuscript, and gave me much useful advice.

Linda Hayes, of Columbia Literary Associates, provided support from the moment the idea of this book was conceived through the anguishing moments as deadline approached.

Very special thanks go to Kathleen Moloney, my editor at Times Books, for her utmost patience and faith in me, and also for offering encouragement and guidance when it was most needed. Her expertise was invaluable, as always.

In addition, my sincere gratitude goes to coordinating editor Rosalyn T. Badalamenti, who painstakingly sorted out every detail of the manuscript and brought it all together, to Tracy Bernstein for her very helpful editorial assistance, and to Janis Capone for expertly designing this book. I am also indebted to others at Times Books, including Sandee Brawarsky, Pam Lyons, Marjorie Anderson, and Linda Navarro.

Illustrator Linda Tunney provided the excellent drawings that add clarity and depth to several of my recipes.

Finally, and most of all, I want to thank those who were closest to me throughout both the ecstasies and difficulties of working on a project of this dimension—my dear husband, Geoffrey, and young sons, Dylan Joshua and Trevor Stanley. Their love and total support sustained me at all times, and made this book possible.

PREFACE

When I first became cooking editor of the *Baltimore Jewish Times* in 1980, I had no intention of writing a Jewish cookbook. I thought that the subject was already well covered. But, during the next few years, my extensive research on the subject of Jewish food taught me otherwise.

I found it necessary to peruse many volumes whenever I wanted to write an in-depth article about the culinary customs of any particular Jewish holiday. What I was able to glean from the available literature was often scanty or inconsistent; and most "traditional" holiday recipes were so vaguely written that they could hardly be followed by the uninitiated expert, let alone the novice cook.

Furthermore, the information was almost always about Ashkenazic (Eastern European-Jewish) cuisine. There was very little material available on the culinary heritage of the Sephardim (those Jews whose ancestors were generally from Spain or the Middle East).

I began to interview Jewish cooks who had immigrated to the United States from many different countries. Furthermore, whenever I traveled—to Israel, Turkey, Canada, and many other places—I made it a point to contact Jewish cooks.

During my trips and at home, I searched bookstores for obscure, out-of-print Jewish cookbooks. I also mail-ordered unusual cookbooks published by the sisterhoods of Jewish, particularly Sephardic, congregations.

I tested and adapted a multitude of Jewish recipes from all over the world and wrote out the very best with clear and precise directions, so that even the complicated techniques did not have to be learned at one's mother's knee.

When the results of all these endeavors began to appear in my cooking columns, the reader response was overwhelmingly positive and satisfying. I was repeatedly told that my recipes were excellent and easy to follow, and that my articles were interesting and informative—even by those who never touched a skillet.

Thus, I was inspired to collect and organize enough material for a comprehensive Jewish cookbook. This book is a fascinating reference for both Jews and non-Jews who want information on Jewish culinary culture. And, it provides practical, delectable recipes that can bring this culture to life in your own dining room. I hope it will fill a gap in current Jewish culinary literature and will give pleasure to all.

Columbia, Maryland   —Gloria Kaufer Greene
September 1985

CONTENTS

Introduction   3

A Note on Transliterations Used in This Book   10

A Word About Ingredients   11

1. SHABBAT   15

2. THE DAYS OF AWE: Rosh Hashanah Through
   Yom Kippur   61

3. SUKKOT (Including Hoshanah Rabbah),
   SHEMINI ATZERET, AND SIMHAT TORAH   105

4. HANUKKAH   147

5. TU B'SHEVAT   185

6. PURIM   204

7. PESACH (Passover)   237

8. YOM HA'ATZMAUT (Israel's Independence Day)
   AND YOM YERUSHALAYIM (Jerusalem Day)   287

9. LAG B'OMER   315

10. SHAVUOT   336

Index   377

THE
JEWISH HOLIDAY
COOKBOOK

INTRODUCTION

In recent years, international cooking and dining have become very chic among Americans. "Gourmets" with sophisticated palates are finally looking beyond classic French cuisine, and adding a whole world of ethnic foods to their culinary and gustatory repertoires. Yet Jewish cuisine has had an international flavor for more than two thousand years, ever since the beginning of the Diaspora. Early Jews were exiled from their homeland in Judea, first by the Assyrians and Babylonians, and later by Roman conquerors. By the year 300, Jews, who then numbered about three million, had settled in almost every part of the immense Roman Empire. From there, a constant succession of expulsions and dispersions, as well as voluntary migrations, eventually scattered Jews to most areas of the civilized world.

Throughout history, religious dietary laws, local customs, and limited finances have often put severe limitations on the types of foods available to Jews. Rather than stifling their culinary creativity, however, these restrictions have stimulated the Jewish people to develop an international kosher cuisine that is as delicious as it is diversified. No other single "nation" or ethnic group can claim such fantastic variety!

Indeed, Jewish cooks have always been resourceful. When they couldn't prepare a desirable dish, for whatever reason, they invariably found a way to make something else do. Thus, wherever they have lived, Jews have adapted the best and most available local foods in such a way as to make them distinctly Jewish. And, many times, they carried these specialties to other lands, where further modifications and improvements made the dish barely recognizable from the original.

So, then, just what is *Jewish cuisine?*

Until a decade ago, I thought it meant only the Ashkenazic foods that were the mainstay of my Jewish upbringing. Ashkenazim—those Jews whose ancestors dwelled primarily in Eastern and Central Europe—now comprise the vast majority of American Jewry. Thus, their cuisine is what most Americans—Jew and non-Jew alike—think of as "Jewish food." It includes chopped liver, pot-roasted brisket, chicken soup with matzo balls, kreplah, mandlen, kugel, tzimmes, blintzes, and latkes, to name just a few favorites. Most Ashkenazic dishes have Yiddish names, because that was once the common language spoken by all those who prepared them.

The term *Ashkenazim* comes from *Ashkenaz,* which is an old Hebrew word for "Germany." By the tenth century, Jews who had settled along the southern borders of Germany during Roman rule had migrated northward across the Alps and established the Ashkenazic tradition in Jewish centers along the Rhine River.

During the next several hundred years, however, periodic expulsions or flights from persecution, as well as migrations necessary for economic survival, brought the majority of these Jews to Poland and such nearby areas as Lithuania, Bohemia, and Russia. *Yiddish*—medieval German with some Hebrew and local vernacular thrown in—developed during this period.

The climate was, for the most part, cold and uncompromising, and food supplies in the *shtetls* (small villages), where most Ashkenazic Jews lived, were often quite meager. Nevertheless, cooks found ingenious ways to stretch whatever they had into tasty dishes that not only satisfied and sustained, but made life a bit more pleasant, as well.

When times were more prosperous, the Ashkenazim refined their cuisine and indulged in the luxuries of fresh fish, fruits, vegetables, sweets, and more. Migrations to the Austro-Hungarian Empire further influenced Ashkenazic cooking and introduced, among other things, elegant pastries and tortes.

When I became seriously involved in food writing, I began to learn about the "other type" of Jewish food—the kind prepared and prized by Sephardim. I did not, however, delve deeply into its mysteries until 1980, when I became cooking editor of the *Baltimore Jewish Times*.

In my weekly columns, particularly those about the Jewish holidays, I decided it would be interesting and culturally valuable to discuss not only Ashkenazic culinary customs, which most of my readers already knew, but also those of Sephardic origin. Naturally, I wanted to include traditional recipes from both heritages. This led to much research and recipe testing, during which I discovered a bounty of fascinating information about the foods eaten by the Sephardim.

Sephardic Jews form a far more heterogeneous group than their Ashkenazic brethren. Though they are often identified as "Jews who are not Ashkenazic," this definition is really too simplistic.

The Hebrew word *Sepharad* originally referred to an area of Asia where some exiled Jerusalemites went after the destruction of the First Holy Temple. During the Middle Ages, however, it came to mean Spain, and *Sephardim* were the Jews who lived there peacefully under Moslem rule for many centuries. After the heinous Spanish Inquisition, those Jews who had been expelled from the Iberian peninsula, and also all their descendants, became generally known as Sephardim, no matter where they eventually resettled.

Most of the deported Sephardim sailed eastward to the Balkans and central areas of the Ottoman Turkish Empire, where they and their extensive talents were needed and welcomed. Another large group made new homes along the northern coast of Africa, particularly in Morocco. Smaller numbers went to Italy and some Middle Eastern areas. Later, new Sephardic communities were established in other parts of the world, such as Holland and its colonies, several major cities of Europe, and even North America, whose first Jews were Sephardim.

During their brilliant "Golden Age" in Iberia, Sephardic Jewry had developed a sophisticated culture, complete with elaborate culinary skills. Throughout their exile, the Sephardim maintained many of these skills, while adapting their cuisine to local ingredients, and adding native cooking techniques to their own repertoire. In return, the Sephardim often had a positive influence on the cooking of the countries in which they resided.

As with Ashkenazic cuisine, climate also played an important role in the types of foods eaten. Sephardim have generally lived in warm areas with long, abundant growing seasons, and so an amazing variety of fresh vegetables and fruits is prominent in their cuisine. Also, foods are typically cooked in olive oil, not the rendered animal fat (or *schmaltz*) that was, of necessity, usually used by Ashkenazim.

The names of most Sephardic dishes reflect their conglomerate origins. Many are Judeo-Spanish, or *Judezmo*, as it is sometimes called. *Ladino*—the liturgical form of this language—is basically Castilian Spanish with some Hebrew mixed in. Like Yiddish, it is written in Hebrew characters. Over the centuries, conversational Judeo-Spanish has picked up many words from local languages, particularly Turkish. Thus, the transliterated Judeo-Spanish names of dishes often include words that resemble Spanish or Turkish words, but have slightly different spellings or pronunciations.

In addition to the true Sephardim, there is another group of non-Ashkenazic Jews, sometimes referred to as "Oriental Jews," whose ancestors never lived in Iberia or any part of Europe, but, rather, stayed in the Middle East or returned to it after they were deported from ancient Judea. Because this area has long been dominated by Arabs, the Jewish cuisine took on an Arabic flavor and many of the dishes have Arabic names.

Small, early communities of Jews were also established in the Near East, India, and even the Orient, as well as in some obscure regions. And, in each place, the local cuisine was absorbed and adapted.

The non-Ashkenazic Jews who have Iberian ancestors actually far outnumber those who don't. Thus, to simplify matters and avoid confusion, all of them are usually grouped together, in modern parlance, as "Sephardim."

Although the Sephardim and Ashkenazim have different culinary backgrounds, they are all Jews, with the ancient Hebrews as their common ancestors. Their cuisines, therefore, have the same primary basis—namely, the dietary rules, or laws of *kashrut*.

The word "kosher," or *kasher* in Hebrew, means "ritually fit." Thus, kosher food is simply fit for consumption according to Jewish law. The laws of *kashrut* are based on biblical injunctions, and any health value is considered to be coincidental. They have been followed by Jews, without question, for millennia, and have shaped Jewish cuisine in a truly unique fashion.

The laws specifically state which animals may be eaten and which may not. According to Leviticus, ". . . any animal that has true hoofs, with clefts through the hoofs, and that chews the cud—such you may eat." Cattle and sheep are thus permitted, for example, but pigs, rabbits, and horses are not. Also, ". . . anything in water, whether in the seas or in the streams, that has fins and scales—these you may eat." Thus, most vertebrate fish are permitted, but shellfish are not.

Almost all "crawling" and "swarming" things, such as reptiles and most insects, are also forbidden, as are certain enumerated birds (and their eggs), "animals that walk on paws," and any animal that has died of disease or natural causes.

Permitted animals and birds (but not fish) must be ritually slaughtered in a manner which ensures both that the animal dies as quickly and as painlessly as possible and that most of the blood drains from the animal's carcass. After being slaughtered, the carcass is examined to certify that the animal was healthy.

The consumption of blood is absolutely forbidden. Therefore, shortly after butchering, raw meat must be soaked in water, treated with coarse salt, and drained well; then it must be thoroughly rinsed to ensure that all possible blood has been removed. This process is called *kashering*. Because it is impossible to kasher liver in this manner, it must be broiled instead. Broiling is considered an alternative to salt kashering, and may also be used with other cuts of meat. (Fish does not need kashering of any type.)

Also forbidden are certain fats and the sciatic nerves and connected tendons in the hindquarters of permitted animals. Dissecting these parts out of the meat is difficult and time consuming; therefore, in the United States, the hindquarters are virtually always sold to non-kosher butchers. However, in Israel and some other countries, where meat is relatively scarce and expensive, the tedious dissection is done, and kosher cuts from the hindquarters are thus available.

A strict prohibition against eating meat and dairy (that is, milk products) together in any form comes from the biblical statement, "You shall not boil a kid in its mother's milk." This injunction is repeated twice in Exodus and once in Deuteronomy. To ensure that the law will not be violated, all kitchen equipment, utensils, and dishes used to prepare and eat meat must be kept completely separate from those used for dairy.

Certain foods are considered to be neither meat nor dairy, and are "neutral" or *pareve* (pronounced "pahr-vuh" or "par-reh-vuh"). This category includes all fruits, vegetables, and grains—that is, anything that grows from the earth—as well as eggs and fish. Because they are "neutral," *pareve* foods may be mixed with either meat or dairy products. (It is a long-established custom, however, for many Jews not to cook fish and meat together or eat them from the same dish, though they may be included in separate courses of the same meal.)

For convenience, all the recipes in this book have been designated (P) for *pareve*, (M) for meat, or (D) for dairy.

In addition, the recipes have been categorized, in chapters, according to the Jewish holiday (*hag* or *yom tov,* in Hebrew) when they would be most appropriately served. Of course, most of the dishes are so appealing and versatile that it is unnecessary to restrict them to certain holidays. For easy reference, therefore, the index also lists all the recipes in the book by the type of dish.

I chose to arrange the recipes by holidays because, throughout the ages, many Jewish foods have been traditionally identified with religious rituals, and thus symbolically came to be associated with specific holidays. More important, in many modern Jewish households, holidays seem to be the major focus for culinary endeavors revolving around ethnic foods. Even those Jews who are generally not observant celebrate many of the holidays with a special family meal. And, holidays are the time when many Jews take particular pride in their roots and want to pass on this heritage to their children.

Of course, the traditional Jewish foods served on holidays need not be only those from one's own culinary background. Though my husband and I are both Ashkenazic Jews, it has become our family custom, in recent years, to enjoy at least one traditional Sephardic dish (and usually more) at each holiday meal. Holidays in our home have thus become adventures in international dining. And, because we make a point of discussing with our children the origin of each dish and any symbolism connected to it, our meals are also tasty lessons in worldwide Judaic culture.

The recipes in this book are an international collection of culinary treasures awaiting discovery and delectation by both Jews and non-Jews alike. They have been culled and adapted from a number of sources. Several of the Ashkenazic recipes were taught to me by expert cooks in my own family. While I had to look elsewhere for the Sephardic recipes, it was a fascinating experience that was deliciously worthwhile. I interviewed many Jewish cooks from all over the world, most of whom now live in the United States, Canada, or Israel.

The majority of these people create wonderful dishes by instinct and memory alone, their only measurements being "a handful of this" or "a pinch of that." Consequently, I had to test every recipe a number of times in my own kitchen. Often, I adjusted ingredients to increase flavor or nutritional value, and I sometimes simplified technique. Yet, I always tried to retain the basic integrity and authenticity of each dish.

In so doing, I followed in the footsteps of other Jewish cooks throughout the ages, who have constantly modified and improved Jewish cooking. The process is a continuous one and is especially evident in modern-day Israel, where the multi-faceted, international cuisines of immigrants are gradually being transformed by a brand-new style of innovative, local cooking that takes superb advantage of indigenous foods.

Thus, Jewish cooking has come full circle. The ancient birthplace of Jewish cuisine is where its newest dishes are currently being created.

Jewish food is, of course, inseparable from the traditions, customs, history, and lore of the people who cook it. Therefore, I have attempted to make this cookbook as rich in culinary culture as it is replete with recipes. It has been designed to provide sustenance for the mind and soul, as well as the body. And it can help carry on a culinary legacy that began more than two thousand years ago.

So, as they say in Israel, *"B'tayavon!"* Good appetite!

A NOTE ON TRANSLITERATIONS USED IN THIS BOOK

Hebrew, Yiddish, and Ladino (or Judeo-Spanish) are all customarily written in Hebrew characters. Therefore, words from these languages must be transliterated for English-speaking readers. Because there is no universal standard, transliterations are quite inconsistent from source to source.

In this book, I have usually tried to spell words from the above languages as they sound, with one major exception. Because the "ch" connotation for the Hebrew/Yiddish guttural "h" sound is so confusing, and is often misunderstood to be the "ch" of "chair," I have decided to use a plain "h" instead. (For example, I say "kreplah," not "kreplach"; and "Hanukkah," not "Chanukah.") However, I have left the guttural "ch" in a very few words (such as "challah" and "Pesach") where it is virtually always used, or where leaving it out makes a word incomprehensible.

Occasionally, I have included a phonetic pronunciation, where I felt this would be helpful.

Transliterations of Hebrew words are based on the Sephardic pronunciation commonly used in modern Israel.

For the convenience of those who observe the dietary rules of *kashrut*, all recipes have been designated (P) for *pareve*, (M) for meat, or (D) for dairy. In a few cases where there is a choice of ingredients, the recipes may be designated (D) or (P).

A WORD
ABOUT INGREDIENTS

This brief glossary includes only those ingredients that are called for in more than one recipe and that may need more explanation than that which is given in the text.

Almonds: Almost all the almonds called for in this book are *blanched* almonds, meaning that the brown skin has been removed from the almond kernel. Raw, blanched almonds can usually be purchased either *whole* or *slivered*. (*Sliced* almonds are *not* blanched.) Sometimes, blanched almonds are available finely ground; however, they usually taste best if they are ground just before they are used. For best keeping, store almonds in the freezer, but be sure to let them come to room temperature before chopping or finely grinding them. When the measurement of almonds is critical to a recipe, weight is more reliable than volume. However, if a kitchen scale is not available, the following can be used as a guide:

1 cup blanched *whole* almonds = 5⅓ ounces.
10 ounces blanched *whole* almonds = 1⅞ cups.
1 cup blanched *slivered* almonds = 4⅓ ounces.
10 ounces blanched *slivered* almonds = 2⅓ cups.
1 cup blanched *finely ground* almonds = 4 ounces.
10 ounces blanched *finely ground* almonds = 2½ cups.

Bulgur Wheat: Also called *burghul,* this is kernels (or "berries") of whole wheat that have been steamed, dried, and cracked into small pieces. Bulgur is available at most health-food stores and some supermarkets. For best keeping, store it in the freezer. (Note: Cracked wheat looks like bulgur; however, it has not been steamed.)

Cardamom: This "sweet-smelling" spice is available at most supermarkets in its ground form. It comes from small seed pods, which are sold whole at some specialty stores.

Chick-peas: These are also known as *garbanzo beans, humus, nahit, bub, arbes, ceci,* and other names. They are used extensively in Jewish cooking, particularly Middle Eastern Sephardic cuisine. Chick-peas are available precooked and canned at most supermarkets. Dried chick-peas may also be available there, or they may be found at health-food or specialty stores.

Coriander (or coriander seed): This spice is frequently used in Middle Eastern cuisine. It is available ground in some supermarkets and specialty stores (Note: Coriander *leaves*—also known as "cilantro"—are not the same as the spice, and they cannot be used interchangeably in recipes.)

Cumin: This brownish-gold spice is used quite often in Middle Eastern cuisine. (For instance, it gives Israeli *falafel* a deliciously distinctive taste.) It is available ground in most supermarkets.

Farmer Cheese: Though it occasionally has other meanings, in this cookbook, *farmer cheese* always refers to a soft, unripened cheese that is similar to very fine, dry cottage cheese. This type of farmer cheese is usually sold in rectangular, soft plastic packages that weigh 7½ to 8 ounces each. It may also be sold loose, in bulk, at some stores. It is used instead of cottage cheese, because it is finer and drier and does not release liquid when cooked. It is traditionally used in many Ashkenazic Jewish recipes.

Feta Cheese: This "salt-cured" white cheese is available at many supermarkets, and can also be special-ordered from several distributors of kosher cheese in New York City.

Filo (pronounced "fee'-low"): This is a very thin dough which looks and feels remarkably like white tissue paper. Filo (also spelled *fillo, phyllo,* or *fila,* and sometimes called *strudel leaves*) usually comes in a long, narrow box which contains 1 pound of sheets folded together and sealed inside a plastic bag. Filo can be purchased in the frozen food sections of some supermarkets, as well as in most Greek or Middle Eastern ethnic grocery stores and gourmet specialty stores. The packaged sheets should always be brought to room temperature before they are unwrapped, unfolded, and used. If they have been frozen, they must first be thawed in the refrigerator overnight.

The delicate sheets of filo dry out extremely quickly. Therefore, whenever they are removed from their sealed plastic bag, they should be kept in a stack between two slightly damp (but not wet) dish towels and used as soon as possible for best results. If filo is handled correctly, it is easy and fun to use. However, if it is thawed improperly or allowed to dry out, it may crumble and become impossible to work with. Any unused sheets of filo should be folded and returned to their plastic bag. Seal the bag well with tape, and store the filo in the refrigerator (for a week or two) or return it to the freezer.

Kasha: This word can mean almost any type of cereal; however, to Ashkenazic Jews it almost invariably means *buckwheat groats.* Although buckwheat is botanically not a grain, it is usually cooked like one. "Kasha" can be purchased in most supermarkets as whole groats, coarsely cracked, or finely ground.

Kaskaval Cheese: This Balkan cheese is very popular among Sephardic Jews who hail from Turkey, Greece, and nearby areas. It has become commonplace in Israel, where it is sometimes called *katzkaval* or *kashkeval.* Similar cheeses, which may be used instead, are *kasseri* and *caciocavallo.* The cheeses may be available at specialty stores, and some of them may also be special-ordered from a few distributors of kosher cheese in New York City.

Olive Oil: For best results, particularly in salad dressings, olive oil should be a very good-quality type, which has a rich, "fruity" taste that adds to the flavor of food. The highest quality olive oil is labeled "virgin," and a lower quality is "pure." Good olive oil is often slightly green in color. Store olive oil in a dark place, and, for best keeping, buy it in small bottles.

Pine Nuts: Often called by their Italian name, *pignoli,* these are frequently used in Mediterranean and Middle Eastern cuisine. There are basically two types: The European ones are cylindrical and slightly resemble slivered almonds. The southwestern American type (which are less expensive) are more triangular shaped. Both are soft and very rich tasting; however, the European type is generally preferred by gourmets. Pine nuts can be purchased at some supermarkets as well as health-food and specialty stores. Though they are expensive, a little goes a long way. Store them in the freezer.

Rose Water: This unusual flavoring, which is extracted from rose petals, is occasionally used in Middle Eastern and Near Eastern cooking. It can be purchased at many specialty stores.

Seeds (Anise, Caraway, Poppy, and Sesame): Although all these seeds are usually available at supermarkets, large quantities are often much less expensive at health-food stores. Store seeds in the freezer, where they will keep for at least a year.

Tahini: This is a plain paste ground from hulled sesame seeds just as peanut butter is made from peanuts. Tahini is available at most health-food and specialty stores, as well as many supermarkets. Once opened, it will keep for several months in the refrigerator, if the plastic lid is resealed on the can. A newly opened can of tahini should always be stirred very well before being refrigerated, to re-suspend any separated sesame oil. The tahini should then stay well mixed for quite a while. (Note: In Israel, this is called *tahina,* as is a dip made from it.)

SHABBAT

"What is Shabbat? Shabbat is taste:
The warm flavor of homemade soup;
The rich taste of Challah;
The sweetness of Shabbat cake,
And, perhaps, the taste of the world to come.
This is Shabbat."
—from a poem by Yochanan ben Avraham

Shabbat (Hebrew for "Sabbath"), the most important holiday of the Jewish calendar, begins every Friday evening at sundown and lasts until nightfall on Saturday. Throughout Jewish history, the best foods and the nicest clothes have always been reserved for Shabbat, the most splendid day of the week. New fruits and vegetables of the season were sometimes not eaten on weekdays so that they could be relished on Shabbat. And poor Jews often scrimped throughout the rest of the week just to have a decent Shabbat meal.

On Shabbat, unlike other days or holidays, it is considered a *mitzvah*—a very good deed—to eat *three* main meals (not including breakfast). These are the Friday night meal, the midday meal on Saturday, and an early evening meal on Saturday known as *Se'udah Shelisheet* (meaning the "third meal"). This tradition is said to have come about because of a verse in Exodus that quotes Moses saying the word "today" three times in referring to eating manna on Shabbat. The Talmud tells us that one who partakes of these three meals will receive favorable judgment in the world to come.

The first two meals (and sometimes the third) begin with the *kiddush*, a special prayer said over a cup of wine. This is followed by the blessing for bread, two loaves of which are always on the Shabbat table (except during Pesach, when leavened bread is forbidden). The bread is dipped into salt before it is eaten, to recall the ancient Temple in Jerusalem, where salt was present on the sacrificial altar.

It is quite customary for the main course on Friday evening to be meat or poultry. In times past, when many Jews were impoverished, these foods were luxuries and they were served in relatively large quantities only on Shabbat.

Fish is also usually on the menu. In fact, it is suggested by the Talmud that fish, at the very least, must be eaten on Shabbat, and a Yiddish proverb says, "Shabbat without fish is like a wedding without dancing." Jewish sages have determined several symbolic reasons for this custom. Some said that since God created fish on the fifth day, and humankind on the sixth, and the Sabbath followed on the seventh, the three should be kept together, with people eating fish on Shabbat. Others noted that the Hebrew letters in the word for fish, *dag,* numerically add up to seven, the day of the week on which we observe Shabbat. Also, in Genesis, God repeatedly blesses people and fish and tells both to "be fruitful and multiply"; therefore, fish has also come to stand for fertility and immortality. In the past, some pious Jews refrained from eating fish during the week just so that it would be particularly enjoyable on Shabbat.

For the Friday evening meal, Ashkenazic Jews also typically serve soup, usually golden-yellow chicken broth; whereas, Sephardic Jews prefer a large selection of cooked and chilled vegetable salads. After such a large, multi-course holiday meal, dessert is often kept light—egg cookies, sponge cake, or fresh fruit.

On Shabbat, according to Jewish law, a fire may not be kindled and no work is permitted. Therefore, the observant Jewish cook must prepare all food for the entire day ahead of time. However, it is also important to have at least two hot, cooked meals for the holiday. For many centuries, this seeming dilemma has been deliciously solved by serving as the midday dinner on Saturday a hearty stew that is assembled and partially cooked on Friday before sundown, and then allowed to slowly simmer overnight. (For more details, see the recipes for *cholent* and *dafina,* pages 38 and 40.)

The late Saturday afternoon meal, or *Se'udah Shelisheet,* is usually lighter than the other two. It is generally a non-meat meal, featuring bread, smoked or pickled fish, hard-boiled eggs, kugel, and cakes. After eating, very Orthodox Jews known as *Hasidim* sometimes gather to discuss nuances of the Torah and Talmud and to sing Shabbat songs.

Because Shabbat is a day exalted above all others in the week, pious Jews are always very unhappy to see it come to an end. Therefore, after *havdalah,* the ceremony held at the conclusion of Shabbat, Hasidim often have yet another light meal (or snack) called *Melavah Malkah,* during which they celebrate any recent joyous occasions, such as a bar mitzvah or engagement. (For more details, see the recipe for *Spicy Apple Coffee Cake,* page 58.)

Many of the recipes in this chapter have been chosen because of their traditional symbolism with regard to Shabbat. Others are simply in keeping with the spirit of the holiday. Because several of the dishes served during other Jewish holidays are also very appropriate for Shabbat, be sure to look through the rest of this cookbook for more ideas.

GRANDPA'S CHALLAH (P)

When I was a child, my paternal grandfather, Joseph Kaufer, was renowned throughout the Jewish community of northeastern Pennsylvania as an amateur baker *par excellence.* As far back as my Dad—the youngest of thirteen children—can remember, his father was the best baker in the family and remained so almost until his death at age 83.

Grandpa's specialty was yeast-raised breads and cakes. For Shabbat, he always made rich *challot* (the plural of "challah"), like those that follow below. For synagogue picnics, as well as bar mitzvah and wedding celebrations, he prepared gorgeous, perfectly braided challot that were so huge they had to be baked in a professional oven.

Grandpa also mixed up an enormous batch of dough on Saturday evening, then set it out on the porch in a bucket covered with a towel to rise slowly during the night. Any of his children who went out on a date was expected, upon returning home, to punch down the dough and knead it a few times before going to bed. Grandpa would then get up in the wee hours of Sunday morning to concoct wonderful doughnuts, cinnamon buns, onion-laden *pletzels,* and more, so all would be ready in time for a delectable family breakfast.

As with many expert bakers, Grandpa rarely measured ingredients, and most of his recipes are gone forever. Fortunately, one of my aunts, Hannah Kaufer Hafetz, an occasional assistant to Grandpa, and an able baker in her own right, jotted down an approximate list of ingredients for his challah, on which the following recipe is based.

2 packets (about 4½ teaspoons)
    active dry yeast
1½ cups warm (105 to 115 degrees)
    water, divided
⅓ to ½ cup sugar, or to taste
About 6 to 6½ cups white bread
    flour or all-purpose unbleached
    white flour
2 teaspoons salt

½ cup softened pareve *margarine or
    vegetable shortening*
3 large eggs

GLAZE
1 egg yolk, beaten with 1 teaspoon
    water
Poppy seeds (optional)

Mix the yeast with ½ cup of the water and 1 teaspoon of the sugar. Let the mixture rest for 5 to 10 minutes, or until it begins to foam.

Meanwhile, put about 4 cups of the flour into a large bowl with the remaining sugar, salt, and margarine. Use an electric mixer or a pastry blender to combine the ingredients until they form coarse crumbs. Add the yeast mixture, the remaining 1 cup water, and the eggs and beat the loose dough with the mixer or a wooden spoon for about 3 minutes. By hand (or with a heavy duty mixer), slowly stir in just enough of the remaining flour to form a soft, slightly sticky dough. Cover the dough with plastic wrap and let it rest for about 5 minutes.

Turn out the dough onto a lightly floured surface and knead it, adding small sprinkles of flour, if necessary, to keep it from sticking, for about 10 minutes, or until it is very smooth and satiny. Put the dough into an oiled bowl and turn the dough so that all sides are oiled. Cover the bowl loosely with a piece of plastic wrap and then a dish towel, to keep the dough moist and dark. Let the dough rise until doubled in bulk, about 1 to 2 hours (depending on the temperature of the room).

Punch down the dough and knead it a few times to remove any air bubbles. Divide the dough in half, for two loaves. Then divide each half into 3, 4, 5, or 6 pieces, depending on the number of strands desired for each loaf. Cover the dough pieces loosely with plastic wrap and let them rest for 10 minutes.

On a lightly floured surface, roll out each dough piece into a smooth strand and braid the strands following the directions in the section on *The Symbolism and Shaping of Challah.* Carefully set the loaves several inches apart on a very large greased or nonstick spray-coated baking sheet (or on 2 smaller sheets). Gently rub the surface of each loaf with a little oil to keep the dough from drying out. Cover the loaves loosely with wax paper and let them rise at room temperature until doubled in bulk, 45 minutes to 1 hour or longer. (Formed bread dough tends to hold its shape better if allowed to rise slowly at room temperature, rather than in a warm place.)

Gently brush the loaves well with the egg glaze and, if desired, sprinkle them lightly with poppy seeds. Bake the loaves in a preheated 375-degree oven for 40 to 45 minutes, or until the crust is browned and the bottom of each loaf sounds hollow when tapped. (If the loaves are browning too rapidly, loosely cover each one with a tent of aluminum foil.) Remove the loaves from the baking sheet and cool them on wire racks.

Makes 2 large challot, about 1⅔ pounds each.

THE SYMBOLISM AND SHAPING OF CHALLAH

The bread now called *challah* is almost always prominent at Jewish festivals and celebrations (except, of course, during Pesach). In ancient times, the ceremonial loaf probably had more of a flat, round shape, similar to the *pita* bread (page 308) that is still very popular in the Middle East.

During hundreds of years in the Diaspora (particularly in Eastern Europe), challah evolved into the rich, egg-laden, beautifully shaped bread with which we are now so familiar. Jewish scholars, as is their wont, have ascribed symbolism to each bump and cranny in this "staff of life," as well as to the way it is presented on the table.

Thus, much challah tradition is related to the perfect food—manna—that the Jews collected and ate as they wandered in the Sinai desert before entering the Promised Land. For instance, it is said that there are always *two* loaves on the Shabbat table (and at other festivals) to remind us of the double portion of manna given to our ancestors on Friday so they would not have to profane the Sabbath by gathering and carrying food. In addition, it was customary in ancient times for the joyous and abundant Shabbat meal to feature two main dishes (unlike ordinary weekday meals which had only one), and a loaf of bread always accompanied each course.

The seeds often sprinkled on top of challot are supposed to be similar to manna as it is described in the Book of Exodus. When the Shabbat table is set, the twin challot are usually covered with a beautifully decorated cloth which represents the dew that surrounded the manna. (Another, more fanciful, explanation for the covering is that the challot are hidden so they will not be "insulted" or "offended" that the *kiddush* prayer for wine is recited before their own blessing is said.) Both the challah cover and tablecloth are often white, as were the manna and the desert sands upon which it fell, and also because white means purity.

The Torah says that a small portion of the dough from each large batch of homemade bread must be separated and offered to the *kohanim* (or priests) of the Holy Temple. Since the destruction of the Second Temple, observant bakers have symbolically carried on this practice by removing an olive-sized piece of dough and burning it in the oven as they say a special blessing. This act is known as *"taking challah,"* and from it comes the name of this treasured loaf.

Braiding Challah

It is written that twelve loaves of *shewbread* (or showbread), representing the twelve tribes of ancient Israel, were continually displayed in two rows in the portable Tabernacle and later on the altar of the Holy Temple in Jerusalem. Each Shabbat, the loaves were replenished.

The shewbreads are sometimes symbolized by braiding two challot so that six "humps" show on top of each one, or by braiding each loaf with six individual strands of dough. The latter is sometimes accomplished by capping a large three-strand braid with a smaller three-strand braid, then baking the two together as one loaf. However, some bakers prefer to weave six equal strands into a magnificent single braid.

Four-strand loaves have also become commonplace, simply because they look more attractive, rise higher, and are thus often lighter than standard three-strand loaves, yet are easier to braid than the six-strand type.

There are many ways to form slightly differing braids using the same number of strands. Offered here are those with steps that are particularly simple, logical, and easy to remember. Before you try these techniques on bread dough, it is best to practice them with even lengths of thick yarn knotted together at one end. That way, you can determine which method works best for you.

Before braiding the bread dough, roll out very smooth, evenly sized strands that are 12 to 16 inches long. For a loaf that tapers at both ends, make the strands slightly thicker in the center. Lay out the strands parallel to each other, and pinch them together at one end. As you work, keep the braid even and compact. Be careful not to stretch or tear the strands, or the surface of the loaf may develop holes as it rises and bakes. When the braiding is completed, pinch the dough strands tightly at the bottom end to keep them from unraveling. Neatly tuck under both ends of the loaf and place it on a greased baking sheet to rise.

TO BRAID THREE STRANDS
A three-strand challah is slightly flat, but very easy to braid. Keep repeating steps A and B.
   A. Pass the strand on the right over the one in the center.
   B. Pass the strand on the left over the one now in the center.

TO BRAID FOUR STRANDS
   1. This makes a high, attractive challah. Keep repeating steps A and B.
      A. Pass the strand on the far right under the two to the left of it, then back over the one now on its immediate right (Fig. 1A).
      B. Pass the strand on the far left under the two to the right of it, then back over the one now on its immediate left (Fig. 1B).

FIGURE 1   A   B

2. This challah is a bit flatter than the one in method 1. The method is quite simple, though the loaf tends to move toward one side as it is being braided. Keep repeating step A, always beginning on the same side (your choice) and moving in the same direction.
      A. Pass the strand on the far left (or right) over the one next to it, under the one after that, and over the last strand (Figs. 2A and 2B).

 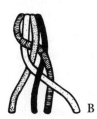

FIGURE 2   A   B

3. This version is slightly more difficult than the first two, but it makes a high, beautiful challah. Keep repeating steps A and B.

    A. Pass the second strand from the right over to the far left position; then pass the strand on the far right over the one now on its immediate left (Fig. 3A).

    B. Pass the strand second from the left over to the far right position; then pass the strand on the far left over the one now on its immediate right (Fig. 3B).

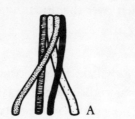

FIGURE 3   A   B

TO BRAID FIVE STRANDS

Keep repeating steps A, B, and C.

    A. Pass the second strand from the left over the one on its immediate right (Fig. 4A).

    B. Pass the strand on the far right over the strand which is now second from the left (Fig. 4B).

    C. Pass the strand on the far left over the two strands to its immediate right (Fig. 4C).

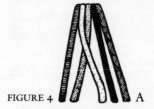

FIGURE 4   A   B   C

TO BRAID SIX STRANDS

1. Many six-stranded braids are much more complicated and confusing than this impressive-looking one. Keep repeating steps A, B, C, and D.

    A. Pass the second strand from the right over to the far left position (Fig. 5A).

    B. Pass the strand on the far right over the two strands now on its immediate left (Fig. 5B).

C. Pass the second strand from the left over to the far right position (Fig. 5C).

D. Pass the strand on the far left over the two strands now on its immediate right (Fig. 5D).

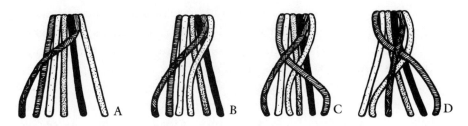

FIGURE 5

2. This is actually composed of two three-stranded braids (for a total of six strands), which are baked together as one loaf.

Divide the dough into four pieces—three that are equal and one slightly larger. Braid the three equal pieces as described above in "To Braid Three Strands." Then divide the remaining larger piece of dough into three equal strands and braid them. Lay the small braid over the large one; then let the two braids rise and bake together.

Creating Other Shapes

Throughout the ages, imaginative Jewish bakers all over the world have lovingly pounded, bent, squeezed, and rolled their challah dough into many other innovative and interesting designs. On Rosh Hashanah, for instance, round challot (page 64) and loaves shaped like ladders are quite popular.

Small pieces of the dough can also be shaped into rolls. Simple round rolls, made from balls of dough, can be baked on baking sheets or in muffin tins. Or the dough can be formed into short strands, and each one tied into a double knot with the bottom end tucked under. For rolls that resemble birds, tie a short dough strand into a single knot and lift up the top end for a head. Just before baking, notch the bottom end of the strand a few times to resemble tail feathers.

Tiny individual loaves, which are each braided from three very small strands of dough, can be great fun for children to shape. In some households, two of these miniature challot are put near each child's place setting on the Shabbat table.

SWEET CROWNS FOR THE SHABBAT QUEEN

(P) or (D)

(Miniature Filled Challah Rolls)

Shabbat is often likened to a beautiful bride or queen who makes a regal appearance only once each week. The Shabbat Queen's crown is occasionally symbolized by forming a long, narrow *challah* braid into a circular, doughnut-like shape. The *challah* may be filled with confections that represent the sweetness of the day.

Following is a simple recipe for a miniature crown bread, which is baked in a muffin tin. It is a perfect project for young children (see Notes on page 25). The crown can be produced with either homemade *challah* dough (see pages 17 and 64) or already prepared dough which can sometimes be purchased from Jewish bakeries. The dough should have risen once and be ready for its final shaping. *Below are instructions for 1 crown.* For more, simply repeat the steps. (All measurements are approximate.)

1 2-ounce piece of challah dough
   (about the size of a small plum)
   (see comment above)
1 teaspoon very soft, stick margarine,
   whipped margarine, or butter
1 teaspoon granulated brown sugar
   (or regular dark or light brown
   sugar)
1/8 teaspoon ground cinnamon
2 to 3 teaspoons of some of the
   following fillings: raisins,
   currants, chopped walnuts or
   pecans, sunflower seeds, shredded
   coconut, chopped prunes, poppy
   seeds, and/or chocolate chips

GLAZE
2 tablespoons confectioner's sugar
1 drop vanilla extract
Water
Colored sprinkles or jimmies
   (optional)

Pat or roll out the dough to a 3- by 6-inch rectangle. Spread the margarine over the top surface of the dough. Sprinkle the brown sugar, cinnamon, and your choice of filling(s) evenly over the margarine. Roll up the rectangle, as for a jelly roll, beginning at one of the longer sides. With the seam on the inside, bring the ends of the roll around to form a doughnut shape and pinch the ends together very tightly. Put the crown in a well-greased or non-stick spray-coated, standard-sized muffin tin or 6-ounce custard cup. Let it rise in a warm place until doubled in bulk, about 45 minutes. Bake the crown in a preheated 350-degree oven for 15 to 18 minutes, or until it sounds hollow when tapped on the bottom. Cool it completely before glazing it.

For the glaze, mix together the confectioner's sugar, vanilla, and just enough water to make a drizzling consistency. Spoon the glaze over the crown. If desired, decorate the top with sprinkles.

Makes 1 miniature crown.

Notes for Those Working with a Group of Very Young Children

With a bit of advance planning, this can be an enjoyable, very successful project. Wrap individual, pre-measured pieces of dough in 12-inch squares of plastic wrap. Draw a dark 3- by 6-inch rectangle on each of several pieces of cardboard or construction paper, so there is one for each child.

Have the children open their packages of dough on top of their rectangles. Instruct them to use their fingers to press out the dough on top of the wrap until it fills the rectangle which is visible through the plastic. Then have the children spread a small amount of very soft margarine over the dough using a tongue depressor or plastic knife. Next, have them use a small spoon to sprinkle the dough with granulated brown sugar (it sprinkles easier than the regular kind). They can shake on a bit of cinnamon right from the can. Let them choose and add the other fillings they want. (Have each type in a separate bowl.)

Assist the children in rolling up the dough and connecting the ends to form a circle. To keep each crown separate and identifiable, cut disposable foil muffin tins into individual cups and use a marking pen to put the name of each child on the outside of a cup. Put one crown in each greased cup. Let the crowns rise; then bake and cool them. If desired, let each child spoon some icing on top of his or her crown, and decorate it.

KUBANEH   (D) or (P)

(Yemenite Shabbat Bread)

Although most people are familiar with cholent-like stews, which are very slowly cooked overnight on Shabbat in order to have fresh hot food on Saturday, I doubt that many have heard of bread being cooked in this fashion. *Kubaneh* is often part of the meal eaten by Yemenite Jews after they return from Saturday morning synagogue services. Sometimes, the *kubaneh* is served with *quishr,* coffee spiced with ginger and perhaps cardamom.

In Israel, special *kubaneh pots* are sold just for making this unusual bread. The deep, aluminum pot is about 8 inches in diameter, and has a close-fitting lid which sits over the outside edge of the pot. An ovenproof 4-quart or similar Dutch oven, saucepan, or deep casserole, which is covered tightly with aluminum foil, can be used instead.

Because it is cooked so long, *kubaneh* does not have the light texture of many yeast-raised breads. Rather, it is heavier, moister, and a bit like *kugel*. It is typically eaten warm, from the oven, although some may prefer it cooled to room temperature.

2 packets (about 4½ teaspoons) active dry yeast
2 cups warm (105 to 115 degrees) water, divided
1 tablespoon sugar
1 tablespoon honey

2 tablespoons butter or margarine, softened (see Note)
2 teaspoons salt
5½ to 6½ cups white bread flour or all-purpose unbleached white flour
4 to 6 tablespoons butter or margarine for the pot

In a large bowl, mix the yeast, 1 cup of the water, and the sugar and honey. Let the mixture stand until it gets foamy. Add the remaining 1 cup water, 2 tablespoons softened butter, and about 5 cups of the flour. Stir to make a soft dough. Cover the dough with plastic wrap and let it rest for about 15 minutes. Then stir in enough additional flour so the dough is not sticky. Knead the dough, adding sprinkles of flour just until it is no longer sticky. Cover the dough again and let it rest for 10 minutes.

Meanwhile, melt the 4 to 6 tablespoons of butter in an 8-inch-diameter, approximately 4-quart, ovenproof pot or deep casserole and let it cool to room temperature. Divide the dough into 4 pieces, and roll each one into a smooth ball. Put the balls of dough next to one another in the pot, rolling each in the butter so it is completely coated. Let the dough rise, uncovered, until it is doubled in bulk, about 1 hour. Cover the pot tightly with aluminum foil and put it in a preheated 200-degree oven. Let the dough bake overnight, 8 to 12 hours or longer. Serve warm.

Makes 12 or more servings

NOTE: If desired, leave the 2 tablespoons of butter out of the dough mixture. Instead, cut it into 4 pieces, and insert one into the center of each dough ball before putting the balls into the pot. (This variation is preferred by some Yemenite Jews.)

HERAIMEH (P)

(Libyan-Style Fish in Spicy Tomato Sauce)

I learned this recipe from Denise Saville Zandman, a Welsh Jew who went to visit Israel in the early 1970s. It wasn't long before she fell in love with the country and also with one of its sabras, Dov Zandman. They married and made their home in Haifa.

Although Mrs. Zandman was primarily familiar with the British-style Ashkenazic cuisine of her birthplace, she found that many of her husband's favorite foods were the exotic Libyan-Jewish dishes that his mother often prepared. After several lessons from her mother-in-law, Mrs. Zandman learned how to expertly cook—and, indeed, to prefer—the wonderfully spicy dishes for which many of the Sephardic Jews of Israel are justly famed.

This is one of her own favorites. It is served at room temperature or chilled, several hours or even the day after it is cooked. And it is always accompanied by plenty of bread to sop up the luscious, rich sauce.

¼ cup good-quality olive oil
1 6-ounce can tomato paste
4 to 5 large garlic cloves, pressed or
* very finely minced*
½ to ¾ teaspoon salt
¼ to ½ teaspoon ground cumin
⅛ to ¼ teaspoon cayenne pepper
About ½ cup water, divided
1 tablespoon lemon juice

1½ pounds firm light-fleshed fish,
* such as grouper, hake, halibut,*
* bass, or mullet, cut crosswise into*
* ¾-inch-thick steaks*

TO SERVE
Italian-style or French-style bread,
* cut into thick slices*

In a large heavy skillet (preferably a non-stick one), combine the oil, tomato paste, garlic, salt, cumin, cayenne, and about ¼ cup of the water. Mix well. Put the skillet over medium heat and cook the thick sauce, stirring often, for about 15 minutes to give the flavors a chance to blend. Stir in ¼ cup more water until it is well combined and bring the sauce to a simmer. Stir in the lemon juice.

Add the fish steaks in one layer; then spoon some of the sauce over them. Cover the skillet and gently simmer the fish in the sauce, stirring occasionally, for about 10 to 12 minutes, or just until the fish is cooked through. (Do not overcook the fish or it may fall apart in the sauce.) If the sauce becomes so thick that it sticks to the bottom of the pan, add a few additional tablespoons of water.

Transfer the cooked fish to a serving dish and pour all of the sauce over it. Chill the fish in the refrigerator, but take it out about an hour before serving, so it can warm to room temperature. Serve it with bread to dip in the sauce.

Makes 4 to 6 servings as a first course.

VARIATION

KAVED EN SHOOMA (M)
(Chicken Livers in Garlic-Tomato Sauce)

For this Israeli adaptation of *heraimeh*, chicken livers are used instead of fish. Prepare the sauce as directed, but substitute *white vinegar* for the lemon juice. Add about *¾ pound cleaned and kashered chicken livers* and simmer them in the sauce, turning occasionally, for about 10 minutes. Cool and serve as you would heraimeh.

EASY "NOUVELLE" GEFILTE FISH (P)

"Old-fashioned" gefilte fish is always made from whole fish; the head, skin, and bones are used for the broth and the flesh is used for the balls. The word *gefilte* is Yiddish for "stuffed," and the dish is so named because, at one time, the minced fish mixture was stuffed back into the skin of the fish before it was cooked. The method was simplified by forming the fish mixture into balls or oblong shapes.

I've taken the liberty of going a few steps further in this recipe, which calls only for fish fillets—a standard in many home freezers. The fillets are ground in a food processor, if one is available, resulting in a fish ball that is very light and delicate.

Gefilte fish became quite traditional for Ashkenazic Jews on Shabbat for an interesting, non-culinary, reason. No work may be done on the seventh day; yet, separating bones from fish in a certain manner was determined, by rabbinic Jewish authorities, to be "work." Thus, to avoid accidental infringement of the religious code, most fish to be served on Shabbat was boned (and often prepared) in advance.

FISH BALLS
1 pound fresh or frozen (thawed) haddock fillets or similar firm white fish
1 medium-sized onion
1 small carrot
1 large egg
½ teaspoon salt
⅛ teaspoon black pepper, preferably freshly ground
Pinch of sugar (optional)
2 tablespoons matzo meal

BROTH
About 5 cups water
1 medium-sized onion, thinly sliced
1 medium-sized carrot, thinly sliced on the diagonal
¼ teaspoon black pepper, preferably freshly ground
2 to 3 vegetable bouillon cubes (or other pareve *bouillon cubes)*

TO SERVE (OPTIONAL)
Lettuce leaves

For the fish balls, coarsely cut the fish, onion, and carrot into chunks. Put them into a food processor fitted with the steel blade and process until almost smooth. Add the egg, salt, pepper, sugar (if used), and matzo meal and process until smooth. (If a food processor is unavailable, grind the fish and vegetables together in a food grinder; then stir in the remaining ingredients.) Set the fish mixture aside while preparing the broth.

Put all the broth ingredients into a deep, straight-sided, 10-inch skillet or similar pan. Bring to a boil over high heat; then lower the heat and simmer, stirring, until the bouillon cubes have dissolved.

With wet hands, shape the fish mixture into 1½-inch-diameter balls, using about ¼ cup of the mixture for each one. Gently drop the balls into the simmering broth. Cover the skillet and simmer very gently for about 1 hour, occasionally turning the balls with a spoon. Remove the skillet from the heat and let the balls cool in the broth.

Use a slotted spoon to transfer the balls to a serving bowl. Scatter the cooked carrot slices around the balls. Strain the broth through cheese-

cloth and pour it over the balls. Chill. If desired, serve the drained fish
balls and carrots on a bed of lettuce.

Makes about 12 fish balls; 4 to 6 servings.

VISCHKOEKJES   (D) or (P)

(Dutch-Style Fish and Potato Cakes)

After Shabbat morning services, Dutch Jews sometimes enjoy these simple pancakes of sorts, which make great use of leftovers from the previous night's meal. They are tasty both hot and at room temperature. For
a dairy meal, they can be accompanied by sour cream.

2 cups boned, skinned and flaked, *¼ teaspoon ground mace or nutmeg*
 cooked white-fleshed fish   *½ teaspoon salt*
1½ cups plain mashed potatoes *⅛ teaspoon black pepper, preferably*
2 large eggs   *freshly ground*
2 tablespoons finely chopped fresh *2 to 4 tablespoons butter or*
 parsley leaves   *margarine*

In a large bowl, mix together all the ingredients, except the butter. In a
large griddle or skillet over medium-high heat, melt about 2 tablespoons
of the butter. Spoon approximate ¼-cup portions of the fish-potato batter onto the griddle, flattening them slightly. Cook the pancakes until
they are browned on the bottom and firm; then turn and cook them on
the second side. Repeat until all the batter is used. If the pancakes are
browning too fast, lower the heat.

Makes 4 to 5 servings.

FISH IN TARRAGON-TOMATO SAUCE   (D) or (P)

A good first course for the Shabbat evening meal, this is also tasty as a main dish on other nights of the week.

1½ tablespoons butter or margarine.
1 medium-sized onion, finely chopped
1 large garlic clove, minced
1 16-ounce can tomatoes, including juice, chopped
½ cup dry white wine
2 tablespoons finely chopped fresh parsley leaves

2 teaspoons dried chives (or 1½ tablespoons chopped fresh chives)
2 teaspoons dried tarragon leaves
½ teaspoon salt
⅛ teaspoon black pepper, preferably freshly ground
1 pound skinless fish fillets, such as cod, haddock, or a similar white-fleshed fish

In a large deep skillet, over medium-high heat, melt the butter; then sauté the onion and garlic until they are tender but not browned. Stir in the tomatoes, wine, parsley, chives, tarragon, salt, and pepper. Simmer, stirring often, for about 15 minutes.

Add the fish fillets to the skillet and spoon a little sauce over each one. Simmer about 10 minutes longer, or until the fish is cooked through and the sauce is thickened.

Serve hot or at room temperature.

Makes about 6 to 8 servings as a first course for Shabbat dinner or about 4 main-dish servings.

MY MOTHER'S CHICKEN SOUP   (M)

During my childhood, my mother, Helene ("Hindy") Kaplan Kaufer, prepared this soup just about every Erev Shabbat. As sure as Friday followed Thursday, Mom would begin her day by plucking any stray feathers from the chicken and cleaning the vegetables.

On a rare occasion, however, she would yearn for variety and prepare a different soup. This inevitably meant rebellion from the rest of the family. Somehow, my father, my sisters, and I all felt that the only way Shabbat could properly begin was by lighting candles, reciting the blessings for wine and *challot,* and eating Mom's delectable, shimmery, golden-yellow chicken soup.

And so it is with my own husband and sons. Though they allow me to experiment every now and then with soups from other Jewish cultures, they consider chicken soup the only "authentic" soup for Friday night.

Following is the very basic recipe that my mother still uses. I sometimes add other herbs, and perhaps a few additional vegetables, such as a leek or a turnip.

The trick in having a richly flavored, translucent broth is in very slowly simmering the soup for at least four hours. If the broth is allowed to boil rapidly, it may become cloudy.

1 large chicken (3½ to 4 pounds),
preferably a pullet, cut into large
pieces, with the large pieces of fat
removed
Chicken neck and gizzard, cleaned
(optional)
Boiling water
About 12 cups water
2 medium-sized onions, peeled but
left whole
2 to 3 celery stalks, left whole
3 to 4 medium-sized carrots, peeled,
if desired, and cut into 2-inch-
long sections

1 bay leaf (optional)
Dried dillweed to taste (optional)
Salt and freshly ground black pepper
to taste

TO SERVE
Cooked noodles, rice, mandlen,
farfel, galushka, *or* meat kreplah
(pages 80, 77, 34, and 78)

Put the chicken into a colander and pour boiling water over it. Then clean it well and pluck out any remaining feathers.

Meanwhile, bring the 12 cups of water to a boil in a large soup pot over high heat. Add the chicken, chicken neck, and gizzard (if used) to the water. Lower the heat so that the water just simmers. Cook the chicken, uncovered, for 10 to 15 minutes, stirring occasionally. While the chicken is cooking, use a spoon or strainer to skim off the white foam that floats to the top of the soup. When there is no more foam, add the onions, celery, carrots, and bay leaf (if used). Cover the pot and turn the heat to low, so that the soup simmers very gently. Simmer the soup for 4 to 8 hours (the longer, the better). Shortly before serving, use a slotted spoon to remove and discard the celery, onions, and bay leaf (if used), but not the carrots. If desired, skim any excess fat from the top of the soup. Season the soup to taste with dillweed (if used), salt, and pepper.

Serve the soup with the cooked carrots, some of the chicken meat, and noodles or other suggested "garnishes."

Makes 8 to 10 servings.

RED LENTIL SOUP (M)

Various types of lentil soup are popular among Sephardim, who often call it *sopa de lentijas* in Judeo-Spanish. The recipes sometimes use brown lentils instead of red and may substitute tomato sauce or paste for canned tomatoes. Also, the seasonings vary greatly.

I've chosen the particular herbs and spices in this version because they give it a wonderful Mediterranean flavor. Red lentils, which are smaller than brown ones and actually bright orange in color, are available at many specialty and health-food stores. They partially disintegrate during the cooking, making the soup thick and giving it a lovely color.

1½ tablespoons olive or vegetable oil
1 medium-sized onion, finely chopped
1 garlic clove, minced
5 to 6 cups beef broth (or more, if needed)
2 cups (about ¾ pound) red lentils, sorted and rinsed

1 16-ounce can tomatoes, including juice, finely chopped
½ teaspoon ground cumin
¼ teaspoon ground coriander
1 tablespoon lemon juice
Salt and freshly ground black pepper to taste

In a large saucepan or 4-quart soup pot, heat the oil; then cook the onion and garlic, stirring, until they are tender but not browned. Add the broth, lentils, tomatoes, cumin, coriander, and lemon juice. Bring to a boil; then lower the heat and simmer the soup, covered, for about 40 minutes, or until the lentils are very tender and the soup is thick. If the soup becomes too thick, add a little more broth. Season the soup with salt and pepper to taste.

Makes about 6 servings.

GALUSHKA or SPATZLE or NOCKERL (P)

(Tiny Noodle Dumplings)

As my mother-in-law, Freda Michaelson Greene Cantor, watched me prepare these delicate, irregularly shaped Eastern European dumplings, she exclaimed in surprise, "You're making *trifleh,* like my mother used to make!" Apparently, there are many names for these easy-to-prepare little "trifles." They are delicious as a soup garnish and can also be served with stews. Or they may be tossed with butter and grated cheese for a nice dairy side dish.

2 cups all-purpose white flour,
  preferably unbleached
½ teaspoon salt

2 large eggs
About 5 to 6 tablespoons cold water

In a medium-sized bowl, combine the flour and salt. Make a well in the center of the flour. Put the eggs and 4 tablespoons of the water into the well and beat them together gently with a fork. Then gradually mix in the flour. Stir in just enough additional water to make a soft, slightly sticky dough. Gather the dough into a ball and wrap it in plastic wrap. Let it rest at least 10 minutes at room temperature, or up to overnight in the refrigerator.

In a large pot, over high heat, bring several quarts of water to a boil. Spread about one third of the dough on a small plate (see Note). Dip a small spoon into the boiling water; then use it to scoop a tiny bit of the dough off the plate into the water. Continue until all the dough on the plate has been used. Boil the small dumplings for 3 to 6 minutes, or until they are just tender throughout. If overcooked, the dumplings become mushy. Remove the dumplings with a slotted spoon and transfer them to a bowl. Repeat until all the dough is used. For the best flavor and texture, serve the dumplings as soon as possible. If necessary, they may be reheated in boiling water.

Makes about 3½ cups of cooked dumplings.

NOTE: If desired, the dough may be formed into dumplings by pressing it through a special "spatzle machine" or a grater with very large holes. Cook as directed above.

ZIPPY CRANBERRY POT ROAST (M)

This combination of ingredients may seem a little unusual, but the sweet-and-sour sauce tastes great. In fact, this roast has become a favorite in my own family.

SAUCE
1 16-ounce can tomato sauce
1 16-ounce can whole (or jellied) cranberry sauce
1 tablespoon prepared horseradish
1 teaspoon powdered mustard
3 tablespoons apple cider vinegar

¼ cup dry red wine, cranberry juice, or water
1 tablespoon vegetable oil

MEAT
1 approximately 3-pound boneless chuck (or similar) roast, trimmed of all fat

Combine all the sauce ingredients in a Dutch oven or large deep skillet with a cover. Over high heat, bring the sauce to a boil; then lower the heat and simmer the sauce, uncovered, for about 5 minutes. Put the roast into the sauce and cover the pot tightly. Simmer the pot roast over low heat, basting it often with the sauce, for 2 to 3 hours, or until the meat is very tender. (If the roast is very thick, turn it once or twice during the cooking period.)

Transfer the cooked roast to a serving platter. Raise the heat and quickly cook down the sauce to the desired thickness. Spoon some of the sauce over the roast and put the remainder in a bowl to serve on the side. Cut the roast across the grain into thick slices before serving.

Makes about 8 servings.

MAFROUM (M)

(Libyan-Style Stuffed Vegetables)

This tasty dish is often served on Shabbat by Libyan Jews, such as Liora Ben-Chaim Zandman, a resident of Jerusalem. Just a year after Israel became a state, Mrs. Zandman and her family left their home in Tripoli and made *aliyah*. In her adopted country, she married and raised a family, but still kept cooking the delicious dishes of her native land.

Though many of her favorite foods are obviously Middle Eastern in style and taste, they have distinctively Jewish touches, such as the matzo meal in the following meat stuffing.

In this recipe, potato and eggplant slices are stuffed, then fried in a tasty coating that helps hold them together, and finally simmered in a flavorful tomato sauce. If desired, *mafroum* can be prepared using only eggplant *or* potatoes.

STUFFING

1 pound very lean ground beef or lamb

1 to 2 medium-sized onions, grated

2 to 3 garlic cloves, minced

1/4 cup finely chopped fresh parsley leaves

2 large eggs

1 teaspoon ground cinnamon

1/2 to 1 teaspoon salt

1/4 to 1/2 teaspoon black pepper, preferably freshly ground

About 1/4 cup matzo meal

VEGETABLES

1 medium-sized eggplant (about 1 pound)

2 to 3 large "boiling" or "all-purpose" potatoes

Vegetable oil for frying

All-purpose white flour, preferably unbleached

1 to 2 large eggs, lightly beaten

SAUCE

1 large onion, thinly sliced

1 6-ounce can tomato paste

3 cups water

Salt, ground black pepper, and cinnamon to taste

For the stuffing, combine all the stuffing ingredients in a large bowl and mix very well with your hands until the mixture is quite smooth and well blended. (A food processor may be used for this step.) Set the stuffing aside.

Prepare the vegetables as follows: Use a sharp knife to cut off the ends of the eggplant; then cut it crosswise into 3/4-inch-thick slices. Carefully slit each slice almost in half to form two thin slices which are connected at one end. (It may be easier to do this by cutting 3/8-inch-crosswise slices from the whole eggplant, but only slicing every other one completely through [Fig. 6].)

FIGURE 6

Peel the potatoes; then cut them lengthwise into ½-inch-thick slices. Slit the slices almost in half, as with the eggplant (Fig. 7A).

FIGURE 7   A   B

To stuff the vegetables, use your fingers to firmly pack the meat stuffing inside each slit slice, forming "sandwiches" which look like partially open clam shells. The stuffing layer should be about ⅜ to ½ inch thick (Fig. 7B). It will be slightly more difficult to stuff the potatoes, as they do not "give" as easily as the eggplant.

In a large Dutch oven, soup pot, or very large deep skillet, heat about 2 to 3 tablespoons of oil. Lightly coat each sandwich first with flour and then the beaten egg. Fry the sandwiches in the oil, in batches, until they are golden brown on both sides. Set them aside on a plate. (If desired, the recipe may be prepared ahead of time up to this point and the sandwiches refrigerated until about an hour before serving time.)

For the sauce, pour all the oil from the pot except about 1 tablespoon (or add more oil, if necessary). Add the onion and cook, stirring, until it is tender but not browned. Stir in the tomato paste, water, and seasonings to taste. Bring the sauce to a simmer. Carefully add all the fried sandwiches to the sauce, trying to have no more than 2 layers. The sauce should almost, but not completely, cover them. Add a bit more water, if necessary.

Cover the pot and simmer the vegetables sandwiches for about 1 hour, or until they are tender and the meat is cooked through. Occasionally baste the top vegetables with some of the sauce.

To serve, use a slotted spoon to remove the stuffed vegetables from the pot to a serving platter. If the sauce seems to be too watery, quickly boil it down until it reaches the desired consistency. Adjust the seasonings to taste. Pour some of the sauce over the vegetables and serve the rest on the side.

Makes about 6 servings.

CHOLENT (M)

(Long-Cooked Meat Stew)

Although Jewish law prohibits kindling a fire on Shabbat, it is nevertheless considered a *mitzvah* to eat a hot meal at midday on Saturday. Over the centuries, Jews throughout the world have worked out a number of ingenious solutions for this dilemma. All involve cooking food overnight at a very low heat. In the past, a hot fire was started in the baker's oven (or home oven) before Shabbat and then left to slowly burn itself out over a long period of time.

There are so many different versions of the Sabbath stew that a whole book could be written about them alone. The medieval word *cholent* (pronounced "tshoh'-lent") may have come from the Old French word *chald,* which meant "warm," or, less likely, from the Yiddish *shul ende,* which describes when the cholent is eaten—"after synagogue." The German word *schalet* probably has the same origin.

The standard, Eastern European *cholent,* as follows below, usually contains meat, lima and/or white beans, barley, and potatoes, and sometimes also a piece of *kishka* or "stuffed derma" put on top of the other ingredients just before the *cholent* is put into the oven.

In Israel, a similar stew (which is often made with chicken instead of red meat, due to the high cost and relative scarcity of the latter, and cooked on top of the stove rather than in the oven) is usually called *hamim* from the Hebrew word for "hot." Similarly, the Italian version of the stew is known as *hammin.* Some Greek Jews have a version called *fijonicas.* Moroccans have a variation that is usually called *dafina* (page 40).

Iraqi Jews have an unusual long-cooked Shabbat dish called *pacha,* which is tripe stuffed with lamb and an assortment of seasonings, including cardamom, cinnamon, cloves, turmeric, and rose petals. A similar filling (without the lamb) is used for *tabeet* (page 43), an Iraqi Sabbath specialty made with a whole chicken. Iranian Jews have a different version of stuffed tripe called *geepa,* which features dried yellow peas, rice, leeks, herbs, and spices.

There is nothing like waking up to the wonderful aroma of *cholent* simmering in the oven. Though this recipe makes a lot, the leftovers reheat quite well.

1 cup dry baby lima beans, sorted
and rinsed

1 cup dry white beans, such as navy
beans or Great Northern beans,
sorted and rinsed

2 tablespoons vegetable oil

Water

2 large onions, finely chopped

About 2½ pounds chuck roast,
brisket, top of the rib, or other pot
roast, trimmed of all visible fat
and cut into 4 to 6 large chunks

⅔ cup pearl barley

½ cup dry lentils, sorted and rinsed

3 garlic cloves, minced

1½ teaspoons paprika

1 teaspoon salt

¼ to ½ teaspoon black pepper,
preferably freshly ground

½ teaspoon ground ginger

1 bay leaf

About 6 small thin-skinned "new"
red or white potatoes, well
scrubbed

About 7 cups boiling water (or as
needed)

The day before serving the cholent, put the lima beans and white beans into a large saucepan with water to cover them by at least 2 inches. Cover and bring to a boil. Boil for 2 minutes; then remove from the heat. Let the beans soak in the water for 1 to 3 hours. (Alternatively, unboiled beans may be soaked in water for 8 to 12 hours.) Drain the beans well before using them.

In a 6- to 8-quart non-aluminum, ovenproof stock pot or Dutch oven, heat the oil; then cook the onions, stirring, until they are just beginning to brown. Add the meat to the pot and brown the pieces on all sides. (see Note). Add the soaked beans, barley, lentils, garlic, paprika, salt, pepper, ginger, and bay leaf. Put the potatoes on top. Add enough water so that everything is almost covered, but there is at least 1 inch headroom at the top of the pot.

Over medium heat, bring the cholent to a boil; then cover it tightly and put it in a preheated 350-degree oven. Bake it for 1 hour; then lower the oven temperature to 225 to 250 degrees, and bake it overnight (12 to 20 hours). The cholent can be served at any time, at your convenience, after the minimal 12 hours. Do not stir the cholent while it is cooking.

Serve the cholent in soup bowls, giving each diner a portion of each of the ingredients. Spoon the broth on top.

Makes 8 to 10 hearty servings.

NOTE: If desired, cholent can be cooked overnight in a very large slow cooker. After browning the onions and meat, transfer them and the remaining ingredients to the slow cooker. Cook on high for 1 hour; then turn the heat to low and cook overnight.

DAFINA (M)

(North African-Style Long-Cooked Meat Stew)

North African Jews have a variation of *cholent* (page 38), which is called *dafina, s'hena, sefrina,* or *frackh,* depending on the cook and the city of origin. Like many other Shabbat stews, it has meat, potatoes, and beans (usually chick-peas), but differs from them in that it traditionally includes a calf's foot, a cloth bag of rice or wheat berries, and a giant meatball or dumpling called *coclo* or *kouclas.* The dumpling may be stuffed into a chicken neck, packed into a cloth bag, or partially poached or browned ahead so it will hold its shape without any covering. (Interestingly, both the name and the dumpling are similar to the type of Ashkenazic *kugel* which is occasionally cooked with *cholent.*)

Almost all *dafinas* also include delicious eggs cooked in their shells on top of the stew. Called *huevos haminados* (see page 248 in the Pesach chapter for directions on how to cook the eggs alone), the eggs are sometimes removed from the stew on Saturday morning and served as a hot breakfast.

Another type of Shabbat stew eaten in North Africa is called *orissa* and usually features whole wheat berries. In some areas, *orissa* may be made with sweet potatoes, honey, and cinnamon.

I based the following recipe for *dafina* on those of several Moroccan Jews who came from different parts of that country. All the recipes had the basics in common, with each person adding his or her own special touch. One told me that dates were the secret, adding flavor and color, but not sweetness. (He was right! They are included below.) Others used brown sugar or caramelized white sugar for the same purpose.

The dumplings added to the stew were all different—most made with meat, rice, and herbs, but others with just seasoned bread crumbs and fat. At any rate, I decided to forgo the dumpling, as the stew is quite filling without it. Also, since most of the Moroccans lamented the difficulty of getting kosher calves' feet in the United States, I omitted them as well. However, I was careful to retain the special combination of seasonings that makes *dafina* so special.

One devotee of *dafina* who enthusiastically shared his recipe with me is Rabbi Joshua Toledano, religious leader of Philadelphia's Congregation Mikveh Israel, one of the oldest Sephardic synagogues in the United States. Rabbi Toledano, descendant of a long line of rabbis which he has traced back to pre-Inquisition Spain, has also carried on the heritage of the family's *dafina,* which became "famous" in Morocco in the early 1960s.

As Rabbi Toledano tells the story, King Hassan II had just come into power and was touring Morocco to officially proclaim his reign. Rabbi Toledano's maternal grandfather, a wealthy businessman of Meknes, was among those who welcomed the king at the gates of the city. He was also a good friend of the governor of Meknes, who happened to be the king's uncle.

The king arrived on a Friday afternoon and, during an audience with his uncle demanded to have "the Jewish dafina" for his evening meal. The governor went to his Jewish friend and explained the situation. Ten prominent rabbis got together and decided that the Jewish community could profane the Shabbat, just this once, for the king. Together, many people prepared a huge *dafina* that they were able to cook only for 3 to 4 hours because of the time limitation.

The king loved it. In fact, he enjoyed it so much that the next day he requested *dafina* for his midday meal. Again, the governor came to see his Jewish friend. This time, Rabbi Toledano's grandfather called upon the families of all nine of his children, who combined their own individual *dafinas,* already prepared for Shabbat, into a magnificent one fit for a king.

King Hassan II left Meknes happy and satisfied, and the governor was forever indebted to Rabbi Toledano's family.

1½ cups dry chick-peas (garbanzo beans), sorted and rinsed
Water
About 2½ pounds chuck roast, brisket, top of the rib, or other pot roast, trimmed of all visible fat and cut into 4 to 6 large chunks
2 medium-sized onions, finely chopped
3 cloves garlic, finely minced
¼ cup chopped pitted dates
½ teaspoon ground cinnamon
½ teaspoon ground allspice
¼ teaspoon ground ginger
¼ teaspoon ground turmeric
1 teaspoon salt
¼ teaspoon black pepper, preferably freshly ground
1 cup uncooked white or brown rice or whole wheat berries
6 to 8 small thin-skinned "new" red or white potatoes, well scrubbed
6 to 8 unshelled large raw eggs
About 7 cups water

The day before serving the dafina, put the chick-peas into a medium-sized saucepan with water to cover them by at least 2 inches. Cover and bring to a boil. Boil for 2 minutes; then remove from the heat. Let the beans soak in the water for 1 to 3 hours. (Alternatively, unboiled beans may be soaked in water for 8 to 12 hours.) Drain the beans well before using them.

In the bottom of a 6- to 8-quart non-aluminum, ovenproof stock pot or Dutch oven (see Note), spread the soaked chick-peas. Put the meat on top of the beans. Scatter the onions, garlic, dates, spices, and seasonings around the meat. Cut a very large square from a double thickness of cheesecloth. Put the rice or wheat berries in the center of the square. Then bring up the edges of the cloth and tie them tightly at the top with heavy cord to form a bag. There should be enough room in the bag for the grains to at least double in size. Put the bag in the center, on top of the meat. Surround it with potatoes and eggs, alternating them so the potatoes "cushion" the eggs. Add enough water so that everything is almost covered, but there is at least 1 inch of headroom at the top of the pot.

Over medium heat, bring the dafina to a boil; then cover it tightly and put it in a preheated 350-degree oven. Bake it for 1 hour; then lower the oven temperature to 225 to 250 degrees and bake it overnight (12 to 20 hours). The dafina can be served at any time, at your convenience, after the minimal 12 hours. Do not stir the dafina while it is cooking.

The dafina is usually served in "courses." First, the eggs are shelled and served with the potatoes and a little broth. (Moroccans like to chop the eggs and potatoes together.) This is followed by the rest of the dafina. Sometimes, the meat and rice (or wheat) are eaten from a plate, and the beans are served in the rich broth as a "soup."

Makes 8 to 10 hearty servings.

NOTE: If desired, the dafina can be cooked in a very large slow cooker. Put all the ingredients in the cooker in the order listed above. Cook on high heat for 1 hour; then turn the heat to low and cook overnight.

TABEET (M)

(Iraqi-Style Chicken and Rice)

Years ago in Baghdad, this dish was prepared as a type of *cholent* to be served after services on Shabbat. Rachel Muallem Gabes, a native of Iraq, recalls that it was cooked very slowly overnight on a stove fired with fine charcoal and wood.

In 1942, when the German army was about to enter Egypt, Mrs. Gabes and her family fled to Iran. In 1950, the family again became endangered because of her father-in-law's participation in an underground movement to help Russian Jews escape to Israel. This time, they traveled to the United States and eventually became naturalized citizens.

Mrs. Gabes no longer prepares *tabeet* as an overnight dish. Instead, she may cook it for several hours during the day and serve it on Friday night or at a dinner party. For added flavor and color, she may steam some vegetables and fruit, such as turnips, fresh beets, and apples, on top of the rice surrounding the chicken.

The following simplified version of *tabeet* is an amalgam of recipes I learned from Mrs. Gabes and other Iraqi Jews. As in traditional versions, the chicken contains a rice stuffing which is seasoned differently from the rice that surrounds the chicken. Also, it forms the "crust" on the bottom of the pan which is so prized by both Iraqis and Iranians. However, it only takes about 2 hours to cook.

(Note: The rice in this dish is partially cooked and then rinsed to remove excess starch, which may cause stickiness.)

2 cups long-grain white rice
4 cups cold water

STUFFING SEASONINGS
⅛ teaspoon each *ground cinnamon,*
allspice, cardamom, cloves,
turmeric, salt, and black
pepper
Heart and gizzard from the chicken,
finely chopped (optional)
1 teaspoon crumbled dried rose petals
(optional)
2 tablespoons water

CHICKEN
1 whole 4-pound (approximately)
chicken, cleaned to remove as
much fat as possible
½ teaspoon ground turmeric

RICE SEASONINGS
3 tablespoons tomato paste
¼ teaspoon ground cinnamon
Pinch of ground allspice or cloves
½ teaspoon salt
¼ teaspoon black pepper, preferably
freshly ground
1½ cups water

Put the rice and the 4 cups water in a large saucepan over high heat. Bring to a boil; then lower the heat and simmer for 5 minutes. Remove the saucepan from the heat and drain the rice in a colander. Rinse the rice with cool water and drain it well.

Put ¾ cup of the partially cooked rice into a small bowl. (Reserve the remainder.) Add all the *stuffing seasonings* including the giblets and rose petals (if used), and water and mix well. Loosely stuff the chicken with the rice mixture and enclose it by sewing together the skin flaps, or skewer them closed with round wooden toothpicks (the sturdy type that are pointed at both ends).

Put the chicken, breast up, in a large soup pot or Dutch oven with about 1 inch of water. Sprinkle the ½ teaspoon turmeric over the chicken and into the water to give extra color. Bring the water to a boil over high heat; then lower the heat, cover the pot tightly, and steam the chicken for about 45 minutes, or until it is almost tender but not falling apart. During the cooking period, baste the chicken often with the cooking water and poke a few deep holes through it with a metal skewer to release fat and to allow some juices to enter the cavity containing the stuffing.

Use 2 large spoons to carefully remove the cooked chicken from the pot. Set it aside on a platter. Discard the cooking liquid (it will be greasy) and wipe out the pot. Put the reserved partially cooked rice into the pot and add all the *rice seasonings* and water; then stir well. Put the chicken on top of the rice. Bring to a boil over medium-high heat, cover tightly, and turn the heat to low. Steam the rice and chicken for about 45 minutes to 1 hour without disturbing the rice. It will form a crust on the bottom of the pot.

To serve, carefully transfer the chicken to a serving dish. Use a metal spatula or pancake turner with a large flat blade to remove the rice in the pot, turning the rice over so the crust is on top. Serve it with the chicken and stuffing. (For ease in removing the rice crust, sprinkle a tablespoon of water over the rice, cover the pot, and set it in some cool water for a minute.)

Makes about 6 servings.

OAF TAPOOZIM (M)

(Israeli-Style Orange Chicken)

This easy, delicious main dish uses two foods which are quite popular in Israel, oranges and almonds.

2 tablespoons pareve *margarine or vegetable oil*

5 *medium-sized or 4 large chicken breast halves, skinned, boned, and cut into 1-inch squares (about 1¼ pounds chicken meat)*

1½ *tablespoons cornstarch*

¼ *teaspoon ground cinnamon*

¼ *teaspoon ground ginger*

1¼ *cups orange juice*

3 *tablespoons dry white wine or dry sherry*

1 *tablespoon honey*

2 *teaspoons soy sauce*

1 *tablespoon grated orange rind (colored part only)*

1¼ *cups peeled and seeded fresh orange sections*

½ *cup slivered or sliced almonds*

TO SERVE
Hot cooked white or brown rice

In a large skillet, over medium-high heat, melt the margarine; then brown the chicken lightly on all sides.

Meanwhile, in a large measuring cup (or a bowl), combine the corn-starch, cinnamon, and ginger. Stir in a small amount of the orange juice to make a paste with the cornstarch mixture; then stir in the rest of the juice, the wine, honey, and soy sauce.

Add the juice mixture to the skillet. Continue heating, stirring occa-sionally, until the sauce thickens and comes to a boil. Cover the skillet and lower the heat. Simmer the chicken for about 20 minutes, basting it often with the sauce, until it is very tender. Stir in the grated orange rind, orange sections, and almonds and cook for about 2 minutes longer, or until the oranges are heated through. Serve the chicken mixture over hot cooked rice.

Makes about 4 servings.

SYRIAN-STYLE CHICKEN AND SPAGHETTI (M)

This is a dish that Jews of Syrian ancestry often enjoy as part of their Friday evening meal. All the seasonings can be adjusted to taste.

About 3½ pounds meaty chicken pieces (remove skin, if desired)
2 cups cold water
1 large onion, diced
2 to 3 garlic cloves, minced
½ teaspoon ground paprika
1 teaspoon ground cinnamon
¼ teaspoon ground allspice

½ teaspoon salt
¼ to ½ teaspoon white or black pepper, preferably freshly ground
1 pound thin spaghetti, broken into 3- to 4-inch lengths
1 tablespoon olive oil
1 6-ounce can tomato paste
½ teaspoon dried oregano leaves

Put the chicken pieces into an ovenproof, 6-quart or similar soup pot or Dutch oven. Mix the water with the onion, garlic, paprika, cinnamon, allspice, salt, and pepper and pour the mixture over the chicken. Bring the liquid to a boil over high heat; then cover the pot and lower the heat. Simmer the chicken for about 1 hour, or until it is quite tender.

Meanwhile, cook the spaghetti according to the package directions, but a few minutes less than indicated, so it is still quite firm. Drain the spaghetti well and rinse it briefly under cold water; then drain again. Toss the spaghetti with the oil so the strands do not stick together. Set aside.

Use tongs or a slotted spoon to remove the cooked chicken from the broth in the pot. Set the chicken aside momentarily. (If desired, it may be cooled slightly and boned.) Add the tomato paste and oregano to the broth and stir until they are completely mixed in. Bring the sauce to a simmer for 5 minutes, stirring; then remove it from the heat. Stir the partially cooked spaghetti into the sauce; then bury the chicken pieces in the spaghetti. Cover the pot loosely with aluminum foil and put it in a preheated 350-degree oven. Bake for about 45 minutes, or until the sauce is absorbed.

Makes about 6 servings.

CHICKEN WITH BRANDIED CHERRY
SAUCE (M)

Loosely adapted from a popular entrée once served at the Holland Glory
Restaurant in Amsterdam, this impressive, yet easy, dish is sure to be a
hit among cherry fanciers.

2 *tablespoons* pareve *margarine or*
  vegetable oil
6 *medium-sized chicken breast halves*
  (remove skin, if desired)
1 *16-ounce can dark sweet cherries,*
  including liquid

⅓ *cup cherry-flavored brandy, sweet*
  cherry wine, or cream sherry
1 *tablespoon cornstarch*
1½ *tablespoons cold water*
1 *to 2 teaspoons sugar (optional)*

In a large skillet, over medium-high heat, melt the margarine; then
brown the chicken pieces with the meaty side facing down. Drain the
liquid from the cherries into a small measuring cup. There should be
about ⅔ cup; if not, add water to make that amount. (Reserve the cherries.) Pour the liquid over the chicken in the skillet. Cover the skillet
tightly, lower the heat, and simmer the chicken in the cherry juice for
about 40 minutes, or until the chicken is tender. Use tongs or a slotted
spoon to remove the chicken from the skillet to a warm serving platter.
Add the cherry-flavored brandy to the skillet; then raise the heat and
bring the liquid to a boil while scraping up any browned bits on the
bottom of the pan. Mix the cornstarch with the water and add the mixture to the skillet while stirring. Simmer the sauce until it thickens, 1 to 2
minutes. Add sugar, if desired, and stir until it dissolves. Gently stir in
the reserved cherries for about 1 minute, or until they are heated through.
Spoon the cherry sauce over the chicken breasts.

Makes 4 to 6 servings.

ROCK CORNISH HENS WITH
CUMBERLAND GLAZE (M)

These make very impressive company fare, yet are a cinch to prepare and
take only a short time to roast. If desired, the hens may be filled with
your favorite stuffing or pilaf before roasting. When stuffed, they will

need about 20 to 25 minutes more roasting time. Brush them with the glaze during the last third of the cooking period.

3 Rock Cornish hens or "Rock
  Cornish broiler chickens"
  (approximately 1½ pounds each;
  see Note)

CUMBERLAND GLAZE
½ cup dry red wine or cranberry
  juice
½ cup orange juice
2 tablespoons lemon juice

1 tablespoon grated orange rind
  (colored part only)
½ teaspoon powdered mustard
¼ teaspoon ground ginger
⅛ teaspoon ground cloves
Pinch of cayenne pepper (optional)
½ cup red currant jelly
2 teaspoons cornstarch
1 tablespoon cold water

Use heavy string or cord to tie the legs of each hen together and close to the body of the bird. Tie the wings so they rest against the body. Place the hens, breast up, on a rack in a shallow roasting pan, leaving some room between them for the heat to circulate. Roast, uncovered, in a preheated 375-degree oven for 1 hour.

Meanwhile, prepare the Cumberland glaze. In a small saucepan, over medium-high heat, combine the wine, orange juice, lemon juice, orange rind, powdered mustard, ginger, cloves, and cayenne (if used) and bring to a simmer. Stir in the currant jelly and cook, stirring, until it is melted. In a small cup, combine the cornstarch and cool water; then stir this into the mixture in the saucepan. Continue cooking, stirring constantly, until the glaze boils and thickens. Remove it from heat and cool it to room temperature.

After the hens have roasted for 1 hour, brush them with the prepared glaze. Roast the hens, periodically brushing them with the glaze, about 30 minutes longer, or until the juices run clear (not pink) when a thigh is pricked and a leg twists easily. To serve, cut each hen in half lengthwise. If desired, reheat any leftover glaze and serve it as a sauce with the hens.

Makes about 6 servings.

NOTE: If smaller hens are used, they will need less time to roast. For instance, 1-pound hens take only about 1 hour. Periodically brush them with the glaze during the last 30 minutes of roasting time.

ROASTED PEPPER AND TOMATO SALAD (P)

Chilled vegetable salads, such as this, are very popular with Moroccan and Middle Eastern Jews. Several salads are always on the Friday evening Shabbat table and are served at most other holidays as well. They are usually accompanied by fresh bread.

In the past, the peppers for this salad were always roasted over an open fire. Here, the technique has been simplified, using a broiler or gas flame. Sweet red peppers may be substituted for some of the green ones; however, they should be watched carefully during broiling as they usually take less time. If desired, unseasoned, peeled roasted pepper pieces may be frozen and used at a later time.

4 or 5 medium-sized sweet green peppers

2 medium-sized tomatoes, preferably vine-ripened, peeled, seeded, and cut into small pieces

2 thin scallions, including green tops, thinly sliced

2 garlic cloves, finely minced

1 tablespoon finely chopped fresh parsley leaves

2 tablespoons good-quality olive oil

2 tablespoons lemon juice

¼ teaspoon salt

Pinch each of ground cumin and paprika (optional)

Freshly ground black pepper to taste

Put the peppers in a foil-lined baking pan (such as a jelly roll pan), and place the pan about 6 inches under a heated broiler element. Broil the peppers, rotating them often with tongs, for 15 to 25 minutes, or until the skins are completely blistered and charred. (Alternatively, spear each pepper on a fork and roast by rotating it over a gas flame for 3 to 4 minutes.)

Use tongs or a large spoon to transfer the roasted peppers to a brown paper bag. Fold over the top of the bag and let the peppers cool. The steam in the bag helps loosen the skins. (Moisture may seep through the bottom of the bag, so keep it in the sink if possible.) Rinse each pepper under cool running water, while you remove and discard the skin, stem, and seeds. (Be careful of the steam that may remain inside the pepper.) Drain the peppers very well.

Cut the peppers into small pieces. Put them in a bowl with the remaining ingredients and toss to combine. Chill the salad several hours or overnight to give the flavors a chance to blend. For the best flavor, remove the salad from the refrigerator about 1 hour before serving time. Stir the salad before serving.

Makes about 6 servings.

BAMIA (P)

(Okra in Tomato Sauce)

Okra, which is very popular among Sephardim, appears on the table at most festive meals. Those who are unfamiliar with this vegetable will be pleasantly surprised at how tasty it can be when prepared using Sephardic techniques. Sometimes the okra is part of a large vegetable stew, which contains such varied vegetables as sweet green peppers, eggplant, green beans, and tomatoes. On other occasions, the preparation is simpler.

Following is one of the most popular and easiest okra dishes. It is tasty both hot as a side dish or cold as a salad; it can be varied by using tomato sauce or fresh tomatoes instead of canned ones.

About 1½ pounds fresh small okra (or 2 10-ounce packages frozen okra, slightly thawed)
2 tablespoons olive oil
1 large onion, finely chopped
2 garlic cloves, minced

1 16-ounce can tomatoes, including juice, chopped
2 tablespoons lemon juice
⅛ teaspoon black pepper, preferably freshly ground

Wash the fresh okra well. Cut off the stems and tiny bottom tips, being careful not to expose any seeds. (No preparation is necessary for frozen okra, although you may wish to trim any stems that are still intact.)

In a medium-sized saucepan, heat the oil over medium-high heat. Cook the onion and garlic, stirring, until they are tender but not browned. Add the okra, tomatoes, lemon juice, and pepper. Bring to a boil; then lower the heat and simmer, covered, for about 10 minutes. Remove the cover and continue simmering until the okra is tender and most of the liquid has evaporated to form a thick sauce, about 10 to 20 minutes longer. Serve hot as a side dish or chill and serve cold or at room temperature as an appetizer or salad.

Makes 6 to 8 servings.

HERBED KASHA-MUSHROOM PILAF (M)

Kasha is just another name for toasted buckwheat groats. Though botanically not a grain, kasha is usually cooked and eaten just like one. It is a favorite of those Jews with Russian backgrounds, and is often served with "bow tie" noodles and gravy. The following is a different way to cook kasha. Serve it as a side dish or use it to stuff poultry before roasting.

¼ cup pareve *margarine or vegetable oil*	*3 cups chicken broth or bouillon made from cubes or powder*
1 large onion, finely chopped	*3 tablespoons finely chopped fresh parsley leaves*
2 celery stalks, diced	
1½ cups chopped fresh mushrooms	*½ teaspoon ground sage*
1½ cups whole or coarse kasha (buckwheat groats)	*½ teaspoon dried thyme leaves*
1 large egg, lightly beaten	*Salt and freshly ground black pepper to taste*

In a saucepan, over medium-high heat, melt the margarine; then cook the onion and celery, stirring, until they are tender but not browned. Add the mushrooms and cook, stirring, 1 minute longer. Mix the kasha with the egg and add this to the saucepan. Cook, stirring, 1 to 2 minutes longer, or until the kasha seems dry. Then stir in the remaining ingredients.

Bring the broth to a boil; then cover the saucepan and lower the heat. Simmer the pilaf for 15 to 20 minutes, or until all the liquid has been absorbed and the kasha is tender.

Makes 6 to 8 servings.

FRIJOLES NEGROS (P)

(Cuban-Style Black Beans)

Almost seventy years ago, when she was only two, Regina Korenstein and her family left their native home in Poland, with hopes of immigrating to the United States. However, U. S. quota restrictions made this impossible and so they decided to live in Cuba. There, they became part of a large, active Jewish community. Regina grew up in Cuba, and married another Jewish immigrant, David Gershgorn, who had left Russia (and his family) to escape conscription into the army.

During the late 1940s, an American tourist visiting Cuba mistook David Gershgorn for a friend of hers who lived in the United States. It was indeed an incredible coincidence that the woman's friend turned out to be Mr. Gershgorn's brother, Morris Gordon, whom he hadn't seen or heard of since childhood. The "Yankee" brother eventually persuaded Mr. Gershgorn and his entire family to move to the United States, and adopt the Americanized version of their surname—just a few years before the Communist takeover of Cuba.

In Philadelphia, Mrs. Regina Gordon continued to cook the unique Cuban-European cuisine she had learned during her youth, and that her family favored. Mrs. Gordon passed away a short while ago. But loving memories of her linger on in recipes, such as the one here, which I got from her daughter-in-law, Sharon Cantor Gordon, who enthusiastically carries on the family's culinary traditions.

On Friday nights, recalls Sharon, Mrs. Regina Gordon often served this dish with chicken soup, Eastern European-style brisket or rib roast, avocado salad, and thinly sliced, fried *plantano* (or plantain), a banana-like vegetable, which is popular in the Caribbean.

The bean mixture is typically served over perfectly cooked long-grain *white* rice. However, the combination of beans with a whole grain, such as brown rice, actually provides enough complete protein to serve as a delicious main course. (Note: If you cannot find black beans with the other dry beans in the supermarket, look in the specialty section featuring Spanish foods.)

1 pound (2½ cups) dry black (turtle) beans, sorted and rinsed well
1 large bay leaf
Cold water
2 tablespoons vegetable or olive oil
1 large onion, finely chopped
4 to 5 garlic cloves, minced
1 large sweet green pepper, finely chopped

1 teaspoon salt
⅛ teaspoon black pepper, preferably freshly ground

TO SERVE
Hot cooked white or brown rice, preferably "converted" rice
Finely chopped onions to taste (optional)

Put the dry beans and bay leaf into a very large saucepan or small Dutch oven and add about 6 cups water or enough to cover the beans by approximately 1 inch. Bring the water to a boil over high heat; then cover the saucepan and lower the heat. Simmer the beans, covered, for 1 hour. Then continue cooking them for about 1 hour longer, periodically adding small amounts of very hot or boiling water, as necessary, to keep the level of liquid just as high as the beans but not higher.

Meanwhile, heat the oil in a large skillet over medium-high heat; then sauté the onion, garlic, and green pepper until they are tender but not browned. Set the vegetables aside.

When the beans are very soft, stir in the sautéed vegetables. Continue cooking the beans over low heat, uncovered, stirring often, for about 30 minutes longer, or until they become slightly mashed and form a creamy sauce and the vegetables are blended into the beans. Season the bean mixture with the salt and pepper, adjusting them to taste. Serve the beans over hot cooked rice. If desired, top them with freshly chopped onion.

Makes 8 to 10 servings as a side dish.

BROWN RICE PILAF (M)

This dish is a great way to introduce brown rice to a skeptical family.

1½ tablespoons pareve *margarine or vegetable oil*
1½ cups long-grain brown rice
3 cups hot chicken broth or bouillon made from cubes or powder
½ teaspoon ground allspice
¼ teaspoon ground cinnamon
⅛ teaspoon ground cloves
1 teaspoon lemon juice
¼ teaspoon salt
⅛ teaspoon black pepper, preferably freshly ground
½ cup slivered almonds
½ cup dark raisins

In a medium-sized saucepan, over medium heat, melt the margarine. Add the uncooked rice, and stir constantly for about 2 minutes. Slowly add the hot broth while stirring. Then stir in the remaining ingredients. Bring to a boil; then lower the heat and cover the pan tightly. Simmer the rice for 45 to 50 minutes, or until all the liquid has been absorbed. (For drier rice, remove the lid during the last 5 minutes of cooking.) Use a fork to fluff and stir the rice once before serving, making sure the raisins and almonds are evenly distributed.

Makes 6 to 8 servings.

FRUITY TOFU LOKSHEN KUGEL (P)

(Noodle "Pudding")

Although this looks and tastes something like a dairy *kugel*, it is *pareve* and perfect for a Shabbat or other meat meal. Thanks to the tofu (which is made from soybeans and available in many supermarkets and most health-food stores), the following *kugel* has more protein than most non-dairy versions and less cholesterol than most dairy ones.

8 ounces medium-wide egg noodles
3 large eggs, lightly beaten
¼ cup vegetable oil
¼ cup honey
¼ cup orange juice, apple juice, or water
2 teaspoons ground cinnamon
¼ teaspoon salt

1 pound hard (firm) tofu, well drained and crumbled
1 large apple, finely diced (it is not necessary to peel it)
1 cup dark or light raisins
¼ cup coarsely chopped walnuts (optional)

Cook the noodles as directed on the package; then drain them well.

Meanwhile, in a large bowl, stir together the eggs, oil, honey, juice, cinnamon, and salt until well combined. Mix in the tofu, apple, raisins, and walnuts (if used). Add the noodles and stir until completely mixed in. Turn out the mixture into a greased or non-stick spray-coated, 7- by 12-inch or equivalent baking dish. Bake in a preheated 350-degree oven for about 45 minutes, or until set. Serve warm or at room temperature.

Makes about 8 servings.

JA'ALAH (P)

(Mixed Fruit and Nuts)

Before and after the Shabbat meal (and other festive meals), Yemenite Jews often partake of this delicious mixture so they can say blessings thanking God for the fruit of the tree, the vine, the earth, and other foods.

Their main course on Shabbat is likely to be *shawayeh,* meat roasted on a grill and flavored with *hawayiz* (a seasoning mix of black pepper, caraway seeds, cardamom, and turmeric). The bread may be *lakhuah* (a very flat sourdough loaf made on a griddle like a pancake). Also likely to be included are *hilbeh* (a paste of fenugreek seeds, garlic, coriander leaves, and cumin); *zhoog* (a spicy-hot mixture of chili peppers, garlic, coriander, cumin, cardamom, and water); or a relish made by combining the two with tomatoes. Yemenite Jews claim that all these seasonings help prevent heart disease and gastrointestinal problems.

After such a spicy meal, one is sure to welcome the sweet mixture that follows. *Ja'alah* is also served to postpartum mothers to help them regain strength. Sometimes, soaked and toasted beans, such as chick-peas, are added to it.

Shelled roasted peanuts	*Raisins*
Whole shelled almonds	*Dried apricots or similar dried fruit*
Hulled sunflower seeds	*Assorted candy or candied fruit*

Mix the above in any proportions desired and put the mixture in a bowl on the Shabbat table along with fresh fruit.

EIR KICHLAH (P)

(Egg Cookies or "Bow Ties")

There are dozens of variations of these very popular light cookies. Some are made with a stiff, rolled dough, others with a softer dough that is "dropped" onto the baking sheet. Some use copious amounts of oil, others use none at all. Some call for baking powder, others don't. Some are barely sweet, others are very sweet. Some are cut into simple squares, rectangles, or circles, others are cut into fancier diamonds or twisted into bow ties.

With their Yiddish name, these treats are obviously Ashkenazic. But Sephardic Jews of Turkish and Greek origins use an almost identical dough to make ring-shaped cookies which are coated with sesame seeds. The latter are sometimes called *biscochos de huevo,* which translates the same as *eir kichlah.* And Jews in the Sephardic community on the island of Curaçao serve a similar crisp sponge cookie called *panlevi* (page 57) on holidays and other special occasions.

The following *eir kichlah* recipe is my own combination of many versions. The cookies are light, pleasantly but not excessively sweet, and easy to make. (This recipe may be doubled; roll it out in two batches for best results.) The method for *biscochos de huevo* is also included below.

2 large eggs
¼ cup sugar (plus more for rolling
*   and topping)*
3½ tablespoons vegetable oil

¼ teaspoon vanilla extract (optional)
1¾ cups all-purpose white flour,
*   preferably unbleached*
1 teaspoon baking powder

Use an electric mixer to beat the eggs with the ¼ cup sugar for several minutes until very light and fluffy; then beat in the oil and vanilla (if used). Stir in the flour and baking powder and mix until combined. If the dough is still very sticky, add a little more flour. Gather the dough into a ball and wrap it in plastic wrap or wax paper. Let it rest for 5 to 10 minutes.

Using extra sugar, instead of flour, to keep the dough from sticking, roll out the dough to about a ¼-inch thickness. Sprinkle more sugar on top and gently press it in with the rolling pin. Using a sharp knife or pastry wheel, cut the dough into small squares, rectangles, or diamonds. Transfer the cookies to a greased or non-stick spray-coated baking sheet, keeping them at least ½ inch apart.

To make bow ties, cut the dough into rectangles about 1 inch wide by 2½ to 3 inches long. Carefully twist each rectangle twice in the center so that the sugared surface faces upward. Place the bow ties on the prepared baking sheet.

Bake the cookies in a preheated 350-degree oven for about 20 minutes, or until they are lightly browned. Remove them from the sheet and cool them on a wire rack.

Makes about 3 dozen small, flat cookies or about 2 dozen bow ties.

VARIATION

BISCOCHOS DE HUEVO   (P)
(Sesame Ring Cookies)

Increase the sugar in the dough to ⅓ cup (or up to ½ cup for sweeter cookies). Use floured hands to shape the dough into ½-inch-diameter ropes. Cut the ropes into 4-inch-long sections and pinch the ends of each section together to form a ring. Beat *1 egg* with *1 teaspoon each of cold water and sugar*. Dip the top surface of each ring into the egg mixture and then into *hulled sesame seeds*. Place the rings on a greased or non-stick spray-coated baking sheet with the seeds facing upward. Bake as directed for eir kichlah.

Makes about 3 dozen cookies.

PANLEVI (P)

(Crisp Egg Cookies)

Five centuries ago, during the period of the heinous Inquisition, many Jews fled from Spain and Portugal to countries which were more tolerant. A number of Jews went to live in Holland and, from there, small groups eventually settled in almost all the Dutch colonies.

One such settlement was on the island of Curaçao, part of the Netherlands Antilles in the Caribbean. Today, the oldest surviving synagogue and Jewish cemetery in the Western Hemisphere are located there, along with a thriving Jewish community.

Cookies like that which follow have been served for centuries by the Sephardim of Curaçao on holidays and other special occasions. Interestingly, it has become a "New World" tradition to accompany them with a drink of hot chocolate at the celebration of a *brit milah* (circumcision).

Those with Ashkenazic backgrounds may notice that these cookies are quite similar to one version of *eir kichlah* in which the dough is dropped rather than rolled.

2 large eggs
⅓ cup sugar
⅛ teaspoon ground cinnamon
⅛ teaspoon ground mace

½ teaspoon vanilla extract
¾ cup all-purpose white flour, preferably unbleached
¼ teaspoon baking powder

In a medium-sized bowl, use an electric mixer to beat the eggs with the sugar until very thick and light. Beat in the cinnamon, mace, and vanilla. By hand, stir in the flour and baking powder. The batter will be loose.

On greased and lightly floured or non-stick spray-coated baking sheets, drop the batter by generous teaspoonfuls, pushing it off the spoon with your fingertip (see Note). Leave at least 1½ inches between each cookie.

Bake in a preheated 350-degree oven for about 18 to 20 minutes, or until the edges of the cookies are browned. Immediately use a metal spatula to remove the cookies from the baking sheet to a wire rack. They should become crisp as they cool. If the cookies are too soft, return them to a low oven for a few minutes to crisp.

Makes about 20 (2-inch) cookies.

NOTE: For larger cookies, use about twice as much batter and bake them a little longer.

SPICY APPLE COFFEE CAKE   (D) or (P)

During the *havdalah* service, which signifies the end of Shabbat, several sweet-smelling spices (or *besamim*) are sniffed by all those present. The spices represent the wonderful "fragrance" of Shabbat, and are said to help us get over our disappointment that the symbolic "Shabbat Queen" is departing. Some Jews, particularly Hasidim, give her a royal send-off with a special meal called *Melavah Malkah* (which means "accompanying the queen"). This may be a large feast, or simply an assortment of cake and cookies. The following delicious cake contains the same spices often used for *havdalah,* and would be perfect for *Melavah Malkah* or any time during Shabbat.

FILLING AND TOPPING
⅔ cup finely chopped walnuts or
  pecans
¼ cup sugar
1 teaspoon ground cinnamon
1 large apple, peeled, cored, and
  thinly sliced

BATTER
½ cup butter or margarine, softened
¾ cup sugar

3 large eggs
1 teaspoon ground cinnamon
¼ teaspoon ground allspice
¼ teaspoon ground cloves
1 cup apple cider or richly flavored
  apple juice
2 cups all-purpose white flour,
  preferably unbleached (may be
  half whole wheat flour, if desired)
1 teaspoon baking powder
1 teaspoon baking soda

In a small bowl, make the filling and topping by mixing together the nuts, sugar, and cinnamon. Set the mixture aside with the apple slices.

For the batter, use an electric mixer to cream the butter and sugar until light and fluffy. Beat in the eggs, one by one, and stir until well combined. Beat in the cinnamon, allspice, and cloves. Alternately add the cider and flour, mixing after each addition. Then mix in the baking powder and soda until completely combined.

Pour half the batter into a well-greased or non-stick spray-coated 9-inch-square or equivalent baking pan. Sprinkle the batter with half of the filling-and-topping mixture. Arrange the apple slices on top. Spread the remaining batter over the apples and sprinkle it with the remaining filling and topping. Use your fingertips to lightly press the topping into the batter.

Bake the cake in a preheated 375-degree oven for 30 to 35 minutes, or until a toothpick inserted in the center comes out clean. Cool in the pan on a wire rack. Cut into squares to serve.

Makes 16 squares; about 8 servings.

LINZERTORTE   (D) or (P)

(Jam-Filled Tart)

Jews of Austro-Hungarian heritage are justly proud of wonderful pastries such as this. The *linzertorte,* which is actually more like a jam tart than a torte, can be made ahead, and keeps very well for several days. It also freezes nicely.

1⅔ cups all-purpose white flour, preferably unbleached
1 cup (about 4 ounces) very finely ground almonds
1 teaspoon baking powder ·
¾ teaspoon ground cinnamon
¼ teaspoon ground cloves
¼ teaspoon salt
½ cup butter or margarine, softened
¾ cup granulated sugar
1 large egg
2 tablespoons lemon juice
1 teaspoon grated lemon rind (yellow part only)

¼ teaspoon almond extract (optional)
2 tablespoons plain dry bread crumbs or matzo meal
1 10-ounce jar (about 1 cup) red or black raspberry jam

GLAZE
1 egg yolk, beaten with 1 teaspoon water

GARNISH (OPTIONAL)
Confectioner's sugar

In a medium-sized bowl, mix together the flour, almonds, baking powder, cinnamon, cloves, and salt and set aside. Cream the butter and sugar with an electric mixer or by hand until smooth. Add the flour mixture and mix until fine crumbs are formed. Add the egg, lemon juice, rind, and almond extract (if used) and mix very well to form a stiff dough. Wrap the dough in plastic wrap and chill it for about 30 minutes, or until it has firmed slightly. Press about two thirds of the dough evenly into the bottom and 1 inch up the sides of a greased 9-inch springform pan or tart pan with a removable bottom. Sprinkle the bottom of the pastry shell with the bread crumbs. Stir the jam to soften it and then spread it over the crumbs in the shell.

Roll out the remaining dough between two sheets of wax paper until it forms a 9½- by 4½-inch rectangle. Leave the dough in the paper, and chill it in the freezer for about 5 minutes, or until it is quite firm.

Lay the chilled, rolled-out dough on a cutting board, and use a sharp knife or scissors to cut it lengthwise into 8 ½-inch strips right through the paper and dough. Peel the paper off one side of a strip; then lay the strip, dough side down, across the filled pastry shell. Peel off the second piece of paper. Continue with the remaining strips, crisscrossing them to form a lattice. Press the ends of the strips against the pastry shell and trim off any overhanging pieces. Brush the glaze over the lattice and the edge of the shell.

Bake the torte in a preheated 350-degree oven for about 45 minutes, or until the crust is browned and quite firm. Cool the torte in the pan on a wire rack for about 30 minutes; then remove the sides of the pan and slide the torte off the pan base onto the rack to cool completely. Just before serving, it is customary, but not necessary, to sprinkle the torte lightly with sieved confectioner's sugar.

Makes about 8 servings.

THE DAYS OF AWE

Rosh Hashanah Through Yom Kippur

"L'shanah tovah tikatevu!" "May you be inscribed for a good year!" During the "Days of Awe" (or *Yamim Nora'im,* in Hebrew)—the ten days beginning with Rosh Hashanah and ending with Yom Kippur—this optimistic greeting is frequently exchanged by Jews all around the world.

Rosh Hashanah, the Jewish "New Year," takes place on the first and second days of the Hebrew month of Tishri, which usually occur in September or early October. Yom Kippur, the "Day of Atonement," is on the tenth of Tishri. Jewish communities everywhere celebrate these "High Holy Days," as they are sometimes called, in basically the same way. At synagogue services, the *shofar* (ram's horn) is sounded amidst solemn prayer, while those present reflect on the past and on their hopes for a bright future. According to traditional Judaism, divine judgment on each person's life is made and rendered during the Days of Awe.

The meals of Rosh Hashanah and those before and after the fast of Yom Kippur are times for feasting, and there are many culinary customs associated with them. One of the oldest and most widespread is the eating of sweet foods, particularly honey, to symbolize a universal hope that our lives will be sweet in the coming year.

Both Ashkenazic and Sephardic Jews dip apples and *challah* (pages 17 and 64) into honey. Dried fruit, sugar, and honey are used to sweeten many dishes, including main courses and vegetables. And, of course, several types of honey-laden desserts are favored for the Days of Awe.

Fish is often served as a symbol of fertility and immortality. Among Sephardic Jews, a whole fish is usually served with its head intact as a reminder that we should strive to be at the "head" of our peers and an example of righteousness to all. With this same idea in mind, Italian Jews eat ravioli filled with calves' brains, and Moroccans cook the brains into fritters. Greeks prefer savory pastries filled with hard-boiled eggs and brains. Jews from several different cultures partake of calves' or lambs' tongue in a variety of sauces. Yemenites and Afghans may even serve a whole sheep's head highly seasoned with fenugreek.

Many Sephardim (and some Ashkenazim) perform a special ceremony during the main meals of Rosh Hashanah in which they say blessings over certain foods. Seasonal vegetables which are plentiful and grow rapidly are always featured, because they are considered symbols of abundance. Leeks are also sometimes eaten for "luck"; whereas, large winter squash express the hope that the participants may "grow in fullness of blessing."

Some foods are included because their Hebrew names are puns on words in holiday prayers. For instance, the word for dates sounds like part of the blessing in which we ask to be cleansed of sin. Dates are also eaten because they are sweet, and because some consider them symbols of beauty and peace.

Some Israelis cook ordinary green "bottle" squash into a special holiday dish because its name sounds like part of the prayer which asks that our enemies be chopped down.

Other foods, such as carrots and beets, are eaten for similar reasons. Details are included with the holiday recipes for these foods in this chapter.

On the *second* night of Rosh Hashanah, at least one fruit not yet sampled in the season, is usually eaten. Unlike other Jewish holidays, the two days of Rosh Hashanah are considered to be one extended day. Thus, the *sheheheyanu* prayer for new experiences, in which we thank God for allowing us to reach this important moment of life in peace and health, might be "wasted" if it were repeated on the second evening without the "experience" of enjoying a "new" fruit.

In many Jewish households, this fruit is either grapes or a pomegranate, two favorites of both ancient and modern-day Israel. The exotic and succulent pomegranate also represents the hope that we will be privileged in the coming year to perform as many worthy deeds and pious acts as the pomegranate is replete with seeds.

The seeds also symbolize fertility and fruitfulness, as do sesame seeds and many other types of edible seeds enjoyed on Rosh Hashanah. Yemenites, for example, always eat a sauce made of fenugreek seeds, and many Moroccans dip dates in anise and/or sesame seeds.

Although the vast majority of culinary customs associated with this holiday are positive, optimistic ones, there are a few in which certain foods are purposely avoided. For instance, sour and bitter foods are not eaten, and some Jews avoid black-colored food, such as black olives and eggplant, as well. Some Iraqi Jews do not eat fish on Rosh Hashanah because the Hebrew word for "fish" *(dag)* is very similar to the word for "worry" *(da'ag)*. And certain Ashkenazic Jews avoid nuts because the total numerical value of the letters in a Hebrew word for "nut" is quite close to that of a word for "sin."

Also, the ceremonial challah is not dipped into salt as during the rest of the year, but into honey instead. In fact, in some homes, all the salt on the holiday table is replaced with sugar.

As the divine judgment made on Rosh Hashanah is said to be rendered on Yom Kippur, most of the culinary traditions are followed throughout the Days of Awe. However, there are a few special ones for the meals that immediately precede and follow the 25-hour Yom Kippur fast.

It's actually considered a *mitzvah*—a very good deed—to feast on the day before Yom Kippur. When we fast, we are supposed to feel hunger pangs, to be acutely aware of how difficult it is to atone for our sins. This is all the more obvious if we have dined well beforehand. Thus, in biblical times, Jews sometimes held great banquets prior to fasting.

More recently, it has become very traditional for Jews worldwide to partake of chicken soup at the pre-fast dinner. Boiled chicken—like all the foods usually eaten at this meal—is bland and easily digested, thus preventing undue thirst and indigestion during the long hours of prayer in the coming day.

Ashkenazic Jews usually serve *kreplah* (meat-filled dumplings) in the soup. (See the recipe on page 78 for more details.)

For the festive meal following Yom Kippur—the "break-the-fast" as it is sometimes called—Ashkenazim typically enjoy a light, dairy meal, which invariably includes pickled and/or smoked fish. This custom apparently came about because the fish supposedly helps restore the salts and minerals lost from the body during fasting. Many of the dairy dishes at such a meal—including *lokshen kugel* and *cheese blintzes* (pages 368 and 358)—are the same as those served during the holiday of Shavuot.

Italian Jews often break their fast with fried doughnuts coated with sugar. The round shape, like that of the round challah eaten during the Days of Awe, symbolizes hope for a well-rounded year, as well as good luck the whole year round. Since the doughnuts actually have a "double round" form, they additionally symbolize a hope for happiness all around the world. Similarly, Syrian Jews eat *ka'ak* (page 67), doughnut-shaped unsweet cookies that are coated with sesame seeds.

Some Moroccan Jews and also those from the island of Curaçao in the Netherlands Antilles break the fast by drinking coffee topped with a fluffy mixture of beaten egg yolks and sugar. Iraqi Jews prefer to sip *hariri* (page 102), a sweet non-dairy "milk" made from almonds.

At the post-fast meal, Moroccan and other North African Jews often partake of a hearty meat, bean, and vegetable soup called *harirah*—a custom adapted from local Arabs, who eat the soup to break the Moslem fast of Ramadan. Also enjoyed is *djadja zetoon* (page 85), a dish of chicken cooked with olives and pickled lemons.

And, Greek and Turkish Jews are fond of eating a very light lemon-flavored chicken soup called *avgolemono* (page 76), which is usually preceded by a sweet drink made of melon seeds, called *pepitada* (page 104).

It is also customary for Jews of all cultural backgrounds to break their fasts with many of the same sweet, spicy cakes and cookies that are traditional for Rosh Hashanah. Recipes for several of these, as well as many other symbolic holiday dishes, are included in this chapter.

"YOM-TOV" ROUND CHALLAH (P)

("Holiday" Egg Bread)

Two beautiful loaves of bread are customary at almost every Jewish holiday meal. For the Days of Awe, many Jews all over the world form the favored *challah* into a round shape instead of braids. The roundness symbolizes a universal wish for a well-rounded, full, and wholesome year. And the round loaves often spiral upward in the center, to show that we want our prayers to ascend to heaven.

More elaborate breads may be adorned with dough ladders or birds for the same reason. Sometimes, the dough is shaped into a long, narrow braid, and the ends looped together to make a circular loaf.

During the Days of Awe, when the blessing for the bread is said, it is dipped into honey (not salt, as on Shabbat), in hope of a sweet year to come. Also, extra sugar and honey, as well as raisins, are often added to the dough. Sephardic Jews, particularly those from the Mediterranean area, may include anise seeds and/or sesame seeds for flavor and because they represent fruitfulness. Italian Jews sometimes use a combination of olive oil and anise seeds to produce a bread with a deliciously exotic flavor.

The following is an amalgam of sweet egg bread recipes from both Ashkenazic and Sephardic cultures. It is traditionally eaten not only on Rosh Hashanah, but also to break the fast of Yom Kippur.

(Note: If desired, the dough may be shaped into braided loaves following the directions in the Shabbat chapter.)

2 packets (4½ teaspoons) active dry yeast
1⅔ cups warm (105 to 115 degrees) water
⅓ cup sugar
¼ cup honey
½ cup vegetable oil (may be half olive oil)
3 large eggs
2 teaspoons salt
About 7 to 7½ cups white bread flour or all-purpose unbleached white flour

½ cup dark or light raisins (optional)
1 tablespoon each anise seeds and sesame seeds (or 2 tablespoons of either one) (optional)

GLAZE
1 egg yolk, beaten with 1 teaspoon water

In a large mixing bowl, combine the yeast with ⅔ cup of the water and 1 teaspoon of the sugar. Let the mixture rest for 5 to 10 minutes, or until it begins to foam. Add the remaining water, sugar, honey, oil, eggs, salt, and about 4 cups of the flour. Beat the loose dough with an electric mixer or a wooden spoon for about 3 minutes. Mix in the raisins and/or seeds, if desired. By hand (or with a heavy duty mixer), slowly stir in just enough of the remaining flour to form a soft, slightly sticky dough. Cover the dough with plastic wrap and let it rest for about 5 minutes.

Turn out the dough onto a lightly floured surface and knead it, adding small sprinkles of flour if necessary to keep it from sticking, for about 10 minutes, or until it is very smooth and satiny. Put the dough into an oiled bowl and turn the dough so that all sides are oiled. Cover the bowl loosely with a piece of plastic wrap and then a dish towel, to keep the dough moist and dark. Let the dough rise until doubled in bulk, about 1 to 2 hours (depending on the temperature of the room).

Punch down the dough and knead it a few times to remove any air bubbles. Divide the dough in half, for two loaves. Cover the dough pieces loosely with plastic wrap and let them rest for 10 minutes. Then form each piece into a round loaf using one of the four following methods. Be careful not to stretch or tear the dough as you shape it, or the surface of the loaf may develop holes when it rises and bakes.

Method 1: On a lightly floured surface, roll the dough into a very smooth 24-inch-long "snake" of even thickness. Bring one end around to form a circle that is about 5 inches in diameter. Continue winding the rest of the snake on top of the circle so that it spirals inward and upward, finishing in the center. Tuck the end of the "snake" into the center.

Method 2: On a lightly floured surface, roll the dough into a very smooth 24-inch-long "snake" that is much thicker at one end and tapers down to the other. With one hand, raise the thicker end of the "snake" so it points upward, and use your other hand to neatly wind the rest of the "snake" around it in a spiral fashion. Tuck the narrow end neatly under the bottom.

Method 3: On a lightly floured surface, roll about two thirds of the dough into a large ball. Form the remaining dough into a miniature spiral, as above, or into a small ladder or bird. Center the spiral, ladder, or bird on top of the ball.

Method 4: Divide the dough into 3 pieces and, on a lightly floured surface, roll each into a smooth narrow strand about 18 to 20 inches long. Braid the strands; then bring the ends of the braid around to form a circle and attach the ends tightly together.

When each loaf has been shaped, carefully transfer it to a small, greased or non-stick spray-coated baking sheet or 9-inch-round cake pan and gently rub a little oil over the exterior surface of the loaf to keep the dough from drying out. Cover the loaves loosely with wax paper and let them rise at room temperature until doubled in bulk, 45 minutes to 1 hour or longer. (Bread dough tends to hold its shape better if allowed to rise slowly at room temperature, rather than in a "warm" place.)

Gently brush the loaves with the egg glaze; then bake them in a pre-heated 350-degree oven for 40 to 45 minutes, or until the crust is browned and the bottom of each loaf sounds hollow when tapped. (If the loaves are browning too rapidly, loosely cover each one with a tent of aluminum foil.) Remove the loaves from the baking sheets or pans and cool them completely on wire racks.

Makes 2 large loaves, about 1¾ pounds each.

KA'AK (P)

(Savory Sesame-Anise Rings)

These crunchy pastries, which are like anise-flavored pretzels, are staples in the households of Syrian Jews. I first tasted them at the home of Ginger Kassin, whose ancestors hail from Aleppo, Syria. Mrs. Kassin and her family are part of a very large, tightly knit, Syrian-Jewish community in the Deal, New Jersey, area.

Many Syrian Jews still follow culinary customs that have been practiced for generations. For instance, *ka'ak* are served at just about every festival (except, of course, Pesach), as well as religious occasions, such as *oneg Shabbat* and *brit milah*. Furthermore, a guest in any home is always offered *ka'ak* as a courtesy.

And, *ka'ak* are eaten to break the fast after Yom Kippur. They are perfectly suited for this, as they are not sweet, but are subtly flavored with a variety of refreshing spices. The sesame seeds on top represent the hope that the coming year will be fruitful and replete with good deeds.

Very similar sesame "rings" are also eaten by Jews from other Middle Eastern countries, such as Iraq and Egypt.

Following is my adaptation of a recipe for *ka'ak* that appears in *Deal Delights,* a cookbook compiled by the Sisterhood of the Deal Synagogue. The *ka'ak* are baked twice, to dry them out and make them crunchy. They keep quite well, and thus can be made several days in advance and stored at room temperature. Or they can be frozen for 3 months or longer.

1 package (2¼ teaspoons) active dry
  yeast
1 teaspoon sugar
1¼ cups warm (105 to 115 degrees)
  water
4 to 4½ cups all-purpose unbleached
  white flour (may be half whole
  wheat flour, if desired)
2 tablespoons anise seeds
Generous ½ teaspoon ground cumin
Generous ½ teaspoon ground
  coriander seeds (optional)

2 teaspoons salt
⅔ cup vegetable shortening
1 tablespoon vegetable oil

GLAZE AND TOPPING
1 large egg, lightly beaten with 1
  teaspoon water
About ⅓ cup sesame seeds

In a small bowl, dissolve the yeast and sugar in the warm water and let the mixture rest for 5 to 10 minutes, or until it is foamy.

In a large bowl, combine 4 cups of the flour, the anise seeds, cumin, coriander (if used), and salt. Cut in the shortening and oil with a pastry blender or electric mixer until the mixture resembles coarse crumbs. Add the yeast mixture and mix to make a firm dough. Turn out the dough onto a lightly floured surface and knead it for 5 to 10 minutes, or until it is smooth and elastic. Add sprinkles of flour, as necessary, to keep the dough from sticking.

Put the dough into an oiled bowl and turn it so that all surfaces are oiled. Cover the bowl loosely with plastic wrap and a dish towel and let the dough rise until it has doubled in bulk, about 1½ to 2 hours.

Punch down the dough; then divide it in half. Form one half into a log about 2 inches in diameter. Cut the log into approximately ½-inch-thick slices. Roll each slice into a rope that is ½ inch thick and 4 to 6 inches long. (If you want all the rings to be exactly the same size, cut the ropes to the same length.) Bring the ends of each rope together to form a small ring and pinch the ends tightly together.

FIGURE 8   A   B

Dip the top (only) of each ring into the egg-water glaze and then into the sesame seeds (Fig. 8A). Place the rings, seeded side up, about 1 inch apart on a large lightly greased or non-stick spray-coated baking sheet. (For a "fancy" look, use a small sharp knife to cut notches about ½ inch apart around the outside of each ring [Fig. 8B].) Bake the rings in a preheated 400-degree oven for 10 minutes.

Meanwhile, shape the remaining dough into rings, place on another baking sheet, and bake as above. When the rings are done baking, make sure they are loosened from the baking sheets, but leave them in place. Lower the oven temperature to 300 degrees.

Return the rings to the oven. (One baking sheet can be put on the top oven shelf, and the other on the bottom.) Bake the rings for an additional 20 to 40 minutes (rotating the two sheets every 10 minutes for more even baking), or until they are dried out and crisp, like "hard" pretzels. Cool them completely on wire racks; then store them in an airtight container.

Makes 4 to 5 dozen rings.

BRITISH-STYLE FRIED GEFILTE FISH (P)

When I first asked Pauline Rubens Saville, a native of Birmingham, England, and a long-time resident of South Wales, for a typical British-Jewish recipe, she wasn't sure how to respond. Having an Ashkenazic background similar to my own, she assumed that both of us prepared traditional foods in the same manner. But, when we compared recipes, I found out that she, and, indeed, most British Jews, prefer their gefilte fish fried, not poached, as do Americans.

In fact, Mrs. Saville told me that poached gefilte fish is usually only eaten when fried fish might be too heavy, such as to break the fast on Yom Kippur.

Another difference is that Mrs. Saville usually uses cod combined with either haddock or hake (steakfish) in her minced fish mixture, rather than carp and pike. She feels (and I concur) that the British combination is more subtle tasting and lighter in texture and color than its American-Eastern European counterpart. (White gefilte fish is also in keeping with the "purity" of the Days of Awe.)

The following gefilte fish mixture is actually quite versatile. It can be made with any combination of cod, haddock and/or hake, and in any proportions desired, depending on the fish that is available. Sometimes, Mrs. Saville adds a bit of ground almonds to it, particularly if it seems to be rather wet. She shapes the mixture into large patties for meals, or small balls for hors d'oeuvres (see Note). She may coat the patties or balls with seasoned matzo meal or just leave them "bare." Occasionally, she even saves the heads, bones, and skin from the fish, and makes a broth in which to poach some of the gefilte fish. No matter how she prepares it, Mrs. Saville always serves gefilte fish with red *hrain* (horseradish).

FISH MIXTURE
1½ pounds skinless cod fillets
½ pound skinless haddock or hake (steakfish) fillets
2 medium-sized onions, cut into eighths
2 large eggs
1 tablespoon vegetable oil
1 teaspoon salt
1½ teaspoons sugar
⅛ teaspoon ground white pepper
1 to 2 tablespoons finely ground almonds (optional)
About 4 to 6 tablespoons matzo meal
Vegetable oil for frying

COATING (OPTIONAL)
½ cup matzo meal
1 tablespoon all-purpose white flour, preferably unbleached (or very fine matzo cake meal)
Salt and ground white pepper to taste

TO SERVE (OPTIONAL)
Prepared horseradish, preferably the "red" type with beets

Cut the fish into pieces and finely grind it in a food processor (fitted with the steel blade) or with a food grinder. Grind the onions in the same manner and add them to the fish. Mix in the eggs, 1 tablespoon oil, salt, sugar, and white pepper. Add the ground almonds (if used) and just enough matzo meal so that the fish mixture can be easily handled and is not sticky. Form the fish mixture into plump patties, using about ¼ cup to ⅓ cup of the mixture for each one.

If a coating is desired, put the coating ingredients into a large plastic bag, close the top, and shake until mixed. To coat each patty, put it into the bag, close the bag, and shake gently until the patty is lightly coated.

To fry coated or uncoated patties, heat oil that is about ⅛ to ¼ inch deep in a large skillet over medium-high heat. Fry the patties until they are lightly browned on both sides. Drain them on paper towels. Refrigerate the patties until serving time and serve them chilled, with horseradish if desired.

Makes 16 to 20 patties; about 8 servings as a first course.

NOTE: For gefilte fish hors d'oeuvres, form the fish mixture into 1-inch balls. If desired, coat them with matzo meal. To preserve their round shape, *deep-fry* the balls in hot oil. Drain them on paper towels. Serve them chilled, on toothpicks.

QUICK CHOPPED HERRING (P)

The spread known as "chopped herring" is very popular among Ashkenazic Jews, and has always been one of my own personal favorites. I can still remember watching my maternal grandmother, Lillian Levine Kaplan, prepare it years ago when I was a young child. In those days, "Mama Lil" (as she is affectionately known by her grandchildren and great-grandchildren) would purchase a special selection of whole pickled herrings, which she boned and put through a hand-operated grinder along with the other ingredients. Her entire kitchen smelled wonderful. (Or at least *I* thought so!)

Very few people, including my grandmother, make chopped herring "from scratch" any longer. Most buy it at the delicatessen or supermarket. However, with a food processor, the following "modernized" version can be prepared in seconds. It takes a little longer with a food grinder, but it's still a cinch. Either way, it tastes great.

2 slices toasted whole wheat or rye bread (or challah), torn into pieces
1 16-ounce jar (or 2 8-ounce jars) herring fillets in wine sauce
2 hard-boiled eggs, coarsely chopped
2 large apples, peeled, cored, and cut into eighths

2 tablespoons sweet red wine (optional)

TO SERVE
Lettuce leaves
Challah or other bread or crackers

With a food processor, put the bread into the processor bowl fitted with the steel blade and process until the bread becomes fine crumbs. Drain the herring, reserving the onions and some of the liquid. Add the drained herring fillets, onions from the jar, eggs, and apples to the food processor and process until the mixture is almost smooth. If it is too thick, add a little of the reserved liquid or the wine. If it is too wet, add more bread crumbs. Process until the mixture is smooth.

With a food grinder, grind the drained herring, onions from the jar, eggs, apples, and bread, in that order. (The bread helps to push the other ingredients through.) Then mix everything well. If the mixture is too thick, stir in some herring liquid or wine.

Put the chopped herring into a covered bowl or container and refrigerate it for several hours, or until serving time. (It can be stored in the refrigerator for up to 3 days.) Serve it on a bed of lettuce accompanied with bread or crackers.

Makes about 8 servings.

MOROCCAN-STYLE FISH BAKED WITH STUFFED DATES (D) or (P)

Fish is very popular in Morocco, especially in some of the coastal communities where many Jews have lived. In fact, it is said in those parts, that Jonah was disgorged by the "big fish" on the coast of Morocco, where the Massa River meets the Atlantic.

When the following indescribably delicious dish is prepared according to the classic method, dates stuffed with a spiced almond-rice mixture are sewn inside the fish's abdominal cavity. However, this is inconvenient, and it limits the number of dates that can be used. Therefore, I have suggested putting only a few of the dates in the cavity and spreading the rest around the fish.

Though Arabic in origin, this dish has been adopted by some Moroccan Jews, who always eat dates (for sweetness) at the New Year. The fish should be brought to the table with the head left on to symbolize each celebrant's desire to be at the head of his or her peers during the coming year. A white-fleshed fish, blanched almonds, and white rice are used because white means purity.

ALMOND-RICE STUFFING FOR
DATES
1¼ cups (5 ounces) very finely
 ground blanched almonds
¾ cup cooked and cooled white (or
 brown) rice
2 tablespoons butter or margarine,
 softened
2 teaspoons sugar
1 teaspoon ground ginger
½ teaspoon ground cinnamon
¼ teaspoon black pepper, preferably
 freshly ground

DATES, FISH, ETC.
1 pound large whole pitted dates
 (preferably soft ones)
1 approximately 4-pound whole
 dressed fish, such as red snapper,
 grouper, striped bass, croaker, or
 other white-fleshed fish (with head
 and tail intact)
1 small onion, finely chopped
¼ cup water
3 to 4 tablespoons butter or
 margarine
About 1 teaspoon ground cinnamon

For the almond-rice stuffing, combine all the stuffing ingredients in a medium-sized bowl and mix well to form a paste. (If a food processor with a steel blade is available, use it to grind the almonds. After measuring out the correct amount of ground almonds, return them to the food processor bowl, and add the remaining stuffing ingredients. Process until a paste is formed.)

Cut a lengthwise slit in the side of each date. Form the stuffing into small elongated "balls" and stuff one into each date, dividing the stuffing evenly among the dates. (The dates may be stuffed ahead of time and refrigerated, covered, so they don't dry out.)

Shortly before baking the fish, rinse it well and pat it dry with paper towels. Put it in a shallow well-greased or non-stick spray-coated baking pan (diagonally, if it fits better that way). Scatter the chopped onion around the fish; then pour the water over the onion. Put some of the stuffed dates into the fish's abdominal cavity and surround the fish with the remainder. Dot the fish and the dates with the butter; then lightly sprinkle them with cinnamon.

Cover the pan loosely with aluminum foil. Bake the fish in a preheated 400-degree oven for 20 minutes. Remove the foil and continue baking for 20 to 25 minutes longer, or until most of the liquid has evaporated and the skin of the fish is crisp and golden. Serve each person some fish (preferably without bones) and several dates.

Makes 8 to 10 servings as a first course.

PESCE ALL'EBRAICA (P)

(Italian-Style Sweet-and-Sour Fish)

The Italian name of this interesting dish means "Jewish-style fish." Italian Jews traditionally serve it for Rosh Hashanah and to break the Yom Kippur fast. Small whole fish are fried, and then gently simmered in a delicate sweet-and-sour sauce. For a baked version, which uses fillets instead of whole fish, see the variation below.

About 6 whole small dressed fish, such as rainbow trout
All-purpose white flour, preferably unbleached
Vegetable or olive oil for frying
⅓ cup water
1 to 2 tablespoons honey
3 tablespoons red wine vinegar (or lemon juice)

2 tablespoons good-quality olive oil
⅓ cup light (or dark) raisins
2 to 4 tablespoons pine nuts (pignoli) or slivered almonds, preferably lightly toasted
1 teaspoon dried mint leaves (or 1 tablespoon chopped fresh spearmint leaves)

Lightly dredge the fish in the flour. In a very large skillet, over medium-high heat, heat vegetable oil that is ⅛ inch to ¼ inch deep. Fry the fish, in batches if necessary, until they are golden brown on both sides. Remove the fish from the skillet and drain them on paper towels. Discard any oil remaining in the skillet.

Add to the skillet, the water, honey, vinegar, olive oil, raisins, nuts, and mint leaves. Bring the mixture to a simmer and cook, stirring, for 1 to 2 minutes to blend the flavors. Return the fish to the skillet and spoon the "sauce" over it. Simmer the fish, basting often, about 5 minutes longer.

Makes about 6 servings as a first course.

VARIATION

For *"baked* pesce all'ebraica," substitute *1¼ pounds skinless fillets of firm white-fleshed fish, such as flounder, perch, haddock, or cod* for the whole fish. Omit the flour and vegetable oil. Put the fillets, in one layer, in a greased or non-stick spray-coated baking dish. Sprinkle the raisins and nuts over the fish. Decrease the water to 1 tablespoon (baked fillets usually give off plenty of liquid). Combine the water, honey, vinegar, and olive oil and mix very well. Pour the mixture evenly over the fillets. Bake the fillets, uncovered, in a preheated 400-degree oven for 15 to 20 minutes, or until they are cooked through but not falling apart. Baste once or twice during the cooking period. Makes about 6 servings as a first course.

CHICKEN LIVER PÂTÉ (M)

("Fancy" Chopped Liver)

The alcohol in both the sherry and wine cooks away in this delicious spread, leaving behind only their wonderful flavors. If the sweeter type of wine is used, this pâté, which is smoother than traditional Jewish-style "chopped liver," will have a subtly sweet flavor that is in keeping with the spirit of Rosh Hashanah.

1 pound chicken livers, cleaned
3 tablespoons pareve *margarine or rendered chicken fat*
1 tablespoon vegetable oil
1 large onion, finely chopped
1 large apple, peeled, cored, and chopped
¼ cup dry sherry
¼ cup dry red wine or sweet holiday wine

4 hard-boiled eggs, coarsely chopped
Salt and ground black pepper to taste

TO SERVE
Lettuce leaves
1 sweet red pepper, cut into strips (optional)
Parsley sprigs (optional)

Put the chicken livers on a piece of aluminum foil and broil them close to the heating element just until the outsides are seared, about 3 minutes. Set them aside.

In a large skillet, over medium-high heat, heat the margarine with the oil. Sauté the onion until it is lightly browned. Stir in the chicken livers, apple, sherry, and wine. Cook, stirring constantly, until most of the liquid has evaporated and the apple is soft, about 10 minutes. Stir in the chopped eggs. Remove the mixture from the heat.

Purée the mixture in a food processor, meat grinder, or blender (in batches, if necessary). Season it with salt and pepper to taste. Chill the pâté until it is firm. (It can be refrigerated, covered, for up to 1 week, or frozen for up to 2 months.) To serve, mound the pâté on a large lettuce-lined platter or on small individual lettuce-lined plates. If desired, garnish the pâté with the red pepper strips and/or parsley.

Makes about 3 cups; 6 to 8 servings.

AVGOLEMONO or SOPA DE HUEVO Y LIMÓN (M)

(Egg-Lemon Soup)

Whether they call it by its Greek or Judeo-Spanish name, Sephardic Jews, particularly those with Turkish or Greek backgrounds, often break the Yom Kippur fast with this light, elegant soup. It is very quick and easy to prepare, and is a great way to perk up leftover homemade chicken broth or good-quality canned broth.

6 cups strained chicken broth, seasoned to taste with salt, pepper, and dillweed (optional)
½ cup medium- or long-grain white rice

3 large eggs
2 to 4 tablespoons lemon juice, or to taste

In a 3- to 4-quart saucepan over medium-high heat, bring the broth to a simmer. Add the rice and simmer it, covered, for about 20 minutes, or just until it is tender. Turn down the heat so the broth stays hot but does *not* boil.

In a medium-sized bowl, beat the eggs with a wire whisk or fork until they are light; then beat in the lemon juice. Slowly add about ¾ cup of the hot broth to the egg-lemon mixture while constantly stirring. Gradually add this mixture back to the broth remaining in the pan, stirring constantly. Continue stirring and heating for about 1 to 2 minutes longer, or until the soup thickens slightly. Do not boil the soup or the eggs will curdle.

Makes about 6 servings.

HOMEMADE NOODLE FARFEL (P)

(Egg Barley)

For the same reason that we have circular *challah* during the Days of Awe—our desire to have a well-rounded, fulfilled year—Hasidic Jews often eat "round" (barley-shaped) *farfel* in soup. Also, there is a play on the word *"farfel";* it represents a hope that any misdeeds of the past year will "fall" away in the future.

These tiny noodle dumplings are very tasty and surprisingly easy to prepare—a good project to do with children. Serve them with soup or stew. (Note: Homemade *farfel* is not as "round" as some of the packaged kinds.)

2 cups all-purpose white flour, preferably unbleached	½ teaspoon salt 2 large eggs

Combine the flour and salt in a medium-sized bowl and make a well in the center. Break the eggs into the well and beat with a fork. Gradually beat in the flour from around the edges of the well until the dough is too stiff to use a fork. Then work the flour in with your hands until a very stiff dough is formed. Roll the dough into a thick log; then let it air dry for at least 1 hour, or until it is stiff enough to grate.

Rub the dough across a coarse grater to form pieces the size of barley. Or finely chop the dough using a food processor fitted with the steel blade. If the farfel is at all sticky, toss it with a bit more flour. Then spread it on a dish towel to dry until you are ready to cook it. (If desired, the farfel may be dried completely and stored in an airtight container.)

Cook the farfel in salted boiling water or soup for about 10 minutes, or until tender.

Makes about 8 servings.

MEAT KREPLAH (M)

(Triangular Noodle Dumplings)

It is very traditional for Ashkenazic Jews to include *kreplah* in the chicken soup at the pre-fast Yom Kippur meal. According to one interpretation of this custom, the meat covered with dough symbolizes our hope that on the Day of Atonement, God's strict justice will be "covered" with compassion and mercy.

Kreplah are eaten also on Hoshanah Rabbah (the seventh day of Sukkot) and Purim. Some say that we eat *kreplah* on the three holidays in which someone or something is "beaten," because the meat inside the *kreplah* is prepared by chopping, which is sort of like beating. On the day before Yom Kippur, men may be symbolically flogged while they ask forgiveness for their sins; on Hoshanah Rabbah, willow branches are beaten; and, during the reading of the *Megillah* on Purim, we stamp or beat our feet against the floor whenever the name of the wicked Haman is said.

Be that as it may, *kreplah* are quite tasty and a good way to use up cooked meat. In fact, my mother insists that the *only* suitable filling is made from leftover roast beef, steak, and soup meat, which she saves in the freezer. When she has collected enough for a batch of *kreplah* (about ¾ pound), she thaws the meat, then shreds it in a meat grinder (or food processor), and adds grated onion, 1 egg, salt, and pepper to make a filling.

If leftover meat is not available, fresh ground beef can be cooked for the filling, as in the recipe below.

DOUGH
2 cups all-purpose white flour,
    preferably unbleached
½ teaspoon salt
2 large eggs
About 2 to 4 tablespoons cold water

FILLING
Scant 1 pound lean ground beef
1 small onion, grated or very finely
    minced
1 garlic clove, finely minced
    (optional)
1 large egg, lightly beaten
Salt and ground black pepper to taste

For the dough, combine the flour and salt in a medium-sized bowl. Make a well in the center of the flour. Add the eggs and water to the well and beat them with a fork. Gradually beat the flour into the egg mixture to form a stiff dough. If the dough is dry and crumbly, add a bit more water; if it is too wet, add more flour. Knead the dough for about 5 minutes, or until it is smooth and silky. Wrap it well in plastic wrap and let it rest at room temperature for 20 minutes to 1 hour.

(Note: The dough can be made in a food processor. Process the flour, salt, and eggs until crumbly. Then, with the machine running, add the water. The mixture should form a ball. If it is too dry, add water; if it is too wet, add flour. After the ball is formed, process 30 seconds longer to knead it.)

For the filling, put the ground beef, onion, and garlic (if used) into a large skillet over medium-high heat. Cook the meat, pressing it often with a potato masher or fork to keep the pieces as small as possible. When the meat is completely cooked through, drain off all excess fat. Cool the meat. For a smoother, more compact, filling, process the cooked meat mixture in a food processor or put it through a meat grinder. Stir in the egg, salt, and pepper.

Divide the dough into 2 pieces, and keep the second one wrapped so it does not dry out. On a lightly floured surface, roll out the first piece of dough to a very thin rectangle about 9 by 15 inches. Cut the dough into about 15 3-inch squares. Put about 1 tablespoon of filling on each square, and dab a little water along 2 perpendicular edges. Fold over the dough on the diagonal to form a triangle. Press the top and bottom edges together; then press on the edges with the tines of a fork to tightly seal them closed. Repeat with the second piece of dough, to make about 15 more kreplah.

(Note: If desired, the kreplah may be frozen at this point. Freeze them in a single layer, uncovered, on a baking sheet; then put them into a plastic bag and seal it for storage. Do not thaw them before cooking; just cook them for 5 to 10 minutes longer or until they are done.)

To cook the kreplah, gently drop them into a large pot of lightly salted boiling water and simmer them for 15 to 20 minutes, or until they are just tender but not mushy. (They will increase greatly in size as they cook.) Remove them from the water with a slotted spoon.

To serve the kreplah, reheat them in hot soup. (Or, if desired, drain the kreplah very well; then fry them in a small amount of hot oil, margarine, or rendered chicken fat until they are golden on both sides. Then serve them hot as hors d'oeuvres or as a side dish.)

Makes about 30 kreplah.

MANDLEN (P)

(Soup "Nuts")

Though the Yiddish name of this soup garnish translates literally to "almonds," nuts are not among the ingredients. The little nuggets of pastry simply resemble them. When I was younger, my mother often made *mandlen* for holidays. Her biggest problem, however, was keeping them around until meal time because my sisters and I would sneak into the kitchen and snitch a handful of the delectable treats whenever she wasn't looking.

My mother has always deep-fried the tiny pieces of dough, but I prefer to bake them since it is quicker and easier. Nevertheless, I must admit that the fried ones are somewhat lighter and more delicate than the baked ones. The same dough can be used for either method.

2 large eggs
1 tablespoon vegetable oil
½ teaspoon salt
½ teaspoon baking powder (optional; omit for fried mandlen)

About 1¼ cups all-purpose white flour, preferably unbleached
Vegetable oil for frying (only for fried mandlen, not the baked ones)

Use a fork to beat the eggs with the 1 tablespoon of oil in a medium-sized bowl. Add the salt, baking powder (if used), and about 1 cup of the flour and mix well. Add just enough additional flour so the dough is not sticky when handled.

Divide the dough into 6 to 8 pieces. On a floured surface, roll each piece into a rope that is ⅜ to ½ inch thick; then cut each rope into ½-inch-long "nuggets." The nuggets may be either baked or fried, as follows:

For baked mandlen, arrange the dough nuggets in one layer in a large well-greased or non-stick spray-coated shallow baking pan, such as a jelly roll pan. Bake them in a preheated 375-degree oven for 20 to 25 minutes, or until they are browned and quite firm. (Shake the pan occasionally, so that the mandlen bake evenly.) Remove the mandlen from the pan, and cool them to room temperature before storing.

For deep-fried mandlen, pour enough oil into a saucepan so that it is about 1½ inches deep. Heat the oil until it is very hot, about 375 degrees. Drop some of the nuggets into the oil so they are not too crowded. Fry them until they are slightly puffed and golden on all sides. Remove the mandlen with a slotted spoon and drain them on paper towels. Repeat until all the dough nuggets have been fried. Cool them to room temperature before storing.

Makes about 7 to 8 dozen mandlen.

"YOM-TOV" TZIMMES (M)

(Sweet "Holiday" Stew)

The Yiddish word *tzimmes* has come to mean anything that is a fuss or all mixed up. Well, this wonderful one-pot meal is certainly "all mixed up" with meat, fruit, and vegetables, but it's not really that much of a fuss. The following sweet version is a very traditional Ashkenazic dish, not only for Rosh Hashanah, but also for Sukkot. The long cooking time is necessary to tenderize the meat and blend all the delicious flavors.

3 to 4 pounds boneless chuck roast or brisket, trimmed of all surface fat
1 tablespoon oil
3 cups hot water
1 cup orange juice
3 tablespoons honey
3 tablespoons packed dark brown sugar
¼ to ½ teaspoon ground cinnamon
¼ to ½ teaspoon ground ginger
5 carrots, cut into 2-inch-long pieces

3 medium-sized sweet potatoes, peeled and cut into 1-inch chunks
1 medium-sized butternut squash (about 1½ pounds), peeled and cut into 1-inch chunks
8 ounces pitted prunes (about 25 large)
5 ounces dried apricots (about 20 large)
Cornstarch and cold water (optional)

In a 6-quart or larger ovenproof pot or Dutch oven, heat the oil over medium-high heat; then brown the meat on all sides. Drain off any excess fat. Add the water, juice, honey, and brown sugar, and cover the pot. Bring to a boil; then lower the heat and simmer the roast for 1½ hours. Preheat the oven to 350 degrees toward the end of this period.

Randomly arrange the carrots, sweet potatoes, squash, prunes, and apricots around and on top of the roast. Cover the pot and transfer it to the preheated oven. Bake for 1½ hours; then uncover the pot and bake for an additional 1 to 2 hours, or until the roast is fork-tender.

Use a slotted spoon to remove the vegetables and fruit from the pot and put them in a serving bowl. Carefully transfer the roast to a platter or carving board. If the sauce in the pot is too thin, either quickly boil it down to the desired consistency, or use a thickener. For the latter, combine 1 tablespoon each of cornstarch and cold water, and stir the mixture into the hot broth; then bring the sauce to a boil. If necessary, add more thickener until the desired consistency for the sauce is reached.

Cut the roast into thick slices against the grain of the meat. Pour some of the sauce over the meat and the vegetables. Serve the remainder on the side in a sauceboat or small pitcher.

Makes 8 to 10 servings.

LAMB AND BROWN RICE PILAF (M)

Middle Eastern Jews and those from the Balkan countries often serve lamb for Rosh Hashanah to recall how God tested Abraham's faith by asking him to sacrifice his son, Isaac, but ultimately allowed him to substitute a ram. Some popular dishes include stuffed breast of lamb, lamb shoulder roasts, and pilafs, such as that which follows. The raisins, apple, and spices give it a slightly sweet flavor, making it perfect for this holiday. Brown rice is used in this version because it has a rich taste that goes well with lamb, and a longer cooking time than white rice, which allows the lamb to become tender.

6 tablespoons pareve margarine
2 large onions, finely chopped
3 to 4 garlic cloves, finely minced
4 celery stalks, finely chopped
3 cups long-grain brown rice
2 to 3 pounds boneless lamb,
  trimmed of all fat and gristle, cut
  into ½-inch cubes
6 cups beef broth or bouillon made
  from cubes or powder
2 15- to 16-ounce cans chick-peas
  (garbanzo beans), drained

1½ cups dark or light raisins
1 apple, peeled, cored, and finely
  chopped
1 cup finely chopped fresh parsley
  leaves
1 teaspoon ground allspice
¼ teaspoon ground cinnamon
½ teaspoon dried thyme leaves
½ teaspoon black pepper, preferably
  freshly ground
¼ teaspoon salt

In a 5- to 6-quart pot or a Dutch oven, over medium-high heat, melt the margarine; then cook the onion, garlic, and celery, stirring, until they are tender but not brown. Add the rice and cook, stirring, 1 minute longer. Then add the lamb cubes and stir until they are browned on all sides. Stir in the broth, chick-peas, raisins, apple, parsley, allspice, cinnamon, thyme, pepper, and salt. Bring to a boil; then cover and lower the heat. Simmer, covered, for about 45 minutes, or until all the liquid has been absorbed. Toss with a fork before serving.

Makes about 8 servings.

COUSCOUS AUX SEPT LÉGUMES (M)

(Meat Stew with Seven Vegetables)

This scrumptious stew, which always features steamed semolina pellets (also called *couscous)*, is one of the most popular dishes of Morocco, Algeria, and Tunisia. It is served by North African Jews on Shabbat, festive holidays, and other happy occasions, such as weddings and baby namings.

The dish is very versatile and often varies with the city, or even the household, where it originated. It can be subtle or fiery hot; it can be made with meat, chicken, or fish; or it can be vegetarian. The steamed semolina pellets can even be used for a sweet dessert featuring nuts, dried fruits, and cinnamon (page 163).

Sometimes, elaborately spiced meatballs or stuffed vegetables are added to the main-course stew, a custom that is particularly Jewish.

One-pound boxes of ready-to-cook *couscous* (the semolina) can be found in the gourmet section of most supermarkets, as well as in many specialty and health-food stores. It is often imported from France, where many Moroccans, including Jews, now live.

Couscous is traditionally prepared in a *couscousière*—a special two-section pot which looks like an enormous double boiler. The stew is simmered in the large, bulbous bottom section. A smaller pot with tiny holes in its base sits tightly on top, and is used to cook the semolina in the fragrant steam which rises from the stew. Although this is ideal, a large colander set over a soup pot can be used instead. Directions for both methods are given below.

The following recipe is for a marvelous, slightly sweet *couscous* which is perfectly suited for Rosh Hashanah. North African Jews traditionally eat

"*Sept Légumes*" (seven fresh seasonal vegetables) on this holiday so that a special prayer of hope for the New Year can be said over each one.

In addition, the number seven is considered lucky (or even holy, by some). This is because, among other reasons, Shabbat takes place on the *seventh* day of each week, and Rosh Hashanah occurs on the first day of the *seventh* month.

(Note: If desired, all chicken or all lamb can be used in the following recipe, rather than some of each. The couscous pellets are steamed two times to make them especially light and fluffy.)

About 10 cups water
2 pounds lamb shanks or lamb shoulder (or beef chuck), cut into large chunks and trimmed of all excess fat
2½ to 3 pounds chicken drumsticks and thighs (remove skin, if desired)
1 1-pound box ready-to-cook dry couscous (about 2½ cups)
2 cups lightly salted cold water
2 tablespoons olive or vegetable oil
2 medium-sized onions, cut into fourths through the root end
4 large carrots, peeled and cut into 2-inch-long pieces
2 small white turnips, peeled and cut into quarters
1 teaspoon salt

½ teaspoon ground cinnamon
½ teaspoon ground ginger
¼ teaspoon black pepper, preferably freshly ground
¼ teaspoon ground turmeric
1 small cabbage, cut into eighths through the core
1 small butternut squash, peeled and cut into large chunks
2 small zucchini, cut into 1½-inch-long sections
1 medium-sized tomato, cut into eighths
1 15- to 16-ounce can chick-peas (garbanzo beans), drained
1 cup dark or light raisins
3 to 4 tablespoons pareve margarine, softened and cut into small pieces (optional)

In a 6- to 8-quart soup pot (or the bottom of a couscousière), bring the 10 cups of water to a boil over high heat. Add the lamb. Cover, lower the heat, and simmer gently for 45 minutes. During the first 20 minutes skim off and discard any foam that rises to the surface of the water. Add the chicken and simmer, covered, for 30 minutes longer.

Meanwhile, put the dry couscous into a large bowl and cover it with the 2 cups of salted water. Let it rest for 15 minutes, or until all the water is absorbed. Then use your hands to mix the softened couscous with the oil, carefully separating all the pellets so that they are fluffy and none are stuck together. Set aside.

To the pot with the meat and broth, add the onions, carrots, turnips, salt, cinnamon, ginger, pepper, and turmeric. Bring to a simmer and cook, covered, for 40 minutes; then add the cabbage, squash, zucchini, tomato, chick-peas, and raisins.

Set a large cheesecloth-lined colander (or the steamer part of the couscousière) into the top of the soup pot. The bottom of the colander should not touch the liquid in the pot. If steam is escaping where the colander and pot meet, wedge a towel between them so the steam is forced to come through the center. Gently sprinkle all the soaked couscous into the colander. Steam the couscous, uncovered, for 20 minutes over the simmering stew.

Turn out the couscous into a large bowl and fluff it with a 2-pronged fork (or your fingers), separating the pellets as before. Adjust any seasonings in the stew, if necessary. (If desired, the dish may be prepared several hours in advance to this point. Cover the couscous with a damp cloth, so it does not dry out. About 30 minutes before serving the meal, bring the stew in the pot to a simmer, and continue as follows.)

Once again, sprinkle the couscous pellets into the colander on top of the stew. Simmer the stew for about 20 minutes, steaming the couscous a second time in the process.

To serve, turn out the hot steamed couscous onto a large serving platter and again fluff and separate it with the 2-pronged fork. If desired, toss the couscous with the margarine. Use a slotted spoon to remove the meat and vegetables from the pot and place them on top of the couscous. Spoon some of the gravy from the pot over the stew and serve the remainder of the gravy on the side.

Makes 8 to 10 servings.

DJADJA ZETOON (M)

(Moroccan-Style Lemon Chicken with Olives)

Moroccan Jews often break the fast of Yom Kippur with this wonderfully exotic dish. They usually make it with "pickled lemons," which have been preserved in salt and oil. Although almost all North Africans make and eat pickled lemons, only the Jewish cooks use oil in the pickling process. (The others use just salt.)

For the lemons to be pickled in the Jewish manner, several of them are cut lengthwise into fourths or into slices, and salted very well. Sometimes, they are also sprinkled with paprika (another Jewish touch). Then they are tightly packed into very clean jars and covered with vegetable oil (or a mixture of vegetable oil and olive oil). The tightly covered jars are kept at room temperature. After about two or three weeks, the lemon peels lose most of their bitterness and become softened and translucent. The entire lemon, peel and all, can then be used whenever needed, or stored for up to a year. When used, preserved lemons are usually rinsed and chopped into small pieces.

The following recipe employs a different, "shortcut" technique to soften and mellow the peel of a whole lemon in only 30 minutes (while the chicken is cooking). Actually, the lemon is not pickled, but it looks and tastes something like one that has been, and it can be used in this easy, delicious dish without weeks of advance planning. (Of course, an "authentic" pickled lemon can be substituted, if desired. Chop it into small pieces, and add it to the skillet toward the end of the cooking period, in place of the boiled lemon described below.)

1 cup water
1 small onion, grated
1 small onion, finely chopped
2 to 3 garlic cloves, finely minced
1 medium-sized ripe tomato, peeled, seeded, and finely chopped (optional)
¼ cup finely chopped fresh parsley leaves
2 tablespoons finely chopped fresh coriander (cilantro) leaves, or 2 teaspoons dried coriander (cilantro) leaves (optional)
½ teaspoon ground ginger

¼ teaspoon ground turmeric
¼ teaspoon black pepper, preferably freshly ground
3 to 3½ pounds meaty chicken pieces (remove skin, if desired)
1 medium-sized fresh lemon
About 1 cup green olives, whole or pitted (with any pimiento removed and discarded)
2 tablespoons lemon juice, preferably fresh

GARNISH (OPTIONAL)
1 fresh lemon, cut into thin wedges

In a very large deep skillet or an electric frying pan, mix together the water, grated onion, chopped onion, garlic, tomato (if used), parsley, coriander leaves (if used), ginger, turmeric, and pepper. Add the chicken and bring the liquid to a boil over medium-high heat. Lower the heat and simmer the chicken, covered, for about 1 hour, or until it is very tender. Rotate the chicken occasionally with tongs, so that all sides are in the liquid for part of the cooking period.

While the chicken is cooking, use a small sharp knife to score 4 or 5 very shallow cuts in the surface of the lemon. Put the lemon into a saucepan and cover it with water. Bring it to a boil over high heat; then lower the heat and simmer the lemon, covered, for 30 minutes. Rinse it under cool running water to stop the cooking process and let it cool until it can be handled. If water has gotten into the lemon, squeeze it out. Cut open the lemon (if it hasn't already opened during cooking). Discard any loose lemon pulp that has come free from the peel. Cut the peel (with any attached pulp) into small pieces. Set aside.

While the lemon is cooking, bring the olives to a boil in plain water and simmer them for 3 minutes; then discard the water and let them soak in cool, clean water until needed. This helps remove any excess saltiness and bitterness from the olives.

When the chicken is tender, stir the 2 tablespoons of lemon juice into the sauce. If the chicken has given off a lot of liquid and the sauce is too thin, raise the heat and quickly boil the sauce down until it has thickened to the desired consistency. Turn the heat to low and stir in the olives and reserved pieces of cooked lemon peel. Simmer gently about 5 minutes longer, stirring occasionally and rotating the chicken pieces in the sauce.

To serve, put the chicken on a large platter and spoon the sauce with the olives and lemon pieces over the top. If desired, garnish with the lemon wedges.

Makes about 6 servings.

SPICY CHICKEN WITH TOMATOES AND
SESAME SEEDS (M)

This recipe is based on Moroccan cuisine, which often uses unexpected, yet delicious, spicy-sweet sauces with poultry.

*1 to 2 tablespoons vegetable or olive
  oil
About 3 pounds meaty chicken pieces
  (remove skin, if desired)
1 16-ounce can tomatoes, including
  juice, finely chopped
1 small onion, grated
1 garlic clove, minced*

*1 to 2 tablespoons honey
1 teaspoon ground cinnamon
¼ teaspoon black pepper, preferably
  freshly ground
Pinch of ground ginger
2 tablespoons sesame seeds, preferably
  toasted (see Note)*

In a deep 11- or 12-inch skillet or Dutch oven, over medium-high heat, heat the oil; then lightly brown the chicken pieces on all sides.

Meanwhile, stir together the tomatoes and their juice, the onion, garlic, honey, cinnamon, pepper, and ginger. Pour this mixture over the browned chicken, cover the pan tightly, and lower the heat.

Simmer the chicken, basting occasionally, for 50 to 60 minutes or until it is very tender. Transfer the chicken pieces to a serving plate. If the sauce remaining in the pan is too thin, raise the heat and quickly boil the sauce down to the desired consistency. Spoon the sauce over the chicken pieces. Sprinkle the sesame seeds on top.

Makes 5 to 6 servings.

NOTE: To toast sesame seeds, put them in an ungreased skillet over medium-high heat and stir them often until they are evenly browned and very aromatic. For very best flavor, toast the seeds shortly before using them.

TURKISH-STYLE GREEN BEANS WITH LEEKS AND CARROTS (P)

During the Days of Awe, Turkish Jews and other Sephardim eat leeks to symbolize the hope that they will "never lack in luck" during the coming year. They may serve the following colorful dish chilled, with an assortment of other cooked vegetable "salads," at the beginning of the meal. Or they may prefer to serve it warm, as a side dish. Either way, it tastes great.

1 large bunch (about 4 medium-sized) fresh leeks
2 tablespoons good-quality olive oil
1 medium-sized onion, halved and cut into ½-inch-thick semi-circular slices
3 medium-sized carrots, cut into ¼-inch-thick slices
½ cup water

1½ tablespoons lemon juice
2 tablespoons finely chopped parsley leaves
¼ teaspoon sugar
⅛ teaspoon salt
1 9- or 10-ounce package frozen Italian green beans, thawed slightly

To clean the leeks, cut off and discard the roots and all but 1 to 2 inches of the green tops. Slit the top of each leek in half lengthwise down to the point where the green part meets the white. Gently spread the leaves open and rinse the leeks very well under cool running water to remove any grit. Drain them well. Slice the cleaned leeks crosswise into ½-inch-long pieces and set them aside.

In a medium-sized saucepan, over medium-high heat, heat the oil. Add the onion and cook, breaking up the slices. When the onion is tender but not browned, add the reserved leeks and cook, stirring often, about 5 minutes longer. Then add all the remaining ingredients, except the Italian green beans, and stir gently to combine.

Bring the mixture to a boil; then lower the heat, cover, and simmer for 20 minutes. Gently stir in the green beans; then simmer, covered, for 10 minutes longer, or until all the vegetables are tender. Serve warm. Or, to serve in the Turkish manner, chill completely (several hours or overnight), and serve chilled or at room temperature.

Makes 4 to 6 servings.

BARBA (P)

(Moroccan-Style Beet Salad)

At every festive meal, Moroccan Jews follow the custom of their native land and serve many seasonal vegetable salads. The following salad is often served on Rosh Hashanah because beets are among the fruits and vegetables specifically honored by many Sephardim on this holiday. Naturally sweet beets are eaten not only for a sweet year, but also because the Hebrew word for "beet" sounds like a word in the New Year blessing in which we ask to rid ourselves of (or "beat" back) our enemies.

1 large bunch medium-sized fresh beets (about 1 pound)
3 tablespoons lemon juice, preferably fresh
1½ tablespoons olive or vegetable oil
1 to 2 garlic cloves, finely minced or pressed

2 tablespoons finely chopped fresh parsley leaves
1 teaspoon sugar
Pinch of ground cinnamon
Pinch of ground cumin
Pinch of salt

Cut off the beet greens about 1 inch above the beets. If desired, reserve the greens for the beet greens salad called *Selka* (page 91). Leave the taproots of the beets intact. Scrub the beets well; then put them into a medium-sized saucepan and cover them with cold water. Bring to a boil over high heat. Cover the pan, lower the heat, and simmer the beets for about 30 minutes, or until they are tender enough to be easily pierced with a wooden toothpick.

Let the beets cool in the cooking water, or rinse them under cold running water until they can be handled. Carefully cut off the taproots and stems, and slide the skin off the beets. (Or peel them with a sharp knife, if necessary.) Dice the beets or cut them into strips and put them into a small bowl.

Stir in the remaining ingredients, adjusting the amounts to taste. Chill the salad until serving time, mixing occasionally. Serve chilled or at room temperature.

Makes about 4 small servings.

SELKA (P)

(Moroccan-Style Beet Greens Salad)

As fresh beets are usually sold with their greens, this salad often accompanies the Moroccan-style beet salad known as *Barba* (page 90). Sephardim partake of beet greens on Rosh Hashanah in the hope that any enemies will wither and shrink like the fresh greens do when they are cooked. Beet greens are not only tasty, but healthful as well, providing plenty of vitamin A.

Beet greens (leaves and stems) from 1 large bunch of beets
1½ tablespoons olive or vegetable oil
1 to 2 garlic cloves, very finely minced or pressed

2 tablespoons lemon juice, preferably fresh
Pinch of paprika
Pinch of salt

Wash the beet greens very well, making sure to remove all soil. Cut the leaves and stems into small pieces. Then place them in a medium-sized saucepan. Add cold water to cover. Bring to a boil over high heat; then lower the heat and simmer the beet greens for about 5 minutes, or until they are tender. Drain the beet greens well. When they have cooled enough to handle them, squeeze out all the excess water.

Dry the saucepan well; then heat the oil over medium heat. Add the beet greens and the garlic and cook, stirring, for about 10 minutes, or until the greens are dried out and the garlic is tender. Add the lemon juice, paprika, and salt and stir for a minute longer. Adjust the seasonings to taste. Serve hot, chilled, or at room temperature.

Makes about 2 servings.

SUNSHINE CARROT COINS (P)

Among the vegetables favored for Rosh Hashanah, carrots are probably the most popular in Ashkenazic households. Because the Yiddish word *mehren* can mean either "carrots" or "increase," carrots have come to represent the wish that our merits will be increased in the coming year.

Furthermore, carrots cut into thin, round slices resemble gold coins, and symbolize a hope for future prosperity. And, of course, carrots are sweet—especially when they are cooked with fruit as in the following recipe—for a sweet year.

*1 pound carrots, thinly sliced
   crosswise into circles*
½ cup orange juice
¼ cup dark or light raisins
*2 tablespoons finely chopped fresh
   spearmint leaves (or 2 teaspoons
   dried mint leaves)*
Pinch of ground ginger

Pinch of ground nutmeg
*1 tablespoon shredded orange rind
   (colored part only)*
*1 medium-sized orange, peeled and
   cut into chunks*
1 teaspoon cornstarch (optional)
2 teaspoons cold water (optional)

Put the carrots, orange juice, raisins, mint, ginger, nutmeg, and orange rind into a medium-sized saucepan over high heat. Cover and bring to a boil; then lower the heat and simmer the carrots for about 8 minutes, or until they are crisp-tender. Add the orange pieces and cook, stirring, about 1 minute longer, or until the orange pieces are heated through. To thicken the sauce slightly, dissolve the cornstarch in the water; then add the mixture to the pan. Cook, stirring, until the sauce thickens and just comes to a boil. Remove from the heat and serve.

Makes 4 to 5 servings.

SYRIAN-STYLE OKRA WITH PRUNES AND APRICOTS (P)

I first tasted this unusual, yet very delicious, dish at a fascinating Syrian-Jewish pre-nuptial celebration called a *sweeneh*. The word means "tray," and it represents the tray of goodies traditionally presented by the groom's mother at the bride's pre-marital ritual bath or *mikvah*. In recent years, the sweeneh has often become an elaborate party held at the home of the groom's mother, where exquisite gifts for the bride from her future mother-in-law are elegantly displayed for all to see. Guests are treated to a luncheon of delectable Syrian-Jewish dishes.

The following mixture is so tasty that even those who may be wary of okra will enjoy it. It has been adapted from a recipe in *Deal Delights* by the Sisterhood of the Deal Synagogue in New Jersey. The original calls for *temerhindi,* a sweet-sour sauce made from tamarind pods and seeds, sugar, lemon juice, sour salt, and water. This unusual Syrian-Jewish condiment tastes a bit like thickened, unsweetened prune juice mixed with lemon juice, ingredients which are much more commonly available, and thus have been substituted below.

The combination of sweet fruit and a popular (among Sephardim) fall vegetable makes this recipe perfectly suited to the New Year.

1 tablespoon olive or vegetable oil
About 12 ounces fresh small whole okra, stem ends and tips trimmed so as not to expose the seeds (or 1 10-ounce package frozen whole okra, thawed and patted dry)
⅔ cup unsweetened prune juice

1½ to 2 tablespoons lemon juice
1 tablespoon tomato paste
⅛ teaspoon salt
½ cup (about 3 ounces) pitted prunes
½ cup (about 3 ounces) dried apricots

In a large skillet (preferably non-stick), over medium-high heat, heat the oil; then sauté the okra until it is very lightly browned, about 3 to 5 minutes.

Combine the prune juice, lemon juice, tomato paste, and salt and mix very well. Pour the mixture over the okra. Distribute the prunes and apricots among the okra.

Bring the liquid to a boil; then cover the skillet and lower the heat. Simmer the okra and fruit, stirring occasionally, for 20 to 30 minutes, or until they are tender and the liquid has formed a thick, rich glaze. If necessary, at the end of the cooking time, remove the cover from the skillet and cook down the liquid, stirring often, until it forms a glaze.

Makes 4 to 6 servings.

LUBIYA OR FIJONES FRESCOS (P)

(Black-Eyed Peas in Tomato Sauce)

Because beans are so abundant, they are one of the special foods eaten by many Sephardic Jews on Rosh Hashanah to symbolically express a desire for a fruitful year. Black-eyed peas are a type of cowpea, a bean which is particularly plentiful in the Middle East. In the following recipe, the beans are cooked in a style favored by Turkish Jews.

1 tablespoon olive or vegetable oil
1 medium-sized onion, finely chopped
1 16-ounce can tomatoes, including juice, chopped
1 10-ounce package frozen black-eyed peas (cowpeas), slightly thawed

⅛ teaspoon black pepper, preferably freshly ground
Salt to taste (optional)

TO SERVE (OPTIONAL)
Hot cooked white or brown rice

In a large saucepan, over medium-high heat, heat the oil; then cook the onion, stirring, until it is tender but not browned. Add the tomatoes and their can juice, the black-eyed peas, and pepper. Cover and bring to a boil; then lower the heat and simmer for about 30 minutes. Remove the cover, raise the heat slightly, and lightly boil the beans, stirring often, for 15 to 20 minutes longer, or until they are tender and the liquid has reduced to a thick sauce. Season with salt to taste. If desired, serve over hot cooked rice.

Makes 4 to 5 servings.

SWEET POTATO-PINEAPPLE CASSEROLE   (D) or (P)

One of the vegetables Ashkenazic Jews particularly enjoy during the Days of Awe is sweet potatoes, as they represent a hope for a sweet year. This easy casserole can be assembled ahead of time, and baked just before serving.

About 5 medium-sized sweet potatoes (or "yams")
3 to 4 tablespoons butter or margarine, cut into small pieces
½ cup orange juice
1 teaspoon grated orange rind (colored part only)

1 8-ounce can juice-pack crushed pineapple, including juice
½ cup dark or light raisins
2 tablespoons packed dark brown sugar

Peel the sweet potatoes and cut them into coarse chunks. Put them in a large saucepan with about 2 inches of cold water. Over high heat, bring the water to a boil; then cover the pan tightly and lower the heat. Simmer the sweet potatoes for about 35 minutes, or until they are quite tender. Immediately drain them well.

Coarsely mash the hot sweet potatoes with a fork; then stir in the butter until it is melted. Add the orange juice, rind, pineapple, and raisins, and stir until well combined. Turn out the mixture into a greased 1½- to 2-quart casserole and sprinkle the brown sugar on top. (The casserole may be prepared ahead to this point.) Bake the casserole in a preheated 350-degree oven for about 40 minutes, or until it is hot throughout.

Makes 6 to 8 servings.

HOLIDAY ORANGE-HONEY CAKE (P)

Not a single Rosh Hashanah, Yom Kippur break-the-fast, or *brit milah* in our family goes by without this wonderfully fragrant, dark loaf cake. My mother has made it as long as I can remember, and I have carried on the tradition. It differs from most other Ashkenazic honey cakes in that it contains orange juice, which gives it a wonderfully appealing flavor.

4 large eggs
⅓ cup vegetable oil
1 cup sugar
1 cup honey
1 tablespoon instant coffee granules
(preferably decaffeinated)
1 cup warm water
1 6-ounce can frozen orange juice
concentrate, thawed (but not
diluted)

2½ cups sifted all-purpose white
flour, preferably unbleached
1 cup whole wheat flour (or an
additional 1 cup white flour)
1½ teaspoons baking powder
2 teaspoons baking soda
1 teaspoon ground cinnamon
1 teaspoon ground allspice
⅛ teaspoon salt

Grease or coat with non-stick spray two 8½- by 4½-inch loaf pans. Line the bottom of each pan with wax paper; then grease or spray the paper. Set the pans aside.

In a large mixing bowl, use an electric mixer at medium speed to beat together the eggs, oil, sugar, and honey until completely combined. Dissolve the instant coffee granules in the water and add with the remaining ingredients. Beat, scraping the bowl occasionally, for 3 minutes, or until the batter is very smooth.

Pour the batter into the prepared pans, dividing it evenly. Bake in a preheated 300-degree oven for about 1 hour and 10 minutes, or until a toothpick inserted in the center of each cake comes out clean. Cool in the pans on wire racks for 45 minutes. Run a knife around the edge of each cake to loosen it; then turn each cake out of its pan, and peel the wax paper from the bottom. Invert the cakes so the tops are facing upward. Cool the cakes completely on the wire racks; then wrap them well for storage.

These honey cakes tastes best when allowed to "mellow" for several hours or overnight, before cutting. They keep well for 3 or 4 days at room temperature, or they may be frozen for several months. (Thaw them, wrapped, at room temperature, before serving.)

Makes 2 loaf cakes; 16 to 20 servings.

HONEY-SPICE CHIFFON CAKE (P)

This light, high, tube cake is much like a rich sponge cake, and thus quite different from most honey cakes typically served on Rosh Hashanah.

A relatively recent invention, chiffon cakes were originated in the late 1920s by a baker—coincidentally named Henry Baker—who kept his formula a secret until the 1940s when he sold it to General Mills. Once the basic recipe was made known to the public, easy-to-make, delicious chiffon cakes immediately became popular.

As so many chiffon cake variations are *pareve*, they are particularly convenient for those who observe *kashrut*, because they can be served at both meat and dairy meals.

Chiffon cakes differ from sponge cakes in that they contain oil and baking powder. This particular one stays quite moist, and can be baked a day or two ahead of time if it is kept well wrapped.

7 large eggs, separated
²⁄₃ cup sugar, divided
²⁄₃ cup honey
½ cup vegetable oil
2 cups all-purpose white flour,
  preferably unbleached
1 tablespoon baking powder
¼ teaspoon baking soda

2 teaspoons ground cinnamon
1 teaspoon ground allspice
½ teaspoon ground cloves
¼ teaspoon ground nutmeg
¼ teaspoon salt
²⁄₃ cup cold water
Confectioner's sugar (optional)

Have an *ungreased* 10-inch angel food tube pan handy. If it is not the two-piece type with a removable tube insert, grease the bottom only and cut a doughnut-shaped piece of wax paper to fit in the bottom. (This will make it easier to remove the cake from the pan.)

Put the egg yolks, ⅓ cup of the sugar, and the honey into a large mixing bowl and beat with an electric mixer until light. Beat in the oil until well combined. In a bowl, or on a piece of wax paper, sift together the flour, baking powder, baking soda, cinnamon, allspice, cloves, nutmeg, and salt and add these dry ingredients to the batter alternately with the water. Mix until well blended.

In a clean bowl, with clean beaters, beat the egg whites until frothy; then gradually add the remaining ⅓ cup sugar while continuing to beat just until stiff peaks form. Do not overbeat the whites or they will be difficult to fold into the batter. Stir about one fourth of the whites into the batter to lighten it. Then gently but thoroughly fold all the batter back into the remaining whites.

Pour the batter into the tube pan, and smooth the top. Bake in a preheated 325-degree oven for 60 to 70 minutes, or until the top of the cake springs back when lightly pressed with a fingertip. Remove the pan from the oven, and immediately invert it on its "legs," or fit the tube over the neck of a bottle to cool upside down. When the cake is completely cool, run a knife around the edge of it, and remove it from the pan. (If the pan was lined with paper, peel it off the bottom of the cake.)

If desired, sprinkle the cake lightly with sieved confectioner's sugar shortly before serving.

Makes about 12 servings.

OOGAT SOOMSOOM V'DVASH (D) or (P)

(Honeyed Sesame Cake)

Sesame seeds (*soomsoom* in Hebrew) are a favorite in Israeli cuisine. They are often used in Rosh Hashanah recipes because their abundant numbers symbolize a hope for increased fruitfulness and productivity. The following cake squares are laden with the rich-tasting seeds, and topped with a honey glaze.

CAKE BATTER
1½ *cups sesame seeds*
2 *large eggs*
⅔ *cup vegetable oil*
¼ *cup honey*
¾ *cup all-purpose white flour,*
   preferably unbleached

¾ *cup whole wheat flour*
½ *cup sugar*
1½ *teaspoons baking powder*

HONEY GLAZE
⅓ *cup honey*
3 *tablespoons butter or margarine*

Put the sesame seeds in a large ungreased skillet, and toast them over medium-high heat, stirring often, until they are light brown and aromatic. Set them aside to cool.

For the batter, mix together the eggs, oil, and honey in a large bowl. Add the flours, sugar, and baking powder, and mix well. Add the cooled sesame seeds and stir until they are completely mixed in. Evenly spread the batter (it will be stiff) in a greased or non-stick spray-coated 9- by 13-inch baking pan. Bake in a preheated 375-degree oven for 18 to 20 minutes, or until a toothpick inserted in the center comes out clean.

When the cake is almost done baking, bring the honey and butter to a boil in a small saucepan over medium heat (or in a glass bowl in the microwave); then remove it from the heat. Spoon the glaze evenly over the baked cake; then return the cake to the oven for 2 to 3 minutes, or until the glaze is absorbed. Cool the cake completely in the pan on a wire rack. Cut it into squares to serve.

Makes about 24 pieces.

TAYGLEH or PINYONATI (P)

(Crunchy Dough Nuggets in Honey)

This sticky confection is popular for Rosh Hashanah and the Yom Kippur break-the-fast among both Ashkenazic Jews (who call it *taygleh*) and Sephardic Jews (who call it *pinyonati*). Both groups also enjoy it for Purim. On these same holidays, some Italian Jews enjoy a similar pastry that they call *ceciarchiata,* because the pieces of dough resemble chick-peas (*ceci* in Italian).

In all cases, the dessert is made in basically the same manner. Small nuggets of a noodle-type dough are baked (or fried), just as with *mandlen.* The cooked dough pieces are then simmered for several minutes in a spicy, honey-sugar syrup. Nuts are usually added to the syrup; however, they may be omitted, or candied fruits may be substituted.

Occasionally, the dough is not baked first, but is added directly to the hot syrup to cook. The entire mixture may then be baked to thicken the syrup.

This confection will keep for up to two weeks if stored in an airtight container at room temperature. If it becomes too sticky, it can be refrigerated.

DOUGH
2 large eggs
2 tablespoons vegetable oil
½ teaspoon baking powder
1¼ to 1½ cups all-purpose white
  flour, preferably unbleached

SYRUP AND NUTS
⅔ cup honey
⅓ cup packed dark or light brown
  sugar .
½ to 1 teaspoon ground ginger
¼ teaspoon ground cinnamon
½ to 1 cup walnuts, whole blanched
  almonds, pecans, or hazelnuts

For the dough, mix together the eggs, oil, baking powder, and enough flour to make a smooth dough that is easy to handle and not dry or sticky. Roll the dough into ⅜- to ½-inch-thick ropes; then cut the ropes into ⅜- to ½-inch-long pieces. If desired, roll each piece in the palm of your hand to make it round. Arrange the dough pieces in one layer on a large greased or non-stick spray-coated baking sheet. Bake them in a preheated 350-degree oven for 15 to 20 minutes, or until they are very lightly browned. Remove them from the oven and let them cool slightly on the baking sheet.

Meanwhile, prepare the syrup. Combine the honey, brown sugar, ginger, and cinnamon in a large saucepan and bring to a boil over medium-high heat. Lower the heat, and gently simmer the syrup for 5 minutes. Add the warm dough pieces to the syrup. Simmer, stirring gently with a wooden spoon, for 10 minutes. Stir in the nuts. Continue simmering, while stirring, an additional 15 minutes. Remove the saucepan from the heat and cool the taygleh in the pan, stirring for 5 to 10 minutes, or until the syrup becomes very thick and the dough pieces hold together. Turn out all the mixture onto a lightly oiled baking sheet and let it cool slightly until it can be handled.

Dip your hands into ice water and form the warm mixture into small mounds or balls containing about 4 to 5 pieces of dough (and some nuts) in each. Let the taygleh cool completely before storing.

Makes 15 to 20 portions of taygleh.

HADGI BADAM (P)

(Almond-Cardamom Cookies)

Iraqi Jews like to break the Yom Kippur fast with these tasty treats. For Pesach, they sometimes prepare a slightly different version that does not call for flour, egg yolks, or baking powder. (For this variation, see the *amaretti* in the Pesach chapter, page 284.) *Hadgi badam* are also widely eaten on Purim. When shaping the dough, Iraqis sometimes moisten their hands with fragrant rose water to give the cookies a bit of added flavor.

Cardamom (called *hel* in both Hebrew and Arabic) is a sweet-smelling spice that is very popular in Asia and the Middle East, as well as in Scandinavia. For some obscure reason, it is still relatively unknown in the United States. The following cookies are a nice way to give cardamom a try.

1 cup (4 ounces) finely ground blanched almonds
1 cup all-purpose white flour, preferably unbleached
⅔ cup sugar
½ teaspoon ground cardamom

⅛ teaspoon baking powder
2 large eggs, beaten with a fork until frothy
Rose water (optional)
24 whole almonds or pistachios, split lengthwise (optional)

In a medium-sized bowl, combine the ground almonds, flour, sugar, cardamom, and baking powder. Stir in the eggs and mix for a few minutes to make a very stiff, slightly sticky dough.

Moisten your hands with water (or rose water) and form scant tablespoonfuls of the paste into 1¼-inch balls. Arrange the balls about 2 inches apart on greased or non-stick spray-coated baking sheets. Then flatten each ball slightly with moistened fingertips. If desired, press an almond or pistachio half into the top of each cookie.

Bake the cookies in a preheated 350-degree oven for 12 to 15 minutes, or until they are firm and very lightly browned. Use a metal spatula to remove the cookies from the baking sheets, and cool them on wire racks.

Makes about 30 cookies.

ZIMSTERNE OR ERSTE-STEREN   (D) or (P)

(Spicy Star Cookies)

These cookies, adapted from German-Jewish cuisine, are a tasty reminder that we must wait for the "first stars" of the evening to appear before we can break the fast of Yom Kippur. (*Zimsterne* is German for "to the stars"; *erste steren* is Yiddish for "first stars.")

A small nosh of these crunchy, honey-sweetened treats helps to alleviate hunger pangs while the rest of the post-fast meal is being readied. As the cookies keep well, they can be made several days ahead.

DOUGH
¼ cup butter or margarine
⅔ cup sugar
½ cup honey
3 large eggs
About 3¾ cups all-purpose white
   flour, preferably unbleached (may
   be half whole wheat flour)
2 teaspoons baking powder

½ teaspoon baking soda
1½ to 2 teaspoons ground cinnamon
½ teaspoon ground nutmeg
¼ teaspoon ground cloves

GLAZE (OPTIONAL)
1 large egg, beaten with 1 teaspoon
   water

In a large mixing bowl, cream the butter with the sugar and honey until smooth and fluffy. Beat in the eggs. Combine the remaining ingedients and add to the butter-egg mixture. Mix until well combined. If the dough seems very sticky, add a little extra flour. Divide the dough into 3 pieces, flatten each one into a circle, and wrap them separately in plastic wrap. Refrigerate the dough for several hours (or overnight) until it is quite firm.

Remove 1 piece of dough from the refrigerator and roll it out on a lightly floured surface until it is about ⅛ inch thick. Cut out the dough with a small star-shaped cutter (use a 6-pointed one if available), and carefully transfer the cookies to greased or non-stick spray-coated baking sheets, keeping them 1 inch apart. Reroll the scraps and cut out as above. (Refrigerate any dough that becomes too soft to work with easily.) Repeat the procedure for the remaining dough.

To give the cookies an attractive, shiny top, brush them lightly with the glaze just before baking. Bake the cookies in a preheated 375-degree oven for 8 to 10 minutes, or until they are lightly browned. Cool them on wire racks. (The cookies get crisper as they cool.)

Makes about 4 dozen cookies; the exact number depends on the size of the cookie cutter.

HARIRI (P)

(Iraqi-Style Almond "Milk")

Jews from Iraq break the Yom Kippur fast with a rich, non-dairy drink made from almonds. Even though Bellah Ini and her family left Iraq in 1951, she still prepares this drink each year. Mrs. Ini points out that it satiates her hunger and thirst better than any other food or drink.

When Mrs. Ini makes *hariri*, she first grinds unblanched almonds very finely, then puts them on "very thin cloth" and gathers the edges to make a bag of sorts. She repeatedly dips the bag into a bowl of water until the liquid becomes quite milky from the almonds. She then adds sugar and cardamom to the liquid, and simmers it a few minutes.

Another Iraqi Jew, Rachel Muallem Gabes, uses a slightly different method to get "milk" from the almonds. She grinds the almonds, water, and sugar together in a blender, then strains the mixture through cheesecloth. This latter method produces a slightly richer milk. Sometimes, Mrs. Gabes adds dairy milk and cooked rice to the almond-water mixture.

Mrs. Gabes recalls that in Iraq, *hariri* was often given to pregnant and lactating women to help ensure a plentiful supply of mother's milk, and was also used as a restorative after childbirth.

Following is my adaptation of *hariri* combining both of the above methods. Blanched or unblanched almonds may be used. The former produce a very white drink which is in keeping with the "purity" of Yom Kippur. A drink made with the latter is a bit off-white in color, but has a slightly stronger almond taste. Although it is not "authentic," a very small amount of almond extract can be added to the drink to make up for the lack of intense flavor in American almonds.

Some Jews from the Balkan and Middle Eastern countries break the fast with similar almond drinks, such as *soubya, soumada,* and *mizo.* Occasionally, a thicker version of almond milk is used as a substitute for dairy milk or cream in order to make creamy sauces for meat dishes without violating the rules of *kashrut.*

*About ¾ cup blanched or
    unblanched, slivered or whole
    almonds
3 cups water
About ¼ cup sugar, or to taste*

*⅛ to ¼ teaspoon ground cardamom
    (optional)
1 to 2 drops almond extract
    (optional)*

Put the almonds and water into a blender jar and process at medium to high speed for several minutes, or until the almonds have been ground as finely as possible. Line a large sieve with 3 to 4 layers of moistened cheesecloth and pour the mixture through the cheesecloth into a medium-sized saucepan. When all the liquid has passed through, gather the corners of the cloth together and carefully squeeze out any remaining liquid.

Add the sugar and cardamom (if used) and bring the "milk" to a boil over medium heat. Lower the heat and simmer, stirring occasionally, for 3 minutes, or until the "milk" has thickened and the flavors have blended. If desired, add more sugar and/or cardamom to taste, and heat a few seconds longer to make sure they have dissolved. Let the "milk" cool slightly; then add the almond extract, if desired. Serve warm. If made in advance, chill until serving time; then reheat in a saucepan (or in a glass pitcher in the microwave oven).

Makes about 2½ cups, or about 6 small servings.

PEPITADA (P)

(Sephardic-Style Melon Seed "Milk")

Greek and Turkish Jews, including those whose families once dwelled on the island of Rhodes, often break the Yom Kippur fast with this non-dairy "milk." They save the seeds from cantaloupe, honeydew, and Persian and similar melons eaten during the few weeks before the holiday, wash them well, and air dry them for several days. Sometimes the seeds are then lightly toasted in a low oven to bring out their flavor. Two days before Yom Kippur, preparation of the following melon seed milk is begun.

½ *to 1 cup clean, dry melon seeds,*   *1 quart cold water*
   toasted if desired (see comment   *1 to 3 tablespoons sugar*
   above)   *1 to 2 drops rose water (optional)*

Process the seeds in a blender or food processor until they are finely ground. Put the ground seeds in 3 or 4 layers of cheesecloth. Bring the edges of the cheesecloth together to form a bag that completely encloses the seeds. Twist a clean rubberband around the top of the bag so it cannot open. Put the cold water into a pitcher or bowl and immerse the bag of seeds in the water. Let the seeds steep in the water for about 24 hours in the refrigerator. During this time, occasionally squeeze the bag of seeds to help release the milky liquid; then return the bag to the liquid. At the end of the 24-hour period, squeeze and dip the bag several times to get out as much "milk" as possible. Discard the bag of seeds.

Stir sugar and rose water into the drink to taste. Return the drink to the refrigerator and chill it until serving time. Serve chilled.

Makes about 8 small servings.

SUKKOT, SHEMINI ATZERET, AND SIMHAT TORAH

(Including Hoshanah Rabbah)

Three times during the year, at Sukkot, Pesach, and Shavuot, early Jews made festive pilgrimage to a major sanctuary such as the Holy Temple in Jerusalem. Sukkot, the most joyous and splendid of these thanksgiving festivals, occurred at the conclusion of the autumn harvest. This holiday was so prominent in ancient times that any reference simply to "The Festival" always meant Sukkot.

As with many Jewish holidays, it actually had a number of names. It was called *Hag Ha'Asif* or "Festival of the Ingathering" regarding the gathering of crops, as well as *Zeman Simhatenu* or "The Time of Our Gladness." It was also called *Hag Ha'Sukkot* or "Festival of the Tabernacles." The latter name eventually became shortened to *Sukkot*.

Tabernacles, booths, huts, or cabanas, as the Hebrew word *"sukkot"* is variously translated, became an important part of the festival due to its agricultural nature. In earlier times, families banded together in villages for protection, and went back and forth to farms which were scattered on the outskirts. During the busy fall harvest season, however, there was no time for such travels. So farmers built rough-hewn huts with foliage roofs as temporary on-site residences.

The *sukkot* were given biblical importance with the following verse from Leviticus: "You shall live in booths seven days . . . in order that future generations may know that I made the Israelite people live in booths when I brought them out of the land of Egypt, I am the Lord your God." Thus, *sukkot* came to symbolize the temporary abodes of those who wandered through the desert with Moses after the Exodus.

To this day, Jews all over the world build impermanent foliage-topped booths to celebrate Sukkot, which begins on the fifteenth day of the Hebrew month of Tishri, exactly two weeks after the first day of Rosh Hashanah. According to Jewish law, a *sukkah* (the singular form of *sukkot*) should have at least three sides. And, its roof should be open enough to allow a view of the stars at night, yet still provide more shade than sunlight during the day.

The festival of Sukkot lasts seven days. During that time, orthodox ritual requires that Jewish men eat all their main meals in the sukkah, with the rest of the family joining in as often as possible, particularly on the first day. Feasting is the keynote; indeed, it is forbidden to fast during this happy festival.

To show thankfulness for a successful harvest, the sukkah is profusely decorated with those fruits and vegetables that reach maturity in autumn. As these vary greatly from place to place, so do the sukkot. For instance, a typical American sukkah would probably have apples, pears, cranberries, gourds, and "Indian corn" hanging from its roof and walls. However, an Israeli sukkah would more likely be adorned with pomegranates, quinces, persimmons, fresh figs, fresh dates, avocados, grapes, pomelos (similar to grapefruits), oranges, tangerines, guavas, custard apples, and carambolas (star fruit).

In all sukkot, wherever they are located, an *etrog* and *lulav* are also present. These encompass "the Four Species" of plants that are blessed and carried about during Sukkot.

The etrog (or citron), an ancient citrus fruit considered to be the biblical "fruit of the goodly tree," is the most important of the symbolic plants because it is the only one having both fragrance and taste. It is a sour fruit which looks like a very large, elongated lemon, but has much more rind than flesh. (After the holiday is over, some cooks collect the etrogs of several families, and turn them into delicious preserves or candy.)

The lulav is composed of a willow branch, palm branch, and myrtle branch, all tied together so they can be held in one hand.

The foods eaten during Sukkot reflect the bounty of a harvest celebration. Lavish casseroles, rich stews, and filled pastries are typical, especially those featuring autumnal vegetables and fruits. In the past, fresh produce was available only during the brief harvest period when it was in season. Thus, it became favored for use in special holiday fare. A wide variety of savory and sweet "stuffed foods" is also served, because their extravagance is in keeping with the opulent atmosphere of celebration.

One-dish casseroles are popular for another reason. They are easy to transport from kitchen to sukkah, and stay hot and palatable throughout a meal eaten outdoors. Even on cool nights, they help keep the family warm and satisfied.

On Hoshanah Rabbah, the seventh and last day of Sukkot, the etrog and lulav are carried around the synagogue seven times, rather than just once as on the six previous days. Also, each person present takes a willow branch and beats it on the floor until most of its leaves have fallen off. The fallen leaves symbolize many things, including the falling away of sins, the falling of rain, and renewed life in the spring (when leaves will grow again).

Hoshanah Rabbah is considered the last day when any unfavorable divine judgments of Yom Kippur may be reversed, and when God's final verdict is sealed and "written." Therefore, round challah and honey-sweetened treats are eaten for the same reasons as during the Days of Awe. Sometimes, the *challah* (pages 17 and 64) is shaped like an out-reaching hand to receive the divine decree. As on Yom Kippur and Purim, meat-filled *kreplah* (page 78) are also a traditional part of the meal served after the synagogue service.

In Israel, a sweet dish made with the giant, pumpkin-like squash called calabassah (*dla'at,* in Hebrew) may also be served on this day. The size and abundance of the squash make it a symbol of plenty, and its pleasant taste expresses hope for a sweet year. Also, Jews from the Germanic countries often eat a dish made with cabbage cooked in water (*kohl mit wasser*), as a play on the Hebrew words *kol me'vasser* from a prayer recited when the willow branches are beaten.

Hoshanah Rabbah is immediately followed by Shemini Atzeret, which is linked to the Sukkot festival, but is a separate, independent holiday. On this day, it has become customary to say a solemn prayer for rain. According to tradition, this is when God judges the world's water, so the prayer asks for enough rain to support life but not so much as to cause flooding and famine.

As with several other Jewish holidays, Shemini Atzeret was extended to two days in early times, to allow for a "margin of error" should the exact date of celebration be slightly miscalculated by those far away from the Land of Israel. The second day eventually became known as Simhat Torah, or "Rejoicing in the Law," because this is when the last verses of the Torah—the Five Books of Moses—are read in the synagogue, and the cyclical reading of the Torah is begun anew at Genesis.

The synagogue service for Simhat Torah is one of the happiest and most raucous of the entire year. All the scrolls of the Torah are removed from the Ark and paraded around the sanctuary by adult members. Children gaily march after them, wildly waving paper flags. In many places, it is customary for an apple or beet holding a lit candle to be stuck on the top of each miniature flagpole. Youngsters are also often given bags containing candy, dried fruit, and nuts.

All over Israel (where Shemini Atzeret and Simhat Torah are celebrated on the same day), and in many other places, the Torah procession continues outside into the streets surrounding the synagogue, where observers typically get caught up in the merriment and join in the dancing and singing.

For Simhat Torah, Israeli bakers add a fruity candy called "Turkish delight" to the fillings for pastries such as *strudel* and *fluden,* and street vendors sell candy-coated apples. Worldwide, spicy honey cookies and small cakes filled with fruits and nuts are popular treats, as are etrog preserves and candied etrog peel. Also, seasonal fruits and vegetables are preserved or dried at this time, for the year ahead.

In keeping with the opulent spirit of Sukkot and the holidays that immediately follow it, this chapter is "stuffed" with recipes for delectable fall dishes. It also includes a recipe and detailed directions for constructing a miniature gingerbread sukkah.

MITZAPUNY (M)

(Meaty Split Pea, Bean, and Barley Soup)

The first time my maternal great-grandparents, Rose Dublin and Harry Levine, met was on the day they wed. As with most turn-of-the-century marriages in Russian *shtetls,* theirs had been arranged. Fortunately for them, it was love at first sight. Unfortunately, however, my great-grandfather was about to be conscripted into the Russian army for many years.

So, when they said their goodbyes to family and friends and ostensibly left on a short honeymoon, Bubby Rose and Zaida Harry walked out of the country with only the belongings they could carry. They eventually made their way to England, where they planned to settle. But the cold, damp weather repeatedly left them ill, so they decided to head for America and the "golden opportunities" of New York City.

All through her travels, Bubby Rose carried this recipe in her mind. When times were difficult, she used a few soup bones to make a version that filled the stomach without emptying the purse. In better times, chunks of meat and some fresh vegetables were added (as below) to make it very rich. No matter what, it was always thick and hearty enough to be a very satisfying one-dish meal, more like a stew than a soup.

In trying to track down the meaning of the soup's name, I learned about the Yiddish word *martzapunis*. The word, I was told, literally translates as the name of an exotic fruit, but it has·come to mean anything special and extraordinary. Whether or not that was what Bubby Rose meant years ago, when she used to make this soup for my mother, it is indeed quite special. When the weather is chilly and the wind howls, nothing warms one up like a big bowl of *mitzapuny*. It's the perfect one-dish dinner for Sukkot.

12 cups water
2 to 3 pounds soup meat (such as crosspiece, chuck deckel, flanken, etc.), cut into large chunks and trimmed of all surface fat
1 medium-sized onion, halved through the root end
4 to 5 medium-sized carrots, cut into ½-inch chunks

2 celery stalks, thinly sliced
1½ cups dry green split peas, sorted and rinsed
1 cup dry baby lima beans, sorted and rinsed
½ cup pearl barley, rinsed
1 teaspoon salt
¼ teaspoon black pepper, preferably freshly ground

In a 6-quart soup pot over high heat, bring the water to a boil. Add the meat and lower the heat so the water simmers. Gently cook the meat for 30 minutes, skimming off and discarding all the foam that rises to the surface. Meanwhile, prepare the remaining ingredients.

Add the remaining ingredients, cover the pot, and simmer the soup, stirring occasionally (especially during the end of the cooking period), for about 3 hours longer, or until the split peas have disintegrated, the meat is very tender, and the soup is thick. If it becomes too thick, stir in some hot water. Remove and discard the onion before serving. Adjust the seasonings to taste, if desired.

Makes 8 to 10 servings.

NOTE: Leftovers can be frozen. Thaw before reheating, and add water if the soup has become too thick. Stir the soup often when reheating it, so it does not stick to the bottom of the pot. This problem can be avoided by reheating individual servings of the soup in a microwave oven.

PURÉED APPLE-SQUASH SOUP (M)

This easy soup is a delicious melding of two wonderful fall flavors—tart apples and sweet squash. Sautéed onions provide a tasty counterpoint.

1 large or 2 small butternut squash OR 3 acorn squash (total weight about 4 pounds)
3 cups chicken broth or bouillon (homemade, canned, or made from cubes or powder), or more if needed

¼ cup pareve margarine
1 large onion, diced
4 medium-sized tart apples, peeled, cored, and sliced
Salt to taste

Peel the squash; then cut it into large chunks, removing and discarding all the seeds and fibers. Put the broth into a large saucepan or soup pot and add the squash pieces. Bring to a boil over high heat; then lower the heat, cover, and simmer for 20 to 25 minutes, or until the squash is very tender.

Meanwhile, melt the margarine in a large skillet or saucepan over medium high heat; then sauté the onion until it is tender but not browned. Add the apples and sauté until they are tender.

In batches, using a blender or a food processor (fitted with the steel blade), process the apples, onion, and cooked squash with just enough of the squash broth so the mixture can be easily puréed. (Reserve the remaining broth.)

Stir the puréed mixture back into the saucepan containing the reserved broth. If the soup is too thick, stir in additional broth as desired. (The soup may be made ahead to this point.) Shortly before serving, reheat the soup, stirring often. Season with salt, if desired.

Makes about 8 servings.

HOLISHKES or PRAAKES (M)

(Sweet-and-Sour Stuffed Cabbage)

For many Ashkenazic Jews, stuffed cabbage in sweet-and-sour sauce is essential for Sukkot. It is just one of the many dishes that were developed in the *shtetls* of Eastern and Central Europe to transform an ordinarily mundane ingredient, such as cabbage, into a rich-tasting delicacy. At the same time, precious meat was stretched to serve a few more.

This dish probably became traditional for Sukkot because cabbage is plentiful during the harvest season, and also "stuffed foods" are customarily eaten on the holiday to symbolize abundance.

Depending on the locale where they or their ancestors once lived, Jews have given stuffed cabbage many different appellations. Some of the more popular Ashkenazic ones include *holishkes, holopches, praakes,* and *galuptzi.* Sephardic Jews make a very similar type of stuffed cabbage, occasionally using ground lamb instead of beef. Those from Turkey and nearby areas generally call the dish *dolmas de col* or *yaprakis de kol.* Middle Eastern Jews spice it differently, and sometimes call it *sarmas* or *mishi malfouf.*

As with many other Jewish recipes that have been carried around the world, stuffed cabbage has innumerable variations. For a delicious, satisfying taste, I have added a few innovative ingredients, such as applesauce and mustard powder, to the following basically Ashkenazic version.

1 large head (about 2 pounds) white or savoy cabbage (see Note)

SAUCE

3 cups plain tomato sauce (3 8-ounce cans)

⅓ cup applesauce

1 small onion, finely chopped

2 to 3 tablespoons packed dark brown sugar

3 tablespoons apple cider vinegar

1 tablespoon lemon juice

½ teaspoon powdered mustard

Salt and ground black pepper to taste

¼ cup dark raisins (optional)

FILLING

1 pound very lean ground beef

1 small onion, grated

½ cup long-grain white rice

¼ cup applesauce

1 large egg

¾ teaspoon salt

¼ teaspoon black pepper, preferably freshly ground

Pinch of ground allspice (optional)

Remove and discard the core and any discolored leaves from the cabbage. Very carefully peel off about 15 whole outer leaves. (The exact number needed will depend on their size.) If the leaves will not come off, cut away the core of the cabbage and parboil the entire head in a large pot of water for about 10 minutes, or until the leaves can be loosened. To soften the separated leaves so they can be easily rolled, put them into a pot of boiling water and simmer them for about 5 minutes, or until they are translucent and very flexible. Cut away any very thick, tough ribs from the base of each leaf.

For the sauce, combine all the ingredients in a very large deep skillet, an electric frying pan, or a Dutch oven. Bring to a simmer over medium-high heat; then lower the heat, cover, and simmer gently, stirring occasionally.

Meanwhile, prepare the filling and stuff the cabbage. For the filling, mix together all the ingredients using your hands or a fork until they are well combined and smooth. To stuff the cabbage, put a spoonful of the filling in the center of a leaf (the exact amount depends on the size of the leaf). Fold up the edge of the leaf which was nearest the core; then fold in the sides and roll up the leaf to enclose the filling. Put the roll, seam side down, into the simmering sauce. Continue until all the filling is used. Try to arrange the cabbage rolls in one layer in the pan.

Spoon some sauce over any rolls that are not already covered with it, and cover the pan. Simmer the rolls, basting them occasionally, for 60 to 75 minutes, or until the meat and rice in the filling are cooked through and the sauce is thick. If the sauce gets too thick during the cooking period, add a little water to the pan.

Stuffed cabbage can be made ahead and reheated; it has a deserved reputation for being "even better the next day." It can also be frozen.

Makes 5 to 6 servings

NOTE: If time allows, white cabbage may be softened by freezing it for 2 or 3 days, and then defrosting it in the refrigerator overnight. Parboiling the leaves, as directed above, is not then necessary.

MAHSHI or DOLMAS (M)

(Meat-Stuffed Vegetables)

This type of dish is very popular all over the Middle East as well as North Africa, Iran, and the Balkans. The idea of stuffing meat into vegetables probably originated in Turkey (the word *dolma* is Turkish for "to stuff"), and spread during the time of the Ottoman Empire. Because of its opulent nature, it is likely to have been developed in the court of a sultan. However, it was eventually adopted by the lower classes, and become a dish for all the people, including the Jews, who lived in these lands.

The basic ground lamb or beef filling is sometimes slightly varied with the addition of rice, bulgur wheat, pine nuts, raisins, tomatoes, or chickpeas. Jewish cooks often extend the meat with some matzo meal.

All the vegetables listed below can be "mixed and matched" in one meal. Also, you can adjust the herbs and spices to suit your own taste.

VEGETABLES (4 TO 6 TOTAL)
Sweet green peppers, small zucchini, miniature Italian eggplants (about 5 to 7 inches long), and/or potatoes

STUFFING
1 pound very lean ground beef or lamb
1 small onion, grated or very finely chopped
2 tablespoons finely chopped fresh parsley leaves
1 teaspoon salt
½ teaspoon ground cinnamon

¼ teaspoon ground nutmeg
¼ teaspoon black pepper, preferably freshly ground
⅛ teaspoon ground allspice (optional)
1 large egg
About ½ cup matzo meal

SAUCE
1 16-ounce can tomatoes, including juice, coarsely chopped
2 to 3 garlic cloves, minced
½ cup water
Freshly ground black pepper to taste
Pinch of cayenne pepper (optional)

To prepare the vegetables, cut each one in half lengthwise. For the green peppers, remove the stems, seeds, and ribs. For the zucchini, cut off the stem; then carefully scoop out a depression in the center of each half, leaving a ½-inch-thick shell. (If necessary, you can use larger zucchini which have been first cut in half crosswise.) For eggplants, remove the stem; then peel off some of the skin, leaving stripes of purple (do not remove all the skin or the eggplants may fall apart) and scoop out a depression in the center of each half, leaving a ½-inch-thick shell. For potatoes, peel them and scoop out a depression in the center of each half, leaving a ½-inch-thick shell.

(A metal melon baller or serrated grapefruit spoon is very helpful for scooping the centers from the vegetables. If desired, the edible scooped-out parts of the vegetables may be chopped up and added to the sauce.)

To prepare the stuffing, place all the stuffing ingredients in a bowl; then mix it with your hands or a fork until it is very well combined and smooth. (You may also use a food processor.) Use just enough matzo meal so the stuffing is neither sticky nor dry. Press the stuffing into the prepared vegetables, rounding the mixture on top so that it extends ½ to ¾ inch above each vegetable.

For the sauce, put the tomatoes and their can juice in a deep 10-inch or larger skillet, pot, or Dutch oven. Stir in the remaining sauce ingredients. Gently place the stuffed vegetables in the sauce, stuffing side up. Bring the sauce to a boil; then immediately lower the heat and simmer, covered, for 30 to 40 minutes, or until all the vegetables are tender and the meat is cooked through. (Or, if preferred, the vegetables and sauce may be placed in a 9- by 12-inch baking pan, covered with aluminum foil, and baked in a preheated 350-degree oven for about 40 to 50 minutes.) Occasionally use a spoon to gently move the vegetables around so they do not stick to the bottom of the pan. Toward the end of the cooking period, baste the stuffed vegetables often with the sauce.

Use a slotted spoon to remove the stuffed vegetables from the sauce. If the vegetables have given off a lot of liquid during cooking and the sauce is too thin, boil it down for a few minutes to thicken it. Pour a little sauce over the vegetables and serve the remainder on the side.

Makes 8 to 12 pieces; 4 to 6 servings.

PAPAS RELLENAS   (M)

(Meat-Stuffed Mashed Potato Croquettes)

Michael Gordon was born in Cuba, and spent his early childhood there before emigrating to the United States. Though his family had Ashkenazic roots, they adopted many Spanish customs while in Cuba, just as other Jews have done wherever they have lived in the Diaspora. Thus,

Mr. Gordon was known as Miguel during his youth, and his mother often prepared dishes that were popular in Cuba. But she always added a special "Jewish touch."

Her version of *papas rellenas,* for example, uses matzo meal, unlike most. This "Jewish" variation is made not only by Cuban Jews, but by those from other parts of Latin America as well.

South American Jews also make the dish, often with their own variations. For instance, Peruvian Jews may use a more elaborate meat filling with raisins, almonds, and olives. And those from Chile and other countries may use chicken instead of red meat. Sometimes, the dish is called *patatas rellenas.*

Interestingly, the following recipe is almost identical to one called *uruq batata* or *batata charp,* which is made by Iraqi Jews. The only difference is that the Iraqis omit the green pepper in the filling, and add, instead, lots of chopped parsley and ground spices, such as cinnamon, cloves, cumin, turmeric, and/or coriander.

I have included *papas rellenas* in this chapter because they are in keeping with the tradition of eating stuffed foods on Sukkot. However, the Gordons often eat them on Shabbat, as well.

FILLING
1 pound lean ground beef
1 medium-sized onion, finely chopped
4 to 5 garlic cloves, minced
1 medium-sized sweet green pepper, finely chopped
Salt and freshly ground black pepper to taste

MASHED POTATOES
About 2½ pounds boiling or all-purpose potatoes, well scrubbed

1 large egg
Salt and freshly ground black pepper to taste

COATING, ETC.
1 large egg, lightly beaten with 1 teaspoon water
Matzo meal
Vegetable oil for frying

For the filling, cook the ground beef with the onion, garlic, and green pepper in a large skillet over medium-high heat, until the meat is browned and the vegetables are tender. While cooking the meat, break it up and mash it with a potato masher or similar utensil so that the mixture is as fine as possible. Drain off and discard any excess fat in the skillet. Set the meat mixture aside to cool.

For the mashed potatoes, put the potatoes into a large saucepan and add enough water so it is about 2 inches deep. Bring to a boil over high heat; then cover the pan and lower the heat. Simmer the potatoes for 30 to 40 minutes, or until they are quite tender. Immediately drain off the cooking water and let the potatoes cool just until they can be handled. Peel the potatoes; then mash them well with a potato masher or fork. Stir in the egg and the seasonings, and mix very well to make a sort of dough. (If the potato dough is extremely loose and sticky, stir in a tablespoon or two of cornstarch or flour.)

While shaping the papas rellenas, be sure to keep your hands clean and wet, as this will keep the potato dough from sticking. Put about a 2-inch-diameter ball of the potato mixture on the moistened palm of one hand; then use your other hand to pat it out to a small saucer shape. Put about 1 tablespoon of the filling in the center; then fold up the potato around the filling, completely enclosing it. Form the papa rellena into a ball (for deep-frying) or a flat patty (for pan-frying); then coat it lightly, first with the beaten egg-water mixture, and next with the matzo meal. Repeat until all the potatoes and filling are used.

Deep-fry the balls in a saucepan of hot oil, or pan-fry the patties in oil about ¼ inch deep in a large skillet over medium-high heat, until they are golden brown and crisp on all sides. Drain on paper towels.

Makes about 20 papas rellenas; about 6 servings.

BAKED KIBBEH OR KUBBAH (M)

(Bulgur-Meat Loaf Stuffed with Spiced Meat and Pine Nuts)

This classic Middle Eastern recipe is popular in Israel, particularly among those Jews who emigrated from Syria, Lebanon, Iraq and Kurdistan. There are actually several types of *kibbeh,* all made from basically the same ingredients. The following version is baked in layers in a pan.

More time consuming and difficult to prepare is the *kibbeh* which is formed into small torpedo or pear shapes, filled with a precooked meat mixture, and deep-fried. The outer layer is usually made from ground meat kneaded with bulgur wheat. However, some Jews use matzo meal or rice instead of bulgur, or a meatless mixture made with matzo meal and/or rice. Occasionally, pomegranate seeds are added to the meat filling.

Sometimes, *kibbeh* is eaten raw in the same manner as *steak tartare,* and is considered a delicacy. Syrian Jews make a vegetarian variation of this type of *kibbeh,* using red lentils in place of meat.

Baked *kibbeh* can be made ahead and reheated, and is a great company dish. Though it seems to contain a lot of spices, the flavor is subtle, even a bit mysterious.

Kibbeh is traditionally made with lamb, the most common meat in the Middle East. However, it also tastes quite good with beef.

2½ cups bulgur wheat

FILLING
1 pound lean ground beef or lamb
1 large onion, finely chopped
1 teaspoon ground cinnamon
¼ teaspoon ground allspice
½ teaspoon salt
¼ teaspoon black pepper, preferably freshly ground
½ cup pine nuts (pignoli) or slivered almonds (or a mixture)

BULGUR-MEAT LAYERS
2 medium-sized onions, finely chopped

1 teaspoon ground allspice
¼ teaspoon ground cinnamon
1 teaspoon salt
¼ to ½ teaspoon black pepper, preferably freshly ground
1½ pounds very lean ground beef or lamb
½ cup very cold water

FOR BAKING
3 tablespoons pareve *margarine or vegetable oil*
2 tablespoons water

Put the bulgur into a large bowl and cover it with warm water. Let it soak for 15 to 20 minutes while the filling is being prepared.

For the filling, cook the ground meat with the onion in a large skillet over medium-high heat. Use a potato masher or similar utensil to repeatedly press against the meat and onion, so that the meat breaks down into very small pieces. (The "S"-shaped type of potato masher works quite well.) Stir in the cinnamon, allspice, salt, and pepper. Continue cooking the meat mixture until most of the liquid in the skillet evaporates. Add the pine nuts and stir for 1 to 2 minutes, or until they are lightly toasted. Drain off and discard any excess fat in the skillet and set the meat filling aside to cool while you prepare the bulgur-meat layers.

For the bulgur-meat layers, it is easiest to use a food processor fitted with the steel blade. If you do not have this appliance, a meat grinder may be used instead. Process the onions in the food processor (or put them through the meat grinder) until finely chopped. Transfer the onion to a medium-sized bowl. Add the allspice, cinnamon, salt, and pepper and combine well. Drain the water from the bulgur wheat, pressing out any excess. Add the bulgur to the onion mixture and mix well.

Put about one fourth of the raw ground meat into the food processor bowl with about a fourth of the bulgur mixture. Process, adding 2 tablespoons of the cold water while the machine is running. Process the mixture until it forms a smooth paste. Transfer the paste to a large bowl. Repeat the process until all the meat and bulgur mixture have been used. Mix the batches together so they are well combined. (If using a meat grinder, mix together all the meat, all the bulgur mixture, and the ½ cup of cold water; then put the combination through the fine blade of the grinder to form a paste. Knead the paste with your hands or mix it with a spoon until it is smooth.)

Press half of the bulgur-meat paste into the bottom of a well-greased or non-stick spray-coated 9- by 13-inch baking pan. Keep your hands or spatula wet so the mixture does not stick. Top the bulgur-meat layer with the cooled, precooked meat and nut filling, spreading it evenly, and lightly pressing it in place. Top the filling with the remaining bulgur-meat paste. This is easiest to do if you press a portion of the paste into a flat "patty" on your wet hand; then place several of these patties on top of the filling, like the pieces of a puzzle. Use a wet spatula to blend them together so that the filling does not show and the top is smooth.

Deeply score the kibbeh into large diamonds (see Note) or squares. Mix together the melted margarine and 2 tablespoons water and spoon the mixture over the top so every piece of kibbeh is coated. Bake the kibbeh in a preheated 375-degree oven for 45 to 55 minutes, or until the top is well browned. Carefully drain off and discard any fat that has accumulated around the edges of the meat. Let the kibbeh cool in the pan for about 5 minutes. Cut along the scored marks and serve hot or at room temperature.

Makes 18 to 20 large diamonds or squares; about 8 to 10 servings.

NOTE: To cut diamonds, first cut the kibbeh lengthwise into 4 even strips; then make parallel, diagonal cuts across the kibbeh, forming diamonds.

BESTILA (M)

(Spicy and Slightly Sweet Chicken and Almond Pie in Filo)

This wonder of Moroccan-Jewish cuisine, which may be called *pastilla* or *bisteeya,* is one of my very favorite dishes. It is perfectly suited for Sukkot because it is lavishly stuffed and very rich. *Bestila* not only tastes great, but also looks beautiful, and thus would be very nice for entertaining. In fact, it is served at most Moroccan-Jewish festive celebrations, including weddings and bar mitzvah parties.

Though *bestila* is classically prepared with pigeons (squab), chicken is almost always substituted in the United States. Also, packaged, ultra-thin filo dough is used instead of the *warka* which is hand-made by dexterous cooks in Morocco.

Filo is available refrigerated or frozen at many supermarkets, ethnic groceries and gourmet stores. (Note: For details on using filo dough, see the recipe for *baklava,* page 218.) This *bestila* does not call for an entire 1-pound package, just a few of the sheets. Those left over should immediately be returned to the package, tightly sealed, and refrigerated or frozen for another use.

FOR THE CHICKEN
4 to 5 pounds meaty chicken pieces, skin removed
2 medium-sized onions, grated
1 cup finely chopped fresh parsley leaves
1 teaspoon dried coriander (cilantro) leaves, or 1 tablespoon chopped fresh coriander (cilantro) leaves (optional)
1 teaspoon ground ginger
½ teaspoon ground cinnamon
¾ teaspoon black pepper, preferably freshly ground
¼ teaspoon ground turmeric
½ teaspoon salt
2 cups cold water

FOR THE FILLING
8 large eggs, well beaten
2 cups (about 10 ounces) blanched almonds, toasted lightly in a 350-degree oven, cooled, and finely ground
2 tablespoons granulated sugar
1 teaspoon ground cinnamon

FOR ASSEMBLING AND TOPPING
About ½ cup unsalted pareve *margarine, melted*
10 large sheets filo (about ½ pound) at room temperature
Confectioner's sugar
Ground cinnamon

Put the chicken pieces into a 4-quart or similar pot or Dutch oven. Mix together the remaining ingredients for the chicken, and pour the seasoned liquid over the chicken in the pot. Cover and bring to a boil over high heat. Lower the heat and simmer the chicken for 1 to 1¼ hours, or until it is very tender. Occasionally rotate the chicken pieces so that each is immersed in the broth for part of the cooking period. (Moroccan cooks prefer to hold the lid on tightly with both hands, and give the pot a few quick shakes.)

Use tongs to remove the chicken pieces from the pot (reserving the broth) and set the chicken aside to cool. When it is cool enough to handle, remove the meat from the bones and shred it. Set the meat aside.

While the chicken is cooling, prepare the egg mixture for the filling. Increase the heat under the broth so that it comes to a boil; then boil it, uncovered, until it has reduced by about a third. Lower the heat so the broth simmers; then stir in the beaten eggs. Stir the broth continuously until the eggs are scrambled and cooked into firm curds. Set aside to cool slightly.

Also for the filling, mix together the ground toasted almonds, sugar, and cinnamon. Set aside.

(Up to this point, the bestila can be prepared ahead. Refrigerate the chicken and egg mixtures in separate covered containers and wrap the almond mixture well.)

To assemble the bestila, use a pastry brush to coat the inside of an 12- to 14-inch-round pizza pan (or similar pan) with some of the melted margarine. Lightly brush one sheet of filo with margarine and put it, "buttered" side up, in the center of the pan. (Some of it may hang over the edges.) Top it with a second "buttered" sheet. Then place 6 "but-

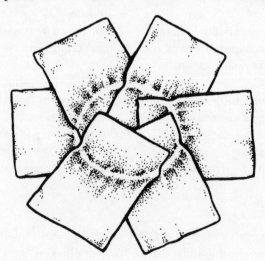

FIGURE 9

tered" sheets around the edge of the pan like the spokes of a wheel, overlapping and arranging them so that about half of each sheet is in the pan and the remainder hangs over the side (Fig. 9).

Sprinkle half of the reserved almond mixture over the filo in the pan. Place the shredded chicken over the almonds. Use a slotted spoon or strainer to remove the egg curds from the broth and spread them over the chicken. Top with the remaining almonds.

Drizzle 2 tablespoons of the broth remaining from the eggs and 2 tablespoons of the melted margarine over the filling to keep it moist. One by one, smoothly fold the overhanging filo sheets over the filling, completely enclosing it. Brush the top with melted margarine; then top it with 2 more sheets of filo, "buttering" each and tucking in the overhanging edges.

Bake the bestila in a preheated 400-degree oven for 25 to 30 minutes, or until the top is golden brown. Invert it onto a large serving platter, draining off any excess margarine. Lightly sift confectioner's sugar on the top; then sprinkle cinnamon over it in narrow, intersecting lines to form a diamond or square pattern. Serve hot, cut into wedges. (If the bestila is not cut, it will stay hot for 15 to 30 minutes.)

Makes 8 to 10 servings.

ORANGE-GLAZED TURKEY WITH FRUIT-NUT STUFFING (M)

Some say that the American holiday of Thanksgiving may have been influenced by the Jewish one of Sukkot. As both are festivals celebrating an abundant fall harvest, this is indeed possible. Interestingly, modern American Jews have turned the tables (so to speak) on the Pilgrims, and now serve many typical Thanksgiving foods, particularly stuffed turkey, during Sukkot.

Actually, this is quite fitting. When Columbus first brought the turkey back from the New World, Sephardic Jewish merchants who dealt in rarities began selling the birds as delicacies, and thus helped spread the turkey throughout Europe. After the fowl was domesticated almost beyond recognition, it was brought back to the Americas to be crossbred with its wild cousins, and eventually became the turkey we have today.

It is also likely that our name for the bird came from an old Hebrew word for peacock, *tuki*. Some say that a Hebrew-speaking member of Columbus' crew dubbed it with the misnomer when he first saw the wild turkey strutting about and flaunting its plumage.

The following turkey recipe features a unique fruit-nut stuffing and orange glaze that are quite in keeping with the Sukkot tradition of eating fruit and nuts.

1 12- to 14-pound turkey
Softened pareve *margarine*

FRUIT-NUT STUFFING
2 tablespoons pareve *margarine*
1 large onion, finely chopped
2 celery stalks, diced
½ cup orange juice
¼ cup sugar
1½ cups fresh or frozen cranberries
12 pitted prunes, coarsely chopped
6 dried apricots, coarsely chopped
1 cup dark or light raisins or currants (or a mixture)
3 medium-sized apples, cored and diced (it is not necessary to peel them)

1½ cups slivered almonds (or other chopped nuts)
2 large eggs, lightly beaten
½ cup finely chopped fresh parsley leaves
1 teaspoon ground cinnamon
¼ teaspoon ground cloves
⅛ teaspoon ground ginger
Salt and ground black pepper to taste

ORANGE-HONEY GLAZE
1¼ cups orange juice
⅓ cup honey
3 tablespoons pareve *margarine*
¼ teaspoon grated fresh gingerroot (or ⅛ teaspoon ground ginger)

Clean the turkey well and discard the giblets (or reserve them for another use). Rub the skin lightly with softened margarine.

For the fruit-nut stuffing, melt the 2 tablespoons margarine in a medium-sized saucepan over medium-high heat; then cook the onion and celery, stirring, until they are tender but not browned. Transfer them to a large bowl. Set aside.

In the same (unwashed) pan, combine the ½ cup orange juice and the sugar and bring the mixture to a boil over medium-high heat. Stir in the cranberries and bring to a boil. Lower the heat and simmer the cranberries, stirring occasionally, for about 10 minutes, or until the berry skins pop. Mix in the prunes, apricots, and raisins and remove the fruit mixture from the heat. Transfer it to the bowl containing the cooked onion and celery. Let the mixture cool to room temperature. Add all the remaining stuffing ingredients and mix well. Adjust the seasonings to taste.

(If desired, the stuffing may be made up to a day ahead and refrigerated, covered. However, the turkey should not be stuffed until just before it is roasted.)

Fill the body and neck cavities of the turkey with the stuffing, allowing some room for expansion. Tuck the legs under the band of skin or the trussing wire at the tail, or tie the legs together with heavy cord. Skewer or sew the neck skin closed against the body. Place the turkey, breast up, on a rack in a shallow roasting pan. Roast in a preheated 325-degree oven for about 3 hours.

Meanwhile, prepare the orange-honey glaze. Mix together all the glaze ingredients in a small saucepan and stir over medium heat until the glaze is well blended. After the turkey has roasted for 3 hours, begin periodically brushing some of the glaze over the turkey while it roasts for 1 to 2 hours longer, or until a drumstick moves very easily and its meat feels very soft when pressed. (Also, the juices released when the thigh is pricked with a fork should be clear, not pink, and the internal temperature of the dark meat should reach 185 degrees, according to a meat thermometer.) If the breast gets browned before the rest of the turkey is done, cover it loosely with an aluminum foil tent. For easier cutting and juicier meat, let the turkey rest for about 15 minutes before carving it.

Makes 12 or more servings.

EAST INDIAN-STYLE SOLE WITH ONIONS AND DILL (D) or (P)

Jews have lived in India for at least a thousand, and possibly over two thousand, years. Jewish communities were established in many cities, particularly those along the coast, such as Bombay, Cochin, and Madras. Historically, many of the Indian Jews were divided into castes based on ancestry and skin color, which generally stayed segregated and did not intermarry.

Before the Second World War, there were about 26,000 Jews in India. However, a large majority have since emigrated to Israel, and a smaller number to England, Canada, and Australia. Of the fewer then 8,000 Jews who remain, most belong to an ancient sect known as the *Bene-Israel,* and live in the Bombay area.

Another prominent group of Indian Jews once resided in Cochin, in an area still known as "Jewtown." Its 400-year-old Paradesi Synagogue, founded by Sephardic Jews fleeing the Inquisition, is still in use, though only a few hundred Jews are left in the community.

The following unusual East Indian recipe would be very appropriate for Sukkot because the fish is "stuffed," like so many of the foods eaten on this holiday.

1 pound small skinless sole fillets
2 tablespoons lemon juice, preferably fresh
Salt and ground black pepper to taste
3 tablespoons butter or margarine
2 medium-sized onions, finely chopped
1 garlic clove, minced

2 teaspoons finely chopped fresh dillweed (or 1 teaspoon dried dillweed)
½ teaspoon grated fresh gingerroot (or ⅛ teaspoon ground ginger)
¼ teaspoon ground turmeric
⅛ teaspoon hot red pepper flakes (or pinch of cayenne pepper)

Sprinkle the fillets with the lemon juice, salt, and pepper. Set them aside.

In a large skillet, over medium-high heat, melt the butter; then sauté the onion and garlic until they are tender but not browned. Stir in the dillweed, gingerroot, turmeric, and hot pepper and sauté 1 to 2 minutes longer. Remove from the heat. Reserve about 2 tablespoons of the onion mixture. Divide the remainder evenly among the fillets, spreading it over the smooth side to which the skin was attached. Enclose the stuffing by rolling up each fillet from its narrow end. Place the rolls in a lightly buttered baking dish, seam side down. Sprinkle the reserved onion mixtue on top of the rolls.

Bake the fish rolls, uncovered, in a preheated 400-degree oven for about 15 minutes, or until the fish is firm when pressed with a fork. (Or bake the fish, covered, in a microwave oven on "high" power, for about 6 minutes. Rotate the baking dish often. Let the fish stand for 2 minutes before serving.)

Before serving the fish, baste it with any pan juices.

Makes about 4 servings.

FRUIT-AND-VEGETABLE TZIMMES (P)

(Autumn Casserole)

The sweet, "mixed-up" stew known as *tzimmes* is just as popular for Sukkot as it is for Rosh Hashanah. The following version is meatless, and meant to be served as a side dish. It features popular fall vegetables and dried fruits.

3 large sweet potatoes (or "yams"),
    peeled and thinly sliced
4 large carrots, thinly sliced
1 small butternut squash, peeled,
    seeded, and thinly sliced
¼ cup dark raisins
¼ cup light raisins
¼ cup pitted prunes

¼ cup chopped dates
Grated rind of 1 orange (colored
    part only)
Juice of 1 orange
2 tablespoons packed dark or light
    brown sugar
¼ cup honey or real maple syrup

In a greased or non-stick spray-coated 9- by 13-inch baking pan, layer the sweet potatoes, carrots, squash, and dried fruit.

Sprinkle the top with the orange rind, juice, brown sugar, and honey. Cover the pan with aluminum foil or a lid and bake it in a preheated 350-degree oven for about 1½ hours, or until all vegetables and fruits are very tender.

Makes 8 to 10 servings.

HARVEST-TIME CRANBERRY RELISH (P)

Because they are a seasonal fall fruit and so brightly colored, cranberries have become a popular decoration for many American sukkot. Children love to string them on threads, and hang up the chains from the roof of the sukkah.

As a food, cranberries go well with many of the fall "harvest" dishes on the holiday table. The following slightly tart relish differs from cranberry sauce in that it requires no cooking, and can be quickly made in a food processor or in batches in a blender. If necessary, the ingredients can even be put through a food grinder.

Also, the relish features an assortment of other fall fruits with the cranberries. It makes an excellent accompaniment to poultry or meat, or it can be used as a side dish with other foods.

(Note: It is not necessary to peel the apple or pear for this recipe. The peels add color, texture, and nutritional value.)

1 medium-sized navel orange
1 12-ounce package (3 cups) fresh cranberries, sorted, rinsed, and drained
1 medium-sized apple, cored and cut into eighths
1 medium-sized pear, cored and cut into eighths

¼ cup walnut or pecan pieces
¼ cup dark raisins or currants
½ cup packed dark brown sugar
2 to 3 tablespoons granulated sugar
1 tablespoon lemon juice, preferably fresh

Use a vegetable peeler or sharp knife to remove the thin colored part of the rind from the orange. Set it aside. Remove and discard all the white pith from the orange; then cut the orange pulp into chunks. Put the orange rind and pulp into a food processor fitted with the steel blade (or a blender) with the remaining relish ingredients, and pulse-process the mixture until the ingredients are finely chopped but not at all smoothly puréed. (If necessary, process the ingredients in batches; then combine all the batches and mix well.) Or put the ingredients through the coarse blade of a food grinder.

Chill the relish, covered, for at least several hours or overnight, stirring occasionally, until the sugar has completely dissolved and the flavors have blended.

Makes about 3½ cups.

PLUM KNEDLIKY OR KNAIDLAH　　　　　(D) or (P)

(Fruit-Filled Potato Dumplings)

These delectable dumplings make a great dessert or tea-time snack. They are very popular in many parts of Czechoslovakia and Hungary, where the choicest small, purple plums grow.

In the United States, fresh Italian prune-plums, which are usually available in early fall, seem to work best in this recipe. The firm, oval prune-plums are only about the size of a walnut, and are very easily pitted. The cavity from which the pit was removed is sprinkled with sugar or cinnamon-sugar, which melts into a tasty sauce as the dumplings cook.

Other fruits, such as peeled, quartered peaches and well-drained canned apricot halves, can be used as well. In a pinch, even a spoonful of fruit preserves can be used for the filling.

The dough that surrounds the fruit contains mashed potatoes, giving it a very good taste and wonderfully chewy texture. The following "modernized" version of this potato dough comes from Judith Erger, a native of Sinover, Czechoslovakia, who now lives in New York City.

When Mrs. Erger first showed me how to make plum dumplings using instant potato flakes, I was a bit astounded to see such an expert "Old World" Jewish cook using a convenience food. But when I tasted the results, I had to agree with Mrs. Erger that she had indeed found a very suitable and delightfully quick substitute for the time-consuming job of boiling, peeling, and ricing potatoes. (What's more, fresh potatoes can be a bit tricky to work with because the water content may vary considerably.)

Mrs. Erger's use of corn flake crumbs instead of the usual bread crumbs in the coating is another tasty, and modern, substitution that also works quite well.

In many classic recipes for *plum knedliky*, the dough is rolled out and cut into squares before filling. But I think Mrs. Erger's technique, which follows, is easier and more foolproof.

DOUGH

1 cup instant potato flakes
1 cup boiling water (or very hot tap water)
1 tablespoon vegetable oil
¼ teaspoon salt
1 large egg
Approximately 1 to 1¼ cups all-purpose white flour, preferably unbleached

FILLING

About 12 small fresh Italian prune-plums
Granulated sugar
Ground cinnamon (optional)

COATING

2 tablespoons butter, margarine, or vegetable oil
¾ cup fine corn flake crumbs or fine, dry, plain bread crumbs

TO SERVE (OPTIONAL)

Preserves or jam, such as apricot or plum, warmed in a small saucepan over low heat or in a heatproof bowl in the microwave oven

Put the potato flakes into a large mixing bowl; then add the boiling water and mix well to make stiff mashed potatoes. Stir in the oil and salt, and set the mixture aside to cool to lukewarm, stirring occasionally.

When the potato mixture is cool, beat in the egg until it is completely combined; then gradually add the flour while mixing. Add just enough flour to form a soft dough that is not sticky. Lightly knead the dough in the bowl for 1 to 2 minutes, or until it is springy. (At this point, if necessary, the dough can be covered well with plastic wrap and set aside for a short while, or it can even be refrigerated overnight.)

Let the dough rest briefly while you prepare the plums. Cut each plum in half lengthwise, along the "groove"; then remove and discard the pit. Keep the mated halves of each plum together, so they can be reassembled later.

Fill a 6- to 8-quart pot three-fourths full of lightly salted water and bring it to a boil while you shape the dumplings.

If the dough has become very sticky while resting, knead in a bit more flour. Using *well-floured hands,* form the dough into about 12 balls approximately the size of golf balls (exact size depends on the size of the plums). Place the balls on a well-floured surface, not touching one another.

In the floured palm of one hand (or on a floured surface), use your other hand to pat out one of the balls into a circle about ¼ inch thick. Set 1 plum half in the center, and sprinkle its cavity with sugar and a bit of cinnamon, if desired. Top it with the matching half, reassembling the plum. Bring the dough up and around the plum and pinch it tightly closed so the plum is completely covered. Roll the dumpling in flour, and shape it in your hands to form a neat ball. Place it, seam side down, on a floured surface. Repeat the steps for the remaining dumplings.

When all the dumplings are shaped, gently drop them into the rapidly boiling water. After about 1 minute, nudge the dumplings gently with a wooden spoon to make sure they don't stick to the bottom of the pot. Angle the cover on the pot so that it is not tightly closed. Adjust the heat so that the water boils gently. Boil the dumplings for 12 to 15 minutes. To test for doneness, try one. The dough should be chewy, but not doughy or gummy.

When the dumplings are almost finished cooking, melt the butter in a large skillet over medium heat; then stir in the corn flake crumbs until completely coated and hot. Remove the skillet from the heat. (If using bread crumbs, sauté them until they are golden brown.)

When the dumplings are cooked through, carefully remove each one from the pot with a slotted spoon, drain it very well, and gently roll it in the crumbs until lightly coated. Serve the dumplings warm, topped with a little heated jam, if desired.

Refrigerate any leftover dumplings and reheat them, covered, in a microwave oven, or in a 350-degree conventional oven until they are hot.

Makes about 12 dumplings.

SLISHKAS (D) or (P)

(Finger-Sized Potato Dumplings)

When I was a child, one of my favorite buffet selections at family bar mitzvah celebrations was buttery, crumb-coated *slishkas*. My cousin Gail and I would meet at the *slishka* chafing dish, and together we would eagerly devour the toothsome treats to our hearts' content.

I had never attempted to make *slishkas* until I realized how easy they would be if I used Mrs. Erger's potato dough from the *plum knedliky* (see page 126). After a little experimentation, the *slishkas* were right on target—just how I remembered them.

Interestingly, a very similar potato dough is also used for the Italian favorite, *potato gnocchi*. However, *gnocchi* (which actually means "knuckles") are usually pressed against a rough surface such as a grater or the tines of a fork before they're cooked, so that rich sauces, based on tomatoes or cheese, cling to them better.

The following slightly chewy dumplings make a great side dish and, of course, they're perfect as part of a buffet meal.

1 recipe potato dough *for the* Plum Knedliky *(page 127)*   *1 recipe crumb* coating *for the* Plum Knedliky *(page 127)*

To make the slishkas, prepare the potato dough as directed in the recipe for plum knedliky. Keeping the dough, your hands, and the surface well floured, roll the dough into ropes that are ½ to ¾ inch thick. Cut each rope into 1- to 1½-inch-long pieces.

Gently drop the pieces of dough into a large pot of salted boiling water. After they rise to the top, boil them, uncovered or partially covered, for 4 to 8 minutes, or until they are chewy and firm, but not doughy. (Overcooking can make them gummy. Taste to check doneness.) Immediately remove them with a slotted spoon and drain them well.

While the slishkas are cooking, prepare the crumb coating as directed in the plum knedliky recipe. When the slishkas are done, toss them in the crumbs. Serve them warm. They may be reheated in the same manner as the plum knedliky.

HERBED WALNUT STUFFING BALLS (M)

Sukkot is indeed the time to eat "stuffed foods." In this recipe, the stuffing is allowed to star on its own.

Of course, this bread stuffing would be fine inside a turkey or chicken. But, the individual balls are more attractive to serve, can be made in advance and reheated, and are even good at room temperature (if you like that sort of thing). What's more, every serving has the "crust" for which family members often vie.

¼ cup pareve *margarine*
1 medium-sized onion, finely chopped
1 garlic clove, minced
6 cups whole wheat bread cubes (cut from about 7 slices)
½ to 1 cup coarsely chopped walnuts
1 teaspoon dried thyme leaves

½ teaspoon marjoram leaves
¼ teaspoon celery seeds
2 large eggs, beaten
¾ cup chicken broth or bouillon made from cubes or powder
Salt and ground black pepper to taste

Melt the margarine in a skillet over medium-high heat; then sauté the onion and garlic until they are tender but not browned.

Meanwhile, toss together the bread cubes, walnuts, thyme, marjoram, and celery seeds in a large bowl. When the onion mixture is ready, remove it from the heat and add it to the bread cube mixture, along with the beaten eggs and broth. Stir until the bread cubes are completely moistened.

Shape the mixture into balls, using about ½ cup for each and place the balls on a well-greased or non-stick spray-coated baking sheet. (Or spoon the mixture into well-greased or sprayed muffin tins or custard cups.)

Bake the stuffing in a preheated 350-degree oven for about 20 minutes, or until it is set. Serve it as a side dish with poultry. If made in advance, reheat in a low oven (or a microwave oven) until warmed through.

Makes about 8 servings.

DOUBLE CORN BREAD   (P)

This moist "quick bread" contains both cornmeal and corn kernels, making it doubly "corny" and tasty. Also, unlike most corn breads, this one is *pareve* and therefore suitable for meat meals. (Cream-style canned corn does not contain any cream; it just looks "creamy.") In fact, it would be perfect to use for a corn bread stuffing for turkey. As a bonus, it takes only minutes to mix up.

1½ cups yellow cornmeal, preferably stone ground
¼ cup all-purpose white flour, preferably unbleached
1 tablespoon sugar
1 tablespoon baking powder

2 large eggs
¼ cup vegetable oil
1 17-ounce can cream-style corn, including all liquid
2 tablespoons water

Preheat the oven to 400 degrees.

In a medium-sized bowl, combine the cornmeal, flour, sugar, and baking powder. Make a well in the center and add the eggs, oil, canned corn, and water. Stir only until completely combined. Pour into a greased or non-stick spray-coated 9-inch-square pan.

Bake the corn bread in the preheated oven for about 25 minutes, or until it is firm and a toothpick inserted in the center comes out clean. Cool it in the pan for at least 5 minutes before cutting it into large squares to serve. This corn bread tastes best shortly after baking; however, it may be made ahead and reheated, if desired.

Makes about 9 servings.

EASY VIENNESE APPLE-NUT STRUDEL   (D) or (P)

Strudel is very traditional for Sukkot because of its lavish use of fruit and nuts. Also, it is "stuffed" like many other holiday foods. This quick version takes advantage of the packaged filo dough available refrigerated or frozen at many supermarkets, ethnic groceries, and gourmet stores. The ultra-thin sheets of dough are also often called, appropriately, "strudel leaves." (Note: For details on using filo dough, see the recipe for *baklava,* page 218.) The following recipe does not use a whole 1-pound package, just a few of the sheets. Those left over should immediately be returned to the package, tightly sealed, and refrigerated or frozen for another use.

If desired, this recipe can be easily doubled or tripled to make two or three strudels.

(Note: For a classic stretched-dough strudel, see the recipe for *Dried-Fruit Strudel* (page 196) in Chapter 5.)

¼ to ½ cup dark or light raisins or currants

3 tablespoons brandy, wine, fruit juice, or water

2½ cups peeled, cored, and finely chopped apples, such as Golden Delicious, Granny Smith, Stayman, or Winesap

½ cup chopped walnuts or pecans

Generous ½ teaspoon ground cinnamon

¼ cup granulated sugar

1 tablespoon melted butter or margarine

1 tablespoon grated lemon rind (yellow part only), optional

⅓ cup apricot jam or preserves

6 large, packaged "strudel leaves" or sheets (also called filo or phyllo), unfolded and at room temperature

Melted unsalted butter or margarine, as needed

½ cup fine dry bread crumbs or cake crumbs

TO SERVE (OPTIONAL)
Confectioner's sugar

Soak the raisins in 2 to 3 tablespoons brandy until plumped. (To hasten the soaking process, heat the raisins and liquid in a microwave oven for about 30 seconds.)

Mix together the apples, nuts, cinnamon, sugar, 1 tablespoon melted butter, and lemon rind. Drain the raisins, reserving 2 teaspoons of the soaking liquid. Add the raisins to the apple mixture.

In a small saucepan, heat the apricot jam with the 2 teaspoons of reserved liquid until warmed and thinned.

Lay 1 strudel sheet on a slightly damp, but *not* wet, dish towel, and brush it very lightly with melted butter. Evenly sprinkle the sheet with 1 tablespoon of crumbs. Top with another buttered sheet and sprinkle with more crumbs. Repeat the layering procedure with 4 more sheets. Put an unbuttered sheet on top. Brush its entire surface with the thinned apricot jam. Then sprinkle it with the remaining crumbs.

Compactly place the apple mixture on the top sheet, keeping it in a narrow strip parallel to one longer side and 4 inches in from that edge. Leave a 1-inch margin on each of the shorter sides. Fold over the 4-inch edge; then fold in the sides. Continue rolling up, jelly roll fashion, using the towel as an aid, if necessary.

Place the strudel, seam side down, in a greased or non-stick spray-coated shallow baking pan. Brush the entire outer surface of the strudel with melted butter. Score the top diagonally *through a few leaves only* into about 12 even pieces. Bake the strudel in a preheated 350-degree oven for about 45 minutes, or until the apples are tender and strudel surface is browned and crisp. Remove the strudel from the oven and let it cool at least to lukewarm before serving. Just before serving, sprinkle the top with sieved confectioner's sugar, if desired. Cut through the scored marks to divide the strudel into serving pieces.

Makes 1 large strudel; about 12 servings.

"RAISED DOUGH" CAKE   (D)

(Filled and Rolled Yeast Cake)

My paternal grandparents immigrated to this country from Eastern Europe at the turn of the century. They met and married in northeastern Pennsylvania, and had thirteen children, of whom my father is the youngest.

My grandmother, Gussie Bransdorf Kaufer (after whom I was named), brought with her this old family recipe for a "raised dough" cake which was always served during the fall holidays. As it was one of my Dad's favorites, my Mom made sure she got the recipe, and she taught it to me.

For as long as I can remember, this treat has been called nothing more than "Raised Dough Cake," probably because the original name was forgotten, and we all knew what the simple title meant. The following recipe makes three large cakes, which freeze quite well. It should be started at least one day ahead of serving, because the dough must be refrigerated overnight.

DOUGH

1 packet (2¼ teaspoons) active dry yeast (or 1 0.6-ounce cake fresh compressed yeast)

½ cup warm (105 to 115 degrees) milk (80 to 90 degrees, for compressed yeast)

1 cup butter or margarine

2 tablespoons sugar

3 large egg yolks (reserve the whites for the filling)

3 to 3½ cups all-purpose white flour, preferably unbleached

FILLING

3 large egg whites (reserved from the dough)

½ cup sugar

1 tablespoon ground cinnamon

1 cup shredded sweetened coconut

1 cup coarsely chopped walnuts

1 cup dark or light raisins (or a mixture)

First, make the dough. Dissolve the yeast in the milk, and set the mixture aside.

In a large mixing bowl, cream the butter with the sugar; then mix in the egg yolks. Stir in the flour alternately with the yeast mixture, mixing well after each addition. Add just enough flour so the dough comes away from the sides of the bowl but is still slightly sticky. Cover the bowl with plastic wrap and refrigerate the dough for at least 8 hours or overnight. It will rise slightly in the refrigerator.

Divide the chilled dough into 3 equal parts and allow it to rest a few minutes at room temperature to soften it slightly. Then roll out each piece of dough on a separate sheet of wax paper to a 9- by 11-inch rectangle.

For the filling, beat the egg whites until foamy; then gradually add the sugar and continue beating until the whites form stiff, shiny peaks. Spread a third of the beaten whites over each rectangle of dough, leaving a 1½-inch border all around. Mix together the cinnamon, coconut, walnuts, and raisins; then sprinkle a third of the mixture over the egg whites on each rectangle.

Using the wax paper as an aid, and beginning with the 11-inch side, roll up each rectangle like a jelly roll. Fold the ends under; then set each roll, seam side down, on a greased and floured or non-stick spray-coated baking sheet. (Two cakes may fit on 1 large sheet; leave plenty of space between them for rising.)

Let the cakes rise at room temperature until not quite doubled in bulk, about 1 to 1½ hours. Bake them in a preheated 350-degree oven for about 30 minutes, or until the tops are golden brown. Carefully remove the cakes from the baking sheets and cool them on wire racks. Cut them into slices at serving time. (If freezing the cakes, cool them completely before wrapping for the freezer. Thaw them wrapped.)

Makes 3 rolled cakes; about 8 servings each.

MANDELBROT (P)

(Almond Rusks)

This popular Ashkenazic almond cookie is "twice-baked" to give it the special crunch that makes it so appealing. Although it is served on Shabbat and many other occasions throughout the year, *mandelbrot* is particularly popular for Sukkot. The following version is quicker and easier than most because the dough is baked in loaf pans, and thus does not need to be shaped into neat rolls. Therefore, each cookie is rectangular and larger than with some other recipes.

3 large eggs
¾ cup sugar, plus 2 tablespoons for
  sprinkling
⅓ cup vegetable oil
1 teaspoon vanilla extract
½ teaspoon almond extract
2¾ cups all-purpose white flour,
  preferably unbleached (1 cup
  whole wheat flour may be
  substituted for 1 cup of the white
  flour)

2 teaspoons baking powder
⅔ cup finely chopped blanched
  almonds

Beat the eggs with the ¾ cup sugar until the mixture is light and lemon-colored. Beat in the oil and the extracts. Mix the flour, baking powder, and almonds together; then stir the flour mixture into the egg mixture to make a stiff, but soft, dough. With floured fingertips, press the dough into 2 well-greased or non-stick spray-coated 8- by 4-inch loaf pans, dividing it evenly between them. Smooth the tops with your fingertips.

Bake the loaves in a preheated 325-degree oven for 35 minutes, or until they are lightly browned and baked through. Remove the pans from the oven and cool them on a wire rack for about 5 minutes. Tap the edges of the pans against a countertop to loosen the loaves; then remove the loaves from the pans and cool them on the rack for 10 minutes. Meanwhile, raise the oven temperature to 400 degrees.

Place the warm loaves on a cutting board; then use a serrated or other sharp knife to cut them crosswise into ½-inch-thick slices, about 16 from each loaf. Lay the slices on ungreased baking sheets so that they do not overlap. Sprinkle the upper surfaces of the slices with the remaining 2 tablespoons of sugar. Toast the slices in the 400-degree oven for about 10 minutes, or until they are lightly browned and dried. Cool the slices on wire racks.

Makes about 32 (2- by 3½-inch) rectangular cookie slices.

SWEET PLUM KREPLAH or VARENIKES (D) or (P)

(Fruit-Filled Noodle Dumplings)

Kreplah are very traditional for Hoshanah Rabbah, which is the last day of Sukkot. The following sweet, fruity version of *kreplah* can be served as a side dish or dessert. Small Italian prune-plums, which are usually widely available and inexpensive in the fall, are perfect for these easy-to-make, round dumplings.

The dough for these *kreplah* is kneaded to give it strength and elasticity for shaping. Resting the dough after kneading makes it easier to roll, and helps keep the *kreplah* tender. The dough can be made in just a few minutes with a food processor, or it can be mixed and kneaded by hand.

DOUGH
2 tablespoons butter or margarine,
  softened
1 large egg
1½ cups all-purpose white flour,
  preferably unbleached
¼ teaspoon salt
¼ to ⅓ cup milk or water

FILLING AND TOPPING
2 tablespoons sugar
½ teaspoon ground cinnamon
Pinch of ground nutmeg
¼ cup finely chopped walnuts
8 to 10 small fresh Italian prune-
  plums

For the dough, put the butter and egg in a food processor fitted with the steel blade or a medium-sized mixing bowl. Process or beat until well blended. (Don't worry if the mixture looks curdled.)

If using a food processor, add the flour and salt to the bowl; then pulse-process until they are completely mixed in. With the machine running, pour ¼ cup milk through the chute and process until a ball forms. If the mixture is dry and crumbly, add a bit more milk. Knead the dough by processing it for 30 seconds to 1 minute longer, or until it is very smooth.

If not using a food processor, stir into the butter-egg mixture the flour, salt, and just enough liquid to form a stiff dough. Knead the dough on a very lightly floured board for about 8 minutes, or until it is very smooth.

In either case, wrap the kneaded dough in plastic wrap and set it aside to rest for 30 minutes at room temperature.

Meanwhile, in a small bowl, mix together the sugar, cinnamon, nutmeg, and nuts for the filling. Set aside.

Cut the plums in half lengthwise, along the "groove," and remove the pits. Keep the mated halves together, so that they can be reassembled later. Sprinkle the plums' cavities with about half of the sugar-nut mixture. Reserve the remainder of the mixture to top the finished kreplah.

After the dough has rested, roll it out on a lightly floured surface to ⅛-inch thickness; then cut out 2¾- to 3-inch-diameter circles. Reroll the trimmings and cut additional circles. There should be about 16 to 20 circles in all.

Reassemble one of the plums, putting the cut sides together; then place the plum on top of a dough circle. Top it with another dough circle. Bring the edges of the two circles together around the center of the plum, and crimp them very well so the dough is tightly sealed. Repeat until all the circles are used.

Fill a 6- to 8-quart pot three-fourths full of water, and bring it to a boil over high heat. Gently drop in the kreplah and lower the heat so the water just simmers. After about 1 minute, the kreplah should float to the surface of the water; gently loosen any that have stuck to the bottom. Simmer the kreplah for about 12 minutes, or until they are tender but not mushy. Taste one to test for doneness. Remove the kreplah with a slotted spoon, draining them well. Sprinkle them with the reserved sugar-nut mixture. Serve them warm or at room temperature. Some may even enjoy them chilled. (If desired, the cooked kreplah may be lightly sautéed in butter or margarine before being sprinkled with the sugar-nut topping.)

Makes 8 to 10 large plum kreplah.

INDIAN PUDDING (D)

(Thick Cornmeal and Molasses Pudding)

Though this recipe is not necessarily Jewish, it is very appropriate for a harvest festival like Sukkot. The dessert actually originated with the early American colonists, not the Native Americans. However, it is so-named because of the British habit of using the word "corn" to identify the major grain of any country. In England, wheat was called "corn." To differentiate wheat flour from cornmeal—the major "grain" of the North American Indians—the latter became known as "Indian corn," or just "Indian" for short.

Since several Jews numbered among the early colonists, it's possible that they enjoyed this dessert after a dairy meal. Though dark brown and almost tarry in texture, Indian pudding is quite delicious when served warm and topped with a scoop of vanilla ice cream. As a bonus, it is a very good source of calcium.

Unlike most traditional recipes for Indian pudding, this quick, easy version is not baked for the usual 2 to 4 hours *after* it is cooked in a saucepan, but is simmered for only about 30 minutes instead.

⅔ *cup stone-ground yellow cornmeal (such as Indian Head)*	*1 teaspoon ground cinnamon*
2½ *cups cold water*	½ *teaspoon ground ginger*
¾ *cup instant nonfat dry milk powder*	½ *teaspoon baking soda*
½ *cup dark unsulphured molasses*	TO SERVE (OPTIONAL)
	4 to 6 small scoops vanilla ice cream

Put the cornmeal into a 2½- to 3-quart saucepan and gradually stir in the water. Add the remaining ingredients and mix until combined.

Put the saucepan over medium-high heat and stir constantly until the pudding thickens and comes to a boil, about 10 minutes. Then turn the heat to low and cook, stirring often, about 10 to 20 minutes longer, or until the pudding is very thick and rich tasting. If it becomes too thick, stir in a little milk or extra water, and cook a few more minutes, until the liquid is mixed in well. Serve warm. If desired, top each serving with a small scoop of ice cream.

Store any leftovers in the refrigerator. The pudding cannot be reheated easily, but it is good chilled, too.

Makes 4 to 6 servings.

MULLED CRAN-APPLE-COT SWIZZLE (P)

When guests come to visit your sukkah, or for any type of holiday open house, offer them a mug of this delicious and soothing hot drink. For best flavor, it should be made with unprocessed apple cider that has not been filtered or had any preservatives added. During the fall, this type of cider is available in many areas of the country.

As cider freezes well, the mulled "swizzle" can also be made for Hanukkah. To freeze cider that comes in plastic jugs, just pour off about a cup of it (to allow for expansion during freezing), and freeze the cider right in its jug. It takes a long time to thaw, so remove it from the freezer a day before using. Don't pour out any of the cider until the entire jug has thawed or the solids won't be distributed evenly. Always shake unprocessed cider before using it.

8 to 10 cups apple cider (preferably unfiltered and unprocessed)
6 cups cranberry juice cocktail
4 cups apricot nectar
3 or 4 cinnamon sticks

About 20 whole allspice "berries"
1 large orange, preferably a navel orange
About 20 whole cloves

Put the cider, cranberry juice, and apricot nectar in a large pot over medium heat. Stir in the cinnamon sticks and allspice. (If desired, they may be tied in a cheesecloth bag; however, they will give more flavor if allowed to float freely.) Cut the unpeeled orange crosswise into ½-inch-thick slices; then stick some cloves into the peel of each slice. Float the orange slices on top of the juices.

Cover the pot and slowly heat the juice mixture until it simmers. Lower the heat so the juice stays just below the simmering point, and let it mull for 1 hour. Leave the pot on the burner over very low heat, and ladle the "swizzle" right from the pot into mugs.

Makes 12 to 14 mug-size servings, or about 20 smaller ones.

GINGERBREAD SUKKAH (P)

It is considered a *mitzvah*—a very good deed—to build a *sukkah* for the holiday named after such dwellings. In fact, construction should begin shortly after breaking the fast of Yom Kippur.

A *sukkah* is a present-day reminder of the rough-hewn huts or booths assembled by early, agrarian Jews so they could stay near their fields at harvest time. It has also come to symbolize the temporary abodes of the Jews who wandered in the desert with Moses.

As a miniature symbol, a gaily decorated gingerbread *sukkah* can be the focal point of some holiday rituals and discussions. Thus, "building" one may be a mini-mitzvah of sorts, especially when the whole family shares in the joy and creativity.

Like any worthwhile construction project, a gingerbread *sukkah* takes some time and effort. But the preparation can be divided into two separate sessions of only 1 to 2 hours each.

And, at the end of the Sukkot celebration, the entire structure can be eaten, providing a tasty "feast" for joyous Simhat Torah!

The following detailed directions are for a finished *sukkah* that is about 5 inches high, 7 inches wide, and 4½ inches deep. It will stay deliciously edible for at least 2 weeks after assembly. (*Be sure to read all directions before beginning.*)

PATTERNS

To easily cut out the raw gingerbread dough for the sukkah, cardboard (or heavy paper) patterns must be made first. These can then be used repeatedly to make many sukkot. Make the patterns as follows, and be sure to label each one for easy identification (Fig. 10).

1. *Front and back walls:* Cut out two 7-inch-wide by 5-inch-high rectangles. In the lower center of the pattern piece you will use for the *front* wall, cut out a doorway that is 1½ inches wide by 2½ inches high. In the center of the *back* wall pattern, cut out a window that is 2½ inches wide by 2 inches high.

2. *Side walls:* Cut out two 4-inch-wide by 5-inch-high rectangles. In the center of each one, cut out a window that is 1½ inches square.

FIGURE 10

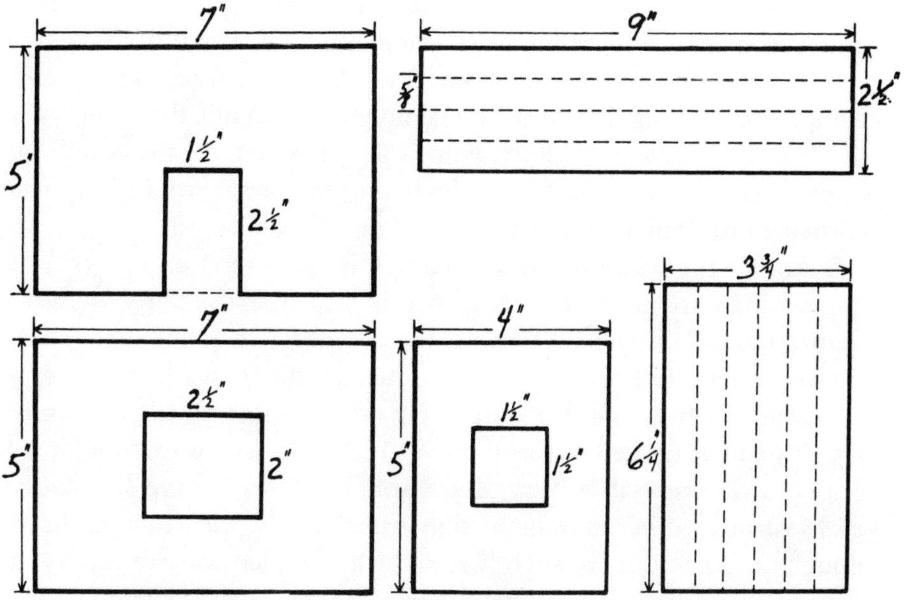

Front and Back Walls   Side Walls   Roof

3. *Roof:* The lattice roof is made from strips of dough which are cut from rectangular sections. For the patterns, cut out one rectangular piece of cardboard that is 9 by 2½ inches, and one that is 6¼ by 3¾ inches.

SPECIAL GINGERBREAD DOUGH
1½ teaspoons ground ginger
½ teaspoon ground cinnamon
½ teaspoon ground nutmeg
½ teaspoon baking soda
¼ teaspoon salt

2½ cups all-purpose white flour, preferably unbleached (To measure the flour, spoon it into the measuring cups; then level the top with a knife.)
½ cup sugar
½ cup white vegetable shortening (NO substitutes)
½ cup light or dark molasses

Put the ginger, cinnamon, nutmeg, baking soda, and salt into a small cup and set aside. Measure out the flour and have it handy.

(Note: Once the following procedure is begun, it cannot be interrupted until the dough has been rolled out.)

Put the sugar, shortening, and molasses into a 2½- to 3-quart saucepan, and mix them together with a wooden spoon just until combined. Set the saucepan over medium-high heat and stir the mixture occasionally until it comes to a full rolling boil. Immediately remove it from the heat and stir in about ½ cup of the flour. Then stir in the spice mixture until completely combined. Add the remaining flour and mix the dough with the wooden spoon until all the flour is incorporated and the dough can be easily scraped away from the sides of the pan. Be sure to reach into the corners of the pan as you mix. The dough will be very stiff.

Turn out the warm dough onto a lightly oiled surface. As soon as it has cooled enough to touch, gather it into a smooth, rectangularly shaped mound. Flatten the mound; then immediately roll it out to a neat 12½- by 15-inch rectangle of even thickness (about ⅛ inch). If necessary, use a pastry wheel or sharp knife to cut off some uneven edges; then re-attach them as needed to form an even rectangle. The warm dough will not be sticky and will be very easy to roll. However, *it must be rolled out while warm,* as it becomes impossibly stiff once it cools. (In a pinch, the dough can sometimes be slightly rewarmed in a microwave oven. But, be sure not to heat it so much that it cooks further.)

CUTTING THE DOUGH

Let the rolled out dough rest for 5 to 10 minutes, or until it is completely cool, so it will be easier to cut and maneuver the pieces. Very lightly flour the top surface of the dough so that the patterns won't stick. Arrange all the patterns on the dough, placing them next to each other and along the edge of the dough so that they will all fit. Trace the patterns with a pastry wheel or small knife; then lift them off. Cut the 9-inch-long roof rectangle lengthwise into 4 strips that are 9- by ⅝-inch each. Cut the 6¼-inch roof rectangle into 6 strips that are 6¼- by ⅝-inch each. (Leftover dough trimmings and window holes may be baked into "cookies," if desired.)

BAKING THE WALLS

Use a large metal pancake turner or spatula to transfer the wall pieces and the door cut from the doorway (but *not* the roof strips) to a large well-greased or non-stick spray-coated baking sheet (or 2 smaller sheets), leaving about 1 inch between each piece. Bake them in a preheated 350-degree oven for 10 to 13 minutes, or until a *light* touch does not leave an imprint in the dough.

Remove the baking sheet from the oven, and *immediately* retrace each pattern with the pastry wheel or knife, cutting off any excess edges of gingerbread that have expanded during baking. This will be easy while the gingerbread is still hot and soft. (It gets quite firm as it cools.)

Leave the gingerbread pieces on the baking sheet for 2 to 3 minutes to cool slightly; then carefully loosen them with the pancake turner and transfer them to a flat surface (*not* a wire rack) to cool completely. (The wall trimmings may now provide sustenance for hard-working cooks who are being driven crazy by the wonderful aroma!)

BAKING THE LATTICE ROOF

Grease well or generously coat with non-stick spray a clean, cool baking sheet. Lay out the 9-inch strips of dough on it so they are parallel to each other and there is a ¾-inch space between each one. Weave the 6¼-inch strips over and under the longer strips (beginning one over, the next under, and so forth), keeping the shorter strips parallel to each other and evenly spaced. The ends of all the strips should stick out only ¾ inch from the main part of the lattice; adjust the strips if necessary (Fig. 11). (This is not only for appearance, but so the roof will correctly fit on top of the sukkah walls.)

FIGURE 11

Bake the lattice in a preheated 350-degree oven for about 11 to 14 minutes, or until browned and well done. Cool it on the baking sheet for about 5 minutes, or until firm. Then very carefully use the pancake turner to loosen the edges and then the middle of the lattice. Transfer it to a flat surface to cool completely.

STORING THE BAKED PIECES

Once the gingerbread pieces are completely cool, they may be assembled, or they may be stored in an airtight container for up to 3 weeks. Store them carefully so they do not break.

DECORATING AND ASSEMBLING THE SUKKAH

First, make a base for the sukkah by wrapping a rectangular piece of heavy cardboard approximately 8 by 12 inches (or a circular one about 11 inches in diameter) with heavy duty foil or white freezer paper. Use tape to secure the edges of the wrap to the underside of the cardboard.

For the sukkah *decorations,* use an assortment of: *shelled nuts,* such as walnut halves, pecan halves, whole almonds, whole cashews, whole hazelnuts; *hulled large seeds,* such as sunflower seeds, pumpkin seeds (they're green and look like little leaves); and *dried fruit,* such as dried apricots, raisins, wedges of dried pineapple, chunks of dried papaya, and banana chips. (Health-food stores often have a good selection of these items.)

Just before assembling the sukkah, mix up a batch of icing (as follows) to glue the pieces together.

BROWN ICING "GLUE"
2 large egg whites
½ teaspoon cream of tartar
2½ cups sifted confectioner's sugar
⅓ cup sifted *unsweetened cocoa powder (or carob powder)*
½ teaspoon vanilla extract

Put the egg whites into a medium-sized mixing bowl with the cream of tartar. Beat the whites until foamy; then gradually add the confectioner's sugar, cocoa, and vanilla while beating. Continue beating for several minutes until the icing increases slightly in volume, lightens slightly in color, and forms very stiff peaks.

Since egg white volumes and individual measuring techniques may vary slightly, the icing consistency may have to be adjusted. If the icing is very loose even after several minutes of beating, beat in a little extra confectioner's sugar. If it is so stiff that it no longer seems sticky like a "glue," beat in a few additional drops of egg white.

Keep the bowl of icing loosely covered with a damp towel so the icing does not dry out, and use the icing soon for best results.

Put some of the icing into a cake decorating bag fitted with a plain ³⁄₁₆- to ¼-inch tip. If this is not available, spread the icing with a small knife.

Before assembling the walls, decorate them with the fruits and nuts. Use small dollops of the icing to attach any desired decorations to what will become the *outsides* of the walls. (Remember, no one will see the inside, as they do with a real sukkah.) Use enough icing to hold each item securely in place. (Be careful not to overdo the decorating; let some gingerbread show!) Allow the decorated walls to dry flat for about 20 minutes, or until the decorations are secure. (Keep the remaining icing at room temperature and covered as directed above.)

When the wall decorations are set, the sukkah can be assembled. (Note: It is helpful to have an assistant for this part.)

Use the decorating bag to squeeze a thick continuous line of icing on the *bottom edge* and on both *side edges* of one of the *side wall* pieces (or spread the icing on with a knife). Stand the wall in place on the prepared cardboard base, with its decorated side facing out. Have an assistant temporarily hold the wall steady, or lean the wall against a small can or bottle.

Next, put a line of icing on the *bottom edge* (only) of the *back wall*. Stand it in place perpendicular to the side wall, with one end leaning against one of the iced side edges of the side wall to form an "L." If correctly placed and with enough icing, these two walls should be able to stand alone without support (Fig. 12).

Put a line of icing on the *bottom edge* and both *side edges* of the second *side wall*, and set it in place with one side edge touching the remaining end of the back wall. Put icing on the *bottom edge* of the *front wall* and lean it against the iced edges of the two side walls to form a rectangular "box." If the box has any weak corners, reinforce them both inside and out with extra icing. Use a moistened finger to spread it along the joints as if it were caulking.

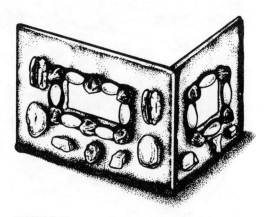

FIGURE 12

Let the walls dry for a few minutes while you prepare the lattice roof for placement. To give the roof extra support so it will not sag at all during an extended period, use icing to glue a thin wooden skewer or craft stick onto the flat underside of each of the 6¼-inch crossbeams of the lattice. The sticks should be about 5½ inches long, so that they will reach from the front wall to the back wall of the sukkah when the roof is in place, but are not obviously seen. (Be sure to remove the sticks before eating the roof.)

To attach the roof to the sukkah, put a heavy line of icing all along the *top edges* of the walls. Center the roof in place (with the supporting sticks concealed underneath), and press down gently so it becomes firmly attached. It will make the structure of the sukkah quite secure. If desired, use icing to attach decorations to the roof where the lattice beams cross each other. Also, the door can be glued against the doorway so it is ajar. (It looks inviting that way.)

Allow the completed sukkah (Fig. 13) to rest for several hours before moving it. The icing will dry "rock hard" (it's still edible), and the sukkah will be relatively sturdy. Once the icing is completely dry, the sukkah can be *very loosely* covered with a plastic to keep off dust. It will stay edible and tasty for 2 weeks or longer.

Makes 1 gingerbread sukkah, about 7 inches wide, 5 inches high, and 4½ inches deep.

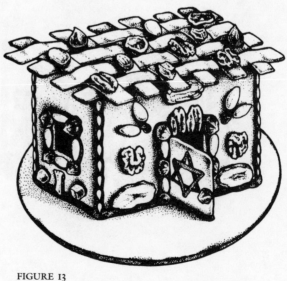

FIGURE 13

HANUKKAH

The first Hanukkah was celebrated in the second century B.C.E. by Judah the Maccabee and his followers. Several years earlier, the Syrian king Antiochus IV, had decreed that all his subjects must become totally Hellenized. He instituted pagan practices in the Holy Temple of Jerusalem and expressly forbade all Jewish ritual on punishment of death.

In the village of Modi'in, the Hasmonean family of Mattathias (a Jewish priest) and his five sons initiated a revolt against the oppressors. When Mattathias died a short while later, his third son, Judah, took over as leader of a small, but determined group of rebels.

Judah, who was known as Maccabee (meaning "hammer") probably because of his persistence or strength, was a brilliant strategist who, after many courageous battles, brought victory to the Jews and an end to tyranny. The Hasmoneans cleansed the Holy Temple and, on the twenty-fifth day of the Hebrew month of Kislev, exactly three years after it had first been desecrated, they re-dedicated it. (The Hebrew word *hanukkah* means "dedication.")

According to tradition, when the sacred Temple *Menorah* (candelabrum) was rekindled during the re-dedication, only enough undefiled oil to last for one day could be found. However, this small amount miraculously burned for eight days and nights until more purified oil could be obtained.

To annually commemorate the miracle of the oil and the inspiring events surrounding it, Jews all over the world burn either small cups of oil or candles in a special Hanukkah menorah—called a *hanukkiyah* in Israel—on each of the eight nights of Hanukkah (which usually occur in

December or possibly late November). Thus, the holiday is also known as the *Festival of Lights*.

Over the years, the relevance of using oil during Hanukkah was further substantiated by Jewish mystics who pointed out that the Hebrew words for "eight" (*shemoneh*) and "Hasmoneans" (*Hashmonayim*) each contains all the letters of the word for "oil" (*shemen*).

Indeed, a variety of foods fried in oil are quite traditional for Hanukkah meals. Among Ashkenazic Jews, pancakes (*latkes,* in Yiddish)—particularly those made with potatoes and onions—have long been the holiday favorite. In the past, when oil was scarce and very expensive, *potato latkes* (page 149) were usually fried in melted goose fat. Geese that had been fattened during the summer and fall were slaughtered shortly before Hanukkah. Most of the rendered fat (*schmaltz*) was put aside for Pesach, but some was always used for Hanukkah latkes. The latkes were often served with roasted goose and sometimes the *gribeness* (skin cracklings) left over from rendering the fat.

For their edible holiday symbols, Sephardic Jews prefer to fry in oil a variety of delectable pastries, many of which are dipped in sweet syrup. In Israel, *soofganiyot* (page 166), jelly doughnuts coated with sugar, are the popular choice.

Another, lesser known, Hanukkah culinary custom is the partaking of cheese and all sorts of dairy dishes in honor of the brave Jewish heroine, Judith. It is written in the Apocrypha that the beautiful widow Judith arranged to dine with an enemy general who intended to destroy her town. During the meal, she fed him great quantities of cheese, and then encouraged him to drink much wine to quench his subsequent thirst. As soon as he fell drunkenly asleep, Judith beheaded him. When his soldiers found out that their general had been slain, they fled in fear, and the town and its people were spared. Judith's valor is said to have inspired Judah the Maccabee and his followers.

Often, the two culinary traditions of Hanukkah—dairy dishes and oil-fried foods—are combined to produce holiday specialties such as cheese latkes, dairy doughnuts, or potato latkes served with sour cream.

On the last day of Hanukkah, some Turkish Jews enjoy a special meal called *merenda,* at which many relatives and friends gather, each bringing a portion of the food to be shared by everyone present.

In the United States, as elsewhere, new holiday customs are still evolving. For instance, it has become popular to make butter cookies shaped like many of the Hanukkah symbols. In that vein, this chapter includes a recipe for soft pretzels that have been especially designed for Hanukkah celebrations. It also features several types of *latkes,* an assortment of Sephardic fried pastries, and a variety of tasty cheese dishes.

POTATO LATKES   (P) or (D)

(Crisp Fried Pancakes)

For American Jews of Eastern European ancestry, these *latkes* have become the quintessential culinary symbol of Hanukkah. However, they are a relatively recent addition to Jewish cuisine. The potato originated in South America, and was not eaten in Europe until after the sixteenth century, when it was first brought back from the New World by early explorers.

The easy-to-grow and inexpensive potato soon became a staple in Ashkenazic cooking. In early winter, when the geese fattened during the previous summer and fall were slaughtered, pancakes made from potatoes and onions were fried in rendered goose fat *(schmaltz)*. The melted fat came to symbolize the oil in the Hanukkah miracle, and the *latkes* became a favorite holiday food. Today, most *potato latkes* are actually fried in vegetable oil, not *schmaltz.*

There are about as many variations of these pancakes as there are Jewish cooks who make them. Some prefer to sauté the onions before making the batter; most do not. Some insist on matzo meal as a thickener; others use flour.

And each *latke* maker seems to favor a certain kind of potato shredder or grater, as well as a specific size of shred. Some *mavins* even insist that the *latkes* won't be "authentic" until one's knuckles are grated right along with the potatoes. Modern cooks, however, are finding that a food processor fitted with a fine shredding blade does a very satisfactory job in a minimal amount of time. (If the food processor has only a coarse shredding blade, but you prefer finely shredded potatoes, return the coarse shreds to the food processor fitted with the steel blade, and pulse-process a few times until the potatoes are the desired consistency.)

BATTER

2½ pounds potatoes, preferably
  "baking" potatoes, such as Russet
  or Idaho, peeled
1 large or 2 small onions
3 large eggs, lightly beaten
1 teaspoon salt, or to taste
⅛ teaspoon black pepper, preferably
  freshly ground, or to taste
About ¼ cup matzo meal (or 2 to 3
  tablespoons all-purpose white flour,
  preferably unbleached)

FOR FRYING
Vegetable oil

TO SERVE
Applesauce, commercial sour cream,
  or plain yogurt

Shred or grate the potatoes alternately with the onion to keep the potatoes from darkening. (The size of the shreds is a matter of personal taste. Coarse shreds produce lacier latkes with rough edges. Fine shreds or grated potatoes produce denser, smoother latkes.) Squeeze the excess liquid from the potato and onion shreds. Mix in the eggs, salt, pepper, and matzo meal. Let the mixture rest for about 5 minutes, so that the matzo meal can absorb some moisture. If the mixture still seems very wet, add a bit more matzo meal.

In a very large skillet, over medium-high heat, heat oil that is about ⅛ to ¼ inch deep until it is very hot but not smoking. To form each latke, use a large spoon to transfer some of the potato mixture to the oil; then flatten the mixture slightly with the back of the spoon. The latkes will be irregularly shaped. An alternative method (which makes more evenly shaped latkes) is to press some of the potato mixture into a large serving spoon; then carefully slide it off the spoon into the hot oil.

Continue making latkes until the skillet is full, leaving a little room between each one. Fry the latkes until they are well browned on both sides and crisp around the edges. Drain them well on paper towels. Repeat the process until all the latkes are fried.

Serve the latkes as soon as possible for the best taste and texture. Accompany the latkes with applesauce, sour cream, and/or yogurt, as desired.

Leftovers can be reheated, but they will probably not be as crisp as freshly made latkes.

Makes about 30 3-inch potato pancakes.

I went to Marki —

— and Ali
but I gave
cell #

EASY WINE-MARINATED BRISKET (M)

Hanukkah *potato latkes* (page 149) go quite well with pot-roasted brisket. Following is an easy, very tasty recipe, which my mother often uses for her holiday brisket or "top of the rib" roast.

MARINADE
1 cup dry red or white wine
2 tablespoons soy sauce
1 small onion, grated
1 celery stalk, thinly sliced
2 garlic cloves, finely minced

MEAT
1 3- to 3½-pound brisket or "top of the rib" roast, trimmed of all excess fat
1 medium-sized onion, thinly sliced

In a glass baking dish or casserole large enough to hold the flat brisket, mix together all the marinade ingredients. Add the brisket and turn it over in the marinade so it is completely coated. Let the meat marinate for several hours, covered, in the refrigerator, turning it occasionally. (Note: A frozen, trimmed brisket can be allowed to thaw at room temperature right in the marinade.)

Transfer the brisket to a roasting pan or large ovenproof skillet. Scatter the sliced onion around it. Pour about half of the marinade over the brisket (reserve the remainder). Cover the pan tightly with aluminum foil or a lid. Roast the brisket in a preheated 325-degree oven, basting it occasionally with the pan juices, for 2½ to 3 hours, or until it is very tender. The meat should produce plenty of juice; however, if it seems dry, add more marinade as needed.

When the meat is cooked, remove it from the oven and let it cool for a few minutes. Thinly slice it against the grain and transfer it to a serving dish. Skim any fat from the pan juices and pour the juices over the brisket.

Makes about 8 servings.

ENJADARA (P)

(Spiced Lentils and Rice)

This Sephardic dish is eaten by Near Eastern and Middle Eastern Jews on festive occasions, and is also traditional for the meatless "Nine Days" which precede the solemn fast day of Tisha B'Av. The simple combination of rice, lentils, and fried onions is also called *mejedrah, mengendrah, megadarra,* and *mujadarah*—variations on the Arabic name.

Iraqi Jews enjoy a slightly different version of this same dish, known as *ketchri,* which is highly seasoned with turmeric, cumin, black pepper, and tomato paste, but contains no onions, and usually has a large amount of melted butter. *Ketchri* is steamed in the same lengthy manner as Iraqi-style rice so that it forms a "crust" on the bottom of the pan.

The following adaptation calls for brown, rather than white, rice because the cooking time for brown rice is the same as that for lentils. What's more, brown rice is more nutritious than white. (If white rice is substituted, add it to the pot after the lentils have cooked for about 20 minutes.)

The combination of lentils and rice provides complete, high-quality protein, so this dish can even be served as a light main course. For a dairy meal in the Sephardic style, accompany *enjadara* with plain yogurt and *huevos haminados* (page 248).

2 tablespoons olive or vegetable oil	1 cup dry brown lentils, sorted and
1 to 2 large onions, finely chopped or	rinsed
very thinly sliced	3½ cups boiling water
1 cup long-grain brown rice	Salt and ground black pepper to taste

In a large saucepan, over medium high-heat, heat the oil; then cook the onions, stirring, until they are lightly browned. Remove half of the cooked onions and set them aside. Add the rice to the saucepan and stir it with the remaining onions for about 1 minute; then add the lentils and water.

Bring the mixture to a boil; then cover and lower the heat. Simmer the mixture for 40 to 45 minutes, or until all the water has been absorbed and the lentils and rice are tender. If the water is absorbed and the lentils are still not tender, add a little more water and cook a few minutes longer.

Gently stir the lentils and rice mixture and season it with salt and pepper to taste. Turn out the enjadara into a serving dish and top it with the reserved browned onions.

Makes about 6 servings.

VARIATION   (P) or (D)

For a spicier dish reminiscent of *ketchri*, add *½ teaspoon ground cumin* and *¼ teaspoon ground turmeric* to the pan with the lentils. Also, if desired, put *2 to 3 tablespoons of butter or margarine* on top of the cooked mixture and steam, covered tightly, about 5 minutes longer.

RICOTTA LATKES   (D)

(Light and Thin Cheese Pancakes)

Both cheese and the fried pancakes called *latkes* are very traditional for Hanukkah. In fact, it is very likely that *latkes* made from cheese actually predate the more popular ones made from shredded potatoes.

The following *latkes* are much more delicate and "refined" than the potato type, and make a tasty breakfast or even a nice dessert, especially when topped with a good jam. As a bonus, these pancakes are high in protein.

BATTER

1 15- to 16-ounce container part-skim or regular ricotta cheese
4 large eggs
6 tablespoons all-purpose white flour, preferably unbleached
2 tablespoons butter or margarine, melted and cooled (optimal)
1 to 2 tablespoons sugar
1 teaspoon vanilla extract

FOR FRYING

Butter, margarine, vegetable oil, or non-stick vegetable spray

TO SERVE

Jam, applesauce, plain or vanilla yogurt, commercial sour cream, or other pancake accompaniments

Put all the batter ingredients in a food processor (fitted with the steel blade) or blender, in batches if necessary, and process until the batter is very smooth, like thick cream. Scrape down the sides of the container a few times during processing. (The batter will be thinner than most pancake batters.)

Preheat a griddle or large skillet over medium heat (*not* hotter), and lightly grease it. Spoon 1½- to 2-tablespoon measures of batter onto the preheated griddle. When a few bubbles have risen to the surface of the pancakes, and the bottoms are golden brown (the pancakes will not rise), turn them once, and cook them briefly on the second side, just until they are golden brown.

Serve the pancakes with your choice of accompaniment.

Makes about 30 2½- to 3-inch pancakes.

QUICK BLINI   (D)

(Thin Buckwheat Pancakes)

These pancakes are becoming commonplace in Israel, having been introduced there by its many Russian-Jewish immigrants. There are probably as many different versions of *blini* as there are Russian cooks. The following *blini* are "quick" ones because the yeast batter rises for only 30 minutes, compared to most traditional batters, which must rise at least three hours, and some as long as overnight. Furthermore, I have simplified the technique of mixing the batter.

For those who are really in a hurry, a variation uses baking powder instead of yeast, and requires no rising at all. Though this version does not have the yeasty flavor that is characteristic of most *blini,* it is nevertheless quite tasty.

Buckwheat flour can be found in most health-food or gourmet specialty stores, as well as in some supermarkets. It can be stored in the freezer for a year or longer. The beige-colored, "light" buckwheat flour produces a *blini* with a mild, deliciously subtle flavor. The brown, "dark" buckwheat flour is much stronger, and should be used only when a very intense buckwheat flavor is desired.

Blini are customarily served with sour cream and caviar or smoked salmon. However, they also make a nice Hanukkah breakfast with a little pancake syrup on top.

1 packet "quick"-type *active dry yeast*

¾ cup plus 2 tablespoons warm (105 to 115 degrees) water

1 tablespoon honey

¾ cup (light) buckwheat flour

¼ cup all-purpose white flour, preferably unbleached

¼ cup instant nonfat dry milk powder

2 tablespoons commercial sour cream or plain yogurt

1½ tablespoons butter or margarine, melted and cooled

2 large eggs, separated

Pinch of salt

FOR FRYING

Butter, margarine, vegetable oil, or non-stick cooking spray

TO SERVE (OPTIONAL)

Commercial sour cream or plain yogurt

Caviar

Very thinly sliced smoked salmon (or "lox")

In a medium-sized bowl, combine the yeast, water, and honey. Let the mixture rest for about 5 minutes, or until it is foamy. Stir in the flours, milk powder, sour cream, melted butter, and egg yolks. Cover the bowl with plastic wrap and let the batter rest for 30 minutes. It will not rise very much, but will form bubbles on the surface.

In a separate, clean bowl, beat the egg whites with the salt just until they form stiff peaks; do not overbeat them, or they may be difficult to fold. Gently, but thoroughly, fold the beaten whites into the batter.

Preheat a griddle or large skillet over medium-high heat and lightly grease it. Spoon 1½- to 2-tablespoon measures of the batter onto the preheated griddle. When bubbles have formed on the surface of the pancakes, and the bottoms are browned, turn them once and cook just until lightly browned on the second side.

Serve the blini with the desired accompaniments, or with pancake syrup.

Makes about 30 2½- to 3-inch blini.

VARIATION

EVEN-QUICKER BLINI (D)

Omit the yeast. In a medium-sized bowl, combine the flours, milk powder, and ½ teaspoon baking powder. Stir in the water (which should be at room temperature), sour cream, honey, melted butter, and egg yolks. In a separate, clean bowl, beat the egg whites with the salt just until they form stiff peaks. Gently, but thoroughly, fold the beaten whites into the batter. Cook the blini as directed above.

CHEESE-RICE LATKES (D)

(Fluffy Pancakes)

These puffed fritters are quite nice for lunch or part of a dairy meal, and a great way to use up leftover cooked rice and bits of cheese.

2 cups cooked *brown or white rice*

3 ounces Cheddar cheese, shredded (¾ cup packed), or your choice of cheese

3 large eggs, separated

3 tablespoons all-purpose white flour, preferably unbleached (or whole wheat flour)

Pinch of salt, or to taste

Generous pinch of black pepper, preferably freshly ground

⅛ teaspoon cream of tartar

Vegetable oil, butter, or margarine for frying

In a medium-sized bowl, mix together the cooked rice, cheese, egg yolks, flour, salt, and pepper.

In another bowl, beat the egg whites with the cream of tartar until they are stiff but not dry. Fold the beaten whites into the rice-cheese mixture until completely combined.

In a large skillet, over medium heat, heat about 2 tablespoons of oil until it is hot. Spoon 2 to 3 tablespoons of the batter onto the skillet for each latke, and flatten it slightly with the back of the spoon. Fry the latkes, turning them once, until they are golden brown on both sides. Repeat with the remaining batter, adding oil to the skillet as needed. Serve hot.

Makes 15 to 18 small latkes; about 4 servings.

BUBBY ROSE'S FARFEL-POTATO DAIRY SOUP (D)

This was one of the first soups my mother ever prepared—something she learned from her maternal grandmother and favorite cooking teacher, my great-grandmother Rose Dublin Levine.

Though Mom used to serve this soup quite often when I was younger, I had completely forgotten about it until we recently had a conversation about the culinary endeavors of Bubby Rose. Mom gave me the recipe, and I promptly tried it in my own kitchen. To my amazement, just one taste of the delicious farfel-potato soup was enough to bring wonderful gustatory recollections of my early childhood to mind.

This quick and easy soup has become so well-liked in my own family that it is now a regular staple in my repertoire. I have modified the original recipe only slightly by chopping the onion and sautéing it in butter (Bubby left it whole and removed it when the soup was done), and using milk powder instead of whole milk.

2 tablespoons butter or margarine
1 medium-sized onion, finely chopped
3 cups hot water
1½ to 2 cups peeled and diced (½-inch cubes) "new" potatoes or all-purpose potatoes (about 2 medium-sized potatoes)

⅔ cup barley-shaped noodles or farfel
¾ teaspoon salt
Pinch of ground white pepper
1 cup instant nonfat dry milk powder
1 cup cool water

In a 2½-quart or larger saucepan, over medium-high heat, melt the butter; then cook the onion, stirring, until it is tender but not browned. Add the hot water, raise the heat to high, and bring the water to a boil. Stir in the potato cubes, barley-shaped noodles, salt, and pepper. Lower the heat and simmer the soup, covered, for 20 minutes, or until the potatoes are tender.

Mix together the milk powder and cool water until smooth. Stir this into the hot soup and continue heating until it simmers, about 2 minutes longer. Serve hot.

Makes 5 to 6 servings.

NOTE: This soup gets thicker upon standing. When reheating leftovers, stir in some milk or water if the soup is too thick.

SPAS (D)

(Russian-Style Yogurt-Barley Soup)

This tangy soup is wonderfully thick and rich-tasting, perfect for a cold winter's night. It's also nourishing and satisfying enough to be a meatless main dish.

2½ cups water
1 cup pearl barley
2½ tablespoons butter or margarine
½ cup finely minced onion
2 tablespoons all-purpose white flour,
  preferably unbleached
3¼ cups milk, any type

2 cups plain yogurt
1 large egg, lightly beaten
1 teaspoon salt

TO SERVE
Chopped fresh chives or thinly sliced
  scallion tops

In a medium-sized saucepan, over high heat, bring the water to a boil; then stir in the barley. Cover the pan tightly, and lower the heat. Simmer the barley for about 45 minutes, or until the water has been absorbed and the barley is tender but not mushy. Set it aside. (The barley may be cooked up to a day ahead of the soup. If the barley is cooked more than a few hours in advance, refrigerate it.)

In a 4-quart or similar saucepan, over medium-high heat, melt the butter; then cook the onion, stirring, until it is tender but not browned. Stir in the flour and cook for 1 minute, stirring constantly. Then very gradually (so that the flour does not form any lumps) stir in the milk. Continue to cook, while stirring, until the mixture thickens slightly and just comes to a boil. Stir in the cooked barley; then cover the pan, lower the heat, and simmer the mixture for 10 to 15 minutes, or until it is very thick.

Meanwhile, stir together the yogurt, egg, and salt. Remove the pan from the heat and stir in the yogurt mixture. Return the soup to very low heat and cook it, stirring, just until it is heated through. (If the soup comes to a boil, it may look curdled; however, it will still taste fine.) If desired, keep the soup warm over very low heat.

To serve, ladle the soup into bowls, and sprinkle some chopped chives or scallions over each serving.

Makes about 8 servings.

CHEESE "COINS" (D)

(Savory Cheese Wafers)

During Hanukkah, it is traditional for Ashkenazic parents to give their children small gifts of *gelt* (Yiddish for "money"), usually in the form of shiny coins. The following recipe produces golden disks of edible Hanukkah gelt. With them, one is sure to get a good return on any "dough" invested in the project. And the holiday game of chance played with a *dreidel* (spinning top) will take on an added dimension when the winnings are so tasty.

Actually, I did not originate the name for this appetizer/snack, which is adapted from a variety of classic British recipes for cheese wafers. The ingredient proportions vary from recipe to recipe, but the names, such as Cheese Coins, Cheese Pennies, or Ha'pennies, invariably have something to do with money.

This version is made in a manner similar to sliced refrigerator cookies.

8 ounces sharp Cheddar cheese, shredded (about 2 cups packed)
½ cup butter or margarine, softened
1 cup all-purpose white flour, preferably unbleached (may be half whole wheat flour)
1 teaspoon Worcestershire sauce
2 tablespoons instant minced onions
Pinch of cayenne pepper (optional)
Sesame seeds (optional)

In a medium-sized bowl, combine all the ingredients, except the sesame seeds. Mix well by hand (or heavy-duty mixer) until a dough is formed. Divide the dough in half and shape each half into a log which is 1 inch in diameter and about 12 inches long. If desired, roll the logs in sesame seeds to completely coat the outside (so that each sliced wafer will be rimmed with seeds). Wrap each log tightly in plastic wrap; then chill for several hours or overnight. (The logs may be frozen at this point; thaw them in the refrigerator before using.)

To bake the wafers, carefully cut each log crosswise into ¼-inch-thick slices. Place the slices on greased and lightly floured or non-stick spray-coated baking sheets and bake in a preheated 375-degree oven for 10 to 12 minutes, or until lightly browned and firm. Use a metal spatula or pancake turner to carefully remove the wafers from the baking sheets. Cool them on wire racks. When the wafers are completely cool, store them in an airtight container to keep them crunchy.

Makes about 7 dozen small wafers.

CHEESE PUFFS (D)

(Savory Cheese Meringues)

Meringues are often sweet and sticky. This savory version is delightfully cheesy instead, and a tasty way to follow the Hanukkah tradition of eating foods made with cheese. They make a nutritious snack or appetizer.

4 ounces sharp Cheddar cheese,
grated (1 cup packed)
3 tablespoons all-purpose white flour,
preferably unbleached (or 2
tablespoons cornstarch)
½ teaspoon powdered mustard

¼ teaspoon baking powder
Pinch of cayenne pepper (optional)
3 large egg whites
⅛ teaspoon cream of tartar
Pinch of salt

In a small bowl, toss the grated cheese with the flour, powdered mustard, baking powder, and cayenne (if used).

In a separate, clean bowl, beat the egg whites with the cream of tartar and salt just until they are stiff but not dry. Very gently fold the cheese mixture into the beaten egg whites, being careful not to deflate the whites too much.

Drop heaping teaspoonfuls of the mixture onto greased and lightly floured baking sheets. Bake in a preheated 325-degree oven for 20 to 25 minutes, or until set. Use a metal spatula or pancake turner to remove the meringues from the baking sheets. Cool them on a wire rack. When the meringues are completely cool, store them in an airtight container.

Makes about 36 cheese puffs.

WELSH RABBIT (D)

(Melted Cheese over Toast)

There seems to be some confusion over the name of this classic British dish, which is also called "Welsh rarebit." It seems that the original moniker—"rabbit"—is a sort of ethnic joke, implying that this dish is the closest some poor Welshmen might ever come to eating rabbit. During the seventeenth century, it was amended to "rarebit," which sounded more proper to some folks.

I think the original name is more fun, simply because it's the closest any observant Jew will ever get to eating rabbit!

The recipe calls for beer and works quite well with "Maccabee" beer imported from Israel. Considering the brand name, this beer is really perfect for inclusion in a Hanukkah meal.

Serve this foudue-like "rabbit" as a snack, appetizer, or light dinner.

1 tablespoon butter or margarine	½ cup beer
12 ounces sharp Cheddar cheese, shredded (3 cups packed)	1 large egg
½ to 1 teaspoon Worcestershire sauce	TO SERVE
¼ to ½ teaspoon powdered mustard	4 to 8 toast triangles or toasted
Pinch of cayenne pepper	English muffin halves

In the top of a double boiler, over simmering water, melt the butter. Add the cheese, Worcestershire sauce, powdered mustard, and cayenne.

In a small bowl, beat together the beer and egg. As the cheese begins to melt, slowly stir in the beer-egg mixture. Continue stirring constantly for several minutes, or until the cheese melts completely and the sauce thickens, but do not let the sauce boil.

For each serving, put 1 or 2 toast triangles or toasted English muffin halves in a soup bowl and spoon some of the cheese sauce on top. (Note: The British like to butter their toast, and then place it, buttered side down, in the bowl before topping it with the cheese sauce.) Welsh rabbit is eaten with a knife and fork.

Makes 3 to 4 servings as a main course, more as an appetizer or snack.

TOPFENKNODEL (D)

(Tiny Cheese Dumplings)

These Viennese dumplings make an appealing side dish when they are served with fresh fruit and sour cream, and a tasty dessert when they are coated with sweet crumbs and served with warmed preserves. The following very easy version is lighter than some which are made with flour instead of the Cream of Wheat.

By the way, these dumplings are served not only by Austrian Jews, but also those from Czechoslovakia and Hungary.

DUMPLINGS
1 7½- to 8-ounce package farmer cheese
1 large egg
⅓ cup "quick" Cream of Wheat cereal
1 tablespoon sugar
¼ teaspoon vanilla extract (optional)

COATING (OPTIONAL)
2 tablespoons butter or margarine

¼ cup corn flake crumbs or fine dry bread crumbs
1 tablespoon sugar (optional)

TO SERVE (YOUR CHOICE)
Warm preserves
Commercial sour cream or plain yogurt
Applesauce with cinnamon
Stewed fruit

For the dumplings, combine the farmer cheese, egg, cereal, sugar, and vanilla (if used) in a medium-sized bowl and mix very well until smooth. Let the mixture rest for about 15 minutes to firm up.

Meanwhile, bring a large saucepan or deep skillet of water to a boil. Lower the heat so the water just simmers.

With wet hands, form the mixture into 1¼-inch balls. Carefully drop the balls into the simmering water and simmer them gently, uncovered, for about 10 minutes, or just until they are firm and cooked through. (Do not let the water come to a full boil or overcook the dumplings, as they are delicate and may fall apart.)

Use a slotted spoon to carefully remove the cooked dumplings from the pot, draining them well. Serve them "as is" with any of the suggested accompaniments. Or, first coat them with buttered crumbs as follows:

In a large skillet over medium-high heat, melt the butter; then stir in the corn flake crumbs and cook, stirring, for about 1 minute, or until they are dry (bread crumbs should be lightly browned). Stir in the sugar (if used) until completely mixed. Turn the heat to low and add the well-drained dumplings. Toss them gently with the crumbs until they are well coated and warmed through. Serve warm or at room temperature with any of the suggested accompaniments.

Makes about 16 dumplings; about 4 servings.

SWEET COUSCOUS WITH DRIED FRUIT AND NUTS
(D) or (P)

The sixth night of Hanukkah is also *Rosh Hodesh* or the "New Moon." It marks the end of a month on the Hebrew calendar and the beginning of the next one. Many Jews observe Rosh Hodesh of every month as a joyous semi-holiday. During Hanukkah, Moroccan Jews often gather with relatives and friends on the evening of the sixth candle for a festive celebration, which usually includes a special meal followed by several desserts.

The main course may feature *couscous* with meats and vegetables, similar to the version in the Rosh Hashanah chapter (see *Couscous aux Sept Légumes* on page 83). Dessert may be *beignets* (page 170), *zlabia* (page 168) or, if *couscous* was not already served during the meal, a rich, sweet *couscous* like that which follows. When served with a dairy dinner or as a midday snack, it is usually accompanied with yogurt or possibly buttermilk.

(Note: The *couscous* is steamed *twice* to fully cook it while keeping it light and fluffy.)

1 ¼ *cups (about ½ pound) ready-to-cook dry couscous*
1 *cup cold water*
1 ½ *teaspoons vegetable oil*
¼ *cup (4 tablespoons) butter or margarine, melted*
½ *cup chopped pitted dates*
½ *cup currants or dark raisins*
¼ *cup sugar*
2 *tablespoons orange juice or sweet wine*

1 *teaspoon grated orange rind, colored part only (optional)*
½ *cup finely chopped blanched almonds*
½ *cup finely chopped walnuts*
¼ *teaspoon ground cinnamon*
Extra ground cinnamon for garnish

TO SERVE (OPTIONAL)
Plain or vanilla yogurt

Put the dry couscous into a large bowl and stir it with the water. Let it rest for 15 minutes or until all the water is absorbed. Then use your hands to mix the couscous with the oil, carefully separating all the pellets so that they are fluffy and none are stuck together.

Set a large cheesecloth-lined colander (or the steamer part of a couscousière) into the top of a large pot (or the bottom of the couscousière) which contains several inches of water. (The bottom of the colander should not touch the water.) Bring the water to a boil over high heat; then lower the heat so the water boils gently. If steam is escaping where the colander and pot meet, wedge a towel between them so that the steam is forced to rise through the center of the colander. Lightly sprinkle all the soaked couscous pellets into the colander. Steam the couscous for 20 minutes.

Turn out the couscous into a large bowl and fluff it with a 2-pronged fork or your fingers, separating the pellets as before. Toss it with 2 tablespoons of the melted butter. (The couscous may be prepared in advance to this point, and set aside for up to 3 hours at room temperature covered with a damp cloth. Continue the preparation about 25 minutes before serving the dessert.)

Into the partially cooked couscous, stir the dates, currants, sugar, orange juice, and orange rind (if used). Bring water to a boil in a pot (or the bottom of a couscousière), just as when steaming the couscous the first time. Sprinkle the couscous mixture into the colander and steam it for 20 minutes. Turn it out of the colander into a large bowl and fluff it as before. Add the remaining 2 tablespoons of melted butter, almonds, walnuts, and ¼ teaspoon cinnamon and toss until well mixed.

Lightly pile the sweet couscous onto a large serving platter so that it forms a mountain-like cone (as is customarily done by Moroccans). Decorate it with a few stripes of ground cinnamon radiating from the center to the perimeter. For the best taste, serve immediately. To serve, spoon into individual bowls. If desired, accompany the dessert with yogurt.

Makes 5 to 6 servings.

HANUKKAH BIMUELOS OR LOUKOUMADES (P)

(Fried Honey Puffs)

This is the most traditional Hanukkah treat for Sephardic Jews who come from Greece and Turkey. *Bimuelos* (or *burmuelos*) is the pastry's Judeo-Spanish name, *loukoumades* (or *loukoumathes*) is its Greek one, and *lokma* is its Turkish one. Sephardic Jews actually use the name "bimuelos" for a number of foods in addition to this one. For instance, it can also mean pancakes or fried patties, or even a type of baked muffins.

The following *bimuelos* are irregularly shaped, yeast-raised "puffs" that are drenched in a honey syrup. Occasionally, they are coated with confectioner's sugar instead of the syrup.

These same pastries are often served on Purim, when they are sometimes called "Purim puffs."

BATTER
1 packet (2¼ teaspoons) active dry
    yeast
1 cup warm (105 to 115 degrees)
    water, divided
½ teaspoon sugar
1 large egg
2 cups all-purpose white flour,
    preferably unbleached
¼ teaspoon salt

HONEY SYRUP
1 cup sugar
¾ cup cold water
½ cup honey
1 tablespoon lemon juice

FOR FRYING AND GARNISH
Vegetable oil
Ground cinnamon

For the batter, mix together the yeast, ½ cup of the warm water, and the sugar in a medium-sized bowl. Let the yeast mixture rest for about 5 minutes, or until it is foamy. Stir in the remaining batter ingredients (including the remaining ½ cup water) until smooth. The batter should be very loose and sticky. Cover the bowl loosely with plastic wrap and let the batter rise for 1 hour. (If necessary, the batter can be stirred down at this point and allowed to rise for another 30 minutes.)

While the batter is rising, prepare the honey syrup. Mix together all the ingredients in a 2-quart or similar saucepan and slowly bring to a boil over medium-high heat, stirring only until the sugar dissolves. Lower the heat slightly and boil the syrup, uncovered and undisturbed, for 5 minutes. Remove from the heat and set aside to cool to room temperature.

When the batter has risen, stir it down. Put enough oil into a large saucepan or a wok so that it is about 1½ inches deep. Heat the oil until it is very hot, about 375 degrees. Dip a teaspoon into the oil, and then use the spoon to scoop up a small portion of the batter. Gently drop the batter into the oil. (Keep your opposite hand moistened, in case you need to nudge the batter off the spoon. The batter will not stick to wet hands.) The dollop of batter will quickly puff up to almost twice its original size. Make more puffs in the same manner, but do not crowd the pan. Fry the puffs, turning them occasionally with a slotted spoon, until they are browned on all sides and very crisp.

Drain them briefly on paper towels or on the rack that attaches to some woks. Then drop 1 or 2 at a time into the cooled syrup (see Note). Use a different spoon or tongs (so the syrup will not get oily) to turn the hot puffs in the syrup until they become completely coated with it. Lift the puffs up, and let the excess syrup drain off. Put the puffs on a large plate. Repeat the frying and dipping process until all the batter is used. Then sprinkle the puffs generously with cinnamon. For best taste and texture, serve them as soon as possible.

Makes about 36 honey puffs.

NOTE: If desired, the honey puffs may be fried in advance, and coated with *hot* syrup just before serving. Some Sephardic cooks prefer to stir about 1 teaspoon cinnamon into the syrup, and then let each guest pour a bit of syrup over his or her own serving of puffs. In some households, purchased pancake syrup is used. Another easy alternative is *1 cup honey* mixed with *¼ to ⅓ cup water,* heated just until blended and hot. Use while warm to drizzle over the puffs.

SOOFGANIYOT (D)

(Jelly-Filled Doughnuts)

In Israel, these light jelly doughnuts are the favorite treat eaten during Hanukkah. They may be made at home or purchased at almost any bakery during the holiday. *Soofganiyot* are also sold, year round, at informal outdoor kiosks, where they are eaten out-of-hand by Israelis, who love to snack. In fact, I once patronized an extremely popular stand in Haifa which had only *soofganiyot* and *g'leedah* (ice cream) for sale.

This version of *soofganiyot* is relatively easy, and requires very little kneading. However, the dough takes a few hours to rise. The time can be filled with holiday activities such as games of "Spin the Dreidel."

DOUGH
2 packets (4½ teaspoons) active dry yeast
1 cup warm (105 to 115 degrees) water, divided

⅓ cup plus 1 teaspoon granulated sugar, divided
⅓ cup butter or margarine, melted and cooled

1 large egg
1 large egg yolk (reserve the white)
1 teaspoon salt
¼ cup instant nonfat dry milk
    powder
3⅓ cups all-purpose white flour,
    preferably unbleached

FILLING
About ¼ cup thick jam (your choice
    of flavor)

FOR FRYING AND COATING
Vegetable oil
Granulated or confectioner's sugar

In a large mixing bowl, combine the yeast, ½ cup of the water, and the 1 teaspoon sugar. Let the mixture sit for about 5 minutes, or until it is foamy; then add the remaining ½ cup water, the ⅓ cup sugar, melted butter, egg, egg yolk, salt, instant nonfat dry milk, and 2⅓ cups of the flour. Beat with an electric mixer at medium speed for 3 minutes; then stir in the remaining 1 cup flour by hand (or heavy-duty mixer) to make a soft dough.

Scrape down the dough on the sides of the bowl; then cover the bowl loosely with plastic wrap and a dish towel. Let the dough rise in a warm place for about 1 to 1½ hours, or until doubled in bulk.

Turn the dough out onto a lightly floured surface, and knead it for about 2 minutes, or until it is very smooth. Let the dough rest for 10 minutes; then divide it in half, and roll out each half to a ¼-inch thickness. Cut out 12 3-inch-diameter circles from each half.

Beat the reserved egg white until frothy; then brush some of it over one of the circles. Place a scant teaspoon of jam in the center of the circle; then top it with another circle, sandwich-style. Pinch the outside edges of the 2 circles together very well to seal them tightly. Place on a floured baking sheet or board. Repeat with remaining circles and jam, for a total of 12 doughnuts. Cover the doughnuts loosely with a dish towel and let them rise until almost doubled in size (about 1 hour).

Put enough oil into a large saucepan or wok so that it is about 2 inches deep. Heat the oil until it is hot, about 350 degrees. Gently drop a few of the doughnuts into the oil so they are not too crowded. Fry them for about 3 minutes on each side, or until they are puffed and golden brown. Drain them well on paper towels; then coat the warm doughnuts with granulated or confectioner's sugar. Repeat until all the doughnuts have been fried and coated.

For the best flavor and texture, serve the doughnuts within a few hours after they are fried.

Makes 12 doughnuts.

ZELEBI OR ZLABIA (P)

(Fried Rosettes Dipped in Honey Syrup)

These pastries are eaten by Jews from all over the Near East, Middle East, and North Africa, who often call them *zlabia*. They are particularly popular among Yemenite Jews in Israel, who usually prefer the name *zelebi* (or *zelebies*). Iraqis may call them *zangoola* or *zingzoola*. In some places, they are sold by street vendors who make them as hungry patrons wait.

Interestingly, an almost identical pastry called *jalebi* is popular in India. The names are so similar that one is probably derived from the other.

Composed of the most basic ingredients, *zelebi* are a very ancient pastry. In fact, there is a mural in the tomb of the Egyptian pharaoh, Ramses III, depicting their preparation.

Before the advent of packaged yeast, the batter was left to ferment on its own for several hours or overnight (in the same manner as American sourdough). Also, since purified sugar was not commonly available in the past, the syrup was often made using only honey.

SYRUP
1²/₃ cups sugar
1 cup cold water
2 tablespoons honey
1 tablespoon lemon juice
1 teaspoon grated lemon rind
  (optional)
1 to 2 teaspoons rose water (optional)

BATTER
1 packet (2¼ teaspoons) active dry
  yeast

½ teaspoon sugar
1¾ cups warm (105 to 115 degrees)
  water
2 cups all-purpose white flour,
  preferably unbleached
¼ teaspoon salt

FOR FRYING
Vegetable oil

First, prepare the syrup so it will have plenty of time to cool. Put the sugar, water, honey, lemon juice, and lemon rind (if used) into a 2-quart or similar saucepan. Slowly bring to a boil over medium-high heat, stirring only until the sugar dissolves. Lower the heat slightly and boil the syrup briskly, uncovered and undisturbed, for 15 minutes. If the rose water is desired, stir it in during the last minute of boiling. Remove the syrup from the heat and set it aside to cool to room temperature before using.

For the batter, mix the yeast and sugar with the warm water in a food processor (fitted with the steel blade) or a mixer bowl, and let the mixture rest for 5 to 10 minutes, or until it is foamy. Add the flour and salt and process or mix with an electric mixer until very smooth and creamy, like very thick cream. Cover the bowl loosely with plastic wrap and let the batter rest for 30 minutes. Beat it by hand for about 2 to 3 minutes, and let it rest for another 10 minutes. Then beat it briefly. It will be very elastic.

Put enough oil into a large saucepan or a wok so that it is about 1½ inches deep. Heat the oil until it is very hot, about 375 degrees. Give the batter a stir to deflate any bubbles and scoop some of it into a pastry bag that has a round tip with a ³⁄₁₆-inch opening. (If this is unavailable, try using a clean, soft plastic ketchup bottle that has had the hole in the top made larger.)

Squeeze out the batter into the hot oil to form a 5- to 6-inch-diameter circle; then squeeze out a little more batter to make zigzags, squiggles, or other designs across the center of the circle (Fig. 14A). The zelebi should have a rough, open, lacy look. If the pan is large enough, make another pastry in the same manner, being careful that it does not touch the first one. Fry each pastry, turning it once with a slotted spoon or fork, about 1½ to 2 minutes on each side, or until it is browned and very crisp (Fig. 14B).

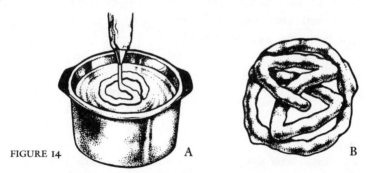

FIGURE 14   A   B

When the zelebi is done, lift it from the oil using the spoon or fork, and drain it briefly on paper towels or on the rack that attaches to some woks. Immediately drop it into the cooled syrup. Use a different fork or tongs (so the syrup will not get oily) to turn the zelebi over in the syrup; then quickly lift it up and let the excess syrup drip off. Put the pastry on a large plate. Repeat the frying and dipping process until all the batter is used. Before refilling the pastry bag with batter, give the batter a quick stir to deflate any bubbles.

The finished zelebi should stay crisp for several hours, possibly even overnight. To store, cover them loosely with aluminum foil. Do not refrigerate them.

Makes 12 to 18 large zelebi.

ZVINGOUS OR BEIGNETS   (D) or (P)

(Fried Fritters in Honey Syrup)

Greek and Turkish Jews sometimes serve these *zvingous* on Hanukkah, in place of *loukoumades* (page 164). North African Jews have very similar treats, which are usually called by their French name, *beignets*. (The French, however, prefer serving this type of beignet with warm jam, rather than dipping it in syrup.)

Though the finished puffs look very similar to *loukoumades,* and are sometimes even called by that name, they are made with a totally different dough—one that is not leavened with yeast, but does contain more eggs. When this dough is put into a pastry bag and squeezed through a notched metal tip directly into hot oil, it produces narrow, ribbed holiday pastries called *tulumbas,* which are dipped in the same syrup and served in the same way as *zvingous.*

HONEY SYRUP
1 *cup sugar*
3/4 *cup cold water*
1/2 *cup honey*
1 *tablespoon lemon juice*
1/4 *teaspoon ground cinnamon*

DOUGH
1/4 *cup butter or margarine*
1 *cup cold water*

1 *tablespoon sugar*
1 *cup all-purpose white flour,*
   preferably unbleached
4 *large eggs*

FOR FRYING AND GARNISH
Vegetable oil
Ground cinnamon (optional)
Finely chopped walnuts (optional)

For the syrup, mix together all the ingredients in a 2-quart or similar saucepan and slowly bring to a boil over medium-high heat, stirring only until the sugar dissolves. Turn the heat to low and simmer the syrup, uncovered and undisturbed, for 5 minutes. Remove it from the heat and set it aside to cool to room temperature.

For the dough, put the butter, water, and sugar into a large saucepan and bring to a boil over high heat. Immediately remove the saucepan from the heat and add all the flour at once. Stir the mixture with a wooden spoon until it leaves the sides of the pan and forms a ball. Return the saucepan to low heat and stir the dough, mashing it against the sides of the pan, for 1 minute. Remove the pan from the heat and use an electric mixer to beat in the eggs, one by one, adding the next egg only after the previous one has been completely incorporated.

Put enough oil into a large saucepan or a wok so that it is about 1½ inches deep. Heat the oil until it is very hot, about 375 degrees. Dip a teaspoon into the oil, and then use the spoon to scoop up a small portion of the batter. Gently drop the batter into the oil. (Keep your opposite hand moistened, in case you need to nudge the batter off the spoon. The batter will not stick to wet hands.) The dollop of batter will quickly puff up to almost twice its original size. Make some more fritters in the same manner, but do not crowd the pan. Fry the fritters, turning them occasionally with a slotted spoon, until they are browned and very crisp.

Drain them briefly on paper towels or on the rack that attaches to some woks. Then drop 1 or 2 at a time into the cooled syrup (see Note). Use a different spoon or tongs (so the syrup will not get oily) to turn the hot puffs in the syrup until they become completely coated with it. Lift the puffs up and let the excess syrup drain off. Put the fritters on a large plate. Repeat the frying and dipping process until all the batter is used. If desired, sprinkle the puffs lightly with cinnamon and/or walnuts. For the best taste and texture, serve them as soon as possible.

Makes about 36 zvingous.

NOTE: If preferred, these may be served with warmed jam instead of being dipped in syrup.

KOEKSISTERS (D) or (P)

(Fried Braided Pastries Dipped in Syrup)

This South African specialty looks like glistening, miniature challah breads. Of all the fried, syrup-dipped pastries in this chapter, *koeksisters* are the most attractive, and one of my favorites. Though they are so popular in South Africa that they are eaten throughout the year (particularly at "tea time"), they seem particularly appropriate for Hanukkah.

The following version of *koeksisters* has been adapted from a recipe I found in a popular South African-Jewish cookbook called *The Singing Kettle,* which was published in South Africa by the Port Elizabeth Branch of the Union of Jewish Women.

SYRUP
1⅔ cups sugar
1 cup cold water
2 tablespoons honey
1 tablespoon lemon juice
Pinch of ground cinnamon
 (optional)

DOUGH
2 cups all-purpose white flour,
 preferably unbleached

1¾ teaspoons baking powder
Pinch of salt
2 tablespoons butter or margarine,
 softened
⅔ cup milk or water
1 large egg yolk

FOR FRYING
Vegetable oil

First, prepare the syrup so it will have sufficient time to chill. Put the sugar, water, honey, lemon juice, and cinnamon (if used) into a 2-quart or similar saucepan. Slowly bring to a boil over medium-high heat, stirring only until the sugar dissolves. Lower the heat slightly and boil the syrup briskly, uncovered and undisturbed, for 15 minutes. Remove the syrup from the heat and let it cool to room temperature; then chill it in the refrigerator.

For the dough, put the flour, baking powder, and salt into a medium-sized bowl and cut in the butter with your fingertips or a pastry blender until the mixture looks like fine meal. Add the milk and egg and mix to form a soft, slightly sticky dough. Turn the dough out onto a lightly floured surface, coat it very lightly with flour, and knead it for 5 to 10 minutes, or until it is very smooth and pliable. Wrap it in plastic wrap and let it rest at room temperature for 30 minutes to 1 hour.

On a very lightly floured surface, roll out the dough to a neat 9-inch square about ¼ inch thick. Use a pastry wheel or sharp knife to cut the square into three 3- by 9-inch sections. Then cut each section crosswise into 9 1-inch strips, for a total of 27 strips, each measuring 1 by 3 inches. For best results, mark the dough with the edge of a clean ruler before cutting.

For each pastry, cut one of the strips lengthwise into 3 equal, narrow "tails," which are joined together at the top (Fig. 15A). Braid the tails compactly and pinch the ends together very tightly so the braid will not unravel during frying.

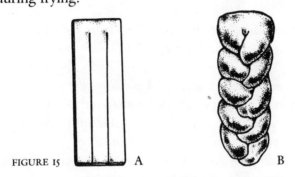

FIGURE 15   A   B

Put enough oil into a large saucepan or a wok so that it is about 1½ inches deep. Heat the oil until it is very hot, about 375 degrees. Gently drop a few of the braids into the oil so they are not too crowded; they will quickly puff up. Fry them about 2 minutes on each side, or until they are browned and crisp (Fig. 15B).

Use a slotted spoon to remove the koeksisters from the oil and drain them briefly on paper towels or on the rack that attaches to some woks. Immediately drop them into the cooled syrup. Use a different spoon or tongs (so the syrup will not get oily) to turn the koeksisters in the syrup until they are completely coated; then quickly lift them up and let the excess syrup drain off. Put the koeksisters on a large plate. Repeat the frying and dipping process until all the dough has been used.

The finished koeksisters can be stored for several days in a loosely covered container at room temperature.

Makes 27 koeksisters.

GULAB JAMUN (D)

(Fried Pastry Balls Soaked in Cardamom Syrup)

This unusual dessert comes from India, where a unique group of Jews called the *Bene-Israel* claim to have lived for at least two thousand years.

There are a number of theories which endeavor to explain the origins of the Bene-Israel. One suggests that they were Israelites who fled ancient Judea to escape religious persecution by Antiochus, the Syrian tyrant who was eventually overthrown by Judah the Maccabee and his followers.

With that possibility in mind, this fried treat seems quite suited for Hanukkah. Though made of pastry, *gulab jamun* fool the eye since they resemble fruit in syrup.

Following is actually a modernized version of a very ancient recipe. Before the advent of milk powder, milk had to be boiled down for several hours until it became thick enough to be made into a dough.

Gulab jamun can be made well in advance, to be served whenever guests decide to drop by for a impromptu Hanukkah visit. In fact, this dessert can be refrigerated for up to two months.

(Note: Unlike the other fried pastries in this chapter, *gulab jamun* are stored and served in their syrup.)

CARDAMOM SYRUP
3 cups cold water
3 cups sugar
7 to 10 whole cardamom pods (if not available, use ½ teaspoon ground cardamom)

PASTRY BALLS
1½ cups instant nonfat dry milk powder

½ cup all-purpose white flour, preferably unbleached
½ teaspoon baking soda
2 tablespoons butter or margarine, softened
¼ to ½ cup cold water

FOR FRYING
Vegetable oil

First, prepare the syrup so that it will have time to cool. Put the water, sugar, and cardamom into a large saucepan and slowly bring the mixture to a boil over medium-high heat, stirring only until the sugar is dissolved. Lower the heat and simmer, uncovered and undisturbed, for 10 minutes. Let the syrup cool to room temperature.

Meanwhile, prepare the pastry balls. Mix together the milk powder, flour, and baking soda. Cut in the butter with a pastry blender or your fingertips until the mixture resembles fine meal. Stir in just enough of the water so that the dough is slightly tacky but comes away from the sides of the bowl. It should be easily handled without sticking to your fingers. If it becomes too wet, add a bit of extra milk powder. If it is too dry, add more water. The exact amount of each depends on the brand of milk powder and the humidity.

Form the dough into about 36 smooth ½- to ¾-inch-diameter balls. Put enough oil into a large saucepan or wok so that it is about 1½ inches deep. Heat the oil until it is hot, about 350 degrees. Gently drop several of the balls into the oil, but do not crowd them; they will quickly puff to almost twice their original size. Fry the balls, rotating them frequently with a slotted spoon, for 5 to 7 minutes, or until they are browned. (Don't worry if they are a little unevenly colored; it adds to their interesting appearance.)

Use a slotted spoon to remove the balls from the oil and drain them briefly on paper towels or on the rack that attaches to some woks. Immediately drop the balls into the syrup and let them soak; *do not remove them.*

Continue until all the balls have been fried and added to the syrup. Let the balls soak in the syrup for 3 to 4 hours at room temperature; then refrigerate them in the syrup. They will further increase in size as they soak. (The whole cardamom pods can be left in the syrup to continue flavoring it, but be sure to remove the pods before serving the dessert.)

To serve the gulab jamun, put 3 or 4 balls (or more) in a small bowl with a little of the syrup. Although this dessert is usually served cold or at room temperature, it is occasionally heated slightly just before serving. If the gulab jamun are stored for more than 1 day, the balls and syrup should be transferred to a covered, liquid-tight container. Store in the refrigerator for up to 2 months.

Makes about 36 balls in syrup; 8 to 12 servings.

SUKARIYOT SOOMSOOM (P)

(Crunchy Sesame Seed Candies)

For some Sephardic families, sesame seed candy is a must at Hanukkah time. It is an ancient confection that is made by Jews from all over the Middle East and North Africa. In Israel, where sesame seeds or *soomsoom* are a national favorite, this treat is also eaten on many other holidays, including Rosh Hashanah and Yom Ha'Atzmaut (Independence Day).

The following version is very easy, and the candy looks and tastes even better than "store-bought." For the best results, try to make it on a cool dry day.

Vegetable oil or non-stick cooking spray for the pan	*½ cup packed dark or light brown sugar*
2 cups sesame seeds (about 12 ounces)	*½ teaspoon ground cinnamon*
½ cup honey	*¼ teaspoon ground ginger*

Coat a 9-inch-square baking pan or dish with oil or non-stick cooking spray. Set aside.

Put the sesame seeds into an ungreased 10-inch skillet (preferably one with a non-stick surface) and stir them over medium-high heat for about 5 to 10 minutes, or until they are lightly browned and aromatic. Temporarily transfer the seeds (they will be hot) to a bowl, making sure that none are left in the skillet. Set aside.

Put the honey, brown sugar, cinnamon, and ginger into the skillet and mix them well. Slowly bring the mixture to a boil over *medium* heat, stirring constantly. As soon as the entire mixture comes to a *full rolling boil,* cook it vigorously for *exactly* 2 minutes. Remove the skillet from the heat and *immediately* stir in the sesame seeds until well mixed. Quickly turn out the hot mixture into the prepared pan and use a metal spatula that has been dipped into cold water to press the candy into a very smooth and even layer.

Cool the candy in the pan for 15 minutes, or until it is solid but still lukewarm. Run the spatula around the edge of the candy to loosen it. Then turn out the whole slab of candy onto a wooden board or other cutting surface. Use a sharp knife to cut the large square of warm candy into very small squares, diamonds, or rectangles.

Cool the candies completely; then store them in an airtight container at room temperature. If a professional look is desired, roll each cooled candy in a small piece of stiff cellophane and twist the ends.

Makes about 64 small candies.

MALAI (D)

(Romanian-Style Corn Bread)

Romanians are great fans of cornmeal, which they usually cook into *mamaliga* (page 366), a solid "cake" of very thick cornmeal mush. However, Romanian Jews also enjoy *malai*, another dish made with cornmeal. This moist, yeasty corn bread is sometimes baked on Friday mornings after the Shabbat challah has come from the oven, and then served as part of Friday's lunch.

Occasionally, a *pareve* or meat version of *malai* is made with water or broth and fried onions. When served during Hanukkah, this type used to be spread with *schmaltz* (rendered fat) from freshly slaughtered geese.

A dairy *malai*, such as that which follows, uses cheese and milk, and is thus also quite appropriate for Hanukkah. It tastes best right out of the oven, each piece split open and slathered with butter or spread with sour cream.

To make *malai*, Romanians usually add hot milk to the dry cornmeal mixture, and then crumble in cakes of compressed fresh yeast. The use of dry yeast and milk powder in this version is my own adaptation, and makes *malai* especially easy for modern-day cooks.

2¼ cups yellow cornmeal, preferably stone ground
¼ cup all-purpose white flour, preferably unbleached
⅔ cup instant nonfat dry milk powder
1 packet (2¼ teaspoons) active dry yeast
3 tablespoons sugar

½ teaspoon salt
1½ cups hot (120 to 130 degrees) water
2 large eggs, beaten
1 cup small-curd cottage cheese

TO SERVE (OPTIONAL)
Softened butter or commercial sour cream

In a large bowl, combine the cornmeal, flour, milk powder, yeast, sugar, and salt. Slowly add the water, while stirring, to produce a thick batter. Cover the bowl loosely with plastic wrap and let the batter rise for 15 minutes. Stir in the eggs and cottage cheese. Pour the batter into a well-buttered or non-stick spray-coated 9-inch-square pan. Bake the malai in a preheated 350-degree oven for about 50 minutes, or until it has risen slightly and is quite firm. Cut it into large squares and serve hot. If desired, cut each piece in half crosswise and top with butter or sour cream. As with most corn breads, malai tastes best when first made.

Makes about 9 servings.

KASHA MUFFINS (D)

(Muffins with Buckwheat Groats)

Although the word "kasha" can be used for almost any cereal, to Russian and Polish Jews it almost invariably means toasted buckwheat groats. Buckwheat (which, botanically, is not a grain, but a type of herb) is an extremely hearty plant that prefers a cool climate. Therefore, kasha was relatively plentiful in the *shtetls* of Eastern Europe, and it was eaten daily. Imaginative cooks used it in every possible dish, including porridge, knishes, kreplah, blintzes, strudel, and cholent.

A side dish called *kasha varnishkes* was often served on Hanukkah and other holidays. It is still a favorite of many Ashkenazic Jews. Chopped onions are sautéed in rendered poultry fat, and whole or coarsely ground kasha stirred in until it is richly browned; then boiling water is added and the groats are simmered until they are soft. Freshly made noodles, usually shaped like bow ties, are then stirred into the cooked kasha.

Another delicious treat made with kasha is the following easy muffins, which call for the *finely ground* type of groats to give the muffins a light texture. If only coarsely ground or whole kasha is available, either can be pulverized in just seconds with a blender or food processor.

As a bonus, kasha is very nutritious, with generous amounts of protein, iron, B vitamins, and fiber.

¾ *cup finely ground kasha (see*
comment above)
1 cup commercial buttermilk
¼ cup vegetable oil
2 tablespoons light or dark molasses
2 tablespoons honey

1 large egg
1½ cups whole wheat flour or
unbleached white flour
2 teaspoons baking powder
½ teaspoon baking soda
½ teaspoon salt

Put the kasha and the buttermilk into a medium-sized bowl. Let the kasha soak for 5 minutes, or until it is slightly softened and some of the buttermilk is absorbed. Add the oil, molasses, honey, and egg and stir until they are well blended. Add the flour, baking powder, soda, and salt and stir only until combined.

Divide the batter evenly among 12 greased, or non-stick spray-coated, or cupcake paper-lined muffin cups. The cups should be about three-fourths full. Bake the muffins in a preheated 400-degree oven for about 20 minutes, or until a toothpick inserted in the center of one of them comes out clean. Serve the muffins warm or at room temperature. Leftover muffins freeze well.

Makes 12 muffins.

VARIATION

KASHA-AND-APPLE MUFFINS (P)

These kasha muffins are *pareve*, and can be used with meat or dairy meals. Substitute *apple juice or cider* for the buttermilk and add *½ teaspoon ground cinnamon* and *¼ teaspoon ground allspice* to the batter. When the batter is mixed, stir in *1 peeled and diced medium-sized apple*. Bake as directed above.

SOFT PRETZELS FOR HANUKKAH (P) or (D)

Making pretzels shaped like Judaic and Hanukkah symbols can be an enjoyable project for parents and children. As the dough is formed, the story of Hanukkah can be told, and the experience can be very satisfying and educational at the same time.

Offered here are recipes for two types of pretzels. The basic dough for both contains a bit of oil to remind us of the miraculous oil which burned for eight days in the Holy Temple of Jerusalem (and it also helps keep the pretzels fresh). One type features cheese as a reminder of the story about the heroic Judith. And both types use whole grains, a good way to show children that nutritious snacks can also be delicious.

Preparation of the dough requires only a few minutes' kneading (which can be done with a heavy-duty mixer or food processor, if desired), and there's no rising or boiling in water (as with some other pretzels).

The basic recipe that follows is for *Whole Wheat Pretzels (with Cheese)*. Also included is a variation using some rye flour.

DOUGH
1 packet (2¼ teaspoons) active dry
    yeast
1 tablespoon honey or sugar (see
    Variation)
1½ cups warm (105 to 115 degrees)
    water
1 tablespoon vegetable oil
1 teaspoon salt
2 cups whole wheat flour (see
    Variation)

4 to 6 ounces sharp Cheddar cheese,
    coarsely shredded (1 to 1½ cups
    packed), optional (see Variation)
2 to 2½ cups white bread flour (or
    unbleached flour)

GLAZE AND TOPPING
1 egg, beaten with 1 teaspoon water
Coarse (kosher) salt, very coarse
    pretzel salt, or seeds, such as poppy,
    caraway, or sesame (your choice)

In a large bowl, mix the yeast and honey with the warm water. Let the mixture sit for about 5 minutes, or until it is foamy. Stir in the oil, salt, whole wheat flour, cheese (if used), and about 2 cups of the white flour, or enough to make a soft dough. Turn out onto a lightly floured board and knead it for 5 to 10 minutes, or until it is smooth and just a bit tacky. Add small amounts of flour as necessary. (Note: The dough may also be mixed and kneaded in a heavy duty mixer or in a food processor, if desired. Follow the manufacturer's directions.)

Grease or coat with non-stick spray some baking sheets. Preheat the oven to 425 degrees.

To make the pretzel shapes, pinch off a piece of dough; then roll it on a flat surface until it forms a rope that is ⅜ inch to ½ inch thick. Shape the pretzels on a flat surface; then immediately transfer each one to a greased baking sheet as soon as it is made. Keep the pretzels about 1 inch apart.

For a large, *standard-shaped pretzel,* make a rope about 20 inches long. Bend the rope into a "U" shape. Cross over the arms of the "U" to form an approximately 4-inch-diameter circular loop at the bottom. Then cross over the arms once more at the point where they intersect, so that they intertwine and each arm comes back to the side of the "U" where it first began. Finally, press the end of each arm down against the bottom curve of the "U." The completed pretzel will be upside down (Fig. 16).

FIGURE 16

For a *Hanukkah menorah* (*hanukkiyah* in Israel) with candles, first make one rope about 24 inches long. Form a very large "U" and double-twist it into a loop as if beginning a standard-shaped pretzel (see above). Move the extended arms of the "U" outward to become the top of the menorah where the candles will be placed. Bend the bottom loop into a triangular base for the menorah (Fig. 17A).

Make another rope about 19 inches long. Cut it into 9 pieces—eight 2-inch lengths, and one about 3 inches long. Set the longer piece in place above the triangular base, as the *shamash* candle (the one used to light the others). Evenly place 4 shorter candles on both sides of it. If desired, press a whole almond into the top of each candle for a "flame" (Fig. 17B).

FIGURE 17

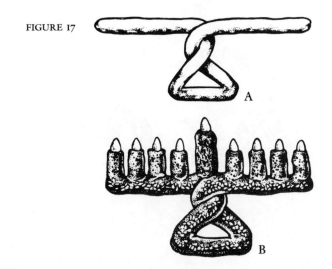

A

B

For the spinning top known as a *dreidel* (*sevivon* in Hebrew), make a rope that is 6 to 15 inches long, depending on the size of dreidel desired. Shape it into an inverted triangle, which points downward and has a flat top. Then make a short rope, and attach it to the flat top of the dreidel as a straight or looped handle. If desired, form another short rope into one of the traditional Hebrew letters—*nun, gimel, hay,* or *shin*—and put it inside the dreidel, attaching it to the sides so it will not fall out when the dreidel is baked (Fig. 18).

FIGURE 18

For a *Star of David* (*Magen David* in Hebrew), make two equal ropes, each 12 to 20 inches long. Directly on the baking sheet, form one rope into a triangle that points upward. Then form the second rope into a triangle that points downward, and place it right on top of the first one. Press the ropes together at the 6 places where they touch.

For a fancier star, lay out the first triangle as above; then weave the second rope over and under the arms of the first one, pinching its ends together to form an inverted triangle (Fig. 19).

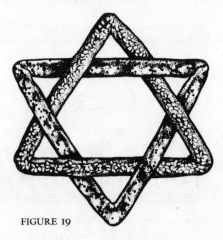

FIGURE 19

Use your imagination to create additional shapes, such as the battle shields carried by the Maccabees, an oil flask, *hai* (the Hebrew letters *het* and *yud,* meaning "life" [Fig. 20]), or a stemmed wine cup.

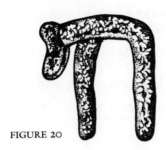

FIGURE 20

Brush the top of each pretzel with some of the egg glaze; then sprinkle it with coarse salt or your choice of seeds. Vary the seeds used on the different parts of a single pretzel, for an interesting and attractive look.

For chewy pretzels with well-defined shapes, bake them immediately, without rising, in a preheated 425-degree oven for 15 to 20 minutes, or until they are browned and well done. (They will rise slightly in the oven.)

(For softer, fatter, bread-like pretzels, let them rise in a warm place for 30 to 45 minutes, or until they are almost doubled; then bake them as above until they are lightly browned.)

Immediately remove the pretzels from the baking sheets (gently loosening them with a metal spatula, if necessary), and cool them completely on wire racks. Store them in an airtight container.

Makes about 16 large, standard-shaped pretzels; the number of holiday shapes depends on their size.

VARIATION

For *Caraway-Rye Pretzels,* substitute *light or dark molasses* for the honey, *rye flour* for the whole wheat flour, and *2 tablespoons caraway seeds* for the cheese in the dough. The remaining ingredients and the technique are the same.

MEXICAN-STYLE HOT CHOCOLATE DRINK (D)

There are almost 40,000 Jews in Mexico, most of whom live in Mexico City. When the Hanukkah menorah has been lit and it's time to relax, they may enjoy sipping some special hot chocolate, spiced with cinnamon.

In more northern climes, where Hanukkah nights are cold and blustery, this delicious drink is a perfect way to "warm up." It is sure to delight holiday guests.

1½ ounces (squares) unsweetened baking chocolate
1 cup instant nonfat dry milk powder
3 tablespoons sugar

¾ teaspoon ground cinnamon
2⅔ cups boiling water
1 large egg, beaten
1 teaspoon vanilla extract

Finely chop or grate the chocolate. Put it into a medium-sized saucepan with the milk powder, sugar, and cinnamon. Add the boiling water and stir until the chocolate is almost melted. Remove a small amount of the chocolate mixture from the pan and mix it into the beaten egg. Add this back to the rest of the chocolate mixture while stirring vigorously with a wire whisk. Stir in the vanilla extract.

Put the saucepan over medium heat and cook the mixture, whisking constantly, for about 2 to 3 minutes, or until it is hot and frothy and the chocolate is completely melted. While heating the mixture, do not allow it to come to a boil or the egg may curdle. Serve hot.

Makes 3 to 4 servings.

TU B'SHEVAT

Rosh *Hashanah Le'Ilanot*—the "New Year of the Trees"—is a minor, but joyous, festival that is commonly known by the abbreviated form of its date on the Hebrew calendar. Thus, it is usually called *Tu B'Shevat,* which is short for *Hamishah-Asar B'Shevat,* the fifteenth day of the month Shevat.

The date was used during ancient times for measuring the maturity of fruit trees in reckoning the tithe. Though it usually falls in late January or early February, when most Americans are enduring the worst of winter's chill, it is approximately the time when the sap begins to flow in Israel's previously dormant fruit trees. In fact, over two thousand years ago, the great Rabbi Hillel is said to have moved the date of the botanical "new year" from the first of the month to the fifteenth just so it would be more likely to coincide with this seasonal occurrence.

To celebrate the "New Year of the Trees," it has become customary for Jews, worldwide, to eat fruits and nuts indigenous to ancient Israel, such as almonds, carob, dates, figs, grapes, citrus, and pomegranates. Because in many areas of the Diaspora it was once difficult or even impossible to obtain fresh fruit at this time of year, dried fruit became the popular choice for the holiday.

In some Ashkenazic households, *fifteen* different types of fresh and dried fruits and nuts, symbolic of the date, are displayed and eaten throughout the day. Sephardic Jews, who sometimes call the holiday *Las Frutas* in Judeo-Spanish (or "Feast of Fruits"), may have as many as *fifty* varieties.

Another custom involves the late-night studying of passages from Jewish texts which refer to trees, fruit, and the fertility of the earth. Between sessions, it is traditional to snack on the fruits and nuts discussed. In honor of the holiday, many Americans also donate money to the Jewish National Fund's reforestation program in Israel. On Tu B'Shevat, a great number of saplings are actually planted by Israeli children, who proudly march out to the fields wearing garlands of flowers.

For the holiday, homes are often decorated with fresh flowers and foliage clippings. Some Turkish and Greek Jews, as well as other Sephardim, set out an elaborate assortment of dried fruit and nuts for guests. Children are usually allowed to take a sampling of the treats home—sometimes in special hand-made drawstring bags.

In addition, it is traditional for many Sephardim to read from a Ladino version of an ancient kabbalistic manual called, in Hebrew, *P'ri Etz Hadar* ("Fruit of the Goodly Tree"), and to perform its ritual steps for eating various types of fruit.

Actually, it is becoming increasingly popular for American Jews of all backgrounds to follow the seventeenth-century custom of a symbolic Tu B'Shevat *Seder* (or "order" of service for a ritual meal). Most "modern-day" Tu B'Shevat Seders are based on the above text (in Hebrew and English translation) but also may include readings from the Talmud, poems, and parables related to trees and the fruitfulness of Spring.

At a typical Tu B'Shevat Seder, four different types of wine (or fruit juice) are drunk, and fifteen to thirty different fruits—fresh, dried, or canned—are tasted. The fruits are typically divided into three categories of "ascending spirituality." Each fruit is cut into small pieces, and arranged on platters to be passed around. The Seder usually begins with the prayers for wine and new experiences, which are always said on holidays. During the Seder, alternating samplings of wine and fruit are interspersed with selected readings.

The first cup of wine is dry, white, and chilled, to symbolize winter when nature is slumbering and all is dry and cold. It is followed by the "lowest level" of fruit, that which has an inedible covering (such as pomegranates, almonds and other nuts, coconuts, pineapples, avocados, bananas, melons, and kiwi fruit), and represents the simple physical being: a body "covering" a soul.

The second cup of wine is very pale (such as golden sherry or very light rosé), and it signifies the early thaw as the sun beats down upon the earth and the sap begins to rise in the trees. Next, comes fruit which is edible except for a pit or stone (such as plums, prunes, dates, apricots, peaches, olives, papayas, mangoes, cherries, and carob), and symbolizes that the heart is protected or inaccessible.

The third cup of wine is more deeply colored but is still light (such as dark rosé), and is symbolic of blooming trees and seeds being sown. It is followed by the highest level of fruit, which can be eaten in its entirety (such as blueberries, strawberries, pears, apples, figs, citrus fruit with candied rind, grapes, and persimmons), and is closest to pure spiritual creation or emanation.

The fourth and final cup of wine is richly red, and represents the fertility of trees abundant with fruit, as well as crops ready to be harvested.

Children who are present at the Seder may substitute the following juices for the wines: white grape juice, apple or orange juice, cranberry juice, and purple grape juice.

Sometimes, the fruit served at a Tu B'Shevat Seder may be categorized as to whether it is fresh, dried, or canned, with nuts considered a fourth group. Also, only white and red wine may be used, and mixed together in different proportions for the second and third cups sampled at the Seder.

Some of the fruits eaten on Tu B'Shevat have their own special symbolism in Jewish folklore. The brightly colored apple, for example, represents the magnificent splendor of God. The almond shows how swiftly God punishes sinners, because the first tree to blossom in Israel is the almond, and also because it is written, in Numbers, that God made Aaron's inert staff sprout almonds as a warning to those who might challenge his right to be High Priest.

The three textures of nuts—soft, medium, and hard—signify that there are three "textures" of Jewish character. Pomegranates and figs stand for peace, prosperity and fertility. And the carob, sometimes referred to as "poor man's bread," is the symbol of humility and repentance.

There is no particular "Jewish" cuisine that is traditional for Tu B'Shevat meals. Therefore, this chapter features a variety of recipes that use many different types of dried fruits and nuts, as well as carob powder. All these items can be stored in the freezer for a year or longer, and do not need to be thawed before using. In fact, frozen dried fruits are often easier to chop (by hand) than those at room temperature, because they are less sticky.

PICADILLO (M)

(Spicy Ground Beef with Fruit and Almonds)

The flavorful meat mixture known as *picadillo* (pronounced "pee-kah-dee'-yoh") is very popular all over Latin America, particularly in Cuba and Mexico. It is sometimes used as a stuffing for green chili peppers, empanadas (turnovers), and enchiladas. And, it is eaten alone as a main course.

Serve the following version of *picadillo* with warmed-up corn tortillas, flour tortillas, or *Double Corn Bread* (page 131). Or stuff it inside *pita bread* (page 308) for a Mexican dinner with an Israeli touch.

2 pounds lean ground beef	½ teaspoon ground cinnamon
1 large onion, finely chopped	¼ teaspoon ground cloves
2 to 3 garlic cloves, minced	⅛ to ¼ teaspoon ground cumin
1 16-ounce can tomatoes, including juice, finely chopped	½ teaspoon salt
2 medium-sized apples, peeled (if desired) and diced	⅛ teaspoon black pepper, preferably freshly ground
1 medium-sized sweet green pepper, diced (optional)	⅔ cup pimiento-stuffed green olives, cut in half crosswise
½ cup dark raisins	½ cup slivered almonds, preferably toasted
½ teaspoon chili powder	

In a very large deep skillet, over medium-high heat, brown the meat with the onion and garlic, breaking up the meat with a fork. When the meat has browned and the onion is tender, drain and discard all excess fat from the pan. Add all the remaining ingredients, except the olives and almonds.

Lower the heat slightly and cook, uncovered, stirring occasionally, for about 30 minutes, or until most of the liquid has evaporated from the pan. Add the olives and almonds, and stir about 2 minutes longer, or until they are heated through.

Makes about 6 servings.

MEAT, FRUIT, AND PEANUT CURRY (M)

The unusual mélange of people in South Africa—native Africans, Malaysians, Indians, Dutch, British, French, and Ashkenazic Jews—has produced an intriguing selection of delectable local dishes, such as this stew, which is quite appropriate to serve on Tu B'Shevat. Similar curries are often eaten by South African Jews throughout the year.

2 tablespoons vegetable oil
1 medium-sized onion, finely chopped
1½ pounds chuck or other beef stew meat (or boneless lamb shoulder), trimmed of all excess fat and cut into 1-inch cubes
1½ cups water
2 tablespoons lemon juice or apple cider vinegar
1 tablespoon curry powder
½ teaspoon salt
¼ teaspoon ground ginger

¼ teaspoon ground cinnamon
1 8-ounce package mixed dried fruits (or a combination of dried apples, prunes, dried apricots, and/or dried pears)
½ cup dark raisins
2 small just-ripe bananas
½ cup roasted peanuts or cashews, preferably unsalted

TO SERVE
Hot cooked white or brown rice

In a very large deep skillet, over medium-high heat, heat the oil; then sauté the onion until it is tender but not browned. Push the onion to one side of the skillet and add the meat cubes. Brown them on all sides. While they are browning, combine the water, lemon juice, curry powder, salt, ginger, and cinnamon in a large measuring cup. When the meat has browned, add the liquid mixture to the skillet along with the mixed dried fruits and raisins. Stir so that the onion, meat, and fruit are evenly distributed.

Bring the liquid to a boil; then cover the skillet tightly and lower the heat so that the liquid just simmers. Cook the curry, stirring occasionally, for about 1 hour, or until the meat and fruits are very tender, and the liquid has formed a thick sauce. (If the skillet cooks dry before the meat is tender, add a bit of water.) Dice one of the bananas and stir it gently into the curry.

Transfer the curry to a large serving platter. Cut the second banana into thin crosswise slices and put the slices around the curry as a garnish. Sprinkle the peanuts on top. Serve the curry with hot cooked rice.

Makes about 6 servings.

ISRAELI-STYLE CHICKEN WITH
KUMQUATS (OR APRICOTS) (M)

In Israel, fruit is often cooked with chicken or meat to produce delicious dishes, such as this one, which has been adapted from a recipe by Israeli author Molly Lyons Bar-David. The light, orange sauce has some chopped chili peppers (or a bit of hot pepper seasoning) added for piquancy.

Preserved kumquats for the dish can be homemade (see the recipe on page 191) or purchased from a gourmet specialty store. If preserved kumquats are not available, dried apricots may be substituted. The latter should be soaked in orange juice before they are cooked, so that they don't absorb all the liquid in the skillet.

About 3 pounds meaty chicken pieces (remove skin, if desired)
All-purpose white flour, preferably unbleached
2 tablespoons pareve margarine
1 small onion, finely chopped
1¼ cups orange juice
3 tablespoons honey
¼ teaspoon powdered mustard
½ teaspoon salt
1 to 2 tablespoons chopped fresh or canned chili peppers (or about ⅛ teaspoon hot red pepper sauce), or to taste

10 to 15 drained, preserved whole kumquats (see comment above), OR dried apricots that have been soaked in orange juice until plump
¼ cup whole (or slivered) blanched almonds (optional)

TO SERVE (OPTIONAL)
Hot cooked white or brown rice

Lightly coat the chicken pieces with the flour. Set them aside momentarily.

In a very large deep skillet, over medium-high heat, melt the margarine; then sauté the onion until it is tender but not browned. Add the chicken and cook it until it is browned on all sides.

In a small cup, combine the orange juice, honey, powdered mustard, salt, and hot pepper sauce, and pour this over the chicken. Bring the liquid to a boil. Cover the skillet tightly; then lower the heat and simmer the chicken for 30 minutes, basting often with the cooking juices. Scatter the kumquats (or apricots) around the chicken and continue cooking, covered, for 20 to 25 minutes longer, or until the chicken is very tender.

Use a slotted spoon to transfer the chicken and fruit to a serving platter. If the sauce remaining in the skillet is too thin, raise the heat and rapidly boil it down to the desired consistency. Stir in the almonds, if desired. Pour the sauce over the chicken and serve. Accompany with rice, if desired.

Makes about 5 servings.

PRESERVED WHOLE KUMQUATS   (P)

The kumquat is a tiny, bright-orange citrus fruit that looks something like a miniature elongated orange. Unlike any other citrus, it has a tender, sweet rind and slightly tart flesh. Thus, it is usually eaten whole, and is used to garnish all sorts of foods. Occasionally, kumquats are made into attractive appetizers by halving them, and removing the pulp. The edible shell is then stuffed with a slightly sweetened cream cheese mixture or other filling.

In Israel, which is known worldwide for its citrus fruits, kumquats are often preserved when they are plentiful, so they can be eaten year round. Preserved kumquats can be served whole (or halved) with meat or poultry (see the recipe for *Israeli-style Chicken with Kumquats,* page 190), or they may be chopped and used in cake fillings, ice cream, and other desserts. If desired, their syrup can also be used as a flavoring.

Among some Sephardim, preserved whole kumquats may be offered to special guests on *la tavla de dulce,* the traditional "tray of sweets," which usually contains an assortment of homemade preserves, confitures, and marmalades. The "sweets" are put into beautiful glass bowls, and attractively arranged on the hostess' most splendid tray. This is passed around, along with silver teaspoons, which guests use to sample the *dulce* of their choosing. Small cups of rich Turkish coffee and a variety of sweet pastries are generally served with the *dulce.*

(Note: In the United States, kumquats are typically "in season" from late fall through early spring, and are available at several supermarkets and gourmet grocery stores.)

2 cups cold water	1 pound (about 4 cups) fresh
1¼ cups sugar	kumquats, washed and stems
¼ cup honey	removed

In a heavy 2-quart saucepan, combine the water, sugar, and honey, and heat over medium-high heat, stirring occasionally, until the sugar dissolves. Bring the syrup to a boil; then lower the heat and gently boil the syrup, uncovered and undisturbed, for 10 minutes.

Meanwhile, use a small, sharp knife to cut a ¼-inch-deep "X" in the blossom end (opposite the stem end) of each kumquat.

When the syrup is ready, add the kumquats and stir them so they are well coated with the syrup. Gently boil the kumquats, uncovered, swirling the pan occasionally to make sure the kumquats cook evenly, for 30 minutes to 1 hour, or until the kumquat skins look translucent. Remove the pan from the heat and immediately cover it tightly. Let the kumquats cool in the covered pan for at least 1 hour without disturbing them. (This helps to keep the kumquats plump, as they tend to "collapse" while cooling.)

When the kumquats are cool, ladle them into sterilized jars. Tightly cover the jars and store them in the refrigerator. Kumquats in sealed jars will keep for about 1 year in the refrigerator.

To use the kumquats, remove them from the jar with a small spoon, allowing any excess syrup to drain back into the jar. If desired, cut the kumquats in half and take out any seeds.

Makes about 3½ cups.

DRIED-FRUIT LOKSHEN KUGEL (P)

(Noodle "Pudding")

Lokshen kugel is popular all through the year, but this delectable one is especially appropriate for Tu B'Shevat. It is not overly sweet, and makes a perfect side dish for a holiday dinner or buffet meal.

1 8-ounce package medium-wide egg	4 large eggs
noodles	⅓ cup sugar
4 tablespoons vegetable oil, divided	1 cup orange juice

¼ teaspoon ground cinnamon
⅛ teaspoon ground ginger
Pinch of salt
¾ to 1 cup diced mixed dried fruits,
 such as prunes, apricots, dates,
 and/or figs

¼ cup dark or light raisins
1 medium-sized apple, peeled (if
 desired) and diced (about 1 cup)

Cook the noodles according to the package directions. Drain them well; then put them in a bowl (or back into the pot), and toss them with 2 tablespoons of the oil to keep them from sticking together. Set aside to cool slightly.

In a large bowl, beat the eggs with the sugar until well mixed. Beat in the remaining 2 tablespoons of oil. Then beat in the orange juice, cinnamon, ginger, and salt. Add the mixed dried fruits, raisins, and apple. Add the cooked noodles and stir until all the ingredients are evenly distributed. Transfer the noodle mixture to a greased or non-stick spray-coated 10-inch-square casserole or equivalent. Cover the casserole with a lid or aluminum foil and bake the kugel in a preheated 350-degree oven for 40 minutes. Remove the lid or foil and bake the kugel, uncovered, for 10 to 20 minutes longer, or until it seems to be firm and set. Let it cool slightly before cutting it into squares to serve. Serve warm or at room temperature.

Makes about 9 servings.

KOFYAS (P)

(Sephardic-Style "Wheat Berry" Pudding)

Sephardic Jews from Turkey often eat this dessert on the evening of Tu B'Shevat, and say the prayer in which we thank God for wheat. Similar wheat puddings called *suffah, prehito,* and *trigo kotcho* may also be prepared by Sephardim for this holiday. Often, chopped dry fruits are added to the basic, sweetened wheat mixture.

Some Greek Jews make an almost identical wheat pudding called *kolliva,* which they may serve on the first evening of Rosh Hashanah because the honey symbolizes a sweet year and the expanding wheat grains represent the growth and sustenance of life.

Occasionally, either bulgur or cracked wheat is substituted for the whole grains of wheat known as "wheat berries." (A variation using bulgur wheat follows below.)

Because the cooked whole wheat berries resemble tiny teeth, *kofyas* is also served to celebrate the appearance of a baby's first tooth. Sometimes, the "lucky" person who discovered the new tooth prepares the pudding. For this same occasion, Syrian Jews make *slihah,* a sweet wheat pudding which contains raisins, caraway seeds, and pistachios or walnuts. And some North African Jews make a very similar barley pudding called *be- lila,* that features pine nuts, almonds, and pistachios, and is flavored with rose water.

(Note: Whole wheat berries are available at most Greek or Middle Eastern groceries and some health-food stores.)

1 cup whole wheat berries	*¼ cup chopped dates (optional)*
4 cups cold water	*¼ cup dark raisins, plumped in*
¼ cup honey	*water (optional)*
½ teaspoon ground cinnamon	*1 cup coarsely chopped walnuts*

Put the wheat berries and water into a large saucepan and bring to boil over high heat. Cover tightly, lower the heat, and simmer the wheat berries for 2 to 3 hours, or until they have split open and are only slightly chewy. Drain off any excess water. Add the honey, cinnamon, dates (if used), and raisins (if used) to the cooked wheat berries and stir over low heat for about 2 minutes. Remove from the heat and stir in the walnuts. Serve warm or at room temperature.

Makes 4 to 6 servings.

VARIATION

For a much quicker wheat pudding that has a slightly similar taste to the one made with wheat berries, but a completely different texture, sub- stitute *1 cup bulgur wheat* for the wheat berries. Simmer the bulgur in only *2 cups boiling water* for about 12 minutes, or until all the water has been absorbed. Then continue as above. (Cracked wheat may be used in place of bulgur, but it will take slightly longer to cook.)

FUDGIEST-EVER CAROB BROWNIES (D) or (P)

While in Israel a few years ago, I made a determined search for whole carobs, and finally found some of the brownish-black, dried pods at the Arab market in Jerusalem. Since then, I have seen them occasionally at specialty stores in the United States.

Carob pods come from an evergreen tree which is indigenous to the Mediterranean area but also found in many other parts of the world. The dried pods are usually 6 to 7 inches long and about 1 inch wide, and are flat and leathery looking. They are sweet and very chewy, with a flavor vaguely similar to chocolate. My children and I find them quite appealing, but my husband, like many other people, has reservations.

Carob became particularly traditional on Tu B'Shevat for Jews in Eastern European *shtetls* because it was one of the few "fruits" from Israel that was available during mid-winter. In the wonderful Yiddish stories of writer Sholom Aleichem, dried carob pods were the *bokser* that young children, particularly *yeshiva* boys, often enjoyed as special treats.

Since dried carob pods keep almost indefinitely in the freezer, I store several there, and take out a few each year just for Tu B'Shevat. However, I have found that most people prefer to eat baked goods made from carob powder, which is available at most health-food stores.

Following is a recipe for rich, moist, fudgy carob brownies that are sure to delight everyone. But please, don't compare them to chocolate brownies! Carob has a unique flavor that should be enjoyed on its own merits.

½ cup butter or margarine
⅔ cup sugar
1 large egg (see Note)
1 teaspoon vanilla extract
½ cup carob powder, preferably the "dark" style (sifted, if lumpy)

½ cup all-purpose white flour, preferably unbleached (or whole wheat flour)
¼ teaspoon baking soda
1 cup coarsely broken walnuts

In a medium-sized saucepan (or medium-sized microwave-proof bowl), melt the butter over medium heat (or in the microwave oven on high). Remove the melted butter from the heat. Stir in all the remaining ingredients, except the walnuts, and mix until very well combined. Then stir in the walnuts until evenly distributed. The batter will be very thick.

Turn out the batter into a greased or non-stick spray-coated 9-inch-square baking pan and spread it evenly. It will not be very deep. Bake in a preheated 350-degree oven for about 20 minutes, or until a toothpick inserted in the center comes out clean. Cool the brownies in the pan on a wire rack; then cut them into squares.

Makes 25 small or 16 larger brownies.

NOTE: If the number of eggs is increased to 2, the brownies will be less fudgy and more cake-like.

DRIED-FRUIT STRUDEL (D) or (P)

Most of the filling ingredients for this delectable treat have been specifically chosen because of their association with Israel, where this type of *strudel* is a very popular Tu B'Shevat dessert.

However, other nuts and dried fruits, such as chopped dried apricots, prunes, papaya, pineapple, and apples, can be substituted. Actually, some of the dried fruit-nut mixtures available in bulk at many supermarkets and health-food stores would probably be suitable. Whatever the choice, the combination of chopped dried fruits, nuts and coconut should measure 5½ to 6 cups.

This recipe uses the classic method of stretching dough, which is explained in detail below. If the directions are followed carefully, even those who have never tried this technique before should be successful—and produce very satisfying results.

(Note: *Strudel* is sometimes made with purchased "filo dough" or "strudel leaves." For a strudel using this technique, see the recipe for *Easy Viennese Apple-Nut Strudel,* page 132.)

DOUGH
1 large egg
¼ teaspoon salt
½ cup tepid water
2 tablespoons butter or margarine,
  melted, or vegetable oil
Approximately 2 cups all-purpose
  unbleached white flour

FILLING
1 cup dark or light raisins or
  currants
1 cup chopped dates
1 cup chopped dried figs
½ cup chopped candied citrus peel
  (orange, lemon, or grapefruit),
  OR 2 tablespoons grated fresh
  citrus rind (colored part only)

1 cup shredded or flaked coconut
1 cup slivered or chopped almonds
½ cup chopped walnuts or pecans
⅓ cup orange juice or sweet wine
4 large eggs, separated
Approximately ½ cup butter or
  margarine (preferably unsalted),
  melted
¼ cup graham cracker crumbs, dried
  cookie or cake crumbs, or plain
  bread crumbs
3 tablespoons packed dark or light
  brown sugar
¼ teaspoon cream of tartar
⅓ cup granulated sugar

GARNISH (OPTIONAL)
Confectioner's sugar

For the dough, use a fork to beat the egg with the salt, water, and melted butter. Gradually add the flour, while stirring with the fork, until a soft dough forms. Begin kneading the dough in the bowl, adding a little extra flour if the dough becomes sticky.

Turn out the dough onto a lightly floured surface and continue kneading, occasionally lifting the dough and slapping it down hard against the surface. After about 10 to 15 minutes, the dough should lose all stickiness and become very smooth and elastic. It may also have some blisters under the surface. Form the dough into a smooth ball and wrap it in plastic wrap. Cover the dough with an inverted bowl and let it rest, in a warm place if possible, for 30 to 45 minutes.

Meanwhile, begin to make the filling. Put the raisins, dates, figs, candied (or fresh) peel, coconut, almonds, and walnuts into a large bowl and mix. Then add the juice and mix again. When the dough is almost ready, beat the egg yolks lightly and add them to the fruit-nut mixture, combining well. Put the egg whites into a clean mixing bowl, but do not beat them yet.

Cover a large surface (such as a kitchen table) with a smooth tablecloth or sheet and flour the cloth lightly. Using a rolling pin, roll out the scantily floured dough as thinly as possible into a square. Brush the top of the dough with melted butter. Remove all jewelry from your hands and lightly flour your fists.

With your palms facing down, reach under the dough, and very gently stretch it from underneath using the backs and bent knuckles of both your hands, but not your fingertips. Continuously work all around the dough, starting in the center and moving toward the edges, trying to keep the thickness of the dough even. (Don't be concerned about the slightly thicker edge which tends to form around the perimeter of the dough.) Pinch the dough promptly to patch any small holes before they are stretched into larger ones.

You should be able to stretch the dough into a translucent 2½- to 3-foot square. (Experts may be able to make it even larger!) Use kitchen shears or a sharp knife to trim off any very thick edges.

Brush the entire surface of the dough with melted butter. Mix together the crumbs and brown sugar and evenly sprinkle them over the dough. Let the dough rest briefly while you complete the filling.

Beat the reserved egg whites with the cream of tartar until frothy; then gradually add the granulated sugar and continue beating the whites until they form stiff, shiny peaks. Fold the whites into the fruit-nut mixture until combined. Heap the filling along one edge of the stretched dough square, keeping it about 4 inches from that edge and 1 to 2 inches from each side.

To roll the strudel, use both hands to lift up the cloth so the uncovered 4-inch margin of dough flips over the filling, enclosing it. Continue lifting the cloth so that the strudel evenly rolls up away from you. Tuck under the two ends of the roll so that the filling cannot come out.

Carefully transfer the strudel, seam side down, to a very large greased or non-stick spray-coated baking sheet (or the bottom of an inverted roasting pan), gently bending the roll into a horseshoe or loose spiral so it can fit on the baking sheet. Generously brush the outer surface of the strudel with butter.

Bake the strudel in a preheated 375-degree oven for about 35 minutes, or until the top is browned and crisp. If desired, baste the roll with any leftover melted butter or margarine about halfway through the baking period.

Cut the baked strudel, on the baking sheet, into 1½- to 2-inch sections while it is still warm. If desired, sprinkle the top with sieved confectioner's sugar just before serving. Serve warm or at room temperature.

Leftovers may be reheated in a 375-degree oven until warmed through and crisp.

Makes 15 or more servings.

CAROB LAYER CAKE WITH CAROB ICING (D)

This is rich and luxurious and a perfect treat for celebrating the "New Year of the Trees." If desired, the top can be decorated with several of the dried fruits, nuts, and seeds eaten on Tu B'Shevat.

CAKE BATTER
½ cup butter or margarine, slightly softened
1¼ cups granulated sugar
2 large eggs
1 teaspoon vanilla extract
¾ cup carob powder, preferably the "dark" style (sifted, if lumpy)
2¼ cups all-purpose white flour, preferably unbleached
1 teaspoon baking soda

1 teaspoon baking powder
1½ cups commercial buttermilk

CAROB ICING
⅓ cup butter, softened
3 cups confectioner's sugar
½ cup carob powder, preferably the "dark" style (sifted, if lumpy)
⅓ cup hot milk, any type
½ teaspoon vanilla extract

For the cake, grease or coat with non-stick spray two 8- or 9-inch-round cake pans. Line the bottom of each pan with a circle of wax paper, then grease or spray the paper. Set the pans aside.

In a large mixing bowl, use an electric mixer at medium speed to cream the butter with the sugar until light and fluffy. Add the eggs, one at a time, beating well after each addition. Beat in the vanilla.

In a separate bowl (or on a large piece of wax paper), combine the carob powder, flour, baking soda, and baking powder. Sift the carob-flour mixture together, making sure any lumps have been pressed out of the carob powder. Add the carob-flour mixture to the batter alternately with the buttermilk, mixing after each addition.

Pour the batter into the prepared pans and smooth the top. Bake in a preheated 350-degree oven for 30 to 35 minutes, or until a toothpick inserted in the center of a cake comes out clean and the cake is beginning to come away from the sides of the pan. Cool the cakes in the pans on wire racks for about 5 minutes. Unmold the cakes onto the racks, remove the wax paper, and let the cakes cool completely before icing and assembling them.

For the icing, use an electric mixer to beat the butter until it is light and fluffy. Then add the remaining ingredients and beat until they are completely mixed and the icing does not taste or feel gritty. If it is too thick, beat in a bit more milk; if too thin, add more confectioner's sugar. Spread the icing between the cake layers and over the exterior of the cake. Use the back of a spoon to make peaks and swirls in the icing, if desired.

Makes 1 large layer cake; about 10 to 12 servings.

APRICOT-FIG BARS (D) or (P)

Fruit and nut filling tops the crunchy base of these rich squares, which make a great holiday snack or dessert.

BOTTOM CRUST
1 cup all-purpose white flour,
 preferably unbleached (or whole
 wheat flour)
¼ cup granulated sugar
½ cup butter or margarine, softened

TOP LAYER
½ cup all-purpose white flour,
 preferably unbleached (or whole
 wheat flour)

¼ cup packed dark brown sugar
2 large eggs
1 teaspoon vanilla extract
½ teaspoon baking powder
½ cup finely chopped dried apricots
½ cup finely chopped dried figs
½ cup slivered almonds

For the bottom crust, combine all the ingredients in a mixing bowl or a food processor (fitted with the steel blade) and mix or pulse-process until they are completely combined and crumbly. Press the mixture evenly into the bottom of an ungreased 9-inch-square baking pan. Bake the crust in a preheated 350-degree oven for about 20 minutes, or until it is very lightly browned.

Meanwhile, prepare the top layer. In the same bowl as above, combine the ½ cup flour, brown sugar, eggs, vanilla extract, and baking powder.

Beat or process until very well mixed. Add the dried fruits and almonds, and mix just until stirred in.

When the bottom crust is lightly browned, remove it from the oven and evenly spread the fruit-nut mixture over it. Return the pan to the 350-degree oven and bake for about 25 minutes longer, or until the top layer is firm. Remove from the oven and cool completely in the pan on a rack. When cool, cut into squares.

Makes 16 squares.

CAROB DROP COOKIES (D)

These cookies, which have a soft, cake-like texture, form smooth, rounded tops as they bake. When they are completely cool, the flat bottoms of half the cookies can be spread with your favorite icing and paired with the remainder to form filled cookie "sandwiches."

½ cup butter or margarine, softened
⅔ cup sugar
1 large egg
½ teaspoon vanilla extract
½ cup commercial buttermilk
½ cup cold water
½ cup carob powder, preferably the
  "dark" style (sifted, if lumpy)

1 teaspoon baking soda
½ teaspoon baking powder
¼ teaspoon salt
2 cups all-purpose white flour,
  preferably unbleached

In a medium-sized mixing bowl, cream the butter and sugar with an electric mixer at medium speed. Beat in the egg and the vanilla extract. Add the buttermilk, water, and carob powder and beat until well combined. Add the baking soda, powder, salt, and flour and beat until completely incorporated into the batter.

Using a measuring tablespoon of batter per cookie, drop the batter into rounded mounds about 2 inches apart on greased or non-stick spray-coated baking sheets. Bake in a preheated 400-degree oven for 8 to 10 minutes, or until the top of a cookie springs back when lightly touched in the center. Use a metal spatula or pancake turner to remove the cookies from the baking sheet and cool them completely on a wire rack.

Makes about 24 cookies.

CREAMY DATE PUDDING WITH WALNUTS (D)

Dates give this very easy and nutritious dessert a delicious sweet taste.

2 cups cold water
⅔ cup instant nonfat dry milk
    powder
1 large egg
Generous ½ cup pitted dates, cut in
    half (about 4 ounces)

2 tablespoons honey
2½ tablespoons cornstarch
½ teaspoon vanilla extract
¼ cup finely chopped walnuts

Put all the ingredients, except the walnuts, into a blender or a food processor (fitted with the steel blade) and process until the dates are finely chopped. Pour the mixture into a 2½-quart or similar saucepan over medium heat. Cook the pudding, stirring constantly, until it thickens and just comes to a boil. Remove the pan from the heat and pour the pudding into individual small bowls. Sprinkle the walnuts on top. Cool the pudding slightly at room temperature; then refrigerate it. Serve chilled.

Makes about 5 servings.

CAROB-SESAME HALVAH (P)

This confection is a wonderful snack to have on hand in the refrigerator, since it makes a quick, nutritious snack. In addition to carob, it features three other Israeli favorites—sunflower seeds, sesame seeds, and tahini. All are available at most health-food stores, as well as at many supermarkets. Be sure to stir the tahini well before using it, as the sesame oil from the paste tends to float to the top. If the tahini is refrigerated after being well mixed, it will not settle out as easily. Tahini will keep up to a year (or longer) in the refrigerator.

¼ cup finely shredded unsweetened
    coconut
⅓ cup rolled oats, any type
¼ cup unsalted sunflower seeds
3 tablespoons tahini (pure sesame
    paste)

2 tablespoons honey
2 tablespoons carob powder,
    preferably the "dark" style (sifted,
    if lumpy)
¼ teaspoon ground cinnamon
About ¼ cup sesame seeds

Put the coconut, rolled oats, and sunflower seeds in a food processor (fitted with the steel blade) or a blender and process until powdery. Transfer the mixture to a bowl and add the tahini, honey, carob powder, and cinnamon. Mix to form a stiff mass. Knead with your hand or a wooden spoon for a few minutes, or until smooth and malleable. If the mixture is very dry, add a bit more honey or tahini.

Form the mixture into 2 logs, each about 1 inch in diameter and about 6 inches long. Roll each log in sesame seeds so the outside is completely coated. Wrap the logs in plastic wrap and refrigerate them for several hours, or until they are firm. (They can be stored in the refrigerator for a week or longer.)

To serve the halvah, cut each log crosswise into slices approximately ½ inch thick.

Makes about 2 dozen pieces.

FRUIT-NUT CONFECTION BALLS (P)

Several of the dried fruits favored on Tu B'Shevat are featured in this easy uncooked treat, which is loved by young and old alike.

½ cup dried apricots
½ cup pitted dates
½ cup dried figs
½ cup pitted prunes
½ cup walnut pieces

¼ cup shredded coconut, preferably
* unsweetened*
2 tablespoons honey (or as needed)
Granulated sugar (optional)

Finely chop the apricots, dates, figs, prunes, and walnuts in a food processor (fitted with the steel blade), or put them through the coarse blade of a food grinder (the nuts will help push the sticky fruit through). Or, if desired, finely chop them by hand.

Stir in the coconut and honey and mix until well combined. If the mixture seems very crumbly, add honey as needed, but do not use too much or it will become very sticky.

Form the mixture into compact 1-inch-diameter balls and, if desired, roll each one in sugar to coat it. Store in the refrigerator, but serve at room temperature for the best taste.

Makes about 3 dozen balls.

PURIM

When it comes to having lots of light-hearted, good-natured fun, Purim is one holiday that really stands out! Young and old alike enjoy the masquerade and mockery that highlight the day, as well as the delicious food gifts exchanged among family and friends.

Purim celebrates the triumph of ancient Persian Jews over their arch-enemy, Haman, as related in the Scroll of Esther, or the *Megillah* (Hebrew, for "scroll"), as it is usually called.

Haman was an ambitious and conniving minister who gained enormous power by taking advantage of the easily influenced King Ahasuerus. When the king commanded that everyone in the kingdom must bow down to Haman, a Jew named Mordecai refused. This infuriated the anti-Semitic Haman, who convinced the king that all the Jews were disloyal and should be exterminated on a date determined by the casting of "lots" or, in Hebrew, *purim.*

Neither Haman nor the king knew that the beautiful and much beloved Queen Esther was a Jew, and also Mordecai's cousin. When Esther learned of the plot, she prepared a great feast for the king and Haman, and, at the risk of her own life, told the king that Haman wanted to have her and all her people killed.

The king finally recognized that Haman was the real danger, and had him hung on gallows which Haman had prepared for Modecai. The king also allowed the Jews to take vengeance on their enemies on precisely the date set for their destruction—the thirteenth of Adar. On the following day, the Jews in most of Persia rejoiced over their deliverance. But, in the capital city Shushan, fighting continued for another day, and so celebration there did not occur until the fifteenth.

It has become customary for most of the world's Jews to observe Purim on the fourteenth day of the Hebrew month of Adar, (which usually occurs in March). However, those who live in cities that were surrounded by walls in ancient times, as was Shushan, celebrate on the *next* day, which is called *Shushan Purim.*

Thus, Israelis living in Jerusalem are supposed to have their Purim festivities on a different day than those in Tel Aviv. Actually, the holiday is such a major event in Israel that many people celebrate *both* days, just in case their home may have once been inside a walled city!

A huge carnival and parade called *Ad'lo'yada* is held annually in Tel Aviv. The name comes from the Talmudic suggestion that one should drink enough wine on Purim so as "not to be able to distinguish" between the names of Mordecai and Haman.

Worldwide, the drinking of wine (or, perhaps, spiked punch made with *arak* or *raki*) is just one way that Jews enjoy the happy and jovial spirit of this day. Children and adults also dress in masquerade, and often act out spoofs, called *Purimshpiels* in Yiddish, which poke fun at everyone, even rabbis.

For breakfast on Purim, a bread fritter moistened in milk and coated with beaten egg, and sometimes called "Queen Esther's Toast," is eaten by some Sephardim. Quite similar to what Americans call "French toast," this fritter is also served throughout the year to new mothers.

In the afternoon, near the end of the holiday, a feast called a *Purim Se'udah* is held. Merriment is the keynote of the meal, and singing, joking, and silliness are encouraged just this once, making it a particular favorite among youngsters.

Kreplah (page 78) are usually on the menu, as they are for the pre-fast Yom Kippur dinner and for Hoshanah Rabbah. Also, the *challah* (see pages 17 and 64) is often shaped into a tremendous braid called a *keylitsh,* which symbolizes the rope used to hang Haman. The length of the loaf may be six feet or longer!

Purim is also a time to give charity and exchange edible presents, because Mordecai says in the *Megillah* that the holiday should be observed as "a day of feasting and gladness, and of sending portions, one to another, and gifts to the poor." The "rule," according to tradition, is to send at least two portions of ready-to-eat food to each relative and friend and also give some money to at least two less fortunate people.

In some places, the custom of "sending portions"—in Hebrew, *mishloah manot* (or *shalah manot,* as it is more commonly called)—is elegantly executed on beautiful platters wrapped in rich cloths. On display at the

Israel Museum in Jerusalem is a magnificent nineteenth-century silver plate from Austria that was used only for *shalah manot*. It is designed in the shape of a fish, symbolic of the month of Adar. More commonplace, nowadays, are cardboard boxes decorated specifically for Purim food exchange.

In some communities, particularly in Israel, *shalah manot* is a major undertaking, with the preparation of baked goods beginning several weeks ahead of the holiday. Many of the sweet treats made for Rosh Hashanah and Hanukkah are also popular for Purim. These may include, for instance, *loukoumades,* which are sometimes called "Purim puffs," *taygleh* or *pinyonati, hadgi badam,* and *zelebi* (pages 164, 99, 100, and 168). In addition, Iraqi Jews make a dry, rolled type of baklava called *malfoof* and a star-shaped coconut macaroon known as *masafan.*

Some Purim specialties which mock Haman are the Ashkenazic triangular cakes called *hamantaschen* (page 214), Sephardic fried pastries known as *orejas de haman* or "Haman's ears" (page 216), very fine egg noodles tossed with lemon sauce and called *caveos di aman* or "Haman's hair," and evil-looking gingerbread Hamans baked by some Dutch and Scandinavian Jews.

Costumed children, particularly in Israel, often have the "chore" of delivering food gifts. They are frequently rewarded for their labors with special holiday goodies. Among many Sephardic Jews, these treats may include *huevos de haman,* hard-cooked eggs which are each baked inside a pastry basket that may be decorated to depict some aspect of the Purim story.

The recipes in this chapter include a wealth of "goodies" that are ideal for *shalah manot,* and also several dishes for a jovial *Purim Se'udah.* Many are served specifically on Purim because of additional holiday symbolism, which is described with the specific recipe.

ISRAELI-STYLE TURKEY SCHNITZEL   (M)

Turkey is traditionally eaten on Purim because it represents King Ahasuerus. The turkey, considered to be the most foolish fowl, is called *tarnegol hodu* in Hebrew, which literally translates as "cock of India." Likewise, it is written that the oft foolish King Ahasuerus "reigned from India unto Ethiopia."

In the following recipe, turkey looks and tastes remarkably like veal. In Israel, where turkey is plentiful and less expensive than most other meats, restaurants are more likely to offer this version than the "authentic" wiener schnitzel. And, many people (including my family) actually prefer it.

For the best results, the turkey breast cutlets used should be about ⅜ to ½ inch thick. They can be purchased prepackaged at some supermarkets or a butcher can cut them from a whole turkey breast.

1½ pounds thinly sliced, boneless raw
turkey breast cutlets
About ¼ cup all-purpose white flour,
preferably unbleached
2 large eggs
1 tablespoon water
About 1¼ cups fine dry bread
crumbs, seasoned to taste with salt,
black pepper, garlic powder,
chopped parsley leaves, and other
herbs, if desired
Vegetable oil for frying

TO SERVE
Sprigs of fresh parsley leaves
1 lemon, cut into wedges

Put the turkey cutlets between 2 sheets of heavy plastic wrap and pound them with a rubber mallet, rolling pin, or meat mallet until they are about half their original thickness. Be careful not to tear the meat. Lightly coat each piece with flour, shaking off any excess.

In a small bowl, beat the eggs with the water. Dip each cutlet into the egg mixture and let the excess drip off. Then immediately coat the cutlet with the seasoned bread crumbs and set it aside on a large platter or a piece of wax paper. For best results, let the cutlets dry for 20 to 30 minutes at room temperature before frying them. (They may be made several hours ahead up to this point and refrigerated.)

In a large skillet, over medium-high heat, heat oil ⅛ to ¼ inch deep, until it is hot but not smoking. In batches, brown the cutlets on both sides. This will take only 2 to 3 minutes on each side; do not overcook the cutlets or the meat may toughen. Drain the cutlets on paper towels. Then transfer them to a serving platter and garnish them with the parsley and lemon wedges.

Makes about 6 servings.

SALOONA (P)

(Salmon and Vegetables in Sweet-Sour Sauce)

Sweet-and-sour dishes are sometimes eaten on Purim because of the dual nature of the episode in Jewish history commemorated by this holiday. When Haman announced to the Jews that they were to be killed, there was much sadness and grief. However, when the tables were turned, and Haman was hanged instead, the Jews were able to celebrate with great joy.

The following delectable recipe is from Bellah Ini, an Iraqi Jew who often prepares it for Shabbat and other holidays.

After Israel became a state, life became difficult for many Jews living in Arab countries. Such was the case for Mrs. Ini, her husband, and young children, and so they left their native Iraq and emigrated to Israel in 1951. A further move in 1975 brought Mrs. Ini to the United States.

To this day, she still prefers to cook the Iraqi-Jewish cuisine she learned as a young bride. Though she now lives alone, Mrs. Ini often prepares whole Iraqi-style meals, which she shares with her very appreciative children and grandchildren. *Saloona* is one of her specialties.

Other types of fish can be used in the recipe; however, Mrs. Ini prefers salmon, because its flavor goes well with the sauce. Also, all the vegetables, except the onions and tomato, are optional and may be omitted. However, when several vegetables are used, this dish is hearty enough to be a main course.

SAUCE
½ cup plain canned tomato sauce
3 tablespoons granulated white or packed light brown sugar
3 tablespoons white vinegar or apple cider vinegar
2 tablespoons lemon juice
1 garlic clove, finely minced
1 teaspoon curry powder

FISH AND VEGETABLES
1 pound skinless salmon fillets (or about 1¼ pounds salmon steaks)
All-purpose white flour for coating

Vegetable oil for frying
2 *medium-sized onions, halved and thickly sliced*
1 *medium-sized sweet green pepper, cut into strips*
1 *medium-sized carrot, very thinly sliced on the diagonal*
1 *celery stalk, thinly sliced*
1 *large (or 2 small)* cooked *potatoes, cut into thin slices*
1 *small eggplant, peeled and cut into ½-inch-thick slices*
1 *large ripe tomato, thinly sliced*

Combine all the sauce ingredients in a small bowl and mix well. Pour about 2 tablespoons of the sauce into the bottom of a very large deep skillet or an electric frying pan (see Note). Set the remainder of the sauce aside.

Lightly coat the fish with flour. In another large skillet over medium-high heat, heat a few tablespoons of oil until hot. Fry the fish until lightly browned on both sides. Lay the fish on top of the sauce in the first skillet. (If salmon *steaks* are used, remove the bones from the cooked fish before adding it to the sauce.)

Add a bit more oil to the skillet used for the fish, and heat it until hot. Add the onions, pepper, carrot, and celery, and cook, stirring, until the vegetables are tender but not browned. Spread the vegetables on top of the fish. Spoon about 2 more tablespoons of the sauce over the vegetables; then cover them with the potato slices.

Lightly coat the eggplant slices with flour; then fry them in a small amount of oil just until they are lightly browned. Lay the eggplant slices over the other vegetables. Put the tomato slices very neatly on top. Pour the remaining sauce evenly over the tomatoes.

Cover the pan tightly and bring to a simmer over medium heat. Turn the heat to low and gently simmer the fish and vegetables for about 30 minutes, or until most of the sauce has been absorbed.

Makes about 4 servings as a main dish, or more as a first course.

NOTE: If preferred, the sauce, fish, and vegetables may be placed in a 10-inch-square or equivalent casserole, and baked, uncovered, in a preheated 400-degree oven for 20 to 25 minutes, or until most of the sauce has been absorbed.

SAMBUSIK (M)

(Iraqi-Style Chicken or Meat Turnovers)

Years ago, when Rachel Muallem Gabes was a child in Baghdad, her family used to begin preparing foods for Purim two to three weeks ahead of time. Sometimes, she would help her mother make the many sweet and savory pastries that they would serve to holiday guests or offer as gifts for *shalah manot*.

Mrs. Gabes remembers Purim as being particularly joyful and fun for children. The men would read the *Megillah* aloud at her home, and hired musicians would play gay melodies. Young girls such as herself were told to wash carefully on that day so that they would "have the beauty of Esther."

Following is one of Mrs. Gabes' favorite savory pastries—one that her family has always served on Purim. It is filled with a spicy mixture of chicken and chick-peas. Other Iraqi Jews make a very similar filling for *sambusik* using ground meat instead of chicken (see the variation below).

Chicken and meat *sambusik* are customarily deep-fried. However, they may be baked, if preferred, using the directions below. The baked *sambusik* are not as crisp as the fried ones, but they are still very tasty.

(Note: Some Middle Eastern and North African Jews have a non-yeast pastry called *sembussak* or *sanbusak,* which is made from a dough that is more like the one for *borekas* [page 347], and is always baked.)

DOUGH
1 packet (2¼ teaspoons) active dry
    yeast
1 cup warm (105 to 115 degrees)
    water
1 teaspoon sugar
1 cup whole wheat flour
1¾ to 2¼ cups white bread flour or
    unbleached white flour
½ teaspoon salt
¼ cup pareve *margarine, softened*
2 tablespoons vegetable oil

1 large onion, finely chopped
2 cups cooked, skinned, boned, and
    diced chicken meat
1 15- to 16-ounce can chick-peas
    (garbanzo beans), drained
¼ cup water
¼ teaspoon ground cumin
⅛ teaspoon ground turmeric
Pinch of ground ginger
½ teaspoon salt
⅛ teaspoon black pepper, preferably
    freshly ground

CHICKEN FILLING (FOR MEAT
FILLING, SEE VARIATION)
2 tablespoons vegetable oil

GLAZE (ONLY FOR *BAKED*
TURNOVERS)
1 egg, beaten with 1 teaspoon water

For the dough, mix the yeast, water, and sugar in a small bowl and let the mixture rest for 5 to 10 minutes, or until it is frothy.

In a medium-sized bowl, combine the whole wheat flour, 1 cup of the white flour, and the salt; then cut in the margarine until the mixture resembles crumbs. Add the oil and the yeast mixture and stir for about 2 minutes, or until very well combined. Stir in just enough additional white flour to make a very soft, slightly sticky dough. Cover the dough with plastic wrap and let it rest for 15 minutes (so the whole wheat flour can absorb some moisture and become less sticky). Then turn the dough out onto a lightly floured board and knead it for about 5 minutes, or until it is very smooth and only slightly tacky. Put the dough into a lightly oiled bowl and turn it so it is coated with oil. Loosely cover the bowl with plastic wrap and a dish towel and let the dough rise until doubled, about 1 hour.

Meanwhile, prepare the filling. In a large deep skillet, over medium-high heat, heat the oil; then sauté the onion until it is tender but not browned. Add the remaining filling ingredients and mix well. Lower the heat slightly and cook the mixture, stirring occasionally, for about 15 minutes or until all the liquid has evaporated and the flavors have blended. Use the back of a large spoon or a fork to mash the chick-peas with the chicken so the mixture holds together. Set the filling aside to cool.

When the dough has risen, punch it down, and divide it into 24 equal pieces. Form each piece into a ball. One at a time, roll out each ball into an oval, about 4 by 5 inches. Put a generous tablespoon of the filling on one side of the oval; then fold it in half crosswise to cover the filling. Pinch the edges of the dough together very tightly to form a half-moon shape. Repeat until all the dough pieces are filled.

To *fry* the turnovers, put oil about 1½ to 2 inches deep in a large saucepan or wok; then heat it until very hot, about 375 degrees. Deep-fry the turnovers, a few at a time so they are not crowded, until well browned on both sides. Drain them very well on paper towels.

To *bake* the turnovers, put them about 2 inches apart on greased or non-stick spray-coated baking sheets. Brush the tops with the egg glaze; then prick each turnover with a fork so steam can escape. Bake them in a preheated 400-degree oven for 15 to 20 minutes, or until they are well browned.

Serve the turnovers warm. Leftovers of either type may be reheated in a 350-degree oven until warmed through.

Makes 24 chicken turnovers.

VARIATION

For *meat filling,* omit the oil and the chicken, and cook the chopped onion with *1 pound raw lean ground beef,* breaking up the meat with a fork, until the meat has browned and the onion is tender. Drain off and discard all excess fat. Add all the remaining filling ingredients and proceed as above.

MOCK "SPAGHETTI" AND "MEATBALLS"   (P) or (D)

This main dish, which contains neither pasta nor meat, reminds us not only of the jocular nature of Purim, but also that Queen Esther chose to be a vegetarian while she lived in the court of King Ahasuerus, because she could not obtain kosher meat. According to tradition, her diet included many beans, including lentils. Although, it is highly unlikely she ever ate anything like the dish that follows, it would still be fun to serve it at a *Purim Se'udah*. That way, both the guests and the food will be in "masquerade"!

What's more, unlike most spaghetti and meatball dinners, this version may be sprinkled with cheese even by those who observe *kashrut*.

(Note: The meatless balls can be served with real pasta, if preferred.)

MEATLESS BALLS
½ cup dry brown lentils, sorted and rinsed
¼ cup long- or medium-grain brown rice
1½ cups cold water
1 large egg
½ cup seasoned bread crumbs
¼ cup finely ground pecans or walnuts
1 small onion, grated
¼ teaspoon garlic powder
¼ teaspoon dried oregano leaves

½ teaspoon soy sauce or Worcestershire sauce
2 tablespoons chopped fresh parsley leaves

"SPAGHETTI"
1 3- to 4-pound spaghetti squash

SAUCE AND CHEESE TOPPING
Pareve *spaghetti sauce (homemade or store-bought) to taste*
Grated Parmesan (or similar) cheese *to taste (optional)*

For the "meatless balls," put the lentils, rice, and water into a medium-sized saucepan and bring to a boil over high heat. Lower the heat and simmer, covered, for about 45 minutes, or until the lentils and rice are tender. Remove the pan from the heat and let it rest for 10 minutes; then coarsely mash the lentils and rice with any remaining water. Add the remaining ingredients and mix very well.

Shape the mixture into about 30 1-inch balls. Place the balls on a greased baking sheet or jelly roll pan about 1 inch apart. Bake them in a preheated 400-degree oven for about 20 minutes, or until they are firm.

Meanwhile, cook the spaghetti squash. For firm-textured, "pasta-like" strands, it is best to cook the squash whole. Pierce the squash deeply 3 or 4 times with a small knife. Bake it in a preheated 350-degree oven for about 1½ hours. Or cook it in a microwave oven for about 20 minutes, rotating it often; then let it rest for 5 to 10 minutes. Or put it into a large pot and cover it almost entirely with water. Cover the pot and simmer the squash for about 45 minutes.

In all cases, the squash is done when its surface gives to pressure. If the squash is undercooked, the strands will not come out easily. But if it is overcooked, the strands will be mushy and not like spaghetti.

Cut the cooked squash in half crosswise and carefully scoop out and discard the seeds in the center. Then use the tines of a fork to gently pull out and separate the spaghetti-like strands.

To serve, arrange the spaghetti squash in a large platter. Top it with meatless balls and spaghetti sauce. If desired, sprinkle grated cheese on top.

Makes about 4 servings.

SPICY CHICK-PEAS AND RICE (P)

While Queen Esther lived in the palace of King Ahasuerus, she ate only vegetarian fare, particularly peas and beans, so as not to break the dietary laws of *kashrut*. For this reason, chick-peas—*nahit* in Yiddish; *humus* in Hebrew— have become very traditional for Purim.

The following dish uses herbs and spices common in Middle Eastern cuisine to give ordinary beans and rice a wonderfully exotic flavor. Furthermore, it is a great way to use up leftover rice and a perfect side dish for any meal.

The mixture can even be stuffed into pita bread for a light vegetarian main course. When beans and brown rice are combined as in this recipe, they actually provide high-quality protein.

2 tablespoons good-quality olive oil
1 medium-sized onion, finely chopped
1 garlic clove, minced
2 cups cooked *brown rice (or*
    cooked *white rice)*
1 15- to 16-ounce can chick-peas
    (garbanzo beans), drained
½ cup warm water

2 tablespoons finely chopped fresh
    parsley leaves
½ teaspoon dried marjoram leaves
½ teaspoon dried basil leaves
¼ teaspoon ground cumin
¼ teaspoon ground turmeric
½ teaspoon salt
⅛ teaspoon black pepper, preferably
    freshly ground

In a large skillet, over medium-high heat, heat the oil; then sauté the onion and garlic until they are tender but not browned. Stir in the remaining ingredients until well combined. Turn the heat to low and cover the skillet. Simmer the mixture, stirring occasionally, for 15 to 20 minutes, or until the flavors have blended.

Makes about 6 servings as a side dish.

HAMANTASCHEN WITH POPPY SEED FILLING   (D) or (P)

(Filled Triangular Cookies)

For me, Purim simply wouldn't be Purim without *hamantaschen* bulging with a rich, dark, moist poppy seed filling. Though others may prefer *lekvar* (prune jam) or *povidl* (plum jam) or apricot or cherry filling, my all-time favorite is poppy seed, perhaps the "original" filling.

Actually, the record on how *hamantaschen* (which is sometimes spelled "*homentaschen*") came to be a Purim specialty is quite confusing. Some say that poppy seed-filled cakes called *mohntaschen* were already popular in Ashkenazic cuisine—*mohn* meaning "poppy seeds" and *taschen*, "pockets." Because mohntaschen sounded so much like the Yiddish pronunciation of *hamantaschen*, the re-named cookies became associated with Purim.

Others say it happened completely the other way around; that Purim cookies called *hamantaschen* came first. These cookies were eventually filled with poppy seeds just because *Homen* (Yiddish for "Haman") and *mohn* sounded so similar.

Whatever their origin, *hamantaschen* are said to resemble Haman's tricornered hat, or perhaps his pockets filled either with bribes or the lots used to decide which day the Jews would be killed. The triangular shape is also supposed to represent the three patriarchs of Judaism—Abraham, Isaac, and Jacob—who spiritually inspired Queen Esther and gave her inner strength.

Israelis eat these same filled cookies for Purim, but call them *oznai haman,* which is Hebrew for "Haman's ears." (See also the recipe for *orejas de haman,* page 216.)

Those who are not enamored of poppy seeds can substitute another thick filling in the following recipe. Several different types of them—ready-made—can be purchased in most supermarkets.

DOUGH
½ cup butter or margarine, softened
¼ cup packed dark or light brown
   sugar
¼ cup honey
2 large eggs
1 teaspoon vanilla extract
1 teaspoon baking powder
½ teaspoon baking soda
2½ cups all-purpose white flour,
   preferably unbleached (may be
   half whole wheat flour, if desired)

POPPY SEED FILLING
1 cup (about 5 ounces) poppy seeds
½ cup milk or water
½ cup honey
¼ cup dark raisins or currants
1 tablespoon butter or margarine
2 teaspoons lemon juice

For the dough, use an electric mixer at medium speed to cream the butter with the brown sugar and honey in a medium-sized bowl until light and fluffy. Beat in the eggs and vanilla. Then mix in the baking powder, soda, and flour until very well combined. Form the dough into a thick circle, wrap it in plastic wrap or wax paper, and refrigerate it for several hours, or until it is quite firm. (The dough may be made ahead, and refrigerated for up to 3 days.)

Meanwhile, make the poppy seed filling. Grind the poppy seeds in a blender or coffee grinder, or with a mortar and pestle, until most of the seeds are broken up. (If the seeds cannot be ground, they may be used whole; however, the texture of the filling will not be as fine and the flavor not as rich.)

Put the ground poppy seeds into a small saucepan with the remaining filling ingredients. Cook over medium heat, stirring frequently, for about 10 minutes, or until the mixture is very thick and almost all the liquid has been absorbed. Remove the filling from the heat and let it cool slightly; then chill it before using. (The filling may be made ahead, and refrigerated, covered, for up to 3 days.)

Roll out the chilled dough on a lightly floured surface until it is about ⅛ inch thick. (For easier handling, use half the dough at a time and leave the rest in the refrigerator.) Cut out circles about 3 inches in diameter. (Hint: A clean, empty tuna can with both ends removed makes a perfect cutter.) Put a very generous teaspoon of poppy seed filling (or your choice of other filling) in the center of each circle (Fig. 21A). Fold up the edges of each circle in thirds to form a triangular base and pinch the edges together tightly (Fig. 21B), leaving a small opening in the center of the cookie where the filling can be seen. The cookie should resemble a "tricorn" hat (Fig. 21C).

  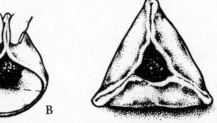

FIGURE 21

Put the hamantaschen about 1 inch apart on greased or non-stick spray-coated baking sheets and bake in a preheated 350-degree oven for about 15 minutes, or until lightly browned. Cool on a wire rack.

Makes about 24 hamantaschen.

OREJAS DE HAMAN (P)

(Sephardic-Style Fried "Haman's Ears" Cookies)

During Purim, different parts of Haman are symbolically cooked and eaten as a way to mock this wicked enemy of the Jews. For instance, Ashkenazic Jews nosh on *hamantaschen*, which represent his hat or pockets. In Israel, these same triangular baked cookies are called *oznai haman*, or "Haman's ears," implying that the man had pretty strange ears. Actually, the term probably came about because it was an old custom to cut off a condemned criminal's ears before execution.

Jews from many other countries also eat "Haman's ears," but these are usually made of twisted, fried noodle dough, which does tend to resemble that designated part of Haman's anatomy. All are quite similar to the Sephardic *orejas de haman* that follow, though some are shaped in a slightly different manner. Among these Purim treats are: North African *hojuelos de haman*, Turkish-Greek *shamlias*, Swiss *schunzuchen*, Dutch *hamansooren*, German *hamman-mutzen*, Italian *orecchi di aman*, and Austrian *heizenblauzen*.

Interestingly, Jews from Persia (Iran), where the story of Esther took place, eat no hamantaschen or "Haman's ears" of any type for Purim, but rather an assortment of other rich cookies.

1 large egg	*Pinch of salt*
1 tablespoon vegetable oil	*About 1 cup all-purpose white flour,*
1½ tablespoons cold water	*preferably unbleached*
1½ tablespoons granulated sugar	*Vegetable oil for deep frying*
½ teaspoon baking powder	*Confectioner's sugar for coating*

In a small bowl, use a fork to beat together the egg, oil, water, sugar, and baking powder, and salt. Gradually beat in enough flour to make a soft, slightly sticky dough. On a lightly floured board, knead the dough for 2 to 3 minutes, or until it is very smooth. Wrap it in plastic wrap and let it rest for 30 minutes to 1 hour.

On a lightly floured surface, roll out the dough until it is very thin and translucent, no more than ¹⁄₁₆ inch thick. If it becomes resistant, cover it with plastic wrap so it doesn't dry out, and let it rest a few minutes; then continue to roll it out.

In a saucepan or wok, heat oil about 1½ inches deep until it is very hot, about 375 degrees. While it is heating, use a pastry wheel (preferably one with a corrugated edge) or a sharp knife to cut the dough into 1-inch-wide strips about 4 inches long, or into random shapes approximating that size. Pick up one of the dough pieces, and twist it once or twice for an interesting look. Then carefully drop it into the hot oil.

For a cookie that more closely resembles a pair of "ears," use the side of a round 2½- to 3-inch cookie cutter to cut crescent shapes from the edge of the dough. Pinch each crescent in the center like a bow tie, to form two attached, ear-like shapes. (Note: Because these cookies also look like a pair of little "leaves," they are sometimes called *hojuelos* in Judeo-Spanish, which means "leaflets.")

Fry only a few cookies at a time, so that they are not crowded. They will puff considerably as soon as they are dropped into the oil. Turn the cookies with tongs or a slotted spoon so that they cook evenly. As soon as they are lightly browned (about 1 minute or less), remove them from the oil, and drain them well on paper towels (or on the rack that attaches to some woks). When all the cookies have been fried, coat them well with sieved confectioner's sugar. Store them in an airtight container.

Makes 3 to 4 dozen cookies, depending on their size.

BAKLAVA OR BAKLAWA   (D) or (P)

(Many-Layered Pastry with Nuts and Honey)

This luscious, flaky dessert is a Purim favorite of Sephardim from many lands. It is also very popular during the Days of Awe, because it contains honey, and thus signifies a hope for a sweet year.

Each group of Sephardim uses a slightly different filling and honey syrup for the pastry. The following version is based on that of Turkish and Greek Jews, who typically call it *baklava*.

Those from the Middle East often prefer pistachio nuts in the filling, and rose water in the syrup. Iraqi and Iranian Jews usually use almonds and cardamom in their filling, instead of walnuts and other spices, and they also like rose water-flavored syrup. Jews from Arabic countries usually call the dessert *baklawa*, its Arabic name.

Though the recipe is a bit time consuming, it makes many pieces, which will keep for at least a week at room temperature or can be frozen for several months.

This dessert is made with filo (pronounced "fee'-low"), a very thin dough which looks and feels remarkably like white tissue paper. Filo (also spelled "fillo," "phyllo," or "fila," and sometimes called "strudel leaves") usually comes in a long, narrow box which contains 1 pound of sheets folded together and sealed inside a plastic bag. Filo can be purchased in the frozen food sections of some supermarkets, as well as in most Greek or Middle Eastern ethnic grocery stores and gourmet specialty stores. The packaged sheets should always be brought to room temperature before unwrapping, unfolding, and using. If they have been frozen, they must first be thawed in the refrigerator overnight.

The delicate sheets of filo dry out extremely quickly. Therefore, whenever they are removed from their sealed plastic bag, they should be kept in a stack between two slightly damp (but *not* wet) dish towels, and used as soon as possible for best results. If filo is handled correctly, it is easy and fun to use. However, if thawed improperly or allowed to dry out, it may crumble and become impossible to work with. Any unused sheets of filo should be folded and returned to their plastic bag. Seal the bag well with tape, and store the filo in the refrigerator (for a week or two) or freezer.

FILLING
4 cups (about 1 pound) finely chopped walnuts (or a mixture of walnuts and almonds)
¼ cup sugar
2 teaspoons ground cinnamon
¼ teaspoon ground allspice
¼ teaspoon ground cloves

PASTRY
10 tablespoons (1¼ sticks) unsalted butter or margarine

1½ tablespoons vegetable oil
2 teaspoons warm water
1 1-pound package filo sheets at room temperature

HONEY SYRUP
1 cup sugar
1 cup cold water
Shredded peel (yellow part only) from 1 medium-sized lemon
½ cup plus 2 tablespoons honey
Juice of 1 medium-sized lemon

For the filling, mix together the chopped nuts, sugar, cinnamon, allspice, and cloves. Set aside.

In a small saucepan, over medium-low heat, slowly melt the butter; then stir in the oil and the 2 teaspoons of water. Cover the pan and keep the mixture warm over very low heat until it is needed.

Remove the filo from its plastic package and unfold it so it lies flat. Keep it covered with a slightly damp dish towel as described above. Dip a large pastry brush into the butter mixture and use it to grease the bottom and sides of a 10- by 15- by 1-inch jelly roll pan or slightly larger pan. (If necessary, a 9- by 13- by 2-inch baking pan can be used.) Use a sharp knife (or scissors) to trim the stack of filo so that the sheets are just slightly larger than the pan. (Discard the trimmings or reserve them for another use.)

Spread out 1 sheet of filo in the bottom of the pan. Brush it lightly with the butter-oil mixture. Cover with another sheet, and butter that one. Repeat the procedure until there are 5 stacked, buttered sheets. Sprinkle about ⅔ cup of the nut filling evenly over the filo.

Stack 2 more sheets on top, buttering each; then sprinkle with another ⅔ cup of the filling. Repeat this process—that is, stack 2 sheets and sprinkle them with filling—4 more times, using up all the nut filling. Top with the remaining sheets of filo (there should be 5 to 10), buttering each.

To "score" the pastry, use a small sharp knife to cut halfway down (not all the way through) the layered sheets. Cut diagonal rows to make diamonds (the traditional shape), or cut the pastry into triangles or squares. Sprinkle any remaining butter mixture on top; then sprinkle on a few drops of water. Bake the baklava in a preheated 350-degree oven for 1 hour. (If the top is browning too rapidly, cover it loosely with a piece of aluminum foil.)

As soon as the baklava is in the oven, prepare the syrup (so it has time to cool). In a medium-sized saucepan, combine the sugar, water, lemon peel, and ½ cup of the honey. Slowly heat the mixture over medium heat, while swirling the pan, until the sugar dissolves; then simmer it, undisturbed and uncovered, for 10 minutes (or until it reaches 212 degrees on a candy thermometer). Remove the syrup from the heat, and stir in the remaining 2 tablespoons of honey and the lemon juice. Set the syrup aside to cool.

When the baklava is done baking, remove it from the oven and immediately pour the syrup evenly over the top. Cut all the way through the scored lines to separate the pieces. Leave the baklava in the pan and let it rest, loosely covered with aluminum foil, at room temperature for at least 4 hours (preferably overnight) before eating it. Store at room temperature for up to 1 week.

(For a longer period, wrap the baklava well and freeze. Thaw it in the refrigerator; then store at room temperature.)

Makes about 40 pieces.

MOHN KICHLAH (D) or (P)

(Queen Esther's Cookies)

These light, crunchy, poppy seed cookies are eaten by many Ashkenazic Jews throughout the year. During Purim, however, they are particularly favored, and sometimes called "Queen Esther's cookies" to remind us how she eschewed the non-kosher food in King Ahasuerus' palace and lived, instead, on ordinary beans and seeds, including poppy seeds. Occasionally, these cookies are cut into the shapes of the characters in the *Megillah.*

½ cup butter or margarine, softened	*¼ to ⅓ cup poppy seeds*
½ cup sugar	*2 cups all-purpose white flour,*
1 large egg	*preferably unbleached (may be*
1 tablespoon water	*half whole wheat flour, if desired)*
½ teaspoon vanilla extract	*½ teaspoon baking powder*
¼ teaspoon almond extract	

In a medium-sized bowl, cream the butter with the sugar until light and fluffy. Beat in the egg, water, and vanilla and almond extracts. Then mix in the poppy seeds. Add the flour and baking powder and mix to form a very stiff dough. The dough may now be used for the traditional rolled out cookies, or it may easily be made into drop cookies.

For *rolled cookies:* Form the dough into a thick circle, wrap it in plastic wrap or wax paper and refrigerate it for several hours, or until it is quite firm. Roll out the dough on a lightly floured surface until it is about ⅛ inch thick and cut it into any desired shapes. Squares, circles and triangles are most common; however, cookie cutters may be used for more elaborate designs. (Re-chill any dough that becomes difficult to handle.)

Use a large metal spatula or pancake turner to carefully transfer the cut out cookies to lightly greased or non-stick spray-coated baking sheets, leaving about ½ inch between each cookie. Bake the cookies in a preheated 350-degree oven for 10 to 12 minutes, or until they are firm with lightly browned edges. Remove the cookies from the baking sheets with a metal spatula or pancake turner and cool them on wire racks.

For *drop cookies:* (These should be made as soon as the dough is mixed; chilling is not necessary.) Drop teaspoonfuls of the dough onto lightly greased or non-stick spray-coated baking sheets; then flatten the mounds slightly with a fork or your fingertip. Bake the cookies in a preheated 350-degree oven for about 15 minutes, or until they are firm with lightly browned edges. Remove the cookies from the baking sheets with a metal spatula and cool them on wire racks. (Drop cookies will be smaller and thicker than the rolled out ones.)

Makes 3 to 4 dozen cookies.

TRAVADOS (P)

(Walnut-Filled Crescent Cookies)

This is another of the delectable sweet pastries made by many Sephardic Jews especially for Purim. The oil-based dough is quite similar to that used for savory *borekas* (page 347). After baking, the cookies are traditionally dipped into hot sugar-honey syrup; however, confectioner's sugar is often substituted.

FILLING
1 cup very finely chopped walnuts
3 tablespoons granulated sugar
1/4 teaspoon ground cinnamon
1/8 teaspoon ground cloves
1 1/2 tablespoons honey

DOUGH
1/2 cup vegetable oil
1/4 cup water
1/4 cup granulated sugar
1/4 teaspoon baking soda

2 cups all purpose white flour,
preferably unbleached

SYRUP (OPTIONAL)
2/3 cup granulated sugar
1/3 cup cold water
2 tablespoons honey
1 teaspoon lemon juice

COATING (IF SYRUP IS NOT USED)
Confectioner's sugar

For the filling, combine all the ingredients and mix them well until they hold together. If the walnut mixture is still quite dry and crumbly, add a bit more honey. Set aside.

For the dough, mix the oil, water, and sugar in a medium-sized bowl. Add the baking soda and flour and stir briefly to make a soft, non-sticky dough. If the dough is very sticky, add a bit more flour; if it is crumbly, add a little water. Gather the dough into a smooth ball. Do not knead it or mix it too much. Form the dough into small circles using either of the following techniques:

For the more traditional method, shape the dough into about 25 walnut-sized balls; then, on a lightly floured surface, either pat out each ball with your fingertips or roll it out to an approximately 2½-inch-diameter circle that is ⅛ inch thick. (Usually, with this technique, each circle is filled as soon as it is flattened out.)

For very uniform circles, roll out all the dough on a lightly floured surface until it is ⅛ inch thick. Use a 2½-inch circular cookie cutter to cut out circles. Reroll any scraps and cut them out. There should be about 25 circles.

To fill the cookies, put a teaspoon of the filling on each circle; then fold over the dough to form a half-moon or crescent, and pinch the edges tightly together. Put the cookies about 1 inch apart on greased or nonstick spray-coated baking sheets and bake them in a preheated 350-degree oven for 25 to 30 minutes, or until they are lightly browned. Remove them from the baking sheets and cool them on wire racks.

If syrup is desired, make it while the cookies are cooling. Put the sugar, water, honey, and lemon juice into a 2-quart or similar saucepan and slowly bring to a boil over medium-high heat, stirring only until the sugar dissolves. Lower the heat slightly and boil the syrup briskly, uncovered and undisturbed, for 10 minutes. Use tongs or a slotted spoon to dip each cookie into the hot syrup; then lift the cookie to drain off all the excess syrup. Let the cookies cool on a platter before storing them.

If the syrup is not used, coat the cookies with confectioner's sugar.

Store the cookies in an airtight container.

Makes about 25 cookies.

MENENAS   (D) or (P)

(Date-Filled Cookies)

I first learned about *menenas* from Lily Livne, an Israeli Jew who was born in Egypt. Because Mrs. Livne had a bit of difficulty with English, her teenage daughter acted as interpreter during our interview. As soon as I mentioned Purim, the young girl insisted that her mother give me the recipe for these cookies, a family favorite.

Further research turned up a variety of similar date-filled cookies that other groups of Sephardic Jews traditionally prepare for Purim. For instance, there are Iranian *klaitcha,* Syrian *ras-ib-adivah,* and Middle Eastern *ma'aroot* and *ma'amool.*

The cookies all use a shortbread dough, which is sometimes made with semolina, and may or may not include an egg. And they are filled with dates that have been gently cooked until they "melt" into a soft paste. Chopped walnuts and cinnamon are often added to the filling, and, occasionally, also nutmeg and cloves.

The cookies are formed in a variety of different ways. Often, the dough is rolled out and cut into circles, or shaped into walnut-sized balls, which are each patted out into a circle. A small ball of date filling is put on the center of each circle. The dough is then brought up around the filling to enclose it, and the filled cookies rolled in the hands to form smooth balls. The cookies may be left as balls. Or they may be formed into oblongs or flattened slightly into disks. For ma'amool, each round ball is usually pressed into a wooden mold called a *tabi,* to give it an ornate surface design.

Sometimes, the date filling is shaped into tiny "sausages," which are laid across the circles of dough. The dough is folded over the log to form a semicircle, and the edges pinched tightly closed. Or, the dough may be rolled around the "sausage," and then bent into a crescent shape.

For the easiest cookies of all, a portion of the dough is rolled out into a long, narrow rectangle, and part of the date filling is formed into a large log. The dough is brought up around the log to enclose it. Cookies are cut from this large roll. Details for this technique follow below. (A further variation of this method involves spreading the date paste in a thin layer over the dough rectangle, and then rolling up the dough as with a filled jelly roll.)

DOUGH
½ *cup butter or margarine*
½ *cup granulated sugar*
1 *large egg*
½ *teaspoon vanilla extract*
1¾ *cups all-purpose white flour,*
  preferably unbleached

FILLING
8 *ounces pitted dates, chopped*

2 *tablespoons butter or margarine*
¼ *cup water*
½ *cup finely chopped walnuts*
¼ *teaspoon ground cinnamon*
  (optional)

TO SERVE (OPTIONAL)
Confectioner's sugar

First, prepare the dough. Use an electric mixer at medium speed to cream the butter with the sugar in a medium-sized bowl. Beat in the egg and vanilla. Then stir in the flour to make a stiff dough. Wrap the dough in plastic wrap and refrigerate it for about 30 minutes.

Meanwhile, prepare the filling. Combine the dates, butter, and water in a medium-sized saucepan. Stir the dates constantly over low heat, mashing them with the back of the spoon, until they soften considerably and form a thick paste. (If the dates are very dry, a bit more water may be needed.) Remove the date mixture from the heat and stir in the walnuts and cinnamon (if used). Refrigerate the date filling, stirring it occasionally, until it is very stiff and cool enough to be handled, about 20 minutes.

Divide the chilled dough in half, and roll out each half on a lightly floured surface to a 10- by 4-inch rectangle. Divide the date filling in half, and form each half into a log about 9½ inches long. Place 1 log lengthwise on each rectangle and bring up the dough over the log to enclose it. Pinch the long edges of the dough together and pinch the ends tightly closed.

Put the filled rolls, seam side down, on a large greased or non-stick spray-coated baking sheet, keeping them about 2 inches apart. Prick the tops with a fork. Bake the rolls in a preheated 350-degree oven for about 25 minutes, or until the bottoms are lightly browned and the tops are firm and golden. Cool the rolls for 5 minutes on the baking sheet; then carefully transfer them to a wire rack to cool to room temperature. Put the cooled rolls on a wooden board or other cutting surface and use a sharp knife to cut them crosswise (or diagonally) into ½- to ¾-inch-thick slices. If desired, sprinkle the cookies with sieved confectioner's sugar before serving them.

Makes 24 to 36 cookies, depending on the thickness.

VARIATION

With this version of *menenas,* the date filling has a spiral look. Prepare the dough as directed above and refrigerate it. Prepare the filling as directed, but *omit the walnuts.* Cool the filling at room temperature so that it remains spreadable. Roll out each half of the chilled dough on a lightly floured surface to a *10- by 7-inch* rectangle. Use a spatula to spread half of the filling evenly over each rectangle, keeping it ½ inch from all edges. Roll up the dough, beginning at a 10-inch edge, like a jelly roll. Pinch the ends tightly closed. Bake and slice the filled rolls as directed above.

MOROCCAN-STYLE MARZIPAN "PETIT FOURS" (P)

(Almond Paste Confections)

Many Jews enjoy *marzipan* during Purim, when it may be called "the bread of Mordecai." The following dainty *petit fours* (a French-Moroccan term meaning any small "sweets") feature balls of golden *marzipan* stuffed into dried fruits or sandwiched between nut halves. The completed confections are beautiful and delicious, and are not very difficult to make. In fact, children can help with the project. And, the *petit fours* are truly an excellent choice as holiday food gifts for *shalah manot*.

Marzipan, a rich almond-egg paste (which is sometimes called *masapan* or *almendrada*) is a Sephardic specialty prepared in many different ways. A pure white type, made with egg whites, is a must at many Sephardic weddings and pre-nuptial receptions, and is also offered to new mothers. Sometimes, it is painstakingly shaped into delicate, woven bracelets.

Jews from Morocco generally prefer to use egg yolks, rather than whites, in the paste. Also, Moroccans do not cook the paste before shaping it, as do some other Sephardim. Moroccan Jews enjoy *marzipan* not only on Purim, but also during Pesach and *Meemounah*—the Moroccan-Jewish holiday which immediately follows Pesach.

The technique for the following confections is adapted from that used by Ginette Spier, a Moroccan Jew who caters kosher Sephardic food from her home in Chevy Chase, Maryland.

(Note: When the marzipan paste is first made, it may taste coarse and sugary. For best flavor and texture, it should be allowed to "ripen" overnight. Thus, the *petit fours* can be *shaped* as soon as the marzipan is prepared but, for best taste, they should not be *eaten* until the next day.)

If desired, the marzipan paste can be made way ahead of time, and refrigerated (for up to one week) or frozen. It should be allowed to come to room temperature before being shaped. The completed *petit fours* may also be frozen.

The *petit fours* look particularly attractive when each one is placed in a tiny fluted paper cup (available in gourmet cookware stores and some supermarkets).

1 10-ounce bag (scant 2 cups) whole blanched almonds OR 1 10-ounce bag (about 2⅓ cups) slivered blanched almonds

¾ cup granulated sugar, plus extra for dipping

2 large egg yolks (from very fresh eggs)

½ teaspoon almond extract, or to taste

½ to 1 teaspoon grated lemon rind (yellow part only)

About 2 teaspoons lemon juice, preferably fresh

3 to 4 ounces each of the following (or your choice to total about 1 pound):
Whole pitted dates
Whole pitted prunes
Dried apricots
Perfect walnut halves
Perfect pecan halves

In a food processor fitted with the steel blade, grind the almonds as finely as possible. (If the almonds have been frozen, be sure to let them come to room temperature before grinding them.) The almonds should be almost powdery. Add the ¾ cup sugar and process until the almonds are powdery; then add the egg yolks, almond extract, lemon rind, and 1 teaspoon of lemon juice and process until the ingredients are very well combined and beginning to form a cohesive mass. Test the marzipan mixture by squeezing a tablespoon of it in the palm of your hand. It should feel slightly tacky and should press together into a ball. If the mixture is too dry, mix in enough additional lemon juice, adding it drop by drop, until the marzipan is the proper consistency.

Turn out the marzipan onto a clean flat surface and gather it together into one large ball. Gently knead the marzipan for about 3 minutes, or until it is smooth and malleable, like a very stiff dough. Make the assorted "petit fours" as follows:

For each *date petit four,* cut open a date on one side, and open it to form the bottom of the confection. Pinch off a piece of marzipan about the size of a cherry. Mold it into an ovoid shape and press it in place on top of the opened date. Fold up the edges of the date, and smooth them around, but not enclosing, the marzipan. Decorate the top of the marzipan by pressing it with the tines of a fork—first in one direction and then in the perpendicular direction—or lightly score a leaf design in the marzipan with a small sharp knife.

For each *prune or apricot petit four,* pinch off a piece of marzipan about the size of a cherry and mold it into a ball. Press it tightly in place over the indentation in the center of the prune or on top of the apricot. (If desired, cut the prunes open and put the marzipan inside as with the date petit fours.) Decorate the top of the marzipan as described above.

For each *walnut or pecan petit four,* shape a cherry-sized piece of marzipan into a cube or ball and squeeze it between *two* nut halves to form a "sandwich." If desired, score the exposed surfaces of the marzipan with a fork.

Gently dab the scored marzipan surface of each petit four in additional granulated sugar to give it a pretty, "crystalline" look. Place each finished petit four into a tiny fluted paper cup or arrange several of them on a doily-covered tray. The petit fours will keep for at least 1 week if stored in an airtight container in the refrigerator. (See the Note above.) For best flavor, let them warm to room temperature before serving.

Makes 3 to 4 dozen assorted petit fours.

NAN-E BERENJI   (D) or (P)

(Rice-Flour Shortbread Cookies)

This tasty Iranian cookie might be among the edible presents exchanged on Purim for *shalah manot.* The delicate shortbread is made exclusively with white rice flour, which can be found in the Spanish section of some supermarkets, as well as in Chinese groceries and gourmet specialty stores. Before rice flour became commercially available, the preparation of these cookies was quite laborious. Raw white rice had to be soaked, dried, and ground several times to produce a fine flour. Some older Iranian-Jewish cooks still prefer to make their own rice flour in this traditional manner.

10 tablespoons (1 stick plus 2
   tablespoons) unsalted butter or
   margarine, softened
⅔ cup confectioner's sugar
1 large egg yolk

½ teaspoon ground cardamom
About 1⅓ cups white rice flour
Rose water (optional)
About 1 tablespoon poppy seeds or
   finely chopped pistachios

In a medium-sized mixing bowl, beat the butter until it is light and fluffy. Add the confectioner's sugar and beat until it is incorporated. Beat in the egg yolk and cardamom; then stir in just enough rice flour to make a stiff, non-sticky, dough. Gather the dough into a ball and wrap it in plastic wrap. Let it rest at room temperature for about 1 hour.

Roll scant tablespoonfuls of the dough into 1-inch-diameter balls. Place the balls about 1 inch apart on 1 large or 2 smaller ungreased baking sheets. Moisten the tip of your index finger with some rose water or water; then dip it into the poppy seeds or pistachios. Lightly press a few seeds or pistachios into the top of each ball, flattening the balls slightly.

Bake the cookies in a preheated 350-degree oven for about 15 minutes, or until the bottoms are lightly browned. The tops should stay off-white. Let the cookies cool on the baking sheet for 5 minutes to firm up; then remove them with a metal spatula or pancake turner and cool them completely on a wire rack. Store them in an airtight container.

Makes about 36 small cookies.

POPPY SEED-MERINGUE TRIANGLES   (D) or (P)

With their thin, golden crust and dark poppy seed filling, these delicious bar cookies are very attractive. For Purim, they are often cut into triangles (to resemble *hamantaschen*); for other occasions, small squares work very well.

1 cup (about 5 ounces) poppy seeds
¼ cup butter or margarine, softened
¼ cup granulated sugar
2 large eggs, separated
1 teaspoon vanilla extract

1⅓ cups all-purpose white flour,
  preferably unbleached
1½ teaspoons baking powder
⅛ teaspoon cream of tartar
⅔ cup packed dark brown sugar

Grind the poppy seeds in a blender or coffee grinder, or with a mortar and pestle, until most of the seeds are broken up. (If the seeds cannot be ground, they may be used whole; however, the texture of the meringue filling will not be as fine and the flavor not as rich.) Set the poppy seeds aside.

In a medium-sized bowl, use an electric mixer at medium speed to cream the butter with the sugar; then mix in the egg yolks and vanilla. Add the flour and baking powder and mix until well combined and crumbly. Firmly press the crumbs into the bottom of a greased or non-stick spray-coated 9-inch-square baking pan. Set aside.

In a clean bowl, with clean beaters, beat the egg whites with the cream of tartar until frothy. Then gradually add the brown sugar and continue beating until the whites form stiff peaks. Fold in the ground poppy seeds. Evenly spread the meringue mixture over the dough in the pan.

Bake in a preheated 350-degree oven for 30 minutes, or until the top is set and very lightly browned. Cool completely in the pan on a wire rack. When cool, cut into 4 large squares; then diagonally cut each square into 4 triangles.

Makes 16 large triangular bar cookies.

MACAROON BAR COOKIES (D) or (P)

Perfect for *shalah manot,* or even dessert at a *Purim Se'udah,* these are easy to prepare and quite tasty.

BOTTOM CRUST
⅓ cup butter or margarine, softened
¼ cup dark or light brown sugar
¾ cup all-purpose white flour,
preferably unbleached (or whole
wheat flour, if desired)
½ teaspoon almond extract

TOPPING
1 large egg

⅓ cup granulated sugar
1 tablespoon all-purpose white flour,
preferably unbleached
1 teaspoon vanilla extract
½ teaspoon baking powder
½ cup slivered or coarsely chopped
almonds
½ cup sweetened shredded or flaked
coconut

For the bottom crust, use an electric mixer at medium speed to cream the butter and sugar in a medium-sized bowl; then mix in the flour and almond extract until fine crumbs are formed. Press the crumbs into the bottom of an ungreased 8-inch-square baking pan. Bake the bottom crust in a preheated 350-degree oven for 15 to 20 minutes, or until it is lightly browned and set.

Shortly before the crust is done baking, prepare the topping. In the same bowl, beat the egg with the sugar until mixed; then add the flour, vanilla, and baking powder. Beat until very well combined. By hand, stir in the almonds and coconut.

When the crust is lightly browned, remove it from the oven and evenly spread the topping over it. Return the pan to the oven and bake about 15 minutes longer, or until the top is lightly browned. Cool completely in the pan on a wire rack. Cut into squares to serve.

Makes 16 bar cookies.

MOCK "MARZIPAN" (D)

(Almond-Flavored Oat Balls)

During modern Israel's early "austerity days," many culinary luxuries, including nuts, were often unavailable. So creative Israeli cooks devised recipes such as this, using inexpensive ingredients, to provide their children with occasional treats. The balls taste remarkably like marzipan, even though they lack the almonds and eggs of the real thing. With the jovial, mocking side of Purim in mind, they make a clever holiday treat.

2 cups rolled oats, any type
¼ cup sugar
3 tablespoons butter or margarine, melted

3 tablespoons skim, lowfat, or whole milk
¾ teaspoon almond extract

In a food processor or a blender (in batches, if necessary), process the oats until they are finely ground. Add the sugar to the ground oats and mix well.

In a medium-sized bowl, mix together the melted butter, milk, and almond extract. Add the oat-sugar mixture and stir until it is completely moistened. (If a food processor is used to grind the oats, simply add the sugar and milk mixture to the oats, and process a few additional seconds until the ingredients are mixed well.)

Let the mixture rest for about 5 minutes to allow the oats to absorb the moisture; then form the mixture into balls about 1 inch in diameter. If the mixture seems very dry and crumbly, stir in a few more drops of milk. If it is too wet to shape, add a bit more ground oats.

Store the balls of mock marzipan in the refrigerator, but serve them at room temperature (or only slightly chilled) for best taste and texture.

Makes about 25 balls.

STREUSEL-TOPPED GINGERBREAD GEMS (D) or (P)

(Miniature Cupcakes)

These attractive miniature muffins make very palatable presents for *shalah manot* and would also be perfect for a Purim party.

STREUSEL
2 tablespoons butter or margarine
¼ cup all-purpose white flour,
    preferably unbleached (or whole
    wheat flour, if desired)
2 tablespoons sugar
⅛ teaspoon ground ginger
⅛ teaspoon ground cinnamon

BATTER
¾ cup all-purpose white flour,
    preferably unbleached (sifted, if
    lumpy)

¾ cup whole wheat flour
¼ cup sugar
½ teaspoon baking soda
1 teaspoon ground ginger
½ teaspoon ground cinnamon
¼ teaspoon ground nutmeg
¼ teaspoon ground cloves
¼ cup vegetable oil
½ cup light molasses
⅓ cup hot water
1 large egg, lightly beaten

For the streusel topping, use your fingertips or a pastry blender to combine all the ingredients in a small bowl. The streusel should resemble coarse bread crumbs. Set it aside.

In a medium-sized bowl, mix together all the batter ingredients, except the egg; then beat in the egg until it is completely combined. Spoon the batter into 24 gem-sized (2-inch-diameter), paper cup-lined (or greased) muffin tins, using about 1 tablespoon batter for each muffin. Sprinkle a teaspoon of streusel over the batter in each cup and use the back of a spoon to gently press it into the batter.

Bake the muffins in a preheated 350-degree oven for about 15 minutes, or until a toothpick inserted in the center of one comes out clean. Remove the muffins from the pans and cool them on a wire rack.

Makes 24 miniature (gem-sized) muffins.

POPPY SEED POUND CAKE (D)

This impressive and delectable cake freezes quite well, so it can be made way ahead to have on hand for *shalah manot* during Purim.

BATTER
⅓ cup poppy seeds
1 cup commercial buttermilk
1 cup butter or margarine
1¼ cups granulated sugar, divided
4 large eggs, separated
1 teaspoon vanilla extract
½ teaspoon almond extract
2½ cups all-purpose white flour,
preferably unbleached (may be
half whole wheat flour, if desired)
2 teaspoons baking powder
1 teaspoon baking soda

FILLING
½ cup granulated sugar mixed with
1 tablespoon ground cinnamon

GLAZE
⅓ cup confectioner's sugar
About 2 teaspoons lemon juice,
preferably fresh
1 to 2 teaspoons poppy seeds for
sprinkling

For the batter, mix the poppy seeds and buttermilk in a small bowl. Let the mixture rest for 5 minutes.

Meanwhile, in a large mixing bowl, use an electric mixer at medium speed to cream the butter with 1 cup of the sugar until light and fluffy. Beat in the egg yolks and extracts. Combine the flour, baking powder, and baking soda and add them to the batter alternately with the buttermilk-poppy seed mixture. Mix until well combined.

In a clean bowl, with clean beaters, beat the egg whites until foamy; then gradually add the remaining ¼ cup sugar and beat until the whites form stiff peaks. Fold the beaten whites into the batter. Pour half of the batter into a greased and floured 12-cup fluted tube pan (such as a Bundt pan) or an angel food cake pan. Sprinkle the batter with half of the sugar-cinnamon filling mixture. Cover with the remaining batter. Sprinkle the remaining filling on top.

Bake the cake in a preheated 350-degree oven for 55 to 60 minutes, or until a toothpick inserted near the center comes out clean. Cool the cake in the pan on a wire rack for 10 to 15 minutes; then turn it out onto the rack to cool completely.

For the glaze, mix enough lemon juice into the confectioner's sugar so that the glaze has a "dripping" consistency. Drizzle the glaze in a zigzag pattern over the top of the cake. Sprinkle the glaze lightly with poppy seeds.

Makes about 16 servings.

PYOTA (D)

(Greek-Style Farina Pudding)

This unusual pudding is a Sephardic Purim specialty that raises mundane cooked wheat cereal to new gastronomic heights. In some versions, honey is omitted from the custard mixture, and, instead, a honey syrup is poured over the baked pudding and allowed to soak in. I prefer the following type of *pyota,* which is not excessively sweet, and makes a fairly nutritious dessert. The pudding, which is firm enough to be cut into squares, is often served with sliced fresh fruit.

3½ cups water
⅔ cup "quick" Cream of Wheat cereal
1 cup instant nonfat dry milk powder
2 tablespoons butter or margarine, cut into small pieces
½ cup sugar

⅓ cup honey
½ teaspoon vanilla extract
¼ teaspoon cinnamon, plus extra for topping
5 large eggs

TO SERVE (OPTIONAL)
Sliced fresh fruit (any type desired)

In a large saucepan over high heat, bring the water to a boil. Stir in the cereal and milk powder and immediately lower the heat to medium. Cook the cereal, stirring constantly, for about 3 minutes, or until it becomes very thick. Remove it from the heat and stir in the butter until it is melted. Then stir in the sugar, honey, vanilla, and cinnamon.

In a medium-sized bowl, beat the eggs with a fork until well mixed. While continuing to beat the eggs, slowly add about 1 cup of the hot cereal mixture to them. Then, stirring constantly, add the egg mixture back to the rest of the cereal mixture. (This technique helps keep the eggs from curdling in the hot cereal.)

Pour the mixture into a greased or non-stick spray-coated 8-inch-square pan and sprinkle the top with cinnamon. Bake the pudding in a preheated 325-degree oven for about 50 minutes, or until a knife inserted in the center comes out almost clean. Cool the pudding to room temperature in the pan on a wire rack; then refrigerate it, covered, for several hours or until it is chilled. Serve it chilled, cut into large squares. Accompany it with fresh fruit, if desired.

Makes about 9 servings.

POPPY SEED-ONION CRACKERS (P)

Homemade crackers are not very difficult and they impress family and friends, particularly those folks who think all crackers come from boxes. The following combination of whole wheat, onions, and poppy seeds is particularly tasty. Like many other Purim treats, these crackers are cut into triangular shapes.

1 tablespoon instant minced onions
½ cup poppy seeds
⅓ cup boiling water
1 cup whole wheat flour
1 cup all-purpose white flour,
  preferably unbleached (or an
  additional 1 cup whole wheat
  flour, if preferred)

¼ teaspoon baking powder
¼ teaspoon baking soda
1 teaspoon salt
¼ teaspoon black pepper, preferably
  freshly ground
1 teaspoon honey
⅓ cup vegetable oil
1 large egg, lightly beaten

Put the instant onions and the poppy seeds into a small bowl and pour the boiling water over them. Set aside for 5 minutes.

Meanwhile, in a medium-sized bowl, combine the flours, baking powder, soda, salt, and pepper. Stir in the honey, oil, egg, and the *undrained* poppy seed-onion mixture. Mix well to form a soft dough that comes away from the sides of the bowl.

Grease well or coat with non-stick cooking spray 2 flat baking sheets which each have at least 2 rimless edges (see Note). (Or grease or spray the inverted bottoms of 2 large baking pans.) Divide the dough in half and roll out each half directly on a baking sheet to a 9- by 12½-inch rectangle, about ⅛ inch thick. Try to keep the thickness of the dough as even as possible. Prick the dough all over with a fork.

Use a small sharp knife or pastry wheel to cut each large rectangle into 9 equal, smaller rectangles (like a "tic-tac-toe" board). Diagonally cut each smaller rectangle into 4 triangles. Leave the dough in place on the baking sheets.

Bake the dough right on the baking sheets (or on the inverted pan bottoms; do not turn the pans over) in a preheated 400-degree oven for 15 to 20 minutes, or until the edges are browned and the crackers are firm. (They will crisp more as they cool.) Carefully remove the crackers from the baking sheet with a metal spatula or pancake turner, separating any triangles that are stuck together. Cool the crackers completely on a wire rack; then store them in an airtight container.

Makes 72 crackers.

NOTE: If a large enough baking sheet is available, the dough can be rolled out on to one 14- by 16-inch rectangle. Cut it into 16 equal rectangles; then diagonally cut each rectangle into 4 triangles. Bake as above. This will yield 64 slightly larger crackers.

PESACH

(Passover)

Pesach begins on the fifteenth day of the Hebrew month of Nisan, which usually occurs in late March or April, and lasts for eight days (seven in Israel). For Jews, it is a very special time, when relatives and friends, young and old, gather to share in the joy of our ancestors' redemption from slavery.

In fact, this freedom festival is probably the most widely observed and best loved of all the Jewish holidays. Unlike the majority of them, it is home-based, with its main service, the *Seder,* taking place at the family dinner table, not at the synagogue. Also, food plays a quintessential role at Pesach, not just a peripheral one as with most holidays. Indeed, the entire celebration revolves around the partaking or prohibition of specific foodstuffs.

The holiday as we know it today developed from two ancient spring festivals. The earlier one, *Hag Ha'Pesach,* or "Festival of the Paschal Lamb," was celebrated by nomadic Jewish shepherds who offered their first lambs of the season in ceremonial sacrifice. Later, Jews who had settled down to till the land instituted *Hag Ha'Matzot,* or "Festival of the Unleavened Bread," in which they discarded all sourdough (fermented dough used as leavening) and old bread connected with the previous year's crop, before beginning the new grain harvest.

Eventually, the nomadic and agricultural festivals became inextricably joined into one major pilgrimage festival known simply as *Pesach,* which was ultimately linked with the Israelites' deliverance from bondage in Egypt three thousand years ago. The word *pesach* came to mean "passing over" because God passed over the Jewish homes (whose doorposts were marked with the blood of the paschal lamb), while He struck down the first-born son of each Egyptian family. This plague—the last and most devastating of ten sent down upon the Egyptians—finally persuaded Pharaoh to free the Jewish people.

The unleavened bread or *matzah* (commonly spelled "matzo") of the festival came to represent the "bread of affliction," which did not have time to rise because it was so hastily baked by Jews fleeing from slavery in Egypt.

While the Holy Temple in Jerusalem was in existence, Jews made pilgrimage there for the Pesach holiday, to offer lambs and other sacrifices. The lambs were then roasted and eaten at a ceremonial meal, along with other special foods. When the Second Temple was destroyed, the holiday became more home oriented.

The modern Pesach *Seder* (a Hebrew word for "order"), which is held on the first night of the holiday and often also the second night, follows a ritualistic "order of service" that has been annually repeated by Jews for centuries. It is based on a text called the *Haggadah*. At the Seder, the story of the Exodus is retold, and symbolic foods on the holiday table are explained and tasted. Representative portions of most of these foods are displayed on a special platter, or "Seder plate," which may be ornately designed specifically for this purpose. The following six foods are on most Seder plates:

Karpas—a mild green vegetable, such as parsley or celery (or, among some Hasidim, possibly a root vegetable, such as a potato)—is the "hors d'oeuvre" of the Seder. At the beginning of the ceremony, it is dipped into salt water or vinegar, and sampled. In the time of the Holy Temple, the Pesach meal (and other formal meals) always began with such dipped vegetables. Karpas also symbolizes the new growth of spring. Salt water, preferred by Ashkenazim for the dip, is said to represent the tears shed by enslaved Israelites. Vinegar is the more traditional dip for most Sephardim.

Maror—a bitter herb which is usually horseradish among Ashkenazim, and endive, escarole, romaine lettuce, or a similar green among Sephardim—symbolizes the intense bitterness endured by the Jews during their slavery.

Hazeret—another bitter herb, such as horseradish, watercress, or romaine lettuce—is also on many Seder plates. Some say it is included because, in conjunction with Pesach, the Bible uses the plural word for "herbs," indicating there should be more than one portion. The hazeret, which is usually considered to be optional, may be used in the *koreh* or "sandwich" of matzo and herbs that is eaten as part of the Seder ceremony.

Haroset—most often a sweet spread made from fruit, nuts, and wine—represents the mortar and mud bricks used by Jewish slaves as they labored to build Pharaoh's cities. Some say the sweet taste of haroset is supposed to temper the sharpness of maror as an expression of eternal Jewish optimism.

Jews from various communities make their haroset in a wide variety of ways, as can be seen by the selection of recipes in this chapter. Most haroset mixtures are quite delicious, and highlights of the Seder. However, some Jews prefer to have unsweetened and unadorned haroset, such as that made solely from puréed raisins or currants, because they believe it should be as "plain as the mud" it symbolizes.

Zeroah—a roasted shank bone (or possibly a roasted poultry neck)—represents the paschal lamb that was always sacrificed in the Holy Temple just before the Pesach festival, and then roasted for the main meal. Such a sacrifice was made on the eve of the Exodus from Egypt, and the blood used to mark the doorposts of the Israelites.

(Because the Jewish sacrificial system was abandoned after the Second Temple was destroyed, some modern-day Jews never eat lamb or roasted meat of any kind at the Seder meal. However, others specifically do partake of it, in remembrance of the paschal sacrifice.)

Baytzah—a roasted egg—is symbolic of the festival offering always brought to the Holy Temple and considered a second, supplemental sacrifice on Pesach. The egg, also a symbol of mourning, shows that the loss of the Holy Temple is still lamented by Jews. (For this same reason, many Jews partake of a hard-boiled egg, often in a "soup" of salt water, as their first course of the Seder dinner.)

Also on the Seder table are three special *matzot* (the plural of *matzo*), which are said to symbolize the three religious divisions of the early House of Israel—Kohan, Levite, and Israelite. Actually, two of the matzot serve the same purpose as the two loaves of bread which are generally on the holiday table, that is, to represent the two rows of show-breads that were always on the altar of the Holy Temple. Some say the third matzo is a reminder of the happy nature of the holiday; others say it represents the "bread of affliction." Mostly, it is needed for the *afikoman*. (A fourth matzo, called the "matzo of hope," is sometimes also included to demonstrate concern and fellowship with Soviet Jews who, even today, do not have religious freedom.)

The part of the middle matzo called the *afikoman* is supposed to be the last bit of food eaten at the Seder by each participant. During the ceremony, it becomes the center of attention for the children, and helps keep them alert. In many Ashkenazic families, the leader of the Seder hides the afikoman, and then offers a gift to the children who find it, so the Seder can be completed. Sometimes, the children are expected to "steal" the afikoman away from the leader and hold it for "ransom" until the end of the meal.

In some Sephardic households, the afikoman is wrapped in a napkin and the youngest child present holds it on his or her shoulder to represent the "burden" carried by the Children of Israel when they wandered in the desert after the Exodus. The child is asked a series of questions to which there is a set response. "Where do you come from?" The child answers, "From Egypt." "Where are you going?" "To Jerusalem." "What provisions do you have for the way?" At this, the child points to the afikoman.

As with almost all Jewish ceremonies, wine is an important part of the Seder, and four glasses are drunk by each adult during the service. A special cup of wine is set out for the spirit of the great prophet Elijah, who, it is said, will come to announce the Messianic Age.

At the Seder, it is considered a religious duty to eat matzo. For the remainder of the holiday, however, matzo is optional. Nevertheless, no *hametz,* or leavened grain—that is, wheat, barley, spelt (an ancient type of wheat), rye, or oats that may have had any possible chance to ferment—is permitted at any time during Pesach. Consequently, all foods made from these grains, with the exception of matzo, are forbidden.

The flour intended for use as matzo is carefully watched to be sure that it is not allowed to leaven. By Jewish law, the entire process of matzo preparation—from mixing the flour-water dough until the matzo is completely baked—can take no longer than 18 minutes, because once grain has been exposed to water, this is the amount of time considered necessary for fermentation to begin.

After the matzo has fully baked, no further leavening is thought to be possible. Thus, matzo that is finely ground into meal is often used in place of flour or bread crumbs for holiday cooking.

Actually, very pious Jews, particularly among the Hasidim, prefer not to mix matzo or matzo products with any liquids during Pesach, just in case a minuscule piece of the matzo may not have properly baked and could possibly ferment. They call such "mixed" foods *gebroks,* and partake of them only on the eighth day of the holiday—a day that was added by rabbinic injunction and is not observed in Israel.

During the post-Talmudic period, certain Jewish religious authorities, who felt obligated to take every possible precaution, decided to prohibit additional foods on Pesach because of their similarity to the proscribed grains. Called *kitniyot* (Hebrew, for "legumes"), these foods include actual legumes (beans and peas) of all types, as well as "lesser grains" such as rice, millet, corn, and buckwheat. Thus, for many centuries, consumption of such foods during the holiday has been forbidden by Ashkenazic custom. (Some also consider mustard, sesame and sunflower seeds and oil, safflower oil, and garlic to be kitniyot.)

Most Sephardim never accepted the rabbinic decision, however, because their cuisine was dependent on kitniyot. Therefore, they generally permit these foods during Pesach. But, actual Sephardic custom varies considerably from place to place. For instance, some Sephardim eat rice, but not beans; whereas, others have the reverse preference. And some Near and Middle Eastern Jews specifically avoid chick-peas (garbanzo beans) simply because their Hebrew (and Arabic) name, *humus,* sounds so much like *hametz.*

Over the years, other culinary customs have evolved for the holiday. It was once common for many Ashkenazim to set aside crocks of cleaned beetroots with water shortly after Purim, so that the beets and liquid could naturally ferment over a period of weeks into *rossel.* This was then used for all sorts of Pesach dishes, ranging from *borscht* to red horseradish. A wine fermented from honey, called *med* or *mead,* was also popular. Some say these practices came about as a reaction against those who claimed that all fermented foods, not just grains, should be prohibited during Pesach.

Also prepared ahead of time were many sweets, such as jams, candied fruits, and syrups. Among Egyptian Jews, for instance, coconut jam has long been a holiday favorite because its whiteness symbolizes purity. And some Ashkenazic Jews have enjoyed candy made from such sweet vegetables as beets and carrots.

During Pesach, the rice eaten by certain Sephardim is thoroughly sorted from three to seven times—the number depending on local convention—to be absolutely certain that there is no foreign matter or kernels of proscribed grains in it.

For the Seder dinner, seasonal spring vegetables, such as asparagus or, among some Sephardim, fresh fava beans in the pods, are usually on the menu. Recipes for many other Seder specialties, and also several mid-holiday favorites, are included in this chapter. (Although these recipes come from many Jewish cultures, all have been adapted to follow the more stringent Ashkenazic custom of avoiding kitniyot during Pesach.)

The conclusion of Pesach is observed by Moroccan Jews as a special holiday called *Meenounah,* which is considered a testimony of their faith in God. According to many Moroccans, the name of the holiday comes from *emounah,* a Hebrew word for "faith" or "belief." Others suggest that it commemorates the death in Fez of the father of the great Jewish scholar, Moses Maimonides.

On the evening after Pesach, Moroccan families hold joyous open houses for their friends and relatives. Rabbi Joshua Toledano, religious leader of Congregation Mikveh Israel in Philadelphia, recalls that during his youth in Morocco, he dressed in finery and visited grandparents on both sides of his family.

Because his paternal grandfather was a great rabbi, the congregation always flocked to that home immediately after evening services. The visitors kissed the elderly rabbi's hand, and he blessed them and presented them with some dates, almonds, and walnuts.

At Rabbi Toledano's maternal grandparents' home, the table was set with a platter containing a huge raw fish, the symbol of fertility, which was surrounded by fresh flour. In the flour were coins, representing the hope for a prosperous year. The table was decorated with green wheat stalks, fresh peas in the pods, and beautiful flowers. Moslem friends came to visit, and brought with them freshly baked bread, honey, yeast, milk, and yogurt. Dairy products were included among the gifts because these were not available *kosher l'Pesach,* and so were abstained from during the holiday.

At Meemounah evening open houses, a multitude of sweet cakes and pastries are typically served. Also included are *muflita*—thin, crêpe-like pancakes that are spread with plenty of butter and honey, and then eaten out-of-hand.

The next morning, the celebration of Meemounah continues with community-wide outdoor picnics. This practice has been carried to Israel, where many Moroccan families meet in a huge park in Jerusalem. Together, they enjoy abundant, delectable foods, and spend the day in jubilant singing and dancing. It is a joyous time for all, and a fitting epilogue to the great festival of Pesach.

ASHKENAZIC-STYLE HAROSET—MY WAY (P)

Unlike Sephardim, who have many different types of *haroset* made with a wide variety of ingredients, Ashkenazim usually limit the mixture to apples, nuts, and red wine, which are sometimes flavored with cinnamon and sugar or honey. According to one rabbinic legend, the apples are a reminder of pious Israelite women who went into the apple orchards to give birth, so their babies would not be killed by the Egyptians.

There are so many different variations of this type of *haroset,* that I would never say any particular one was the *right* one. The following recipe is simply the way I make it, and a guide for those who have never done it before.

Until I decided to include this recipe here, I had never measured the amounts of ingredients, especially since I have always enjoyed adjusting them to taste. So, please feel free to do the same yourself. And keep in mind that the consistency of the haroset is also matter of personal preference.

Finally, although I have always used walnuts in my haroset, I recently discovered that others prefer almonds (or even hazelnuts or pecans). Again, the choice is yours.

3 large firm apples, such as Stayman, Granny Smith, Golden Delicious, or Red Delicious, cored but unpeeled	*1 cup walnut pieces* *About ⅓ cup sweet red Pesach wine* *1 teaspoon ground cinnamon* *2 to 3 teaspoons honey*

Put the apples and nuts into a food processor bowl fitted with the steel blade, and pulse-process until they are coarsely chopped. Add the remaining ingredients and process just a few seconds longer until the apples and nuts are finely chopped and the mixture forms a very rough paste. Do not purée it.

If a food processor is not available, very finely chop the apples and nuts by hand or put them through a food grinder. Then transfer them to a medium-sized bowl and stir in the remaining ingredients.

Makes about 2¼ cups.

MOROCCAN-STYLE HAROSET (P)

During a summer vacation to Canada, my family and I were delighted to find a kosher Moroccan restaurant on Bathurst Street in the "Jewish neighborhood" of Toronto. At *Le Marrakech,* we had one of the best meals of our entire trip.

Some inquiries led us to the owners, Ralph and Suzanne Ohayon and their son, Yves. The Ohayon family had moved to Canada from Morocco in 1968 with the aid of the Hebrew Immigration Assistance Service. In Toronto, they found it difficult to get the type of kosher cuisine to which they were accustomed. They thought that others might have the same gustatory desires, and so, in 1983, they finally opened a Moroccan restaurant, with Yves as manager.

Actually, everyone in the family loves to cook, including Ralph Ohayon, who generously shared some family recipes with me. Though we talked for hours about many delicious dishes, his eyes really glowed when he described the following *haroset,* which he annually prepares in very large quantities for family and friends. I have kept his proportions, but cut down the amounts.

Unlike most *haroset,* this delectable dried fruit-nut mixture is formed into little balls, which will keep for weeks in the refrigerator.

(Note: For best results, all the dried fruit should be fresh and soft.)

2 cups walnut pieces	*20 dried apricots*
1 cup blanched slivered or whole almonds	*10 large, pitted prunes*
25 pitted dates	*½ cup shelled pistachios (optional)*
10 large, brown ("calimyrna") dried figs	*¼ cup sweet red Pesach wine, or as needed*
	Ground cinnamon (optional)

Put all the nuts and dried fruit through the fine blade of a food grinder or finely grind them together in a food processor fitted with the steel blade (in batches, if necessary). Mix in just enough wine to make a smooth paste that is soft and malleable. Form the mixture into 1-inch balls. If desired, sprinkle the balls lightly with cinnamon. Store the balls in a tightly covered container in the refrigerator for up to 2 weeks. For best flavor, let them come to room temperature before serving.

Makes about 6 dozen 1-inch balls (about 3 cups of haroset mixture).

ISRAELI-STYLE HAROSET (P)

Many immigrant Israelis continue to make the *haroset* of the countries in which they once dwelled. However, *sabras* (native-born Israelis) often prefer to use ingredients that are more typical of their own country. The following delicious haroset is of the latter type.

*1 medium-sized navel orange
  (preferably Jaffa)
10 pitted dates
½ cup slivered or whole blanched
  almonds (or possibly peanuts,
  among Sephardim)
1 large apple, peeled (if desired),
  cored, and cut into large pieces*

*1 large or 2 small bananas
1 tablespoon lemon juice, preferably
  fresh
1 tablespoon sugar
1 teaspoon ground cinnamon
¼ cup sweet red Pesach wine
About ⅓ cup matzo meal*

Use a grater to remove most of the outer, colored part of the orange rind. Reserve the grated rind. Remove and discard the white pith from the orange. Cut the orange into pieces. Put the reserved grated orange rind, orange pieces, dates, almonds, apple, and banana through the fine blade of a food grinder, or finely grind them together in a food processor fitted with the steel blade. Stir in the lemon juice, sugar, cinnamon, and wine. Then stir in enough matzo meal for the desired consistency. (The mixture will get a bit thicker as it sits.) Refrigerate the haroset in a covered container, and serve it chilled. It will keep fresh for about 2 days in the refrigerator.

Makes about 2½ cups.

TURKISH-STYLE HAROSET (P)

When I demonstrated this recipe at a Hadassah meeting a few years ago, one of the older members delightedly exclaimed that it tasted just like the *haroset* she remembered having during her childhood in Turkey.

1 cup pitted dates, halved
1 cup dark or light raisins (or a
mixture)
1 large apple, peeled (if desired),
cored, and cut into large pieces
½ cup walnut pieces

½ cup blanched slivered or whole
almonds
1 medium-sized navel orange, peeled
and cut into chunks
About 2 tablespoons sweet red Pesach
wine

Put all the ingredients, except the wine, through the coarse blade of a food grinder, or coarsely grind them together in a food processor fitted with the steel blade (in batches, if necessary). Add the wine and mix or process to form a soft, slightly coarse mixture. Refrigerate the haroset in a covered container, and serve it chilled. (The haroset gets slightly firmer when chilled.) It will keep fresh for 2 to 3 days in the refrigerator.

Makes about 3 cups.

SEPHARDIC-STYLE DATE HAROSET (P)

This type of *haroset* is used by many different groups of Sephardim—North Africans, Iraqis, Iranians, and Afghans, among others.

It is always based on a paste made from cooked dates, sometimes with raisins. Chopped walnuts and/or almonds are also often included, either mixed into the paste or sprinkled on top.

Some Sephardim thin out the date paste with red wine, and flavor it with cinnamon. Others make the paste thick enough to be formed into small balls. Occasionally, the balls are coated with edible, dried rose petals.

Iraqi Jews often use more water and no additional ingredients, to produce a thin, date *syrup,* rather than a paste.

The following version of date *haroset* is an amalgam of several of these types.

1 pound pitted dates, chopped (if
desired, dark raisins may be
substituted for up to half of the
dates)
1½ cups warm water

2 to 4 tablespoons sweet red Pesach
wine (optional)
½ to 1 teaspoon ground cinnamon
(optional)
½ to 1 cup finely chopped walnuts
and/or almonds

Put the dates and water into a medium-sized saucepan and let them soak for 1 hour. Then bring them to a boil over high heat. Lower the heat, cover the saucepan, and simmer the dates for 30 to 60 minutes, or until they are very soft and form a paste. During the cooking period, stir the dates often, and mash them with a spoon to help break them down.

To smooth out the paste, press it through a sieve, colander, or food mill, or purée it in a food processor. If the purée it too thin and does not have a rich date taste, return it to the saucepan and simmer it down to the desired consistency, keeping in mind that it will thicken slightly more as it cools.

Let the date paste cool to room temperature. Stir in the desired amounts of wine and cinnamon. Stir in the nuts and/or sprinkle them on top. Store the paste in the refrigerator, tightly covered, for up to 2 weeks. For the best flavor, let it come to room temperature before serving.

Makes about 2 cups.

YEMENITE-STYLE HAROSET (P)

Yemenite Jews like spicy food, and their *haroset* is no exception. It has an intriguing sweet-hot flavor that is worth trying. Yemenites generally use very little sweetener in their cooking and might not use honey in the following *haroset*. However, those with more "Western" tastes will probably prefer to include it.

6 large, brown ("calimyrna") dried figs
6 pitted dates
2 tablespoons sesame seeds (optional)

About 1 teaspoon honey, or to taste
1/2 teaspoon ground ginger
1/8 teaspoon ground coriander seeds
Pinch of cayenne pepper (optional)

Put the figs and dates through the fine blade of a food grinder, or finely grind them together in a food processor fitted with the steel blade, to make a very firm, sticky paste. Mix in the sesame seeds, honey, and spices, adjusting the latter to taste. Store the haroset in the refrigerator, tightly covered, for up to 2 weeks. For best flavor, let it come to room temperature before serving.

Makes about 2/3 cup haroset mixture.

HUEVOS HAMINADOS (P)

(Sephardic-Style Long-Cooked Eggs)

These special hard-cooked eggs are a must at just about all Sephardic holiday celebrations and other functions, including funerals and the Shabbat dairy brunch known as *Desayuno*.

The eggs are simmered on the stove or in the oven for at least 8 hours, which turns the albumen brown, darkens the yolk slightly, and gives the entire egg a creamy texture and deliciously rich, mellow flavor. Sometimes, the eggs are cooked with onion skins, so that the shells take on a warm, brown hue.

In Israel, at outdoor kiosks, warm *huevos haminados* are often sold with *borekas* (page 347), cheese-filled flaky turnovers. The combination makes a great breakfast or lunch for those on the go.

During Pesach, *huevos haminados* are on most Sephardic Seder tables. Before eating them, some families, like the Danas from Istanbul, use the unshelled eggs for a friendly competition. Each Seder guest taps his or her egg against those of the other participants, until only one egg with an uncracked shell remains—and its owner is declared "the winner." The eggs are then served with *bimuelos de massa* (page 254), as the first course of dinner.

(Note: *Huevos haminados* are also included as part of one-pot Shabbat dinners, such as *dafina* [page 40].)

About 12 raw eggs in their shells	*Skins from several onions (optional)*
Water	*About ¼ cup vegetable oil*

Put the eggs in one layer in a large pot, and cover them with several inches of cool water. If desired, add the onion skins to the water to tint the shells brown and subtly flavor the eggs. (Onion skins are not necessary to tint the egg albumen brown. This happens because of the long cooking.)

Pour the oil on top of the water; it helps keep the water from evaporating during the extended cooking period. Slowly bring the water to a boil over medium-high heat; then cover the pot tightly and lower the heat so the eggs simmer very gently. Simmer them on top of the stove, or place the pot in a 225-degree oven, and cook for at least 8 hours or overnight.

Serve the eggs warm, at room temperature, or chilled. They may be reheated by boiling them for 3 to 5 minutes.

Makes about 12 huevos haminados.

PESCADO CON AGRISTADA (P)

(Fish in Egg-Lemon Sauce)

Among Sephardim from Turkey and Greece, this is the traditional fish course for the Seder dinner on *la prima noche de Pesach*—"the first night of Pesach." It is also often served on Shabbat. *Agristada* is the Judeo-Spanish term for a lemony yellow sauce thickened with eggs, called *avgolemono* in Greek.

As with many other Sephardic fish dishes, this one may be made ahead and chilled before serving, making it particularly convenient for a Seder meal. The recipe is based on one I learned from Ida Dana, an excellent Turkish-Sephardic cook.

POACHING LIQUID AND FISH
1½ cups water
2 tablespoons vegetable oil
Juice of ½ of a medium-sized lemon
  (reserve the other half of the lemon
  for the sauce)
2 tablespoons finely chopped fresh
  parsley leaves
½ teaspoon salt
Pinch of ground black pepper
2 pounds skinless fish fillets, such as
  halibut, salmon, flounder, cod,
  striped bass, sea trout, etc., cut
  into serving-sized pieces

SAUCE
2 large eggs, well beaten
Juice of the ½ lemon reserved from
  the poaching liquid
1 tablespoon matzo cake meal
About 3 tablespoons water

To poach the fish, combine the water, oil, lemon juice, parsley, salt, and pepper in a large deep skillet. Add the fish fillets, in one layer, if possible. Bring the liquid to a boil; then lower the heat and cover the skillet. Simmer the fish for 5 to 10 minutes, or until it is just cooked through but not falling apart. (If the fillets are thick, carefully turn them once during the poaching.) Use a slotted spoon to transfer the fish to a deep serving dish. Reserve the broth.

For the sauce, beat the eggs and lemon juice together in a medium-sized bowl. In a small bowl, mix the cake meal and water to make a creamy paste. Stir the paste into the egg-lemon mixture. Then gradually stir in about ½ cup of the hot fish broth. Stirring constantly, add all the egg-lemon mixture back to the remaining fish broth and stir over low heat until the sauce has thickened. Adjust the seasonings, if necessary. Pour the sauce over the fish. Serve hot or, as is more customary, refrigerate the fish and sauce, and serve them chilled.

Makes about 8 servings as a first course.

KEFTES DE PESCADO (P)

(Salmon Croquettes in Tomato Sauce)

Fish cakes, like those which follow, were one of my favorite childhood weeknight meals, and have always been quite popular with my own family. Recently, I learned that virtually the same dish (with a Judeo-Spanish name) is often served by Turkish and Greek Jews on Shabbat night and for Pesach Seders. The Sephardim add a light tomato sauce, which makes these even more special. For extra convenience, the croquettes can be fried ahead of time and reheated in the sauce just before serving.

Interestingly, some South African Jews make similar croquettes called *frikkadels,* which are often seasoned with ginger and nutmeg, instead of with parsley and lemon.

(Note: It is not necessary to remove the bones and skin from canned salmon; both are hardly distinguishable in the cooked croquettes. Furthermore, the bones are a good source of dietary calcium.)

1 15½-ounce can salmon, including liquid
2 large eggs
1 small-to-medium-sized onion, grated
3 tablespoons finely chopped fresh parsley leaves

1 to 2 tablespoons lemon juice, preferably fresh (optional)
About ½ cup matzo meal
Salt and ground black pepper to taste
Vegetable oil for frying

SAUCE
1 cup (or 1 8-ounce can) plain
  tomato sauce
1 to 2 tablespoons lemon juice,
  preferably fresh

¼ cup finely chopped fresh parsley
  leaves
1 garlic clove, finely minced
  (optional)
Salt and ground black pepper to taste

For the croquettes, put the salmon and its liquid into a medium-sized bowl and mash the salmon well with a fork. Add the eggs, onion, parsley, and lemon juice (if used). Stir in enough matzo meal to hold the mixture together. Season the salmon mixture with salt and pepper and mix it very thoroughly. Let it rest for about 5 minutes for the matzo meal to absorb some of the moisture.

In a large skillet, over medium-high heat, heat oil that is ⅛ to ¼ inch deep until it is hot but not smoking. Form the salmon mixture into thick patties, using about ¼ cup for each one, and put each patty into the oil as it is formed (see Note). (If the mixture is too soft to be shaped, stir in more matzo meal.)

Fry the patties in the oil until they are well browned on both sides. Drain them on paper towels. Pour any leftover oil out of the skillet.

In the skillet, combine all the sauce ingredients and mix well. Over medium-high heat, bring the sauce to a simmer. Arrange the browned croquettes in the sauce and simmer them, covered, for 5 to 10 minutes. Baste them occasionally with the sauce.

Makes 9 to 10 2½-inch-diameter croquettes.

NOTE: Before frying the patties, some Sephardim prefer to coat them lightly with additional matzo meal or matzo cake meal, and then with beaten egg. This egg coating is traditional for many types of keftes, and is quite tasty.

GEFILTE FISH LOAF WITH HORSERADISH SAUCE (P)

A few years ago, when Tulkoff's, the giant in the horseradish industry, had just moved to their new headquarters near the Baltimore harbor, vice-president Martin Tulkoff gave me a personal tour of the sprawling plant, while he recounted its interesting history. Though Tulkoff's is now one of the largest processors of horseradish in the world, Mr. Tulkoff explained that the business actually began as a sideline.

Back in the late 1920s, Harry Tulkoff, the patriarch of the family, was a fruit and vegetable vendor, as were many other Russian Jewish immigrants. The work was very difficult, and competition was tough. To attract more customers, Harry Tulkoff began grinding fresh horseradish root on the side. In that era, the pungent concoction was rarely sold bottled.

One day, as Martin Tulkoff tells it, his father had a brainstorm. Harry Tulkoff abruptly announced to his wife, "We're going into the horseradish business." Her reply: "You're *meshuggeh!* How are we ever going to make a living?"

In the old days, Harry and Lena Tulkoff scrubbed the gangling roots one by one, and ground them in a hand-cranked wooden grinder, which collected the horseradish in a drawer. Then they mixed the ground horseradish with vinegar and salt in large wooden barrels, and bottled, capped, and labeled it—all by hand. The original bottles were octagonal with a label that said, in Yiddish, "*hrain,*" which means, simply, "horseradish."

Gradually, specialized equipment, most of it custom designed by family members, took over each task. Today the plant is almost completely automated. And, Tulkoff's horseradish products are distributed throughout the world. However, a special Pesach horseradish mixture is still produced each year just for the holiday, and is very popular among Jewish customers.

After all, virtually every Ashkenazic Seder plate includes some horseradish. And, most Ashkenazim prefer to eat their holiday gefilte fish with horseradish in some form.

Following are recipes for an innovative, easy gefilte fish dish, and a delectable sauce, based on horseradish, to accompany it. (Of course, purists may prefer their horseradish "straight.")

Any firm-fleshed, light-colored fish can be used in the loaf; however, pike, whitefish and/or carp will give it an "old-fashioned" gefilte-fish flavor. Garnished with strips of pepper and carrot circles, the unmolded loaf is quite attractive, and can be served either warm or cold.

HORSERADISH SAUCE
¾ cup mayonnaise
¼ cup plain prepared horseradish
⅓ cup ketchup
Few drops fresh lemon juice or apple cider vinegar to taste
Ground black pepper to taste

FISH LOAF
½ of a medium-sized sweet green pepper, cut into strips
1 small carrot, peeled and cut crosswise into thin circles

1 pound skinless fillets of firm-fleshed white fish, such as pike, whitefish, cod, carp, haddock, etc.
1 medium-sized onion
1 medium-sized carrot
1 large egg
1 tablespoon vegetable oil
2 tablespoons cold water
¼ cup matzo meal
3 tablespoons finely chopped fresh parsley leaves
½ teaspoon salt
⅛ to ¼ teaspoon ground black pepper

For the horseradish sauce, combine all the ingredients in a small covered bowl. Refrigerate the sauce for several hours to give the flavors a chance to blend.

For the fish loaf, grease well an 8- by 4-inch loaf pan. Line the bottom of the pan with a rectangle of wax paper cut to fit; then grease the paper. Use the green pepper strips and carrot circles to form an attractive design on top of the wax paper. For instance, arrange the strips of pepper so they form parallel crosswise stripes; then put 2 or 3 carrot circles between each stripe. Remember, the design will be inverted when the loaf is turned out of the pan, so put the "good" sides of the vegetables facing down.

In a food grinder or a food processor fitted with the steel blade, grind or process the fish, onion, and carrot until they are very finely minced. (If desired, the onion and carrot may be grated by hand, instead.) Add the egg, oil, water, matzo meal, parsley, salt, and pepper and mix until very well combined. (If the food processor bowl is large enough, all this may be mixed in it.)

Gently spoon some of the fish mixture around and over the vegetable design in the pan, being careful not to disturb the vegetables. Press it into place, leaving no air spaces. Then add the remaining fish mixture to the pan, spreading it evenly. Cover the fish mixture with another rectangle of wax paper, which is first greased on the side facing the loaf.

Bake the loaf in a preheated 350-degree oven for about 50 minutes, or until it is firm. Remove it from the oven and let it stand for about 10 minutes. Peel off the wax paper on top; then run a knife around the sides of the loaf to loosen it. Invert the loaf onto a serving dish and lift off the pan. If the second piece of wax paper is attached to the loaf, peel it off. Serve the loaf warm or chilled, cut crosswise into slices. (It will slice easier when chilled.)

Serve the horseradish sauce on the side, as an accompaniment to the gefilte fish loaf.

Makes about 8 servings.

BIMUELOS DE MASSA (P)

(Matzo Meal Pancakes)

These Sephardic pancakes are virtually identical to the more familiar Ashkenazic *matzo meal latkes*. Some Sephardim include them as part of the Seder meal. Others prefer to serve them for breakfast, accompanied by sugar, yogurt, and, possibly, *arrope*—a thick syrup made from raisins, that is also used as *haroset* in some households.

Sometimes Pesach *bimuelos* are made from matzo farfel or crumbled matzos, which are soaked in water to soften them.

4 large eggs	*1 cup regular or whole wheat matzo*
1 cup water	*meal*
½ teaspoon salt	*Vegetable oil for frying*

In a medium-sized bowl, use a fork to mix the eggs, water, and salt together. Stir in the matzo meal. Let the mixture stand for about 10 minutes to thicken slightly.

In a large skillet, over medium-high heat, heat oil that is about ⅛-inch deep. Spoon generous tablespoons of batter into the oil. Fry the pancakes until they are golden brown on both sides.

Makes about 15 2-inch pancakes.

VARIATIONS

1. For "fluffy bimuelos" (my personal preference), separate the eggs. In a medium-sized bowl, combine the egg yolks, water, and salt. Stir in the matzo meal. In another bowl, use an electric mixer to beat the egg whites until they are stiff but not dry. Mix the beaten whites with the matzo meal mixture. Use about 3 tablespoons batter for each pancake.

2. BIMUELOS DE MASSA Y QUESO   (D)
(Matzo Meal Pancakes with Cheese)

For these, use either of the above methods to make the bimuelos, but substitute *milk* for the water. Add *½ cup finely grated hard or semisoft cheese* to the batter just before frying the pancakes. The type of cheese is a matter of personal taste.

SOUP DIAMONDS ROYALE   (M)

(Soup Garnishes)

Based on a classic French recipe, these light, delicate soup garnishes are made by cutting a very easy, baked custard into tiny diamond shapes. When added to shimmery *Chicken Soup* (page 31), the custard pieces look like golden jewels. Their flavor is reminiscent of the special unlaid egg yolks that my mother used to cook in chicken soup when I was a child.

4 large eggs
1 cup lukewarm chicken broth,
  seasoned to taste with salt, pepper,
  and herbs (or pre-seasoned chicken
  bouillon cubes dissolved in hot
  water)

1 tablespoon finely chopped fresh
  parsley leaves

In a medium-sized bowl, use a fork to beat the eggs until well blended. Then slowly beat in the broth and parsley. Pour the mixture into an 8-inch-square or equivalent pan. Set the pan containing the custard mixture inside a larger pan and pour boiling water into the larger pan about as deep as the custard.

Bake the custard in a preheated 325-degree oven for 25 to 30 minutes, or until a knife inserted in the center comes out clean. Remove the pan from the water and cool the custard to room temperature in the pan. Cut it on the diagonal into ½-inch diamonds (or other desired shapes).

To serve, heat the diamonds in chicken soup just before serving. Include several in each bowl of soup.

Makes about 8 servings.

KEFTES DE PRASSA Y CARNE (M)

(Leek and Meat Patties)

In 1969, Ida Revah Dana, her husband, and two children emigrated from their native Istanbul to the United States. Over the years, the Danas have welcomed increasingly large numbers of family and friends to their Pesach Seders, so that the number now averages around fifty people. Mrs. Dana prepares the entire meal herself, except for a few sweets brought as gifts.

As most of the guests are Turkish Sephardim like the Danas, the menu is always based on holiday favorites from this culinary heritage. For instance, there are usually *bimuelos de massa, huevos haminados, pescado con agristada, apio* (pages 254, 248, 249, and 264), and stewed meat or poultry with the following delectable leek-meat *keftes*.

Mrs. Dana prepares these *keftes* ahead of time, and refrigerates or freezes them. Shortly before serving, she tops them with cooking juices from the stewed meat or chicken, and warms them in a 350-degree oven for about 20 minutes, or until they are heated through.

PATTIES
2 large bunches (about 8 medium-sized) fresh leeks
1 pound lean ground beef
2 large eggs, beaten
About ¼ cup matzo meal or matzo cake meal
1 teaspoon salt
¼ teaspoon ground black pepper

FOR FRYING
About ½ cup matzo cake meal, for coating
Vegetable oil
3 to 4 large eggs, beaten

To clean the leeks, cut off and discard the roots and all but 1 to 2 inches of the green tops. Slice the leeks in half lengthwise and rinse them very well under cool running water to remove any grit. Coarsely chop the leeks and put them in a saucepan with water to cover. Simmer them, covered, for 20 to 30 minutes, or until they are very tender.

Drain the leeks well; then cool them until they can be handled. Use your hands to squeeze out all the excess liquid. Grind the leeks in a meat grinder (or very coarsely purée them with a food processor).

In a medium-sized bowl, combine the leeks with the ground beef, eggs, ¼ cup matzo meal, salt, and pepper. Use your hands or a fork to blend them well. The mixture should be soft, but firm enough to be molded into patties. Add more matzo meal, if necessary.

Form the leek-meat mixture into small patties about 2 inches wide and ½ inch thick, coating each with cake meal to make it easier to shape. In a large skillet, over medium heat, heat oil that is about ¼ inch deep until it is hot but not smoking. Dip each patty into the beaten egg to coat it and drain off the excess; then immediately set it in the hot oil. Fry the patties until they are golden brown on both sides.

Makes about 30 2-inch patties.

TONGUE IN SWEET-AND-SOUR SAUCE (M)

Tongue is sometimes included as a side dish or first course at Ashkenazic Seders, as well as at festive meals for many other holidays. On Rosh Hashanah, for instance, it is often served to show that we want to be at the "head" of our peers in the coming year.

The following tasty sauce turns boiled tongue into a special treat.

1 large beef tongue

SAUCE
2 tablespoons matzo cake meal
1 cup beef broth or bouillon made
from cubes or powder
½ cup apple cider vinegar

½ cup packed dark brown sugar
¼ teaspoon ground cinnamon
¼ teaspoon ground ginger
½ cup light and/or dark raisins
¼ cup chopped dates (optional)
1 or 2 thin fresh lemon slices

In a large saucepan, cover the tongue with cold water and bring it to a boil over high heat; then pour off and discard the water. Repeat the process once more to make sure the tongue is thoroughly cleaned. Cover the tongue with clean, cold water once more, and bring to a boil; then cover the pan tightly and lower the heat. Simmer the tongue for 2 to 3 hours, or until it is fork-tender. (If desired, the tongue can be cooked, instead, in a pressure cooker for about 45 minutes at 15 pounds pressure.)

Drain the tongue well and let it cool for 5 to 10 minutes, or until it can be handled. Do not let the tongue cool completely, or it will be impossible to remove the skin. Using paper towels to keep your fingers from slipping, hold the tongue in one hand, and peel off all its skin with your other hand. If necessary, use a small knife to begin the peeling process. Cut off and discard the tip of the tongue, as well as all the gristle and fat. Cut the meat into ¾-inch cubes. (If desired, the tongue can be made ahead to this point, and reheated later in the sauce.)

For the sauce, mix the cake meal and ¼ cup of the broth in a small saucepan to make a smooth paste. Then stir in the remaining broth, vinegar, brown sugar, cinnamon, and ginger. Bring to a boil over medium-high heat; then stir in the raisins, dates (if used), and lemon. Lower the heat and simmer the sauce, stirring often, for 15 to 20 minutes, or until it has thickened slightly and lost its strong vinegar taste. Stir in the cubed, cooked tongue, and simmer 5 to 10 minutes longer, or until the tongue is heated through. If desired, remove the lemon slices before serving.

Makes 6 to 8 servings as a side dish or first course.

ROLLED PARSLEY-STUFFED VEAL BREAST (M)

Moroccan Jews enjoy a wonderfully varied cuisine that transforms ordinary foods into exotic, attractive treats. A good example is the following veal roast, which comes from the expansive repertoire of Ginette Spier.

Mrs. Spier grew up in Mogador, Morocco, as part of an active Jewish community. In 1961, when her family left their native land, they went to live in England because her mother had a British passport. There, Ginette Rosilio married Gerald Spier, an economist with the World Bank, whose career brought them and their two children to the United States in 1973.

Mrs. Spier and her family celebrate all the Jewish holidays with

Moroccan-Sephardic foods that were favorites from her youth. During Pesach, some of these might include candied citrus fruits, deep-fried artichokes stuffed with meat, a layered meat-potato-egg pie called *pastella,* lamb baked with onions and perhaps truffles or Jerusalem artichokes, and *marzipan petit fours* (page 226).

Another popular dish is this veal roast, which is rolled around an unusual mixture of parsley, chopped hard-boiled egg whites, whole hard-boiled egg yolks, and a variety of seasonings. When the roast is cut crosswise, each slice is a colorful work of art. The loaf can be made ahead, and reheated or served at room temperature.

STUFFING

2 to 3 tablespoons vegetable oil

4 to 5 garlic cloves, finely minced or pressed (optional)

2 large bunches fresh parsley (stems removed), finely chopped

½ teaspoon ground nutmeg

¼ teaspoon salt

½ teaspoon ground black pepper

4 large hard-boiled eggs, chilled or at room temperature

1 to 2 large uncooked eggs

VEAL

1 3-pound boned veal breast, in one piece (without a pocket), most surface fat removed

COOKING SAUCE

2 to 3 tablespoons vegetable oil

2 medium-sized onions, finely chopped

2 garlic cloves, minced (optional)

1 large ripe tomato, peeled, seeded, and chopped

1 medium-sized sweet green pepper, diced

Pinch of cayenne pepper or hot red pepper flakes, or to taste

¼ teaspoon salt

¼ teaspoon ground black pepper

¼ cup warm water

½ cup dry white Pesach wine

1½ cups sliced fresh mushrooms

For the stuffing, heat the oil in a large skillet over medium-high heat; then add the garlic, parsley, nutmeg, salt, and pepper, and cook, stirring, for about 5 minutes, or until the mixture is cooked through and tender. Remove it from the heat. Separate the whites and yolks of the hard-boiled eggs, keeping the yolks whole. Set the yolks aside. Finely chop the whites; then stir them into the cooked parsley mixture. Beat 1 of the raw eggs, and stir it into the parsley-egg white mixture. If the mixture does not hold together well, stir in part or all of another beaten egg.

Before stuffing the veal, lace a large sewing needle with a long piece of heavy thread, preferably black so it will be easy to see and remove later. To stuff the veal breast, spread it out on a flat surface, with the nicer side down. Spread the parsley-egg mixture evenly over the top surface. Arrange the reserved whole cooked egg yolks at evenly spaced intervals lengthwise down the center of the stuffing. Bring the longer sides of the veal breast together over the yolks and sew the edges tightly together. Sew both ends of the roll closed. To make the roast more secure, loop heavy cord around the roll several times, and tie it securely in place.

For the sauce, over medium-high heat, heat the oil in a pot or Dutch oven large enough to hold the roast. Add the onions, garlic, tomato, green pepper, cayenne pepper, salt, and black pepper and cook, stirring, for about 1 minute. Add the roast to the pot and brown it on all sides. Then add the water and wine to the pot. Cover the pot tightly and lower the heat so the liquid just simmers. Stew the roast, basting it and rotating it occasionally, for about 1½ hours, or until the veal is very tender. If the pot becomes too dry, add a bit of water. When the veal is tender, add the mushrooms to the sauce and cook for about 5 minutes, or just until they are tender.

Remove the roast from the pot and let it rest for 10 to 15 minutes. Carefully remove all the cord and sewing thread. Cut the roast crosswise into approximately ¾-inch-thick slices. Serve it with the sauce from the pot.

If the roast is not to be served immediately, do not slice it; wrap it well in aluminum foil and chill it first. (It is easier to slice when chilled.) Serve the roast at room temperature or reheat it. To reheat the sliced roast, reassemble the slices and wrap them well in foil; then warm them in a 350-degree oven until they are heated to the desired temperature.

Makes 12 to 15 slices; about 8 servings.

CHICKEN SCALOPPINE WITH ZUCCHINI IN AVGOLEMONO SAUCE (M)

The term "scaloppine" refers to boneless, thinly sliced pieces of meat which are sometimes also called "scallops." Although this particular cut and its quick cooking method are frequently associated with veal, it is not always the case. The following dish shows how wonderfully elegant, yet easy and inexpensive, chicken (or turkey) breasts can be when prepared in this manner. The egg-lemon sauce is based on one that is very popular among Greek and Turkish Jews.

1½ pounds boned chicken (or turkey) breast, cut into ⅜- to ½-inch-thick cutlets

Salt and ground black pepper to taste

1 to 2 tablespoons vegetable oil

1 tablespoon pareve margarine (or additional oil)

3 medium-sized zucchini, washed well, ends trimmed, and cut into ¼-inch-thick crosswise slices

3 large egg yolks

2 tablespoons lemon juice, preferably fresh

1 cup chicken broth or bouillon made from cubes or powder

Put the chicken cutlets between sheets of plastic wrap and pound them gently with a rubber mallet or rolling pin until they are about half of their original thickness. Be careful not to tear the cutlets. Lightly sprinkle them with salt and pepper.

In a large skillet, over medium-high heat, heat the oil with the margarine. Quickly sauté the poultry cutlets, in batches, just until they are cooked through, only about 2 minutes on each side. Do not overcook them or the meat may toughen. Remove the cutlets to a warm platter. Using the fat left in the skillet, sauté the zucchini slices until they are crisp-tender. Put the slices on top of the cooked cutlets. Discard any fat remaining in the skillet but reserve the skillet.

In a small bowl, beat the egg yolks with the lemon juice. In the reserved skillet, bring the chicken broth to a boil. Very slowly pour the hot broth into the egg-lemon mixture in the bowl, while stirring constantly. Then pour the sauce back into the skillet and cook over low heat, stirring constantly, until it becomes slightly thickened. Do not boil the sauce or it will curdle. Return the chicken and zucchini to the skillet and stir them in the sauce just until they are heated through. Serve immediately.

Makes 5 to 6 servings.

TAGINE OF CHICKEN WITH PRUNES AND ALMONDS   (M)

This delectable dish is quite popular with Moroccan Jews, who some-times substituted boned, cubed lamb for the chicken. Those Sephardim who do not abstain from eating rice during Pesach may serve it with this *tagine* (pronounced "tah-jheen"), a general term for any slowly simmered Moroccan stew. The word also means the special type of ceramic cas-serole usually used in Morocco to cook these stews.

2 tablespoons pareve *margarine or vegetable oil*

1 medium-sized onion, finely chopped

About 3½ pounds meaty chicken pieces (remove skin, if desired)

1 cup water

1 to 3 teaspoons ground cinnamon

½ teaspoon ground ginger

¼ to ½ teaspoon black pepper, preferably freshly ground

Pinch of salt

10 to 12 ounces (about 2 cups) pitted prunes

1 tablespoon honey or sugar (optional)

1 cup whole blanched almonds, lightly toasted (see Note)

In a very large deep skillet or a Dutch oven, over medium-high heat, heat the margarine or oil (or use a mixture); then sauté the onion until it is tender but not browned. Add the chicken to the skillet and lightly brown it on all sides.

Mix the water with the cinnamon, ginger, pepper, and salt and pour it over the browned chicken. Bring the liquid to a boil. Cover the skillet tightly, lower the heat, and simmer the chicken for 30 minutes, turning the pieces occasionally. Add the prunes and honey (if used) to the skillet, evenly distributing the prunes around the chicken, and making sure they are covered with liquid. Cover the skillet again, and simmer the chicken and prunes together for about 20 minutes, or until both are very tender. If the sauce becomes too dry and begins to stick to the bottom of the skillet, stir in additional water as needed.

Use tongs or a slotted spoon to transfer the chicken to a large serving platter. Stir about half the almonds into the prune sauce remaining in the pot; then spoon the sauce mixture over the chicken. Garnish the top with the remaining almonds.

Makes about 6 servings.

NOTE: To toast the almonds, spread them in a jelly roll or similar pan and heat them in a 350-degree oven, stirring them occasionally, for about 10 minutes, or until they are lightly browned. Or, to toast them in the Moroccan manner, heat some vegetable oil in a skillet and sauté the almonds in the oil until they are lightly browned; then remove them with a slotted spoon and drain them on paper towels.

SWEET POTATO AND APPLE TZIMMES (P)

(Vegetable-Fruit Casserole)

Most Ashkenazic households have at least one dish similar to this on the Seder table. It can be made ahead and rewarmed shortly before serving.

4 large sweet potatoes (or "yams"), peeled and cut into ¾-inch cubes (about 5 cups)

1 medium-sized butternut squash, peeled, seeded, and cut into ¾-inch cubes (about 2 cups)

4 medium-sized apples, peeled, cored, and coarsely chopped

About 24 pitted prunes (7 to 8 ounces)

⅔ cup sweet red Pesach wine (may be half water)

About ½ cup sugar, or to taste

1½ teaspoons ground cinnamon

½ teaspoon ground ginger (optional)

In a large bowl, combine all the ingredients and mix well. Turn them out into a greased 9- by 11-inch casserole dish or baking pan. Cover the dish tightly with aluminum foil and bake the tzimmes in a preheated 375-degree oven for about 1 hour, or until the sweet potatoes and squash are tender.

Stir the tzimmes before serving to evenly distribute the sauce and slightly mash the apples.

Makes about 8 servings.

APIO (P)

(Celeriac and Carrots)

This is a traditional dish that Sephardic Jews, particularly those from Turkey and Greece, serve on the first night of Pesach. Like most Sephardic vegetable dishes, it can be served hot as a side dish or chilled (or at room temperature) as a salad or first course.

The recipe features celeriac, which is also called "celery knob" or "celery root." This gnarled root vegetable smells and tastes a bit like its cousin, stalk celery; however, the flesh is a creamy white color, its texture is smooth, not stringy, and the flavor is more subtle than stalk celery. Celeriac should be peeled and cut up just before cooking, as it may darken from exposure to the air.

¾ cup water
1 tablespoon olive or vegetable oil
2 tablespoons lemon juice, preferably fresh
1 tablespoon sugar, or to taste
½ teaspoon salt
3 medium-sized carrots, cut on the diagonal into ¼-inch-thick slices (about 1½ cups)

1 large celeriac, peeled, cut crosswise into ⅜-inch-thick slices, and each slice cut into quarters

THICKENER FOR SAUCE (OPTIONAL)
1 tablespoon potato starch
1 to 2 tablespoons cold water

In a medium-sized saucepan, combine the ¾ cup water, oil, lemon juice, sugar, and salt. Bring to a boil over high heat. Stir in the carrots. Cover the pan and lower the heat. Simmer the carrots for 3 minutes. Then gently stir in the celeriac so that all the pieces are coated with the sauce. Cover the saucepan and simmer the vegetables together for about 10 to 12 minutes longer, or until they are just tender.

If a thicker sauce is desired, combine the potato starch and cold water until well combined and stir the paste into the hot sauce. Continue heating and stirring the vegetables just until the sauce thickens and simmers. Remove from the heat. Serve hot, at room temperature, or chilled.

Makes 4 to 6 servings.

MINA DE ESPINACA Y TOMAT (D)

(Spinach-Tomato Matzo "Pie")

During Pesach, Sephardic Jews, particularly those from Turkey and Greece, enjoy many different types of *minas* (pronounced "mee'-nahs"). Each has a base and a top of whole matzo, with various fillings sandwiched in between. Sometimes, as in the recipe which follows, there is a third layer of matzo inside the pie.

Dairy versions, such as this one and the *Mina de Prassa con Queso* (page 266), are usually served for brunch or a light evening meal. A *mina* made with meat (see *Mina de Carne*, page 268) may be part of the Seder dinner.

Minas are particularly convenient in that they can be made ahead, and reheated. They are cut into squares for serving. Following is one of my family's favorite *minas,* which I prepare often during the holiday.

(Note: "Authentic" *minas* are frequently made with large quantities of oil, both in the pan and on top of the pie. I have eliminated most of it. Consequently, this *mina* is not as crisp, but it is lighter, and very tasty.)

3¼ to 4 whole matzot, plain or whole wheat (but NOT egg matzot, because they're too soft)
2 tablespoons butter, margarine, or vegetable oil
1 medium-sized onion, finely chopped
1 to 2 garlic cloves, minced (optional)
1 16-ounce can tomatoes, including juice, chopped

1 10-ounce package frozen chopped spinach, thawed and very well drained
Salt and ground black pepper to taste
1 to 2 tablespoons vegetable oil for the pan
2 large eggs, beaten
4 to 6 ounces hard or semisoft cheese, any kind or combination (such as Muenster, Swiss, mozzarella, American, etc.), grated (1 to 1½ cups packed)

Soak the matzot in some warm water for about 3 minutes; then carefully placed them on paper towels to drain.

Meanwhile, in a large skillet, over medium-high heat, melt the butter; then sauté the onion and garlic (if used) until they are tender but not browned. Add the tomatoes and their juice, along with the drained spinach. Cook the mixture, stirring occasionally, for about 5 minutes, or until most, but not all, of the liquid has evaporated (see Variation). Season the mixture with salt and pepper to taste; then remove it from the heat. Set it aside to cool slightly.

Coat an 8- or 9-inch-square baking pan with the 1 to 2 tablespoons of oil. Pour the beaten eggs into a large platter that has a slightly raised edge. Coat both sides of a softened matzo with the egg; then place the matzo in the bottom of the pan. Use part of a second egg-coated matzo to fill in any spaces. Spread the matzo with half of the cooked vegetable mixture; then sprinkle it with a third of the grated cheese. Cover the filling with another whole egg-coated matzo, filling in any spaces as before. Then top that with the remaining vegetable mixture, and another third of the cheese. Finally, cover with another layer of egg-coated matzo and sprinkle the remaining cheese on top.

Bake the mina in a preheated 375-degree oven for 20 to 25 minutes, or until the cheese is melted and the casserole is bubbly. Remove it from the oven and let it rest for 5 minutes before serving. Cut it into large squares to serve.

Makes about 4 servings as a main course, or more as a side dish.

VARIATION

For a "tuna-vegetable mina," add a *6½-ounce can of tuna (drained and flaked)* to the vegetable mixture in the skillet, when it is almost done simmering.

MINA DE PRASSA CON QUESO (D)

(Leek-Cheese Matzo "Pie")

Turkish and Greek Sephardim usually cook leeks by simmering them in water; however, I think they have even better flavor if they are sautéed in a little butter first, as in the tasty *mina* recipe that follows.

About 3 whole matzot, plain or whole wheat (but NOT egg matzot, because they're too soft)

1 large bunch (about 4 medium-sized) fresh leeks

2 to 3 tablespoons butter, margarine, or vegetable oil

1 medium-sized onion, finely chopped

¼ cup water

1 7½- to 8-ounce package farmer cheese

3 large eggs, divided

Salt and ground black pepper to taste

1 to 2 tablespoons vegetable oil for the pan

About 6 ounces cheese (such as Muenster, Swiss, mozzarella, etc.), cut into thin slices or grated (about 1½ cups packed)

Soak the matzot in some warm water for about 3 minutes; then carefully place them on paper towels to drain.

To clean the leeks, cut off and discard the roots and all but 1 to 2 inches of the green tops. Slice the leeks in half lengthwise and rinse them very well under cool running water to remove any grit. Finely chop the leeks and set them aside.

In a large skillet, over medium-high heat, melt the butter; then sauté the leeks and onions for about 2 minutes. Add the water and cover the skillet. Steam the leeks and onions for about 5 minutes, or until they are tender. Remove the cover and cook the mixture, stirring, to evaporate any moisture. Remove the mixture from the heat and cool it slightly. Stir in the farmer cheese and 2 of the eggs, and mix until well blended. Season the mixture with salt and pepper to taste.

Coat an 8- or 9-inch-square baking pan with the oil. Beat the remaining egg and pour it into a large platter that has a slightly raised edge. Coat both sides of a softened matzo with the egg; then place the matzo in the bottom of the pan. Use part of another egg-coated matzo to fill in any spaces. Spread about two thirds of the sliced or grated cheese over the matzo. Top it with all of the leek-cheese mixture. Cover the mixture with a second layer of egg-coated matzo, and top that with the remaining sliced or grated cheese.

Bake the mina in a preheated 375-degree oven for about 30 minutes, or until the cheese is melted and the filling is firm. Remove the mina from the oven and let it rest for 5 minutes before serving. Cut it into large squares to serve.

Makes about 4 servings as a main course, or more as a side dish.

MINA DE CARNE (M)

(Meat-Potato Matzo "Pie")

This *mina* is sometimes served as part of a Sephardic Seder dinner. It can also stand on its own as a main course for a mid-holiday meal.

About 3 whole matzot, plain or whole wheat (but NOT egg matzot, because they're too soft)
1 pound lean ground beef
1 medium-sized onion, finely chopped
1 to 2 garlic cloves, minced (optional)
2 celery stalks, finely chopped
2 tablespoons finely chopped fresh parsley leaves

1 teaspoon chopped fresh dillweed (or ½ teaspoon dried dillweed), optional
1½ cups plain mashed potatoes
3 large eggs, divided
Salt and ground black pepper to taste
1 to 2 tablespoons vegetable oil for the pan

Soak the matzot in some warm water for about 3 minutes; then carefully place them on paper towels to drain.

In a large skillet, over medium-high heat, brown the ground beef with the onion, garlic (if used), and celery, breaking up the meat with a spoon or fork. When the meat has browned and the vegetables are tender, drain off and discard any excess fat. Remove the meat mixture from the heat and stir in the parsley and dillweed (if used).

In a small bowl, combine the mashed potatoes and 2 of the eggs and mix until well blended. Stir about two thirds of the potato mixture into the meat filling. Season the meat mixture with salt and pepper to taste. Reserve the remaining potato mixture.

Coat an 8- or 9-inch-square baking pan with the oil. Beat the remaining egg and pour it into a large platter that has a slightly raised edge. Coat both sides of a softened matzo with the egg; then place the matzo in the bottom of the pan. Use part of another egg-coated matzo to fill in any spaces. Spread all the meat mixture on top. Cover the mixture with a second layer of egg-coated matzo, filling in any spaces as above. Season the remaining potato mixture with salt and pepper and spread it on top.

Bake the mina in a preheated 375-degree oven for about 30 minutes, or until the top is lightly browned and the filling is firm. Remove the mina from the oven, and let it rest 5 minutes before serving. Cut it into large squares to serve.

Makes about 4 servings as a main course, or more as a side dish.

FRITADA DE ESPINACA (D)

(Spinach-Cheese Casserole)

Although I often see this popular Sephardic dish, which is sometimes called a *quajado*, described as a "spinach soufflé," it is not at all like a puffy, French-style soufflé, because the egg whites are not beaten separately from the yolks. Actually, a *fritada* is much more similar to an Ashkenazic *kugel* or, perhaps, a crustless quiche.

The following tasty *fritada* makes a nice main course for a light lunch or dinner, or a great side dish at a dairy meal. And, it's perfect for a buffet.

(Note: When baked in a 9- by 13-inch baking pan, as directed below, this *fritada* is about ½ inch high. If preferred, it can be baked in a 9-inch-square pan to produce a higher *fritada* that is served in smaller squares.)

4 large eggs, lightly beaten
2 10-ounce packages frozen chopped spinach, thawed and drained of excess liquid, but not squeezed dry
½ cup matzo meal
6 ounces cheese, such as Swiss, Muenster, mozzarella, or kaskaval (the Sephardic favorite), grated (1½ cups packed)
¼ cup grated Parmesan or Romano cheese (or more of the same cheese as above)
1 cup small-curd cottage cheese
About ¼ teaspoon salt
¼ teaspoon ground black pepper
About 2 tablespoons vegetable oil for the pan

In a large bowl, beat the eggs until they are well blended. Add the remaining ingredients, except the oil, and stir well. Coat the bottom and sides of a 9- by 13-inch baking pan with the oil. Evenly spread the spinach mixture in the pan and smooth the top.

Bake the fritada in a preheated 375-degree oven for 40 to 45 minutes, or until it is golden brown and firm. Let it rest for about 5 minutes before serving. Or let it cool longer and serve at room temperature.

Makes about 6 main-dish servings, or 8 to 10 side-dish servings.

GREMSHELISH (P)

(Dutch-Style Sweet Matzo Fritters)

Various types of matzo fritters are popular in both Sephardic and Ashkenazic cuisines. They are known by a number of names, including *chremslach, kremsel, grimsel, gremlinish, gremsjelies,* and *bimuelos.* The delectable Dutch version that follows is laden with raisins and almonds, and flavored with cinnamon and sugar. And, to lighten the fritters, the egg whites are beaten separately from the yolks.

Similar Sephardic fritters sometimes have an assortment of chopped dried fruit added to them. And they may be topped with a sweetened wine sauce that is similar to *zabaglione* (page 272), instead of cinnamon-sugar.

Serve the *gremshelish* for breakfast or as a snack, or increase the sugar and turn them into dessert.

4½ standard-sized matzot, plain or whole wheat
3 large eggs, separated
¾ cup finely chopped almonds (or other nuts)
1 cup dark or light raisins or currants
3 tablespoons vegetable oil
½ teaspoon ground cinnamon
1 tablespoon lemon juice, preferably fresh

1 teaspoon grated lemon rind (yellow part only)
3 tablespoons matzo cake meal
Pinch of salt
⅓ cup sugar
Vegetable oil for frying

TOPPING (OPTIONAL)
¼ cup sugar, mixed with 1½ teaspoons ground cinnamon

In a medium-sized bowl, break up the matzot into small pieces and cover them with cold water. Let them soak until very soft, at least 15 minutes. Drain the matzot well; then use your hands to squeeze out all excess water. Press the softened matzot between your fingers, or mash them with a fork, until they are completely crushed. With a fork, mix in the egg yolks, almonds, raisins, oil, cinnamon, lemon juice, rind, and cake meal.

In a separate bowl, beat the egg whites with the salt until foamy. Gradually add the sugar and continue beating the whites until they form stiff, shiny peaks. Fold the whites into the matzo mixture.

In a large skillet, over medium-high heat, heat oil that is ⅛ to ¼ inch deep. Drop generous tablespoonfuls of the batter into the oil. Fry the fritters until they are lightly browned on both sides, turning them once. Drain them on paper towels. If desired, sprinkle them lightly with some of the sugar-cinnamon mixture.

Makes about 30 2½-inch fritters; about 8 servings.

POIRES BOURGUIGNONNE (P)

(Pears Poached in Red Wine)

This simple, but elegant, French dessert is a perfect light ending to a holiday meal. The wine tints the outside of each pear a lovely rosy-red color, but the inside stays white. The pears can be served warm, at room temperature, or chilled. They make a nice accompaniment to *sponge cake* (page 276) or *zabaglione* (page 272).

(Note: All the alcohol evaporates from the wine syrup during cooking.)

6 medium-sized barely ripe pears, peeled
1½ cups sweet red Pesach wine
⅓ cup honey (or generous ⅓ cup sugar)

1½ tablespoons lemon juice, preferably fresh
2 teaspoons grated orange rind (colored part only)
2 3-inch cinnamon sticks (or ½ teaspoon ground cinnamon)

Remove the seeds from each pear by carving a small hole in the bottom. Leave the pears whole. In a large saucepan, combine the remaining ingredients, and bring to a boil over medium-high heat. Add the pears and cover the pan. Lower the heat and simmer the pears for 15 to 20 minutes, basting them often with the wine syrup. The pears are done when they are tender but not mushy. The exact time will depend on the type of pear.

Cool the pears in the wine syrup. Serve them lukewarm, at room temperature, or chilled, with a little of the cooking syrup poured over each pear.

Makes 6 servings.

ZABAGLIONE (P)

(Italian-Style Foamy Wine Custard)

This fluffy, rich dessert (pronounced "dzah-bahl-yoh'-neh") is delicious as a sauce over *sponge cake* (page 276), or as a pudding accompanied with fresh fruit, *amaretti* (page 284), or other macaroons. A very similar, French-style custard, often made with white wine instead of red, is called *sabayon*.

Zabaglione is a great way to use up leftover egg yolks. (Leftover egg whites freeze quite well and, when thawed, can be used just as fresh ones; but this is not true of the yolks.)

Be sure to use a large enough pan, as the egg-wine mixture will expand considerably as it cooks.

6 large egg yolks
⅓ to ½ cup sugar (depending on the
  sweetness of the wine)

¼ teaspoon ground cinnamon
  (optional)
1 cup sweet red Pesach wine

Put the egg yolks, sugar, and cinnamon (if used) into the top of a large double boiler (or a heatproof bowl that will fit over a saucepan). Beat with a wire whisk (or portable electric mixer) until the yolks are light and thick. Beat in the wine.

Put the double boiler top (or bowl) over the double boiler bottom (or a saucepan) containing simmering water. The water should not touch the bottom of the pan (or bowl) containing the custard. Beat the egg-wine mixture constantly, over simmering water, for 5 to 10 minutes, or until the custard foams and thickens considerably and becomes very fluffy, doubling to tripling in volume. Remove the pan (or bowl) containing the custard from the water, and continue beating the custard for 1 to 2 minutes, so it does not stick to the pan.

As a dessert, zabaglione is customarily served warm in stemmed wine-glasses. As a sauce over cake, it is served warm or chilled.

Makes about 6 servings.

CARAMEL-COATED ORANGE FLAN (P)

(Baked Custard)

This elegant, light dessert has been adapted from Spanish and Mexican cuisines. The molded orange custard is quite impressive, and a delightful change from cake. It can be made up to two days ahead of time, and refrigerated. However, it should not be unmolded until just before serving time.

With this dessert, "caramelized" (or melted) sugar is used to coat the baking pan. Some of the caramel is absorbed into the outer layer of the custard, and the rest makes a wonderful syrup when the dessert is unmolded after being chilled. Though it may sound tricky, it is not very difficult when the directions are carefully followed.

The following recipe makes a flan that will serve about 6 people. If you wish to have more servings, do not increase the amounts, or the custard may not mold properly. Rather, make two or more flans by repeating the recipe.

CARAMEL COATING FOR THE MOLD
½ cup sugar
3 tablespoons cold water

2 cups orange juice, heated until lukewarm (or ½ cup thawed orange juice concentrate plus 1½ cups hot tap water)

ORANGE CUSTARD
5 large eggs
⅓ cup sugar

GARNISH (OPTIONAL)
About 2 tablespoons finely grated orange rind

Have nearby some pot holders and an ungreased 1-quart, ovenproof, ceramic or heavy glass casserole, soufflé dish, or metal baking pan. (A square Corningware casserole works well.)

Put the ½ cup sugar and water for the caramel into a small heavy saucepan. Bring the mixture to a light boil, swirling the saucepan gently by its handle to help dissolve the sugar. When the syrup is clear, boil it rapidly, swirling the saucepan occasionally, until the syrup caramelizes, that is, thickens and turns a light, golden brown color. Watch the syrup carefully, and do not let it get dark brown, or it may have a burnt taste.

Immediately pour the syrup into the ovenproof casserole. *Be careful— the syrup will be extremely HOT!* Quickly pick up the casserole with the pot holders, and carefully tilt it in all directions, letting the syrup coat the bottom and sides, until the syrup solidifies, in about 30 seconds. Set the casserole aside. (The saucepan and any spilled syrup can be cleaned up with hot water. To keep the saucepan from warping, let it cool before immersing it in water.)

For the custard mixture, use a fork to beat the eggs in a medium-sized bowl until they are well blended; then beat in the ⅓ cup sugar. Beat for a minute or two to make sure the mixture is well combined, but not frothy. Slowly add the warm orange juice to the eggs, beating constantly. Pour the custard mixture into the caramel-coated casserole.

Set the casserole into a larger pan; then add enough boiling water to the larger pan so that it comes about halfway up the outside of the casserole. Bake in a preheated 325-degree oven for 50 to 55 minutes, or until a small knife inserted near the center of the custard comes out clean.

Remove the casserole from the water and cool the custard at room temperature for 30 minutes. Then refrigerate it for at least several hours, or up to 2 days. It should be *completely chilled* before it is unmolded.

Shortly before serving the flan, unmold it onto a serving platter which has a raised rim to hold the caramel syrup. To unmold, carefully run a knife around the top edge of the custard to loosen it from the casserole. Invert the serving platter over the casserole and then invert the two together. Lift off the casserole. The syrup from the casserole will flow over and around the flan. If desired, sprinkle freshly grated orange rind on top of the flan.

To serve, use a cake server or a very large spoon to dish out portions of the flan. Include some of the caramel syrup with each serving.

Makes about 6 servings.

SEPHARDIC-STYLE ORANGE-NUT-DATE TORTE (P)

Adapted from a North African Sephardic recipe, this dense, extremely moist torte uses no flour or matzo meal of any type. The oranges in this unusual recipe are used in their entirety, including both the peel and the pulp, to give the dessert a wonderful, rich flavor and a very distinctive texture.

2 large navel oranges
Potato starch (or sugar) for the pan
6 ounces (about 1½ cups) blanched
  almonds or walnut pieces
1 cup sugar, divided
¼ teaspoon ground cinnamon
  (optional)

½ cup very finely chopped dates
6 large eggs, 2 of them separated

GARNISH
Sugar
Peeled thin fresh orange slices

Wash the oranges well; then put them into a medium-sized saucepan and cover them with cold water. Bring the water to a boil, cover the pan, and lower the heat. Simmer the oranges for about 40 minutes, or until they are very soft. Pour off the cooking water; then add cold water to the saucepan and let the oranges soak for about 5 minutes. Drain the oranges well and dry them with paper towels. (The oranges can be cooked up to a day ahead and refrigerated.) Cut each orange into eighths. Remove any seeds and let the orange pieces cool (if necessary) while you prepare the cake pan and grind the nuts.

Grease a 9½- to 10-inch springform pan well, and coat it with potato starch (or sugar), tapping out any excess. Set aside.

Put the nuts and ¼ cup of the sugar into a food processor fitted with the steel blade, and pulse-process until the nuts are very finely ground and powdery. (Or use a food grinder to very finely grind the nuts; then mix them with the sugar.) Add the cinnamon (if used) to the nuts. Set aside.

Use the food processor (or food grinder) to grind the orange pieces, including the entire peel, to a slightly coarse purée. Mix the dates with the orange purée.

In a medium-sized bowl, use an electric mixer to beat the 2 separated egg whites (reserve the yolks) with ¼ cup of the remaining sugar until they form stiff shiny peaks. Set aside.

In a large bowl, use the electric mixer to beat the 4 whole eggs and the 2 reserved yolks with the remaining ½ cup sugar until very light and fluffy. This may take several minutes. Stir in the orange-date mixture and the ground nut mixture. Then fold in the beaten egg whites until no streaks of white remain. Turn out the batter into the prepared pan.

Bake in a preheated 375-degree oven for 50 to 60 minutes, or until the top of the torte is well browned and it is set in the center when lightly pressed with a fingertip. Remove from the oven and run a knife around the edge of the torte to release it from the pan. (It will settle slightly, particularly in the center.) Cool the torte completely in the pan on a wire rack. Then remove the sides of the pan. The well-wrapped torte may be stored overnight at room temperature. (Wrap the torte in plastic wrap or a similar airtight wrap.) For longer storage, refrigerate it. The torte will stay very moist and fresh for several days.

Just before serving, sprinkle the top of the torte lightly with sugar and garnish the center with several orange slices arranged in a circle.

Makes about 12 servings.

PESACH SPONGE CAKE (P)

This is probably one of the most popular cakes made on Pesach by both Ashkenazic and Sephardic Jews. The latter call it *pan de Espagne* (or a variant of that), which means "bread of Spain" and harks back to pre-Inquisition days.

In this version, the egg whites and yolks are each beaten separately, to produce a delicate, light cake that requires no leavening of any kind. The citrus juice gives it a delicious flavor and moistness.

Sponge cake goes quite nicely with stewed fruit or thawed frozen fruit in syrup, as well as with the fluffy, wine custard called *zabaglione* (page 272).

The following recipe has been in my family for many years.

9 large eggs, separated
1¼ cups sugar, divided
¼ cup orange juice
2 tablespoons lemon juice, preferably fresh
1 tablespoon grated orange rind (colored part only)
1 teaspoon grated lemon rind (yellow part only)
⅔ cup potato starch
⅓ cup matzo cake meal

Have an *ungreased* 10-inch angel food tube pan handy. If it is *not* the two-piece type with a removable tube insert, grease the bottom only and cut a doughnut-shaped piece of wax paper to cover the bottom of the pan. (This will make it easier to remove the cake from the pan.)

In a very large mixing bowl, beat the egg whites until foamy; then gradually add ¼ cup of the sugar while continuing to beat the whites until stiff peaks form.

In a medium-sized bowl, with the same beaters, beat the yolks with the orange juice, lemon juice, and grated rinds until very light. Pour the yolk mixture over the whites, and gently fold them together, leaving a few streaks of white. Sift the remaining sugar, potato starch, and cake meal over the batter, and gently but thoroughly fold them in.

Pour the batter evenly into the tube pan, and smooth the top. Tap the pan once against a countertop so that any large air bubbles in the batter will rise to the surface. Bake the cake in a preheated 325-degree oven for about 1 hour and 5 to 10 minutes, or until the top of the cake springs back when lightly pressed with a fingertip. Remove the pan from the oven, and immediately invert it on its "legs," or fit the tube over the neck of a bottle, to cool upside down. When the cake is completely cool, run a knife around the edge of it, and remove it from the pan. (If the pan was lined with paper, peel it off the bottom of the cake.)

To avoid squashing the cake when cutting it, use a serrated knife, and cut with a sawing motion.

Makes about 12 servings.

TISHPISHTI PARA PESACH (P)

(Cake Diamonds Soaked with Syrup)

This is a Pesach version of a very popular cake that is served by Turkish and Greek Jews throughout the year. As with many other Sephardic desserts, the cake is soaked in a sugar-honey syrup after it is baked. For best flavor and texture, *tishpishti* should be made at least one day ahead. It will stay tasty for several days.

DOUGH
1 cup matzo meal
1 cup matzo cake meal
½ cup sugar
½ cup finely ground blanched
  almonds (or walnuts)
½ teaspoon ground cinnamon
Pinch of ground cloves
½ cup vegetable oil
1 large egg

¾ cup cold water
About 16 whole blanched or
  unblanched almonds

SYRUP
⅔ cup sugar
⅔ cup cold water
2 tablespoons honey
1 teaspoon lemon juice, preferably
  fresh

For the dough, combine the matzo meal, cake meal, ½ cup sugar, ground almonds, cinnamon, and cloves in a medium-sized bowl. Add the oil, egg, and ¾ cup water, and mix very well to form a stiff dough. Knead the dough with your hands a few times to complete the mixing. Evenly press the dough into a greased 8-inch-square baking pan. Use a knife to cut the dough into diamonds. First, cut the dough crosswise into about 4 even rows. Then make diagonal, parallel cuts through the rows. (If desired, cut the dough into squares, instead.) Press a whole almond into the center of each piece. Bake the cake in a preheated 375-degree oven for 40 to 45 minutes, or until it is browned and firm.

Meanwhile, prepare the syrup. Put the sugar and water into a small saucepan. Stir over medium-high heat until the sugar dissolves and the syrup comes to a boil; then boil the syrup, uncovered and undisturbed, for 8 minutes. Stir in the honey and lemon juice. Remove the syrup from the heat, and set it aside to cool slightly.

When the cake is has finished baking, remove it from the oven, and re-cut the pieces. Pour the syrup evenly over the hot cake. Let the cake rest for several hours to completely absorb the syrup. After the syrup has been absorbed, cover the cake with aluminum foil or plastic wrap and store it at room temperature.

Makes about 16 pieces.

HAZELNUT-CHOCOLATE VIENNESE TORTE   (P)

This magnificent flourless cake, one of my personal favorites, is the ultimate dessert for dark-chocolate lovers. It stays moist and delicious for several days, and has best flavor and texture if made a day ahead of serving.

The beautiful torte is blanketed with an incredibly shiny chocolate glaze, and trimmed with ground and whole hazelnuts (or other nuts) and chocolate curls. If preferred, the glaze can be omitted, and the torte topped, instead, with a thick layer of *chocolate mousse* (page 281).

(Notes: The grated chocolate and ground nuts in this torte replace flour and, thus, must be very fine and powdery. You can use a rotary grater or a food processor to accomplish this; however, if the latter is used, be sure not to over-grind the nuts or they may get oily and pasty. For the best results, have the nuts at room temperature, and process them in pulses.

Finely ground *un*blanched almonds, pecans, or walnuts may be substituted for the hazelnuts (which are sometimes called "filberts"). Whichever type, there should be at least 2½ cups of powdery ground nuts.)

Potato starch (or sugar) for the pan

BATTER
6 large eggs, 5 of them separated
Pinch of salt
2 teaspoons lemon juice, preferably fresh
¾ cup sugar, divided
2 teaspoons freshly grated lemon rind (yellow part only)
3 ounces very finely grated semisweet (or "dark") bar chocolate (see Note above)
2½ cups very finely ground unblanched hazelnuts, about 8 ounces (see Note above)

FOR TORTE
¼ cup sweet Pesach wine, sherry, or flavored brandy

About ½ cup apricot (or other) jam or preserves

CHOCOLATE GLAZE
⅓ cup water
3 tablespoons vegetable oil
1 cup sugar
½ cup unsweetened cocoa powder

GARNISH
About 1 cup ground hazelnuts, for the sides of the torte
12 whole hazelnuts
1 ounce semisweet (or "dark") bar chocolate (for chocolate curls; see Note below)

Grease a 9-inch springform pan well, and coat it with potato starch (or sugar), tapping out any excess. If desired, line the bottom of the pan with wax paper to make removal of the cake easier. Set aside.

For the batter, in a large mixing bowl, beat the 5 egg whites with the salt and lemon juice until foamy. Then very gradually add ¼ cup of the sugar, and continue beating the whites until they form stiff, but not dry, peaks.

Use the same beaters and another bowl to beat the 5 egg yolks and the additional whole egg with the remaining ½ cup sugar and the lemon rind until they are very light and fluffy. Gently, but thoroughly, fold the beaten whites into the beaten yolk mixture. Then fold in the grated chocolate and ground hazelnuts. Pour the batter into the prepared pan.

Bake the torte in a preheated 325-degree oven for 50 to 55 minutes, or until the top springs back when gently pressed with a fingertip. Leave the torte in the oven, turn off the heat, and open the oven door slightly. After 10 minutes, remove the torte from the oven. Run a knife around the edge of the torte to release it from the pan rim; then cool the torte for 30 minutes longer in the pan. Remove the pan rim, and *cool the torte completely on the pan bottom.* (The center of the torte will settle slightly.)

Cover a 9- or 10-inch cardboard circle with a heavy duty aluminum foil or freezer paper, for a base (or use a cake platter). Invert the torte onto the prepared base and remove the bottom of the pan (and the wax paper, if used). Sprinkle the wine evenly over the torte. Heat the jam (in a small saucepan on the stove, or in a small heatproof bowl in the microwave oven) until it is thinned; then brush or spread the jam all over the torte. (This not only adds flavor, but also evens out the surface of the cake so the chocolate glaze will be perfectly smooth.)

For the chocolate glaze, combine the water, oil, sugar, and cocoa in a small saucepan and mix very well. Cook the mixture over *low heat,* stirring constantly, for 10 to 14 minutes, or until the glaze thickens slightly and is very smooth and shiny. For the best flavor and texture, it should not boil. Remove the glaze from the heat and stir it for 3 to 4 minutes longer, or until it cools slightly and gets a bit thicker. Pour all the glaze in the center of the torte, and immediately use a metal or rubber spatula to evenly spread it all over the top and sides. Wipe up any drips from the cardboard base or serving platter.

Let the torte rest a few minutes until the glaze begins to set, but is still soft. Press handfuls of ground hazelnuts all over the sides of the torte, but *not* the top. Arrange the whole hazelnuts, evenly spaced, in a circle on top of the torte about 1 inch in from the edge. Heap some chocolate curls (or coarsely grated bar chocolate) in the center of the torte (where it may have settled a bit).

Refrigerate the uncovered, completed torte for several hours or, preferably, overnight so that the glaze can set, and the flavors and textures can "mellow."

(Once the glaze has set, the torte can be frozen for up to 3 weeks. Freeze it uncovered; then wrap it in plastic wrap or aluminum foil. Unwrap it before thawing, so the glaze will not stick to the wrapper, and thaw for several hours in the refrigerator.)

For the best flavor and texture, remove the torte from the refrigerator a few hours before serving.

Makes about 12 servings.

NOTE: To easily make *chocolate curls,* hold a piece of solid semisweet chocolate in the palm of your hand a few seconds to warm and soften it slightly. Then run a sharp vegetable peeler across the smooth surface of the chocolate to make each curl. Chill the chocolate curls until they are needed.

"INSTANT" CHOCOLATE MOUSSE (P)

This mousse is especially easy, because the chocolate is "automatically" melted as it whirls in a food processor or blender with boiling water. A bit of coffee serves to heighten the flavor of the mousse.

6 ounces semisweet (or "dark") bar
  chocolate or bits
½ teaspoon instant coffee granules
⅓ cup boiling water
4 large eggs, separated
3 tablespoons sweet Pesach wine,
  Pesach liqueur, or fresh orange
  juice

3 tablespoons sugar
About ¼ cup grated semisweet (or
  "dark") bar chocolate for garnish
  (optional)

Put the 6 ounces of chocolate and the instant coffee into a food processor (fitted with the steel blade) or a blender, and process for a few seconds until the chocolate is very finely chopped. With the machine running, pour the boiling water in through the top, and continue processing for several more seconds until the chocolate is completely melted. Add the egg yolks and wine, and process until well mixed.

In a medium-sized mixing bowl, use an electric mixer to beat the egg whites until foamy; then gradually add the sugar and continue beating until the whites form stiff, but not dry, peaks. Gently, but thoroughly, fold the chocolate mixture into the whites until no streaks of white remain. Turn out the mousse mixture into an attractive serving bowl or about 6 individual bowls. If desired, garnish the top of the mousse with the extra grated chocolate. Chill the mousse for several hours, or until it is firm.

Makes about 6 servings.

COCONUT-HONEY MACAROONS (P)

These Pesach macaroons are easy to prepare and quite delicious, though they differ from their commercially made canned holiday counterparts. The homemade type is chewier and has a bit of crunch.

British Jews form the same batter (or a very similar one made with whole eggs) into small cone shapes, and call the cookies *coconut pyramids*, symbolic of the structures built by Israelite slaves in Egypt.

2 large egg whites
½ cup sugar
2 tablespoons honey

1¾ cups dry, unsweetened, finely
  shredded coconut (see Note)
2 tablespoons potato starch

Grease 2 large baking sheets; then coat them with extra potato starch, tapping off all the excess. Set aside.

In a medium-sized bowl, use an electric mixer to beat the egg whites until they are foamy; then gradually beat in the sugar and honey, and continue beating for several minutes until the whites form very stiff, shiny peaks. Stir in the shredded coconut and potato starch until well combined.

Drop generous tablespoonfuls of the batter into small mounds about 2 inches apart on the prepared baking sheets. For "coconut pyramids," use moistened fingers to form the mounds into cone-like shapes.

Bake the macaroons in a preheated 325-degree oven for 18 to 23 minutes, or until they are firm and lightly browned. Use a metal spatula or pancake turner to remove the macaroons from the baking sheet. Cool them completely on wire racks. Store them in an airtight container at room temperature.

Makes about 30 cookies.

NOTE: Unsweetened, finely shredded coconut is available at most health-food stores; however it may not be *kosher l'Pesach*. To use fresh coconut, grate it very finely; then spread it out on a baking sheet, and dry it in a 200-degree oven for about 3 hours, or until most of the moisture has evaporated.

VARIATION
_____

ALMOND-HONEY MACAROONS   (P)

Substitute 1¾ cups (7 ounces) very finely ground blanched almonds for the coconut. (For tips on grinding the almonds, see the recipe for *amaretti* [page 284].) Drop the batter onto the baking sheets, and bake the cookies as directed above, but for 15 to 20 minutes, or until they are lightly browned. If the baked cookies are very soft, let them cool on the baking sheets for about 1 minute to firm up; then immediately remove them and cool them on wire racks.

Makes about 30 cookies.

AMARETTI (P)

(Italian-Style Almond Macaroons)

These crunchy meringue-like cookies are very popular in Italian cuisine. Since the *amaretti* use egg whites only, they are often served with custard desserts, such as *zabaglione* (page 272), which call for egg yolks. Sometimes, slightly stale *amaretti* are crumbled and used as a filling for baked apples or baked pear halves.

As American almonds are relatively bland-tasting, almond flavoring is usually added to *amaretti* to give them a more intense almond taste. However, most almond extracts are prohibited on Pesach, because they contain alcohol which is made from grain. A special *kosher l'Pesach* almond flavoring may be available in some areas. Of course, the cookies are also quite tasty *without* added flavoring.

A British-Jewish variation of these cookies, called *cinnamon balls* (see Variation), is flavored with ground cinnamon instead of almond flavoring. The batter is customarily rolled into balls, and the baked cookies are coated with confectioner's sugar. (Note: Confectioner's sugar that contains cornstarch is prohibited, by Ashkenazic custom, on Pesach.)

For very popular Sephardic cookies called *marunchinos* (see Variation), the identical ingredients as for *amaretti* are combined using a different technique, which produces a smaller cookie that is much more dense and chewier than *amaretti*. In fact, it is almost like baked marzipan. For an Iraqi-Jewish touch, cardamom may be added to the *marunchinos* to make a Pesach version of *hadgi badam* (see also page 100 in Chapter 2 for a non-Pesach version).

2 large egg whites	*2 cups (8 ounces) very finely ground*
⅔ cup sugar	*blanched almonds (see Note)*
About ½ teaspoon kosher l'Pesach	*1 tablespoon potato starch*
almond flavoring (optional)	

Grease 2 large baking sheets; then coat them with extra potato starch, tapping off all the excess. Set aside.

In a medium-sized bowl, use an electric mixer to beat the egg whites until they are foamy; then gradually beat in the sugar and almond flavoring (if used), and continue beating for several minutes until the whites form very stiff, shiny peaks. Stir in the ground almonds and potato starch until well combined.

Drop generous tablespoonfuls of the batter into small mounds about 2 inches apart on the prepared baking sheets.

Bake the cookies in a preheated 350-degree oven for 17 to 22 minutes, or until they are firm and very lightly browned. Use a metal spatula or pancake turner to remove the cookies from the baking sheet. Cool them completely on wire racks. Store them in an airtight container at room temperature.

Makes about 30 cookies.

NOTE: The almonds may be ground in a food processor fitted with the steel blade, or in a blender (in batches). If the almonds are frozen, let them come to room temperature before grinding them, and be careful that they do not become pasty from over-grinding.

VARIATIONS

BRITISH-STYLE CINNAMON BALLS (P)

Omit the optional almond flavoring, and fold *1 tablespoon ground cinnamon* into the batter with the almonds. If the batter is stiff enough, use moistened hands to form it into approximately 1¼-inch balls. Or drop the batter in generous tablespoonfuls, as directed above. Bake the cookies as directed above.

Makes about 30 cookies.

MARUNCHINOS or PESACH HADGI BADAM (P)
(Chewy Almond Cookies)

Use the same ingredients as for amaretti. (If desired, for hadgi badam, add *¼ to ½ teaspoon ground cardamom*.) To make the cookies, beat the egg whites with a fork just until they are broken up and slightly frothy. Stir in the sugar until combined; then mix in the remaining ingredients (including the cardamom, if desired) to make a very stiff paste. With moistened hands, form scant tablespoonfuls of the paste into 1¼-inch-diameter balls; arrange them on the baking sheets about 2 inches apart. Use moistened fingertips to flatten each ball slightly. Bake the cookies in a preheated 325-degree oven for 15 to 20 minutes, or until they are firm and very lightly browned. Use a metal spatula to remove the cookies from the baking sheets, and cool them on wire racks.

Makes about 24 cookies.

MUSTACHADOS (P)

(Walnut "Macaroons")

These delectable, chewy Sephardic cookies are quite easy to make. They are very similar to macaroons, though a slightly different technique is used. Also, unlike most macaroons, the entire egg, not just the white, is used.

In Istanbul, very similar cookies, called, in Turkish, *cervis kurabiyesi*, are sold by street vendors. They are always paired together, back to back, with no filling in between. Sometimes, the following cookies may stick together in the same manner, if they are paired while they are still hot.

1 large egg
1½ cups (about 6 ounces) very finely
ground walnuts

½ cup sugar
¼ teaspoon ground cinnamon
(optional)

Grease 2 large baking sheets, then coat them with a little potato starch, tapping off all the excess.

In a medium-sized bowl, beat the egg with a fork just until well blended; then add the walnuts, sugar, and cinnamon (if used) and mix to form a very thick paste.

Use moistened hands to form the paste into 1¼-inch-diameter balls or drop the paste by scant tablespoonfuls into small mounds about 2 inches apart on the baking sheets. Use moistened fingertips to slightly flatten the balls or mounds. Bake in a preheated 325-degree oven for 15 to 20 minutes, or until the edges of the cookies begin to brown. Immediately remove the cookies from the baking sheets with a metal spatula or pancake turner, and cool them completely on wire racks.

Makes 24 to 30 cookies.

YOM HA'ATZMAUT AND YOM YERUSHALAYIM

Israel's Independence Day and Jerusalem Day

O n May 14, 1948, the fifth day of Iyar on the Hebrew calendar, the State of Israel was established. Annually, on the Hebrew anniversary of that date (with certain exceptions*), Israelis, and also many Jews throughout the Diaspora, joyously celebrate the creation of the modern-day Jewish state.

Each year, Yom Ha'Atzmaut is immediately preceded by Yom Ha'Zikaron (Memorial Day), when Israelis solemnly honor those who have given their lives for the country. The proximity of this somewhat somber holiday to the very happy one seems to be in keeping with the Jewish philosophy that we must always remember the sorrowful times along with the good ones.

In the morning on Yom Ha'Zikaron, sirens sound throughout Israel, and everyone and everything—even traffic—immediately stops to observe a few moments of silence. At nightfall, the sirens again sound, and 12 torches are lit in Jerusalem to signify that Memorial Day has ended and Independence Day is about to begin.

Because the Chief Rabbinate of Israel has decreed that Yom Ha'Atzmaut be observed as a break in the *Omer* period of semi-mourning be-

---

* When the fifth of Iyar happens to fall on a Friday or Saturday, the celebration of Yom Ha'Atzmaut is moved up to the preceding Thursday, so that the laws of Shabbat will not interfere with the merrymaking that typifies the holiday.

tween Pesach and Shavuot (as is the holiday Lag B'Omer), all sorts of jubilant festivities can take place. In Israel, Yom Ha'Atzmaut is typically celebrated with plenty of proud flag-waving, parades, fireworks, music festivals, a Bible quiz, and family barbecues.

At Dizengoff Square, in the heart of Tel Aviv, special platforms are set up for theatrical groups, musicians, comedians, and other types of entertainment. There are cake, punch, and wine for all, and the mayor of the city personally greets visitors.

Throughout the country, there is much exuberant singing and dancing in the streets, sometimes all through the night. Often, friends get together for *kumzitz* ("come and sit") around neighborhood bonfires.

At their cookouts and picnics, many Israelis enjoy an abundance of favorite local foods (just as we Americans do at our similar "Fourth of July" celebrations). No particular dishes are as yet specifically associated with this rather new holiday; however, several of the same "outdoor" foods eaten on Lag B'Omer (see Chapter 9) are also quite popular for Yom Ha'Atzmaut.

Although the holiday is definitely more patriotic than religious, many Jews throughout the Diaspora celebrate it simply because of a strong sense of identification with the Land of Israel. For the first time in almost two millennia, there is once again a Jewish homeland. Furthermore, it is likely that at least one member of every Jewish family can well remember those frustrating and very difficult years after the Second World War, which culminated in the critical United Nations vote for partition in Palestine and, ultimately, in Israel's Declaration of Independence.

In New York City and some other American cities, special parades are held in honor of Yom Ha'Atzmaut. Jewish communities throughout the United States have lively sessions of Israeli folk dancing and songfests which always include *Hatikvah,* or "Hope," the national anthem of Israel.

Delicious samplings of typical Israeli foods are usually prominent at Diaspora celebrations of Yom Ha'Aztmaut. Thus, this chapter features many dishes which are either indigenous to Israel or have become very much associated with it.

These same foods are also very appropriate for Yom Yerushalayim or "Jerusalem Day," which takes place on the twenty-eighth day of the Hebrew month of Iyar (about 3½ weeks after Yom Ha'Atzmaut). This Israeli national holiday celebrates the anniversary of Jerusalem's reunification after the "Six Day War" in 1967—a monumental occurrence ranking second in importance only to independence itself. Finally, after a two-thousand-year hiatus, the entire city of Jerusalem, including the Temple Mount and Western Wall, was under Jewish control.

As the modern State of Israel is a melting pot, with citizens ingathered from numerous countries around the world, many other international dishes in this cookbook have also become commonplace in that country, and are considered a part of its cuisine. They, too, would be quite suitable for both Yom Ha'Atzmaut and Yom Yerushalayim.

FALAFEL I (P)

(Tiny Croquettes Made with Dried Chick-Peas)

Of all the street foods in Israel—and there are many—*falafel* is without a doubt the most popular. In fact, it's probably the food most often identified with Israeli cuisine.

Falafel is sold at outdoor kiosks which almost always have large "salad bars." (And Americans think we invented that idea!) When a *falafel* sandwich is ordered, the vendor places a few freshly fried *falafel* balls (and, possibly, some French fries) inside a split loaf of *pita,* and hands it to the purchaser, who then adds his or her choice of salads and dressings.

Israeli teens are masters at skillfully stuffing so much into their *pita* sandwiches that the doughy pocket seems on the verge of bursting. They push in the salad with a vengeance, until the *falafel* balls themselves are a mere pittance, squashed almost into oblivion.

Most amazing is that these teens then partake of such meal-sized sandwiches while walking and chatting, losing nary a lettuce leaf in the process. Tourists, on the other hand, sparsely fill their own loaves, but still leave behind a telltale trail of chopped vegetables and dressing.

While visiting Israel, I sampled the wares of several outdoor kiosks. Upon returning home, I tested numerous *falafel* recipes, until I was finally satisfied with this version, one that tastes "authentic."

I knew I had truly hit the mark when my spicy chick-pea balls garnered much praise from an Israeli family temporarily situated in the United States. Before the sampling, they had greatly missed *falafel* but had no idea how to make it. As *falafel* is always so inexpensive and easily available in Israel, they explained, it is rarely prepared at home.

Falafel vendors in Israel often use a cleverly designed, metal gadget to quickly mold the chick-pea mixture into 1-inch-diameter croquettes. When the gadget's plunger is released, a perfectly shaped croquette is ejected. *Falafel* makers come in single and double styles (to make two croquettes at once), and are nice souvenirs from Israel. However, *falafel* can also be molded by hand.

1 cup dry chick-peas (garbanzo
   beans)
⅓ cup bulgur wheat (or Wheatena
   cereal)
2 to 3 tablespoons lemon juice
2 large eggs
3 tablespoons cold water
2 to 3 garlic cloves, chopped
1 to 1½ teaspoons ground cumin
½ teaspoon ground turmeric
2 tablespoons chopped fresh parsley
   leaves
¼ to ½ teaspoon each dried basil
   leaves, dried marjoram leaves, and
   ground coriander

⅛ teaspoon cayenne pepper
1 teaspoon salt
½ to 1 cup fresh bread crumbs
   (preferably made from pita bread,
   in a food processor or blender)
Vegetable oil for frying

TO SERVE
Several loaves of whole wheat or
   regular pita bread (purchased or
   see page 308)
Salat B'Nusah Kibbutz (Kibbutz-
   style Salad), page 295
Tahina, page 293 (optional)

Sort and wash the dry chick-peas well; then put them into a small saucepan with about 3 cups cold water. Bring them to a boil over high heat; then lower the heat and boil them, covered, for 10 minutes. Turn off the heat, and let the chick-peas stand in the covered saucepan for 1 to 3 hours.

Meanwhile, soak the bulgur wheat (or cereal) in warm water to cover for about 20 minutes; then drain it very well. (The easiest way to do this is to put the bulgur into a large sieve; then lower the sieve into a bowl of water until the bulgur is covered. To drain the bulgur, simply lift up the sieve and press out any excess water.)

Drain the partially cooked and soaked chick-peas, and put them into a food processor (fitted with the steel blade) along with the lemon juice, eggs, water, and garlic. Pulse-process until the chick-peas are very finely chopped, but not puréed. (Alternatively, you can very finely chop the chick-peas with a food grinder; then mix them with the other ingredients.)

Put the chick-pea mixture into a bowl and mix in all the herbs and seasonings until well combined. Add the drained bulgur. Stir in enough bread crumbs so that the mixture holds together well. Cover the mixture and let it rest for 15 to 30 minutes to firm up slightly.

Shape the mixture into 1-inch balls; then flatten the balls slightly to make tiny croquettes. (Or use a falafel maker.) Set the croquettes aside on a platter, not touching one another. When all the chick-pea mixture has been shaped, heat oil that is about ¼ inch deep in a large skillet over medium-high heat. Put several of the croquettes into the oil, but do not crowd them. Fry them, turning them once, until they are well browned on both sides. (If preferred, the falafel may be deep-fried, as is usually done in Israel.) Drain them on paper towels. Repeat until all the falafel have been fried.

To serve the falafel, cut open the loaves of pita, and place several falafel inside each pocket. Top the falafel with salad and, if desired, tahina dressing.

Leftover falafel freeze well. Reheat them in a 350-degree oven until they are crisp and heated through.

Makes 50 to 60 1-inch falafel balls.

FALAFEL II   (P)

(Tiny Croquettes Made with Canned Chick-Peas)

The use of canned chick-peas in this *falafel* makes it quicker, though not quite as "authentic," as the recipe for *Falafel I*. This version is also slightly less spicy.

Be careful not to over-process the canned chick-peas in this recipe, because they can easily turn to mush, and *falafel* tastes best if it has some texture.

¼ cup bulgur wheat (or Wheatena
   cereal)
1 15- to 16-ounce can chick-peas
   (garbanzo beans), well-drained
1 to 2 garlic cloves, coarsely chopped
1 tablespoon lemon juice
1 large egg, lightly beaten
2 tablespoons finely chopped fresh
   parsley leaves
½ to 1 teaspoon ground cumin
¼ teaspoon ground turmeric or
   paprika
¼ teaspoon ground coriander
   (optional)

½ teaspoon salt
⅛ teaspoon ground black pepper
½ to 1 cup fresh bread crumbs
   (preferably made from pita bread,
   in a food processor or blender)
Vegetable oil for frying

TO SERVE
Several loaves of whole wheat or
   regular pita bread (purchased or
   see page 308)
Salat B'Nusah Kibbutz (Kibbutz-
   style Salad), page 295
Tahina, (page 293, optional)

Soak the bulgur wheat (or cereal) in warm water to cover for about 20 minutes; then drain it very well. (The easiest way to do this is to put the bulgur into a large sieve; then lower the sieve into a bowl of water until the bulgur is covered. To drain the bulgur, simply lift up the sieve and press out any excess water.)

Put the drained bulgur and chick-peas into a food processor fitted with the steel blade, and pulse-process just until the chick-peas are finely chopped, but not puréed. If the chick-pea mixture sticks to the perimeter of the bowl, use a rubber spatula to push it back into the center. (Alternatively, you can use a food grinder with a coarse blade to grind the chick-peas and softened bulgur together.)

Transfer the mixture to a bowl, and stir in the garlic, lemon juice, egg, and all the herbs and seasonings until well combined. Then stir in enough bread crumbs so that the mixture holds together well. Let the mixture rest for 15 to 30 minutes to firm up slightly.

Shape the mixture into 1-inch balls; then flatten the balls slightly to make tiny croquettes. (Or use a falafel maker.) Set the croquettes aside on a platter, not touching one another. When all the mixture has been shaped, heat oil that is about ¼ inch deep in a large skillet over medium-high heat. Put several of the croquettes into the oil, but do not crowd them. Fry them, turning them once, until they are lightly browned on both sides. (If preferred, the falafel may be deep-fried, as is usually done in Israel.) Drain them on paper towels. Repeat until all the falafel have been fried.

To serve the falafel, cut open the loaves of pita, and place several falafel inside each pocket. Top the falafel with salad and, if desired, tahina dressing.

Leftover falafel freeze well. Reheat them in a 350-degree oven until they are crisp and heated through.

Makes about 40 1-inch falafel balls.

TAHINA (P)

(Lemony Sesame Dip or Dressing)

Tahina (pronounced "tah-hee'-nah" with a guttural second syllable) is very popular in Israel, on its own as a dip for *pita bread* (page 308), and also as a topping or dressing with many different foods.

Its main ingredient is *tahini*—a plain paste ground from hulled sesame seeds just as peanut butter is made from peanuts. Tahini is available at most health-food and specialty stores, as well as many supermarkets. Once opened, it will keep for several months in the refrigerator, if the plastic lid is resealed on the can. A newly opened can of tahini should always be stirred very well before being refrigerated, to re-suspend any separated sesame oil. The tahini should then stay well mixed for quite a while.

In Israel, both the pure sesame seed paste and the "dip" made from it are called *tahina*—the only difference being that the latter is sometimes described as *prepared tahina*. To avoid confusion, I have designated the pure paste *tahini* (with a final "i" instead of an "a"), as it is usually labeled in the United States.

Tahina dip is fun to make with children, not only because it is so simple, but also because fascinating physical changes take place during its preparation. Pure tahini looks much like very thin peanut butter. When a little water is mixed in, however, it mysteriously becomes extremely stiff and hard to stir. Then, as more water is gradually added, it considerably lightens in color, and becomes smooth and creamy like mayonnaise.

½ cup tahini (pure sesame paste)
About ½ cup cold water
2 to 3 tablespoons lemon juice,
*   preferably fresh*
Salt and freshly ground pepper to
*   taste*

About 1 tablespoon finely chopped
*   fresh parsley leaves (optional)*
Other herbs and seasonings to taste,
*   such as finely chopped dillweed or*
*   garlic (optional)*

Put the tahini into a small bowl and add the water in a slow stream, stirring constantly until the mixture eventually becomes very smooth and velvety. (At first, the mixture will become very stiff; then it will thin out and become lighter in color.) Stir in the remaining ingredients, adjusting the amounts as desired for taste and consistency. If the tahina is too thick, add more water; if it is too thin, stir in a bit more tahini.

If time is available, refrigerate the tahina for several hours to give the flavors a chance to blend. (It gets slightly firmer when chilled.) Stir the tahina again shortly before using it. Serve it cold or, preferably, at room temperature, with falafel, or as a dip with pieces of pita bread or sliced raw vegetables. For use as a salad dressing, thin the tahina a bit more.

Makes about 1 cup.

HUMUS (P)

(Chick-Pea and Sesame Spread)

This thick purée—called *humus b'tahina* in Hebrew (meaning "chick-peas in sesame paste") or, more often, simply *humus* (pronounced "hoo'-moos" with a guttural "h")—is one of my favorite appetizers, and it's so easy to prepare that I serve it often. It keeps in the refrigerator for up to a week, and can even be frozen. Although *humus* is quite tasty with crackers and even cut-up raw vegetables, it is customarily eaten on small pieces of *pita bread*.

Chick-peas are a staple in Israel. They are used most often in *humus* and *falafel* (pages 289 and 291). However, many salads also include cooked chick-peas. The most popular is the simplest: drained, cooked (or canned) chick-peas tossed with olive oil, lemon juice, chopped fresh parsley, salt, and pepper—all in amounts to taste.

Chick-peas are also frequently used in Israeli *hamim*—the Shabbat meal-in-a-pot which is quite similar to *dafina* and *cholent* (pages 38 and 40).

1 15- to 16-ounce can chick-peas
   (garbanzo beans), drained
3 tablespoons good-quality olive oil
¼ cup tahini (pure sesame paste)
   (Stir well before using.)
2 to 4 garlic cloves, chopped
About 2 tablespoons lemon juice,
   preferably fresh
2 to 3 tablespoons cold water (or
   more, if needed when using a
   blender)
Salt and freshly ground black pepper
   to taste

GARNISH
Sprigs of fresh parsley leaves
Sliced pitted ripe (black) olives
   (optional)
1 tablespoon pine nuts (pignoli),
   lightly toasted (optional)
Additional olive oil (optional)

TO SERVE
Several loaves of whole wheat or
   regular pita bread, cut into
   triangles (purchased or see page
   308)

Put the chick-peas, oil, tahini, garlic, lemon juice, and water into a food processor (fitted with the steel blade) or a blender. Process until smooth, scraping down the sides of the container a few times. (With a blender, it may be necessary to add 1 to 2 tablespoons more water to avoid clogging the blades.) Add the seasonings to taste.

Spoon the humus into a small serving dish and attractively garnish it with the parsley and the olives or pine nuts (if used). Refrigerate the humus for several hours to give the flavors a chance to blend. (It will get a bit firmer during refrigeration.) Serve it cold or, for the best taste, let it come to room temperature. If desired, sprinkle the top of the humus with a few teaspoons of olive oil just before serving, as is the Middle Eastern custom. Accompany the humus with pita bread triangles.

Makes about 2 cups.

SALAT B'NUSAH KIBBUTZ   (P)

(Kibbutz-Style Fresh Vegetable Salad)

Israel is well-known for its outstanding vegetables, which are grown in three major crops throughout the year. In fact, most Israeli families have gorgeous farm-fresh produce on the table daily.

Many *kibbutzniks*—those who live and work on farm cooperatives called *kibbutzim*—actually help grow some of the succulent vegetables that they eat. In the kibbutz dining room, vegetables are served in many different dishes, both raw and cooked. At most kibbutzim, a raw vegetable salad is offered at virtually every meal. In fact, the ability to chop vegetables to the smallest, most perfect dice, just for these salads, is considered a status symbol among many kibbutz cooks.

Sometimes, an assortment of cleaned, whole vegetables is put out for the kibbutzniks to cut up and dress as they wish. Usually, there is also a large bowl of homemade pickled vegetables on the table, and there may even be some cooked (and chilled) vegetable salads, such as the *salat hatzilim* (page 297) in this chapter.

Not only at kibbutzim, but throughout all of Israel, a salad such as the following one is almost always on the menu for Yom Ha'Atzmaut. The recipe is meant only to be a guide; please feel free to vary the proportions of all the ingredients to taste. For the best flavor, prepare the salad just before serving it.

3 medium-sized tomatoes, preferably vine-ripened, diced

2 medium-sized cucumbers, peeled and diced

1 medium-sized sweet green or red pepper, diced

2 scallions, including green tops, thinly sliced

4 to 6 red radishes, diced

2 medium-sized carrots, coarsely shredded

½ of a medium-sized head lettuce, coarsely shredded

2 tablespoons fresh lemon juice

2 tablespoons good-quality olive oil (or vegetable oil)

Salt and freshly ground black pepper to taste

Put all the prepared vegetables into a large serving bowl. In a small bowl, mix together the lemon juice and oil and pour the mixture over the vegetables. Season the salad to taste. Serve immediately, as a side dish, or with falafel, inside pita bread.

Makes about 6 servings.

GEZER HAI (P)

(Carrot-Citrus Salad)

The Hebrew name of this very easy, tasty salad translates literally as "living carrots." It is a relatively new dish, created and made popular in the modern State of Israel, where it is likely to be on the menu of many Yom Ha'Atzmaut picnics.

SALAD
1 pound fresh carrots, peeled (or scrubbed) and coarsely grated
About ¾ cup fresh orange juice
1 to 2 tablespoons fresh lemon juice
1 medium-sized navel orange (preferably Jaffa), peeled and finely chopped
Sugar or honey to taste
Pinch of salt (optional)
Pinch of ground ginger (optional)

TO SERVE (YOUR CHOICE)
Crisp lettuce leaves
About 6 hollowed-out lemon or orange halves
About 3 medium-sized ripe avocados, halved and seeded
Sprigs of fresh spearmint (optional)

Mix together all salad ingredients. Refrigerate the salad, covered, for several hours or, preferably, overnight, to allow the carrots to absorb the juices and for the flavors to blend. This salad may be kept refrigerated for up to 3 days, and actually improves with storage. Stir it occasionally.

Just before serving, stir the salad well and adjust the seasonings, if necessary. Serve it on lettuce leaves, in lemon or orange "shells," or over avocado halves. If desired, garnish the salad with mint.

Makes about 6 servings.

SALAT HATZILIM (P)

(Eggplant Salad)

Eggplant is extremely popular in Israel and all the other Middle Eastern countries, as well as in North Africa and the countries of the Mediterranean area. In these places, it is prepared in hundreds—possibly thousands—of different ways. In fact, at one time, the worth of an Arab bride was partially determined by how many eggplant dishes she could prepare.

For salads such as this one, whole eggplants are most often cooked over a gas flame or under a broiler until the skin is charred. (In some places, eggplants are still roasted over open campfires as they have been for centuries.) The charring gives the eggplant a characteristic "smoky" flavor.

SALAD
2 medium-sized eggplants (about 1 pound each)
1 to 2 garlic cloves, pressed or very finely minced
2 to 3 tablespoons good-quality olive oil
1 tablespoon lemon juice, preferably fresh
3 tablespoons finely minced fresh parsley leaves

1 tablespoon finely minced fresh spearmint leaves (or 1 teaspoon dried mint leaves), optional
Salt and ground black pepper to taste

TO SERVE
2 ripe tomatoes, cut into thin wedges
Several loaves of whole wheat or regular pita bread (purchased or see page 308), cut into triangles

Prick each eggplant in several places with a fork. (If you don't, they may explode!) Put them on a heavy, foil-lined baking sheet about 6 inches under a heated broiler element. Broil the eggplants, turning them often, for 20 to 30 minutes, or until the skin is blistered and charred, and the pulp is soft and juicy. (Or, alternatively, skewer each whole eggplant on a long fork and slowly rotate it over a gas flame until the outside is charred and the inside is very soft.)

Cut open the eggplants and let them cool until they can be handled. If desired, remove and discard any large clusters of seeds that taste bitter. Peel off and discard the skin and stem. Chop up the eggplant pulp, and put it into a medium-sized bowl.

Add the remaining salad ingredients and stir until well combined. Refrigerate the salad, covered, for several hours or until the flavors have had a chance to blend. Correct the seasonings, if necessary. Garnish the salad with the tomatoes, and serve it chilled or at room temperature with the pita bread triangles.

Makes 4 to 6 servings.

VARIATION

Substitute *mayonnaise* (to taste) for the oil and lemon juice, and omit the mint. If desired, a *chopped or grated Spanish onion,* or some thinly sliced *scallion* may be substituted for the garlic.

MARAK PAYROT   (P) or (D)

(Chilled Mixed-Fruit Soup)

It is not surprising that delectable, fresh fruit soup is commonplace in Israel, where a fantastic variety of produce is plentiful throughout the year.

This version has become one of my favorite ways to begin company meals in late spring and early summer. The rose-colored soup inevitably evokes a happy "Yum!" from guests, who are pleasantly surprised by its delicious taste.

The soup can also be served as a refreshingly light dessert.

2 cups orange juice, divided	*½ pound seedless green or red grapes,*
¼ cup lemon juice	*cut in half*
1 cup cold water	*1½ to 2 pints strawberries, hulled*
About ¼ cup honey or sugar	*and coarsely sliced*
1 medium-sized cantaloupe, seeded,	
peeled, and coarsely chopped	GARNISH
3 large apples, peeled, cored, and	*Whole perfect strawberries*
coarsely chopped (see Note)	*1 to 2 cups fresh vanilla yogurt or*
	commercial sour cream (optional)

In a very large saucepan (about 4 quarts), combine 1 cup of the orange juice, the lemon juice, water, and ¼ cup honey. Add all the fruit and bring the mixture to a boil over high heat. Lower the heat and simmer, uncovered, for about 10 minutes, or until all the fruit is soft.

Purée the mixture in batches in a blender, food processor, or food mill. Stir in the remaining cup of orange juice. If desired, add a bit more honey to taste.

Refrigerate the soup until it is completely chilled, several hours up to overnight. Serve the soup chilled. Garnish each serving with a few straw-berries and, if desired, a dollop of yogurt or sour cream.

Makes 7 to 8 cups; about 8 servings.

NOTE: If a food mill is used, it is not necessary to peel and core the apples.

MARAK TAYMAHNI (M)

(Yemenite-Style Meat and Vegetable Soup)

During a visit to Israel, my husband and I had an interesting dining experience in the Yemenite Quarter of Tel Aviv. It took place at a small, unassuming restaurant, frequented mainly by Yemenite Jews who spoke no English. The short menu was scrawled in Hebrew on a blackboard, leaving us somewhat confused over what to order.

Looking around, we saw that other diners were partaking of hearty meat soup, grilled skewered meat cubes, chopped vegetable salads, and pita bread. Two types of relish sat in small dishes on each table, and everyone was enthusiastically spooning one or both over each course—even over the bread.

The food looked and smelled absolutely wonderful, and we were rav-enous after a long day of sightseeing. But when a young man came to take our order, the language barrier seemed to be insurmountable. As we frantically tried to communicate with the waiter, a man at the next table saw our problem, and kindly offered, in broken English, to assist us. When the food came a short while later, our new-found friend pointed to the relishes, and said simply, "Hot, spicy, be careful."

The entire meal was delicious and, thanks to the polite warning, we did not sear our mouths on the relishes, but sampled just enough to know that when a Yemenite says hot, he means HOT!

The following soup, which makes a great one-dish meal, is often served ladled over pita bread. The bread absorbs some of the broth and becomes deliciously soft. Though the soup does contain a lot of season-ings, it is not very "hot" in the spicy sense. (When Yemenites eat it, they add plenty of *hilbeh,* a relish made with fenugreek and chili pepper.)

7 cups water
1½ to 2 pounds lamb shoulder, beef
   chuck, or other soup meat, cut into
   1-inch cubes and trimmed of all
   fat and gristle
1 soup bone
1 whole onion, peeled (but not cut
   up)
2 whole scallions, including green
   tops (or 1 whole, trimmed and
   well-washed leek)
3 large carrots, cut into 1-inch pieces
2 pounds "new" or all-purpose
   potatoes, peeled and cut into large
   chunks
1 tomato, cut into eighths
1 celery stalk, cut into 1-inch-long
   pieces
2 garlic cloves, finely minced

½ teaspoon curry powder
½ teaspoon ground cumin
½ teaspoon ground turmeric
½ teaspoon salt
⅛ to ¼ teaspoon black pepper,
   preferably freshly ground
⅛ teaspoon ground cardamom
½ cup finely chopped fresh parsley
   leaves
1 to 2 teaspoons dried coriander
   leaves (cilantro) (or about 1
   tablespoon chopped fresh coriander
   leaves or cilantro), optional

TO SERVE (OPTIONAL)
6 to 8 small loaves of whole wheat or
   regular pita bread (purchased or
   see page 308)

In a 5- to 6-quart soup pot or Dutch oven, over high heat, bring the water to a boil. Add the cubed meat and the bone, and lower the heat. Gently simmer the meat, uncovered, for 20 minutes, while skimming off and discarding all the foam that rises to the top. Add all the remaining ingredients, except the parsley and coriander, and bring the soup to a simmer. Simmer gently, covered, for about 1½ hours longer.

Stir in the parsley and coriander (if used), and simmer, covered, for ½ to 1 hour longer, or until the meat and vegetables are very tender. If desired, remove and discard the onion and scallions. Adjust the seasonings, if necessary.

To serve, put a loaf of pita bread into the bottom of each soup bowl. Ladle some broth, meat, and vegetables on top.

Makes 6 to 8 servings.

SPICED GROUND BEEF IN PITA BREAD (M)

The spices in this quick and easy beef mixture give it an appealing Middle Eastern flavor. And pita bread turns it into a delicious dinner in a pocket.

This dish can also be used for buffet entertaining. Keep the filling warm in a chafing dish, and accompany it with several miniature loaves of pita that have already been slit open at the top.

FILLING
1 pound lean ground beef
1 medium-sized onion, finely chopped
2 garlic cloves, minced
1 8-ounce can plain tomato sauce
⅓ cup water
½ teaspoon dried basil leaves
½ teaspoon ground cinnamon
¼ to ½ teaspoon ground cloves
¼ teaspoon salt

⅛ teaspoon black pepper, preferably freshly ground
2 cups cooked brown or white rice
¼ cup dark raisins

TO SERVE
4 or 5 large loaves of whole wheat or regular pita bread (purchased or see page 308)

In a large deep skillet over medium-high heat, brown the ground beef, breaking it up into small pieces with a potato masher or fork. Add the onion and garlic and cook them in the fat from the meat. When the onion is tender and the meat is browned, spoon off and discard any excess fat in the skillet. Stir in the remaining filling ingredients.

Lower the heat and simmer the mixture, stirring often, for 15 to 20 minutes, or until the filling is thick and the flavors have blended. Cut the pita loaves in half and fill them with the meat mixture.

Makes 4 to 5 servings as a main course.

K'TZITZOT BASAR B'AGVANIYOT (M)

(Israeli-Style Meatballs in Tomato Sauce)

This was inspired by a similar dish that was once served at a kosher restaurant in Philadelphia. It is very easy to prepare and would be nice to serve at home on the evening of Yom Ha'Atzmaut.

MEATBALLS

*1 pound very lean ground beef or
lamb*

*1 small onion, grated or very finely
chopped*

1 large egg

*⅓ cup matzo meal or plain dry
bread crumbs*

*2 tablespoons finely chopped fresh
parsley leaves*

*1 teaspoon dried mint leaves (or 1
tablespoon chopped fresh spearmint
leaves)*

½ teaspoon dried marjoram leaves

*¼ teaspoon each ground cinnamon,
nutmeg, and ginger*

½ teaspoon salt

*¼ teaspoon black pepper, preferably
freshly ground*

SAUCE

*1 16-ounce can tomatoes, including
juice, chopped*

*¾ cup beef broth or bouillon made
from cubes or powder*

1 small onion, finely chopped

1 to 2 garlic cloves, minced

*2 tablespoons finely chopped fresh
parsley leaves*

*⅛ teaspoon black pepper, preferably
freshly ground*

Pinch of cayenne pepper (optional)

TO SERVE

Hot cooked brown or white rice

Combine all the meatball ingredients in a medium-sized bowl and mix them very well with your hands or a fork. Or blend the ingredients in a food processor (fitted with the steel blade). Set aside.

In a large deep skillet, combine all the sauce ingredients. Bring the sauce to a simmer over medium-high heat. Form the meat mixture into 1-inch balls and add them to the simmering sauce. When all the meatballs have been formed, cover the skillet, and simmer the meatballs, basting them occasionally, for 45 to 60 minutes, or until they are cooked through and firm, and the sauce has a rich flavor.

Serve the meatballs over the rice, spooning some sauce over each portion.

Makes about 5 servings.

KUBBAH SINEEYA (M)

(Spicy Meat Loaf with Sesame Topping)

This is a popular Middle Eastern recipe, which has been adapted by the Israelis to include the nationally popular sesame paste known as *tahini.* Israelis also use the same sesame topping, which is actually a variation of the dip called *tahina* (page 293), on baked fish.

MEAT LOAF
2 pounds very lean ground beef
1 medium-sized onion, finely chopped
1 garlic clove, minced
2 tablespoons finely chopped fresh
  parsley leaves
1 teaspoon ground cumin
½ teaspoon ground allspice
¼ teaspoon ground cinnamon
½ teaspoon salt
¼ teaspoon black pepper, preferably
  freshly ground

TOPPING
½ cup tahini (pure sesame paste)
  (Stir well before using.)
⅓ cup cold water
1½ tablespoons lemon juice
2 tablespoons finely chopped fresh
  parsley leaves
¼ teaspoon paprika
⅛ teaspoon salt
⅛ teaspoon black pepper, preferably
  freshly ground
About 3 tablespoons pine nuts
  (pignoli) or slivered almonds

In a large bowl, combine all the meat loaf ingredients and mix with your hands until well combined and smooth. Press the mixture into the bottom of a 9- by 13-inch baking dish. Bake in a preheated 400-degree oven for about 15 minutes, or until browned.

Meanwhile, prepare the sesame topping. Put the tahini into a small bowl and slowly add the water, stirring vigorously. (At first the mixture will become very stiff; then it will thin out and become lighter in color.) Stir in the lemon juice, parsley, paprika, salt, and pepper. Adjust these seasonings to taste, if necessary.

When the meat loaf is browned, remove the dish from the oven and carefully drain off any excess fat that has been released from the meat loaf. Spread the prepared sesame topping over the meat loaf. Sprinkle the pine nuts on top.

Return the meat loaf to the 400-degree oven and bake about 10 minutes longer, or until the topping is puffed and lightly browned.

Makes about 6 servings.

OAF MANDARINOT IM AVOCADO (M)

(Tangerine Chicken with Avocado)

In Israel, poultry and citrus fruit are plentiful, and they are often cooked together in a wide variety of dishes. The following one includes tangerines (a type of mandarin orange, which explains the Hebrew name, *mandarinah*), and also features avocado, another Israeli favorite that is frequently used in unexpectedly delicious ways. With the color contrast of orange and green fruits, this dish looks as great as it tastes.

2 to 3 tablespoons pareve *margarine*
About 2½ pounds meaty chicken pieces (remove skin, if desired), or 5 to 6 skinned and boned chicken breast halves
4 teaspoons cornstarch
1½ cups tangerine juice (made from frozen tangerine juice concentrate, if desired) (or substitute orange juice)
¼ teaspoon ground allspice
⅛ teaspoon ground cinnamon

⅛ teaspoon black pepper, preferably freshly ground
Pinch of salt
1 medium-to-large-sized ripe avocado
1 cup tangerine sections, seeds and fibers removed (from about 3 tangerines) (or 1 10½-ounce can mandarin orange segments, drained)

TO SERVE
Hot cooked white or brown rice

In a large skillet over medium-high heat, melt the margarine; then brown the chicken on all sides.

Meanwhile, in a small bowl, mix the cornstarch with a small amount of the tangerine juice to make a paste; then add the remaining tangerine juice, the allspice, cinnamon, pepper, and salt. Add this mixture to the skillet and continue cooking until the sauce thickens and just comes to a boil. Cover the skillet tightly and lower the heat. Simmer the chicken, basting it often, for 45 to 50 minutes, or until it is very tender.

When the chicken is almost tender, cut the avocado in half lengthwise and remove the large pit in the center. Peel each avocado half; then cut it lengthwise into thirds. Cut each piece crosswise into ½-inch-thick slices. (If desired, toss the avocado slices with 1 to 2 tablespoons additional tangerine juice to keep them from discoloring. Drain before using.) When the chicken is tender, stir the avocado pieces and the tangerine sections into the sauce. Raise the heat and simmer the mixture about 2 minutes longer, or until the fruits are heated through.

To serve, arrange the chicken on a bed of rice, and spoon the sauce on top.

Makes about 5 servings.

OAF SOOMSOOM B'ROTEV DVASH (M)

(Sesame Chicken Tidbits with Honey Dipping Sauce)

This easy appetizer dish is quite delectable and perfect for a party or snack.

6 medium-sized chicken breast halves, skinned and boned (about 1½ pounds chicken meat)
6 tablespoons melted pareve *margarine*

6 tablespoons honey
4 teaspoons soy sauce
⅛ teaspoon ground ginger (or ½ teaspoon grated fresh gingerroot)
About 1½ cups sesame seeds

Pat the chicken dry with paper towels. Cut each breast half into 6 to 8 evenly sized pieces. In a small saucepan (or in the microwave oven), melt the margarine; then remove it from the heat and stir in the honey, soy sauce, ginger, and garlic. Mix well. Dip each chicken piece into the sauce; then roll it in the sesame seeds to coat the surface. (Reserve the leftover sauce.)

Arrange the coated chicken pieces in a single layer on a greased or non-stick spray-coated baking sheet. Bake in a preheated 350-degree oven, turning the pieces once or twice, for 20 to 25 minutes, or until the chicken is cooked through.

Put the leftover sauce into a small skillet and bring it to a boil over medium-high heat. Lower the heat and gently simmer the sauce for about 3 minutes. Serve the chicken pieces (hot or at room temperature) with toothpicks, and offer heated sauce on the side for dipping.

Makes 3 to 4 dozen tidbits with sauce.

KUGEL YERUSHALAYIM (P)

(Jerusalem Noodle "Pudding")

This peppery *kugel* (a Yiddish word adopted into the Israeli vernacular) has become a trademark of the Hasidim in Mea Shearim—an ultra-Orthodox area of Jerusalem—and of nearby areas. In fact, preparation and distribution of the delicious noodle pudding are the means of support for a few of its older residents. Jerusalem *kugel* is served at many Israeli weddings and bar mitzvah celebrations, and even at state functions. The unusual recipe calls for caramelizing sugar in oil, to give the *kugel* a golden color and a subtly sweet taste that contrasts perfectly with the pepper.

1 pound fine egg noodles, vermicelli, or very thin spaghetti broken into 2-inch lengths	*1 teaspoon salt*
	¾ to 1 teaspoon black pepper, preferably freshly ground
½ cup vegetable oil	*4 large eggs, beaten*
¼ cup sugar	

In an approximately 6-quart pot, cook the noodles in boiling water according to the package directions. Drain them in a colander. Then rinse them with cool water and let them drain very well.

Dry the pot well; then put the oil and sugar into it. Stir the sugar in the oil over medium-low heat (they will not actually combine) for 5 to 10 minutes, or until the sugar melts and caramelizes, and turns a dark golden brown—the color of caramel candy.

Immediately add all the well-drained noodles to the pot, while stirring them very well, so the oil and caramelized sugar are evenly distributed. If any of the sugar solidifies into chunks, continue stirring the noodles over medium-low heat until the sugar melts. Remove the noodles from the heat and stir in the salt and pepper. Then let the noodle mixture cool for 20 to 30 minutes or until it is lukewarm.

Stir the beaten eggs completely into the noodles. Then turn out the mixture into a very well-greased (or non-stick spray-coated) 9- to 10-inch-square pan. Bake the kugel in a preheated 325-degree oven for 1¼ to 1½ hours, or until the top is golden and very crisp. Let the kugel cool for about 5 minutes before cutting it.

Makes 8 to 10 servings.

WHOLE WHEAT PITA (P)

(Flat, Round "Pocket" Bread)

This bread, which becomes hollow during baking, is a staple in all Middle Eastern countries. In Israel, it is filled with everything imaginable, from *falafel* (pages 289 and 291) to French fries to salads—sometimes all at once! Often, the loaves are cut or torn apart to be used as "dippers" with spreads and salads, such as *humus, tahina,* and *salat hatzilim* (pages 294, 293, and 297).

In the United States, *pita* has become increasingly popular due to its good taste, convenience for sandwiches, and low calorie count. In fact, delicious loaves of *pita* can now be found in most supermarkets. However, it is still an interesting experience to bake *pita* at home, just to watch the thin pieces of dough puff up into bread "balloons," especially if your oven has a window and light.

Though most bread cookbooks do not admit it, baking *pita* can be a bit tricky. Commercially, it is made in huge, very hot ovens, where the bread is baked directly on the oven floor, just as pizza is. It is the blast of high heat that causes the dough to separate and form the characteristic pocket. To simulate this, the home oven and baking sheet must be preheated to a very high temperature.

For best results, it is also important to handle the dough as little as possible, and not to damage the surface once the dough has been rolled out. The dough circles are baked in the same order that they were rolled out, so that all are allowed to rise for similar amounts of time.

The following recipe is written in detail to help you successfully produce delicious loaves of *pita*.

1 packet (2¼ teaspoons) active dry yeast	*1 tablespoon vegetable oil*
1¾ cups warm (105 to 115 degrees) water	*2¼ to 2½ cups white* bread *flour*
	2 teaspoons salt
1 tablespoon honey	*2 cups whole wheat flour*
	Vegetable oil to coat the dough

In a large mixing bowl, combine the yeast, water, and honey. Let the mixture rest for 10 to 15 minutes, or until it is very frothy. Stir in the 1 tablespoon oil, 2 cups of the white bread flour, and the salt and beat with an electric mixer at medium speed (or with a wooden spoon) for about 2 minutes, or until the batter seems to be very elastic. By hand, or with a heavy-duty mixer, mix in the whole wheat flour to make a sticky dough. Scrape the dough down from the sides of the bowl and cover the bowl with plastic wrap. Let the dough rest for 15 minutes, so the flour can absorb some moisture and become less sticky.

Sprinkle a few tablespoons of white bread flour over the dough; then use a rubber scraper to press down around the sides of the dough so flour falls between the dough and the bowl, making removal of the dough easier. Transfer the dough to a lightly floured surface. Knead the dough, adding very small amounts of flour as necessary, for about 8 to 10 minutes, or until the dough is very smooth and elastic and still a bit tacky. Divide the dough into 16 equal pieces, and roll each one in the palms of your hands to a very smooth ball.

Lightly coat the entire surface of each ball with oil. (Coat your hands with oil and roll the balls in them. Or brush the oil on the balls.) Then arrange the balls about 2 inches apart on a large sheet of wax paper. Completely, but loosely, cover the balls with additional wax paper so they will not dry out and let them rise until doubled, about 1 hour.

Meanwhile, adjust one oven rack to the lowest possible position, and a second one about one third of the way down from the top. Put a very heavy, ungreased baking sheet (or 2 lighter baking sheets, stacked one on top of the other) on the top rack. When the balls have risen, preheat the oven and baking sheet(s) to 500 degrees and set a timer for 30 minutes.

Carefully remove the wax paper covering from a few of the dough balls. (Keep the rest covered until they are needed.) From now on, handle each ball as little as possible. Use a metal spatula, dough scraper, or pancake turner to lift one of the balls from the bottom sheet of wax paper. On a well-floured surface, use your fingertips to gently pat out the ball to a 3-inch circle. Then, use a rolling pin to gently roll it out to a circle approximately 5 inches in diameter and ³⁄₁₆ inch thick. Use as few strokes as possible during the rolling and make sure the dough does not stick or pull at all. Lightly coat the dough circle with flour, gently brushing off any excess, and set it aside on a large sheet of wax paper.

Repeat with the remaining balls, keeping the dough circles arranged in the order that they were rolled out. Cover all the circles very loosely with wax paper, and, if the timer has not already rung, let them rise until it does. (This indicates that the first dough circles have had at least 25 minutes to rise.)

During the following baking procedure, it is important to keep the oven temperature high and stable, so open the oven door as little as possible and work quickly. Remove the preheated baking sheet (or stacked sheets) from the oven and set it on top of the stove. (It will be very hot!)

Immediately use a large, well-floured pancake turner to transfer—one at a time—the first 2 dough circles that were rolled out to the hot ungreased baking sheet, keeping them about 2 inches apart. (Do not bake more than 2 loaves at once, even if they will fit on a baking sheet.) Immediately put the baking sheet on the *bottom rack* of the oven. Bake the dough circles for 2½ minutes; then quickly transfer the baking sheet to the *upper rack*. Bake the puffed loaves for an additional 2 to 2½ minutes, or until they are firm and very lightly browned on top.

Quickly remove the finished loaves from the baking sheet and set them aside to cool. Immediately transfer the next 2 dough circles to the baking sheet. Repeat—baking the dough circles in the order in which they were rolled out—until all the loaves are baked. Keep the dough circles loosely covered until they are needed.

As soon as the loaves are cool, gently press them down to deflate them (the pockets will remain) and transfer them to sealed plastic bags. Store at room temperature. If the loaves are not to be eaten within a day or two, freeze them, as they tend to go stale quickly. If desired, reheat them briefly in a 325-degree oven or a microwave oven; do not heat them for too long, or they will get hard.

Makes 16 5-inch loaves of pita.

TOASTED PITA TRIANGLES (D)

The simplicity of these cheesy snacks belies their delicious taste. The triangles can be completed in advance and then reheated shortly before serving, making them great party fare. Store them in the freezer or refrigerator.

*8 5- to 6-inch-diameter loaves of
whole wheat or regular pita bread
(purchased or see page 308)*
½ cup butter or margarine, softened

*About 2 teaspoons finely chopped
mixed fresh or dried herbs, such as
basil, marjoram, thyme, dillweed,
tarragon, parsley, etc.*
*⅓ to ½ cup finely grated Parmesan
or other cheese*

Cut around the edges of each pita loaf, separating the top and bottom into two thin circles. Spread each circle with ½ tablespoon of the butter. Then sprinkle each circle with about ⅛ teaspoon of the herbs and 1½ to 2 teaspoons of the cheese. Use a knife and cutting board (or kitchen shears) to cut each large circle into 4 wedge-shaped "triangles." Arrange the triangles, cheese side up, in one layer on ungreased baking sheets. Toast them in a preheated 375-degree oven for 8 to 10 minutes, or until the cheese is very lightly browned. Serve the triangles warm.

If the triangles are made in advance, reheat them in a 325-degree oven until they are hot and crisp.

Makes 64 appetizer-sized triangles.

OOGIYOT SOOMSOOM (P)

(Sesame Sticks or Rings)

In Israeli cuisine, sesame seeds—*soomsoom*, in Hebrew—are quite popular, and are made into a number of crunchy "snacks," like those that follow. These barely sweet snacks may be munched plain, like pretzels, and they can be served with dips. Or they can be turned into sweet "cookies" by increasing the sugar, as directed below.

2 cups sesame seeds
2 large eggs
*2 tablespoons sugar (for sweet cookies,
increase to ½ cup)*
*½ teaspoon salt (for sweet cookies,
omit all but a pinch)*
1 teaspoon baking powder

*1 cup all-purpose white flour,
preferably unbleached (may be
half whole wheat flour, if desired)*

GLAZE (OPTIONAL)
*1 large egg, beaten with 1 teaspoon
water*

To toast the sesame seeds, put them into an ungreased skillet over medium-high heat and stir them often until they are evenly browned and very aromatic. For the very best flavor, toast the seeds shortly before using them. Set them aside to cool before adding them to the dough.

In a medium-sized bowl, beat the eggs until they are well blended. Mix in the sugar, salt, baking powder, and flour. Then add the toasted sesame seeds and mix well to form a very stiff dough.

For each sesame stick, pinch off a walnut-sized piece of dough and roll it in floured hands or on a lightly floured surface into a "stick" that is ½ inch in diameter and 5 to 5½ inches long. If desired, connect the ends of each stick to form a ring about 2 inches in diameter. Arrange the sticks or rings about 1 inch apart on a greased or non-stick spray-coated baking sheet.

For a shiny surface, brush the tops of the sticks or rings with egg glaze. Bake them in a preheated 375-degree oven for 15 to 18 minutes, or until they are browned and well done. Remove them from the baking sheets and cool them completely on a wire rack. They crisp more as they cool. Store them in an airtight container.

Makes about 24 sesame sticks or rings.

RAF'REFET TAPOOZIM (P)

(Orange Fluff Pudding)

Most puddings and custards contain milk or cream, making them unsuitable for a meat meal. However, this light, refreshing Israeli dessert can be used at any time. And, it can be easily varied, following the suggestions below.

2 large eggs, separated
½ cup (8 tablespoons) sugar, divided
⅓ cup cornstarch
1 6-ounce can frozen orange juice concentrate, thawed

3 juice cans (about 2⅓ cups) very hot tap water
1 teaspoon lemon juice (optional)
½ teaspoon vanilla extract
Sweetened or unsweetened shredded coconut to taste (optional)

In a medium-sized saucepan, use a wire whisk or portable electric mixer to beat together the egg yolks and 6 tablespoons of the sugar until well mixed. Then beat in the cornstarch and orange juice concentrate until the mixture is smooth. Gradually add the hot water while beating. Place the saucepan over medium-high heat and cook, stirring constantly, until the custard thickens and just begins to boil under the surface. Remove the custard from the heat and stir in the lemon juice and vanilla. Set it aside to cool slightly.

In a medium-sized mixing bowl, use clean beaters to beat the egg whites until foamy; then gradually add the remaining 2 tablespoons of sugar and beat just until stiff peaks form. Stir about a third of the beaten whites into the warm custard to lighten it; then add all of the custard to the whites in the mixing bowl and beat a few seconds longer, just until the pudding is smooth. Pour the pudding into 1 large serving bowl or about 6 individual dishes, and sprinkle the top with coconut, if desired. Refrigerate the pudding until it is completely chilled.

Makes about 6 servings.

VARIATION

1. The pudding as made above is soft and fluffy in texture. To make it firm enough for molding, mix *1 packet unflavored gelatin* into the egg-juice mixture before the hot water is added.

2. For a simpler, thicker pudding, do not separate the eggs. Use the 2 whole eggs and the entire ½ cup sugar in the custard. Spoon the cooked custard into 1 large bowl or 6 individual bowls, and, if desired, garnish with coconut as directed above.

3. RAF'REFET TAPOOZIM V'COCUS   (P)
   (Orange-Coconut Pudding)

For this variation, simply stir *½ to 1 cup sweetened or unsweetened shredded coconut* into the cooked custard while it is still hot. The coconut may be added to any version of the pudding.

OOGIYOT TAHINA (P)

(Sesame Tahini-Oat Cookies)

These treats are packed with complete protein and other nutrients, as well as good taste. In Israel, tahini is often used in baked goods.

Another favorite, sunflower seeds, is also included in the cookies. Israelis particularly enjoy eating toasted unhulled sunflower seeds out-of-hand. In fact, cracking sunflower seeds has been humorously described as one of the country's favorite national "sports." Seeds or *garinim,* as they are called in Hebrew, are sold and eaten virtually everywhere. The floors of many buses, movie theaters, and athletic stadiums are constantly littered with discarded shells.

⅓ cup tahini (pure sesame paste)
  (Stir well before using.)
½ cup honey
1 large egg
½ teaspoon ground cinnamon
⅛ teaspoon ground allspice

1⅓ cups rolled oats (any type)
⅓ cup finely shredded sweetened or
  unsweetened coconut)
⅓ cup unsalted hulled sunflower
  seeds
¼ cup dark raisins (optional)

In a medium-sized bowl, combine the tahini, honey, egg, cinnamon, and allspice.

Stir in the oats, coconut, sunflower seeds, and raisins (if used) until well combined. Use moistened hands to form the mixture into 1¼-inch-diameter balls or drop tablespoonfuls of the mixture about 2 inches apart on a greased or non-stick spray-coated baking sheet. Slightly flatten the top of each cookie with moistened fingertips.

Bake the cookies in a preheated 350-degree oven for about 12 minutes, or until the cookies are firm and the bottoms are lightly browned. Use a metal spatula or pancake turner to remove the cookies from the baking sheet and cool them on a wire rack.

Makes about 2 dozen cookies.

LAG B'OMER

For many pious Jews, Lag B'Omer, which takes place on the eighteenth day of the Hebrew month of Iyar (and usually occurs in May), is one island of happiness and jubilation within a sea of solemn weeks.

Omer is a Hebrew word meaning "sheaf" or "measure" of grain. In ancient times, when the Jewish people were predominantly agriculturally oriented, they celebrated the commencement of the grain harvest by offering, in thanksgiving, an omer of barley on the second day of Pesach. They then counted forty-nine days from that one, and celebrated Shavuot on the fiftieth day by offering two loaves of bread made from the first wheat.

Although there have been no grain offerings since the destruction of the Holy Temple in Jerusalem, the "Counting of the Omer" (*Sefirat Ha'Omer,* in Hebrew) still takes place in modern-day synagogues on each day of the Omer interval.

Orthodox Jews also observe the seven weeks of the *Sefirah* ("counting") as a period of semi-mourning. During most of this time, therefore, they do not have haircuts or listen to music, and festivities such as weddings are not permitted. This custom probably developed in ancient times, when the critical weeks before the wheat harvest were filled with anxiety over the success of the season's crop. It is also said to commemorate a tragic episode in Jewish history, which took place during the Sefirah.

In the year 70, the Second Holy Temple was destroyed by Roman invaders, and Jerusalem lay in ruins. About sixty years later, Shimon Bar Kochba and his followers despaired of ever rebuilding the Jewish city while it was under Roman rule, and so they revolted in an effort to regain national independence.

At first, the Jews were victorious and, some say, even began to build the Third Temple. But in the end, Roman military might prevailed. Bar Kochba, as well as several of the foremost scholars of the day, including Rabbi Akiva (a famed spiritual leader of the Jews), met their deaths. The fighting and a concurrent epidemic also took the lives of tens of thousands of Rabbi Akiva's students and disciples.

However, on the *thirty-third day* of the Counting of the Omer (*Lag B'Omer,* for short), the epidemic is said to have miraculously abated, and the rebellion was briefly successful. In commemoration of these happier occurrences, all prohibitions of the Sefirah period are suspended on Lag B'Omer, and it is celebrated with much joyfulness.

The day also has special significance because of other events that occurred during the Roman rule of Judea. It is said the learned Rabbi Shimon Ben Yohai defied decrees against the study of Torah, and bravely continued to teach his pupils. When this endangered his life, he fled with his son to a cave in the mountains of Galilee. There, they lived and studied for thirteen years, and allegedly wrote the *Zohar* or "Book of Splendor," which is the basis for the Jewish study of mysticism called the *Kabbalah*.

According to tradition, Rabbi Ben Yohai's students visited him each year on Lag B'Omer. In order to mislead the Roman soldiers, the students often disguised themselves as hunters carrying bows and arrows.

It is further said that Rabbi Ben Yohai died on Lag B'Omer, but that his last request was for the anniversary of his death to be observed with joyous celebration, not mourning. Also, he is supposed to have revealed many wonderful secrets to his pupils on that day.

Israeli children have no school on this holiday, which has also been designated a "national students' day," because of its many associations with great Jewish teachers and scholars. In imitation of Rabbi Ben Yohai's pupils, the youngsters often play a bow-and-arrow game of "Jews and Romans." They also engage in all types of sports, races, hikes, and other athletic events. Israeli soldiers sometimes have marksmanship contests.

To honor Rabbi Ben Yohai, tens of thousands of Jews make pilgrimage to Meron, an Israeli village near Safed, where he is said to be buried. Many pitch tents and spend the early part of the evening chanting psalms, singing Hasidic melodies, and studying the Zohar.

Huge communal bonfires are lit near the rabbi's tomb, and people gaily sing and dance around the fire until morning. Some three-year-old Hasidic boys have their first haircut on this day, and the clipped locks are tossed into the bonfire.

All over Israel, Lag B'Omer is celebrated with campfires and other outdoor events like those at Meron. Many friends gather for *kumzitz* ("come and sit"), and enjoy barbecues and picnics, just as on Yom Ha'Atzmaut. Treats made with carob are often eaten on Lag B'Omer, because a carob tree is said to have grown outside Rabbi Ben Yohai's cave, and sustained him while he dwelled there.

In the United States and other countries of the Diaspora, community cookouts, complete with outdoor games and sporting competitions, are also popular for Lag B'Omer. The dishes in this chapter are deliciously appropriate for such a celebration.

ENSALADA DE AVICAS Y ENGINARAS (P)

(Herbed White Bean and Artichoke Salad)

This tasty combination of two popular Sephardic salads is great for a picnic, or any time of year. Sephardim from Turkey and many parts of the Middle East actually serve such salads at almost every main meal, as part of the *mezzeh* (or *meze*).

Mezzeh is an appealing assortment of appetizers, hors d'oeuvres, dips, salads, pickles, and possibly smoked or pickled fish, which is served as a first course. Each item is set out in its own small serving dish, so diners can help themselves.

The following salad and most of the other Sephardic vegetable salads and dips in this cookbook might be among the *mezzeh* selections, as well as such delicacies as *yalanji dolmas* (stuffed grape leaves, page 322). Foods for *mezzeh* are almost always prepared in advance, and served chilled or at room temperature.

The *mezzeh* has gained increasing popularity in Israel, where it is sometimes simply called *salatim*, meaning "salads."

3 cups well-drained canned white
   beans or cooked dry white beans
   (any type)
1 can or jar (about 8 ounces,
   drained weight) water-packed
   whole artichokes, well-drained and
   cut lengthwise into quarters
2/3 cup diced sweet red or green
   pepper
1/3 cup coarsely chopped or sliced
   pitted ripe olives
1/4 cup finely chopped red or Spanish
   onion

1/4 cup chopped fresh parsley leaves
1 teaspoon dried mint leaves (or 2
   teaspoons finely chopped fresh
   spearmint leaves)
3/4 teaspoon dried basil leaves (or 1 1/2
   teaspoons finely chopped fresh basil
   leaves)
1/3 cup good-quality olive oil
1/4 cup red wine vinegar
Salt and freshly ground black pepper
   to taste

In a medium-sized bowl, combine the beans, artichokes, sweet pepper, olives, onion, parsley, mint, and basil.

In a small bowl or jar, stir or shake together the oil and vinegar; then toss the dressing with the bean mixture. Season the salad with salt and pepper. Refrigerate the salad, covered, for several hours or overnight, stirring occasionally, to allow the flavors to blend. Serve the salad cold or at room temperature.

Makes 6 to 8 servings.

BABA GANOUSH (P)

(Eggplant-Sesame Dip)

This delicious appetizer dip of Arabic origin is very popular in Israel, as it is all over the Middle East.

2 medium-sized eggplants (about 1
   pound each)
2 garlic cloves, finely minced or
   pressed
1/3 cup tahini (pure sesame paste)
   (Stir well before using.)
2 1/2 tablespoons lemon juice,
   preferably fresh

2 tablespoons cold water
1 tablespoon good-quality olive oil
2 tablespoons finely chopped fresh
   parsley leaves
1/2 teaspoon salt
1/8 teaspoon black pepper, preferably
   freshly ground
Pinch of cayenne pepper (optional)

GARNISH (OPTIONAL)
Sprigs of fresh parsley
Ripe (black) olives

TO SERVE
Several loaves of whole wheat or
regular pita bread (purchased or
see page 308), cut into small
triangles.

Prick each eggplant in several places with a fork. (If you don't, they may explode!) Put them on a heavy, foil-lined baking sheet about 6 inches under a heated broiler element. Broil the eggplants, turning them often, for 20 to 30 minutes, or until the skin is blistered and charred and the pulp is soft and juicy. (Alternatively, skewer each whole eggplant on a long fork and slowly rotate it over a gas flame until the outside is charred and the inside is soft.)

Cut open the eggplants and let them cool until they can be handled. If desired, remove and discard any large clusters of seeds that taste bitter. Peel off and discard the skin and stem.

If a food processor (with the steel blade) is available, put the eggplant pulp into the bowl, along with the remaining dip ingredients. Pulse-process the mixture until it is almost smooth, but not completely puréed. Occasionally scrape down the sides of the bowl during the processing.

If a food processor is not available, very finely chop the eggplant pulp by hand and put it into a medium-sized bowl. In another bowl, combine the remaining dip ingredients and stir until they are very well blended. Then stir them into the eggplant.

Transfer the baba ganoush to a small serving bowl, and, if desired, garnish the top with the parsley and olives. Refrigerate the dip, covered, for several hours or, preferably, overnight to give the flavors a chance to blend. Serve it cold or, for the best taste, at room temperature. Accompany it with pita bread triangles for dipping.

Makes about 2 cups.

TABOULEH (P)

(Bulgur Wheat and Vegetable Salad)

This nutritious salad is popular among Jews from many Middle Eastern countries. The main ingredient is bulgur—precooked wheat kernels that have been dried and cracked into small pieces. For *tabouleh,* the bulgur (which is also called *burghul*) is softened in water, and needs no cooking.

Tabouleh is customarily served with large lettuce leaves, which are rolled around the salad when it is eaten. It is also delicious with pita bread.

1½ cups bulgur wheat
3 to 4 medium-sized tomatoes,
  preferably vine-ripened, diced
1 cup finely chopped fresh parsley
  leaves
1 cup thinly sliced scallions,
  including green tops
½ cup good-quality olive oil
⅓ to ½ cup lemon juice, preferably
  fresh

1 to 1½ teaspoons salt
¼ cup finely chopped fresh spearmint
  leaves (or 2 tablespoons dried mint
  leaves, crumbled)

TO SERVE (YOUR CHOICE)
Large lettuce leaves
Several loaves of whole wheat or
  regular pita bread (purchased or
  see page 308), cut into triangles

Soak the bulgur wheat in warm water to cover for about 30 minutes; then drain it very well, squeezing out the excess water. (An easy way to do this is to put the bulgur into a very large sieve; then lower the sieve into a large bowl of water until the bulgur is covered. To drain the bulgur, simply lift up the sieve and press out any excess water.)

Put the soaked and drained bulgur into a large bowl. Stir in the tomatoes, parsley, scallions, oil, lemon juice, salt, and mint leaves (if used). Mix the salad well. It may seem a bit wet, but the bulgur should eventually soak up most of the liquid.

Refrigerate the salad, covered, overnight so the flavors can blend and the bulgur can soften and absorb the dressing. Stir the salad occasionally during this period, and once again, just before serving.

To serve the tabouleh, heap it on a bed of lettuce leaves. Or put it into a serving bowl and accompany it with lettuce leaves and/or pita bread triangles.

Makes 8 to 10 servings.

PROVINCIAL EGGPLANT SPREAD (P)

This very appealing spread or "dip," which is based on Mediterranean cuisine, is similar to some of the cooked salads eaten in Israel and other Middle Eastern countries. The combination of several vegetables and olives makes this dip especially rich tasting. And, in fact, it's quite diffi-cult to discern the eggplant—a bonus for those who think they dislike that vegetable!

2 tablespoons good-quality olive oil
1 small onion, finely chopped
1 garlic clove, minced
½ medium-sized sweet green pepper, finely chopped
1 cup finely chopped fresh mushrooms
1 medium-sized eggplant (about 1 pound), unpeeled and finely chopped
⅓ cup dry red wine
¼ cup finely chopped ripe (black) olives

1 to 1¼ tablespoons red wine vinegar
½ teaspoon sugar
¼ teaspoon dried oregano leaves
¼ to ½ teaspoon salt
⅛ teaspoon black pepper, preferably freshly ground
2 tablespoons pine nuts (pignoli) or slivered almonds (optional)

TO SERVE
Italian bread or French bread, cut into 1-inch-thick slices

Heat the oil in a very large deep skillet or Dutch oven (preferably non-stick) over medium-high heat; then cook the onion, garlic, and green pepper until tender but not browned. Stir in the mushrooms, eggplant, and red wine. Cover the pan and lower the heat. Simmer, stirring often, for 10 to 15 minutes, or until the eggplant is very soft and reduced in volume. Be careful that it does not stick to the bottom of the pan.

Add the remaining ingredients and cook, stirring often, for 15 to 20 minutes longer to blend flavors and textures. Adjust the seasonings, if necessary. Serve at room temperature or chilled, with Italian or French bread. (The spread may be made in advance and frozen. Thaw it in the refrigerator.)

Make about 3 cups.

COLESLAW FOR A CROWD (P)

Here's an easy recipe that is perfect for a Lag B'Omer picnic. And, be-cause cabbage and carrots are two of the most healthful vegetables, it's nutritious, to boot!

This recipe makes quite a bit of coleslaw, but it tends to go quickly, and any leftovers can be stored for up to 5 days in the refrigerator. For ease in preparation, shred the vegetables in a food processor or with a rotary grater.

2 medium-sized heads white
 cabbage, finely shredded
4 to 5 medium-sized carrots, finely
 shredded or grated
1 small onion, grated
¾ cup mayonnaise (or similar
 "spread")

¼ cup apple cider vinegar
¼ cup sugar
About 1 teaspoon salt
Freshly ground black pepper to taste

In a large bowl, combine the cabbage, carrots, and onion and mix well. Then add the mayonnaise, vinegar, sugar, salt, and pepper. Adjust the amounts to taste, if necessary. Refrigerate the coleslaw, covered, for several hours or overnight to allow the flavors to blend. To redistribute the dressing, stir well before serving.

Makes 8 to 9 cups; about 15 servings.

YALANJI DOLMAS   (P)

(Grape Leaves Filled with Rice Pilaf)

Among Jews from Turkey, Greece, and other Balkan countries, stuffed grape leaves (which look like miniature cabbage rolls) are very popular. They are usually called *dolmas, dolmades,* or *yaprakes*. The grape leaves are typically filled with either rice or meat.

When an herbed rice mixture is used, as here, the stuffed grape leaves are served chilled, as part of a salad or as hors d'oeuvres. When a meat mixture is used, they are served hot, often topped with an egg-lemon sauce.

The brine-preserved "vine" leaves used in this recipe are sold at most gourmet stores and Greek or Middle Eastern groceries, as well as some supermarkets. Several leaves are tightly rolled together, and two or three "bunches" are packed into each jar. Before buying the leaves, make sure that the liquid in the jar is clear, not cloudy.

1 16-ounce jar preserved grape (or "vine") leaves in brine

4 tablespoons good-quality olive oil, divided

2 medium-sized onions, finely chopped

1 cup white or brown rice

2 cups boiling water

½ teaspoon salt

Pinch to ⅛ teaspoon black pepper, preferably freshly ground

½ cup currants or dark raisins

¼ cup pine nuts (pignoli) or slivered almonds

¼ cup finely chopped fresh parsley leaves

1 tablespoon dried mint leaves (or 2 tablespoons finely chopped fresh spearmint leaves)

2 teaspoons lemon juice

½ cup cold water

TO SERVE

2 lemons, cut into wedges

Drain the grape leaves, unroll them, and rinse each one well under cool running water. Trim off and discard any stems. Spread out the leaves in layers on paper towels, with the dull, thickly veined side of each (the back of the leaf) facing upward. Set aside.

To make the filling, heat 3 tablespoons of the oil in a medium-sized saucepan over medium-high heat; then cook the onions, stirring, until they are tender but not browned. Add the rice and cook, stirring for 2 to 3 more minutes, or until well coated with the oil and slightly toasted. Add the boiling water, salt, and pepper. Stir the rice once, cover the pan tightly, and lower the heat. Simmer the rice until it is tender and all the liquid has been absorbed (about 20 minutes for white rice, about 45 minutes for brown rice). Remove the rice from the heat and stir in the currants, pine nuts, parsley, mint, and lemon juice.

Arrange about 10 of the smallest grape leaves and any torn leaves in the bottom of a 3-quart or similar saucepan. To fill each of the remaining grape leaves, place it on a flat surface, dull side up, so that the stem end is toward you. In the center (Fig. 22A), place about 1 heaping teaspoon to 1 tablespoon of the rice mixture (the exact amount depends on the size of the leaf). Fold over the lower left point of the leaf to cover the rice filling; then overlap it with the lower right point (Fig. 22B). Begin to roll up the leaf from the stem end. Fold in the upper left and upper right points of the leaf (Fig. 22C), and continue rolling to the uppermost point of the leaf. (This is much easier to do than to read about!)

FIGURE 22

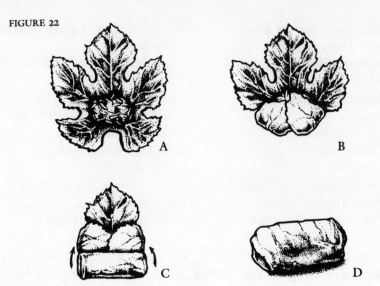

Each completed roll will look like a small log about 2 inches long and about 1 inch in diameter (Fig. 22D). As each roll is formed, put it, seam side down, into the leaf-lined saucepan. Keep the rolls close together and stack them when it becomes necessary.

When all the leaves are filled, sprinkle the rolls with the remaining 1 tablespoon of oil and the cold water. Cover the saucepan very tightly and put it over high heat for *only* 3 minutes; then turn the heat to *low* and steam the rolls for 50 minutes. Uncover the saucepan and let the rolls cool to room temperature. Carefully transfer the rolls to a covered container and refrigerate them.

Serve the rolls chilled or at room temperature. Attractively arrange the rolls on a serving platter, and garnish them with the lemon wedges. If desired, use 1 or 2 of the lemon wedges to squeeze a little fresh lemon juice over the rolls.

Makes 30 to 40 stuffed grape-leaf rolls.

SHASHLIK (M)

(Israeli-Style Kebabs of Lamb or Beef Chunks)

This delicious skewered and grilled meat is basically what Americans call "shish kebab." In Israel, the term *kebab* usually means skewered *ground* meat, whereas *shashlik* indicates that the meat is *cubed*. The latter name is adopted from the Russian term for such grilled meat.

The dish was probably brought to Israel by Russian Jews from the Caucasus and Georgia, where *shashlik* is said to have originated. However, it is so similar to certain Middle Eastern kebabs that it is also considered a specialty of Israelis from Yemen.

In Israel, it has become customary on Saturday evenings for many families to patronize restaurants and outdoor cafés especially for *shashlik* and ground-meat *kebab* (see the recipe for *mititei*, page 327). The grilled meats are usually accompanied with *tahina, humus* (pages 293 and 294), and assorted vegetable salads.

Before cooking *shashlik*, the meat must be marinated for at least several hours or, preferably, overnight. Oil and vinegar in the marinade help to tenderize the meat, and the seasonings give it a delectable flavor.

MARINADE
½ cup red wine vinegar or lemon juice
⅓ cup olive or vegetable oil
1 medium-sized onion, very finely chopped or grated
2 garlic cloves, finely minced or pressed
1 teaspoon salt
¼ teaspoon black pepper, preferably freshly ground
1 tablespoon finely chopped fresh parsley leaves
½ teaspoon dried thyme or dill leaves (optional)

¼ teaspoon dried marjoram leaves (optional)

FOR SKEWERS
2 pounds boneless lamb or beef, trimmed of all surface fat and gristle, and cut into 1- to 1½-inch cubes
3 to 4 small onions, cut into fourths (optional)

TO SERVE
Several loaves of whole wheat or regular pita bread (purchased or see page 308)

In a medium-sized, non-aluminum bowl, combine all the marinade ingredients and mix them well; then add the meat cubes and toss them so they are well coated with the marinade. Cover the bowl tightly. Marinate the meat for 4 to 24 hours, in the refrigerator, stirring it occasionally. The longer the meat is marinated, the more tender and flavorful it will be. Remove the bowl of meat from the refrigerator 30 to 60 minutes before grilling or broiling, to allow the meat to come to room temperature.

Thread the meat cubes onto metal skewers, preferably the flat-bladed type. (Reserve the leftover marinade.) Thread the onion pieces (if used) between some of the chunks of meat.

Grill the meat cubes over hot coals, turning them often and basting them with the leftover marinade, for about 10 to 15 minutes, or until the meat is cooked to the desired doneness. Or, if you prefer, broil the meat cubes about 4 inches from the heat source, turning them often and basting them, for 10 to 18 minutes, or until the meat is cooked as desired. Use a fork to slide the meat off the skewers. Serve with pita bread.

Makes about 6 servings.

VARIATION

"TERIYAKI" MARINADE FOR MEAT (M)

This delicious Japanese-style marinade is perfect, not only for meat cubes, but also for charcoal-grilled steak. If desired, alternate the meat cubes on the skewers with chunks of canned pineapple, in the Oriental manner.

⅓ cup soy sauce
¼ cup dry sherry or dry white wine
3 tablespoons vegetable oil
2 garlic cloves, finely minced or
  pressed

1 teaspoon apple cider vinegar
2 teaspoons honey or sugar
1 teaspoon grated fresh gingerroot
  (or ½ teaspoon ground ginger)

Combine all the ingredients, and use in place of the shashlik marinade in the above recipe. Grill the meat over hot coals, or broil as directed. Serve the grilled meat in pita bread, as above, or with hot cooked rice.

MITITEI or CARNATZLAH (M)

(Grilled Ground-Meat Kebabs)

The Romanian name of these wonderful "skinless sausages"—*mititei*—literally means "very small," and describes their petite size. In Yiddish they are known as *carnatzlah*. Romanian Jews always use a very generous amount of garlic in the meat mixture, and serve *mititei* with red and green chili peppers, dill pickles, and plenty of wine or beer.

Jews from the Middle East and North Africa have a very similar dish called *kofta kebab* or *kefta*. This is usually made with ground lamb instead of beef, and onion instead of garlic, and is served over a bed or rice.

Many Israelis serve their version inside *pita bread* (page 308), and top it with *tahina* (page 293). And, they may call the ground meat morsels *keftedes,* or simply *kebab.* The latter term often confuses American tourists, who tend to think it means skewered, marinated *cubes* of meat. In Israel, however, that dish is known as *shashlik* (page 325).

The delicious meat mixture below is seasoned in the Romanian fashion. For a Middle Eastern or North African flavor, use less or no garlic, and add a small grated onion. The herbs and spices differ everywhere this dish is served, but usually include at least a few of the following: parsley, mint, marjoram, thyme, oregano, coriander, cumin, cinnamon, allspice, cloves, ginger, and paprika, in various combinations depending on the whim of the cook.

1 pound ground beef
2 to 4 garlic cloves, very finely
minced or pressed
¼ teaspoon ground allspice
⅛ teaspoon ground cloves
2 tablespoons finely chopped fresh
parsley leaves

1 teaspoon dried marjoram leaves
¼ teaspoon dried oregano leaves
¾ teaspoon salt
⅛ to ¼ teaspoon black pepper,
preferably freshly ground
¼ cup water

Put all the ingredients in a medium-sized bowl and mix them together very well. For the mititei to have the proper texture, the meat mixture must be mixed until it is soft and almost pasty. To do this, knead the meat with your hands and repeatedly squeeze it through your fingers or mix it in a food processor.

With wet hands, form the meat mixture into finger-shaped sausages, about 4 inches long and 1 inch in diameter. If the meat is to be cooked on a grill with wide grids, form the sausages around flat-bladed skewers and taper the ends of each sausage against the skewer. This helps hold the meat tightly in place, so it will not slide around when the skewers are rotated.

If desired, the formed (and skewered) sausages may be refrigerated overnight, wrapped, to allow the seasonings to better permeate the meat. Remove the sausages from the refrigerator at least 30 minutes before cooking them.

Grill the sausages over very hot coals, turning them often, for 6 to 8 minutes. Or broil them about 4 inches from the heat source for about 5 minutes on each side. They should be well browned on the outside and cooked inside to the desired doneness. If skewers are used, use a fork to slide the mititei off before serving them.

Makes about 10 mititei; about 4 servings.

KLOPS (M)

(Meat Loaf with Whole Hard-Boiled Eggs)

Jews of Germanic background brought this tasty meat loaf to Israel, where it has become very popular. It is often prepared in advance and then chilled, so it can be served at picnics on such festive occasions as Lag B'Omer and Yom Ha'Atzmaut. Potato salad and assorted pickles usually accompany the meat loaf.

When cut into slices, the following version of *klops* is particularly attractive, as each slice features a golden and white cross-section of hard-boiled egg.

(Note: This recipe may be doubled and baked in a 9- by 5-inch loaf pan. Use 6 hard-boiled eggs in the center.)

1 pound very lean ground beef	*⅓ cup plain canned tomato sauce*
1 medium-sized onion, grated	*¼ cup finely chopped fresh parsley*
1 to 2 garlic cloves, minced	*leaves*
1 medium-sized carrot, grated	*½ teaspoon salt*
1 large egg	*⅛ teaspoon black pepper, preferably*
½ cup matzo meal	*freshly ground*

Pinch of ground nutmeg   *About 1 tablespoon* pareve
4 whole hard-boiled eggs, shelled   *margarine*

Mix all the ingredients, except the eggs and margarine, together with your hands or a fork until very well combined. For an especially smooth loaf, squeeze the mixture between your fingers as you mix it. (If the klops will be served chilled, increase the seasonings slightly, as their flavors will not seem as intense.)

Press a little less than half of the meat mixture into the bottom of a greased or non-stick spray-coated 8- by 4-inch loaf pan. Arrange the hard-boiled eggs lengthwise across the top, at even intervals. Pat some additional meat mixture around the eggs to hold them in place; then top them with the remainder of the meat, smoothing the top. Dot the top with the margarine.

Bake the klops in a preheated 375-degree oven for about 1 hour, or until it is browned and shrinking slightly away from the sides of the pan. Hold the pan with pot holders and carefully tilt it over the sink to drain off any released fat. Cool the klops in the pan for about 5 minutes; then unmold it. To unmold, cover the loaf pan with an inverted plate; then invert the two together and lift off the pan. To turn the klops upright, repeat the process with another plate. Serve the klops warm, at room temperature, or chilled. To serve, cut the klops into thick slices. It slices best when chilled.

Makes about 5 servings.

CHICKEN AND BANANA SATE   (M)

(Indonesian-Style Kebabs)

There are many different types of *sate* (pronounced "sah'-teh"), which is the Southeast Asian form of skewered kebab. It can be made with all sorts of meats, chicken, turkey, or even fish. *Sate* (which is sometimes spelled *"satay"*) is also very popular in South Africa, and has been introduced to Israel by South African-Jewish immigrants.

The following version of *sate* uses a soy-peanut marinade/sauce, which is actually a simplified combination of a soy mixture usually used for marinating and grilling *sate* and a peanut dipping sauce usually served with it. Though the mixture may seem strange, it boasts a delicious flavor that is well worth trying.

Sate is customarily prepared on inexpensive thin wooden skewers, which are available at most cooking stores and ethnic groceries.

MARINADE
5 tablespoons peanut butter, preferably smooth
1/4 cup soy sauce
2 tablespoons honey
2 tablespoons lemon juice
2 garlic cloves, finely minced
2 tablespoons vegetable oil
1/3 cup plain canned tomato sauce
1/4 teaspoon ground ginger

1/8 teaspoon cayenne pepper
2/3 cup chicken broth or water

FOR THE SKEWERS
6 medium-sized chicken breast halves, skinned and boned (about 1 1/2 pounds chicken meat)
About 4 medium-sized, very firm, green-tinged bananas

Soak 12 to 18 wooden skewers in water for about 30 minutes, or until they are softened slightly and soaked through. (This helps to ovenproof them.) Or use small metal skewers, preferably those with flat blades.

In a shallow rectangular dish or pan that is large enough to hold the skewers, mix together all the marinade ingredients until well combined. (Or mix the ingredients in a blender and then pour them into the dish.)

Cut the chicken breasts into approximately 1-inch-square pieces. Peel the bananas, and slice them into 3/4-inch-thick circles. Alternately thread the chicken pieces and banana slices on the skewers, beginning and ending with chicken. (If some chicken pieces are very small, thread 2 together.) Leave about 2 inches uncovered at both ends of each skewer. Lay the filled skewers in the marinade, turning them so that all sides are coated. Marinate the sate, covered, at least 2 hours in the refrigerator (or 30 minutes at room temperature), turning them occasionally.

To cook the sate, remove them from the marinade (reserve it), and wrap the ends of each skewer in aluminum foil. Grill the sate over very hot coals, turning them often, for 8 to 10 minutes. Or broil them about 4 inches from the heat source for 4 to 5 minutes on each side. During the cooking period, baste the sate once or twice with the reserved marinade.

Serve the sate on their sticks. If desired, the leftover marinade may be heated to boiling in a small saucepan and served as a sauce on the side, in the Indonesian fashion. If the sauce becomes too thick, stir in a little water.

Makes about 6 servings.

OVEN-BARBECUED CHICKEN (M)

If it happens to rain on Lag B'Omer, all is not lost. Serve this chicken with an assortment of salads, and the "cook-in" will be just as good as any cookout. If you do prefer to cook out-of-doors, this sauce is also great with grilled chicken and meat.

BARBECUE SAUCE
1 8-ounce can plain tomato sauce
⅓ cup apple cider vinegar
2 tablespoons packed dark or light
  brown sugar
1 tablespoon soy sauce
1 tablespoon pareve *margarine*
1 teaspoon salt
½ teaspoon powdered mustard

¼ teaspoon hot red pepper sauce
Pinch of ground cloves
2 garlic cloves, finely minced or
  pressed
1 bay leaf, crumbled

POULTRY
About 3½ pounds meaty chicken
  pieces (remove skin, if desired)

For the barbecue sauce, combine all the ingredients in a small saucepan over medium-high heat. Bring to a boil; then lower the heat and simmer, uncovered, stirring occasionally, for 20 minutes. Cool before using. The sauce may be refrigerated, covered, for up to 4 days or frozen. Thaw it before using.

For easy clean up, line a 9- by 13-inch baking pan with aluminum foil. Pour about one third of the barbecue sauce into the bottom. Arrange the chicken pieces in the pan; then pour the remaining sauce over the top of them. Bake the chicken in a preheated 350-degree oven, basting often, for about 1 hour, or until the chicken is tender and the sauce has thickened and glazed the chicken. If the sauce appears to be drying out too quickly, add a little water to the pan.

Makes about 6 servings.

NO-KNEAD CARAWAY RYE BREAD (P)

Russian and Polish Ashkenazic Jews have carried their love of rye bread with them wherever they have lived. It has even become popular in Israel, though rye is a cool-weather crop and not indigenous to that country.

The following rye bread is very easy and tasty. It is not, however, like delicatessen rye, which has a special coating to make a hard, crisp crust, and is baked in commercial ovens. Nevertheless, this loaf is quite nice for picnic sandwiches on Lag B'Omer, or any other time.

Caraway seeds help give it the typical flavor that we tend to associate with deli rye. The seeds and the rye flour can be found at most health-food and gourmet stores, and also at some supermarkets. If they are stored in the freezer, both will stay fresh for a year or longer.

1 packet (2¼ tablespoons) active dry
  yeast
1¼ cups warm (105 to 115 degrees)
  water
2 tablespoons light or dark molasses
2 tablespoons vegetable oil

2 teaspoons salt
1 to 2 tablespoons caraway seeds
1¾ cups white bread *flour*
1¾ cups rye flour
Vegetable oil to coat the dough

In a medium-sized mixing bowl, combine the yeast, water, and molasses. Let the mixture rest for 5 to 10 minutes, or until it is foamy. Add the oil, salt, seeds, and white bread flour. Beat with an electric mixer on medium speed (or a wooden spoon) for about 2 minutes, or until the batter seems to be elastic. Stir in the rye flour by hand (or with a heavy-duty electric mixer) until well combined.

Scrape down the sides of the bowl with a rubber spatula and press the dough into a rough ball. Sprinkle the top of it lightly with oil; then use the scraper to turn the dough in the bowl so that all sides are oiled. Cover the bowl with plastic wrap and then a dish towel. Let the dough rise until double in bulk, about 1 to 1½ hours.

Stir the dough down until it is completely deflated; then transfer it to a greased or non-stick spray-coated 9- by 5-inch loaf pan. Lightly oil the top of the dough; then cover the pan loosely with wax paper. Let the dough rise until doubled, about 45 minutes. Remove the wax paper and bake the loaf in a preheated 375-degree oven for 40 to 50 minutes, or until the bottom sounds hollow when tapped. Remove the loaf from the pan and cool it completely on a wire rack before storing it. Store it in a plastic bag at room temperature for up to 2 days, or freeze it for longer storage.

Makes 1 loaf.

VARIATION

KNEADED ONE-RISE RYE BREAD (P)

The above dough mixture can be shaped into "free-form" round or oblong loaves after only one rising; however, it must be kneaded first. Mix up the dough as directed; then let it rest in the bowl, covered, for 10 minutes. Turn the dough out onto a floured board and knead it, adding sprinkles of extra white flour when necessary, for about 8 minutes, or until it is smooth and elastic and just a bit tacky. Form it into a ball or oblong and place it on a greased baking sheet. Rub the surface of the dough with oil. Cover the loaf loosely with wax paper and let it rise until doubled, about 1 to 1½ hours. Carefully remove the wax paper and bake the loaf in a preheated 375-degree oven for 25 to 35 minutes, or until the bottom sounds hollow when tapped. Cool as above.

Makes 1 loaf.

EASY CAROB-PEANUT "FUDGE" (D)

Carob is eaten on Lag B'Omer because the great scholar, Rabbi Ben Yohai, is said to have been miraculously sustained by a carob tree, when he hid in a cave for thirteen years. The following confection makes a delicious, and relatively healthful, picnic or hiking snack for the holiday. What's more, it requires almost no cooking, and can be made in a matter of minutes.

*½ cup smooth or crunchy peanut
    butter
½ cup honey
½ cup carob powder, preferably the
    "dark" style (sifted, if lumpy)
½ cup raw or toasted wheat germ*

*¼ cup chopped almonds or walnuts
½ cup unsalted hulled sunflower
    seeds
1 teaspoon vanilla extract
½ cup instant nonfat dry milk
    powder*

In a medium-sized saucepan, over medium heat, warm the peanut butter with the honey, stirring constantly with a wooden spoon, until the mixture is thinned. Remove it from the heat and stir in the carob powder, pressing out any lumps with the spoon. Stir until smooth. Add the remaining ingredients and continue stirring until the fudge is well mixed. It will be quite stiff. If the fudge seems to be very sticky, stir in a bit more milk powder; if it is dry and crumbly, add a little honey.

Press the fudge into a lightly greased or non-stick spray-coated 8- or 9-inch-square baking pan. Chill it in the refrigerator; then cut it into small squares. (Or roll the warm fudge into 1-inch balls; then refrigerate it.)

Store the fudge in a tightly covered container in the refrigerator, but, for best taste, allow it to come to room temperature before serving.

Makes about 36 pieces.

SPICY BEER CAKE (D) or (P)

This loaf cake is a delightful picnic dessert, and one which happens to take advantage of a popular picnic drink—beer! Strange as it may seem to use beer in a sweet cake, it works great and adds rich flavor. In fact, this recipe helps demonstrate a surprising attribute of beer: It is a *pareve* liquid, which can sometimes be substituted for milk in baked goods that are to be served with meat.

½ cup butter or margarine
1 cup packed dark brown sugar
1 large egg
1½ cups all-purpose white flour,
  preferably unbleached (may be
  half whole wheat flour, if desired)
1 teaspoon ground cinnamon

1 teaspoon ground allspice
1 teaspoon ground cloves
1 teaspoon baking powder
¼ teaspoon baking soda
1 cup (lager) beer
½ cup coarsely chopped walnuts

In a medium-sized mixing bowl, use an electric mixer to cream the butter and brown sugar. Beat in the egg. In another bowl, or on a piece of wax paper, combine the flour, spices, baking powder, and baking soda. Add this dry mixture to the batter alternately with the beer, beating after each addition. Stir in the nuts.

Transfer the batter to a greased 8½- by 4½-inch loaf pan. Bake the cake in a preheated 375-degree oven for about 50 minutes, or until a toothpick inserted in the center comes out clean. Cool the cake completely in the pan on a wire rack. Remove from the pan and wrap well in plastic wrap or aluminum foil. For best flavor and texture, cut and serve the cake the day after it is made. To serve the cake, cut it into slices.

Makes 8 to 10 servings.

SHAVUOT

"Shavuot is the wedding anniversary of the Jewish people, and the Torah is the marriage certificate between the Jews and God."
—an ancient rabbi

Like the two other major pilgrimage festivals of ancient times—Pesach and Sukkot—Shavuot had agricultural beginnings. Celebrated on the sixth and seventh days of the Hebrew month of Sivan (only on the sixth in Israel), which usually occur in late May or June, it originally signified the onset of the wheat harvest. One of the many names given to it was *Hag Ha'Katzir,* or "Festival of the Harvest." Among the thanksgiving offerings taken to the Holy Temple in Jerusalem were always two long loaves baked from the new wheat.

Offered, too, were the *bikurim* or choicest "first fruits" of the season, primarily those representing the "Seven Species" for which ancient Israel was famed: barley, wheat, figs, grapes, pomegranates, olives, and honey. Thus, the holiday is also referred to as *Hag Ha'Bikurim,* or "Festival of the First Fruits."

Because it immediately follows the seven-week period when the *Omer* is counted, it received the name most often used today—*Shavuot*—which means "Weeks." Since it occurs on the fiftieth day after the counting begins, it is sometimes called *Pentecost,* a Greek word meaning "fifty."

The holiday also came to be known as *Zeman Matan Torahtenu,* or "The Time of the Giving of Our Law," because tradition says it is the time of year when the Revelation at Mount Sinai took place and God gave the Torah to the Jewish people. Over the years, this monumental event became the dominant theme of Shavuot.

The foods usually served on this holiday are related to both its agricultural and religious facets. One of the oldest and most prevalent culinary customs worldwide is the eating of cheese and other milk products. The simple, agrarian explanation for this custom is that Shavuot occurs in the season when grazing animals give birth and find lush pastures; thus, there is an abundance of milk.

However, with their usual ingenuity, Jewish sages have determined several symbolic reasons, all pertaining to Revelation, for partaking of dairy foods on Shavuot. A popular one is that the Law was given in Israel—"a land flowing with milk and honey," according to Exodus. Also, it is written in the *Song of Songs* that "honey and milk are under thy tongue," implying that the words of the Torah are as sweet as honey and as nourishing as milk. (Honey, one of the "Seven Species," is also eaten on Shavuot.)

Furthermore, some reasoned, the Jewish people did not know about *kashrut* until they received the law. As they did not have time to prepare kosher meat, they had to eat dairy dishes instead.

Others said that the people fasted prior to receiving the Torah, and became so ravenous that they could not wait for a meat meal to be cooked. Still others deduced that while the people were waiting, their milk curdled, and so they immediately made it into cheese.

Mystics construed meaning in the fact that the total numerical value of the letters in the Hebrew word for "milk" (*halav*) is forty, which equals the number of days Moses waited on Mount Sinai for the Torah. And, some noted, the infant Moses would take milk only from a Hebrew wet-nurse. It is also said among some Hasidim that even the wisest scholars are like suckling babes when it comes to real comprehension of the Torah.

Primary among the dairy dishes favored for Shavuot are those in which a sweet or savory cheese filling is encased in some sort of dough. Ashkenazic Jews enjoy *blintzes* (page 358), *kreplah* (page 354), *strudel, knishes, pirogen,* and a pastry known as *topfen.* Sephardic favorites include flaky turnovers called *borekas* (page 347), as well as ravioli-like *calsones* (page 356).

Among the dairy holiday specialties of Kurdistani Jews are wheat cooked in clabbered milk and dumplings filled with cheese and butter.

Another reason why milk products are eaten on Shavuot is that they are usually white and, thus, symbolize the purity of the Torah. Other white foods, particularly rice, are also traditional for many Sephardim. Often, the rice is cooked with milk or honey for a special holiday dish.

Certain Near Eastern and Middle Eastern Jews flavor their Shavuot rice with rose water or garnish it with rose petal jam, because they consider the holiday to be, among other things, the "Feast of Roses." At the synagogue, they may scatter rose petals on the scrolls of the Torah or sprinkle rose water on congregants.

In some communities, it is customary to mix milk or yogurt with the last matzo left over from Pesach, as a reminder that Shavuot was once considered to be the conclusion of the Pesach holiday season, and also that the Revelation at Mount Sinai was the culmination of the Exodus.

Prominent among holiday desserts are cake and cookies shaped like the Two Tablets of the Ten Commandments, as well as cone-like cakes resembling Mount Sinai. Some Sephardim take particular pride in baking *siete cielos* (Judeo-Spanish, for "seven heavens"), which are round, seven-layered cakes or seven-tiered breads filled with fruits and nuts and decorated with symbols of the Revelation. The number of layers corresponds to the weeks in the *Omer* period which precedes Shavuot, as well as to the seven "spheres" of heaven that God is said to have traversed in order to present the Torah to the Jewish people.

Other holiday foods include a pair of extra-long loaves of bread to symbolize the measure of the Law which, according to Job, "is longer than the earth," and also to recall the ancient Shavuot bread offerings at the Temple in Jerusalem. Sometimes, the breads are decorated with ladders, because the numerical value of the Hebrew word for "ladder" is the same as that for "Sinai," and also because a ladder represents Moses' ascent and descent of Mount Sinai. The ladders often have seven rungs for the same reasons that the *siete cielos* have seven layers.

The agricultural side of Shavuot is also specifically recalled in certain aspects of its celebration. For instance, fresh fruits, particularly those that are new to the season, are often included in meals and table centerpieces. In addition, lush foliage and flowers are used to adorn many homes and synagogues, and the scrolls of the Torah may be crowned with garlands.

In modern-day Israel, the custom of collecting "first fruits" is being revived at many kibbutzim and farming towns. The *bikurim* are brought to central points and then distributed to the needy or other worthy groups.

On Shavuot, Ashkenazim from Russia and nearby areas often eat *schav*, a cold soup made from sorrel, an herb which flourishes during late spring. Chilled fruit soups are also popular for this holiday.

In Eastern Europe, it was once customary for Ashkenazic Jews to begin their children's Jewish education on Shavuot. To make the introduction to Torah especially "sweet" and memorable, the children were given honey cakes or candies decorated with Hebrew letters. Or the letters on a child's slate were dabbed with honey for the child to lick off.

Other Shavuot customs include reading the Book of Ruth, and an all-night study session known as *Tikun Leil Shavuot,* during which a small section of every part of Jewish law is studied and discussed. Recently, Shavuot has also become the time when religious schools hold graduation and confirmation ceremonies.

The recipes in this chapter emphasize dairy and fresh fruit dishes, and include a wonderful assortment of hors d'oeuvres, soups, main dishes, and desserts. Many are perfect for buffet entertaining. It would be particularly appropriate to serve them from a holiday table decorated with seasonal greenery, fruit baskets, and freshly picked flowers.

"FIRST FRUITS" RAINBOW SALAD (P)

In ancient times, Jews brought their finest "first fruits" or *bikurim* to the Temple in Jerusalem as a special offering for Shavuot. In remembrance of this, many now serve fresh fruit on the holiday, particularly "new" fruits not yet eaten in the season. Sometimes, whole fresh fruits are arranged in a pyramid-shaped centerpiece to represent Mount Sinai.

Following is a simple, yet delectable fruit salad, which includes fruits mentioned in the Bible or found in modern-day Israel. Feel free to adjust amounts or omit some fruits. Of course, other fruits may be added, such as mango and papaya (tropical fruits now gaining popularity in Israel), avocado, pomegranate, melons, pineapple, dates, and so forth. You can use ten different types of fruit to symbolize the Ten Commandments.

2 grapefruits, peeled and cut into ¾-inch chunks

3 oranges, peeled and cut into ¾-inch chunks

1 tangerine, peeled and sectioned, then each section cut in half

2 apples, cored and diced

½ cup each seedless green and red grapes, cut in half

2 bananas, peeled and diced

2 pears, cored and diced

1 pint strawberries, stems removed and the berries sliced

1 cup fresh or "dry-pack" frozen blueberries or raspberries

3 fresh figs, peeled and cut into fourths (optional)

½ cup coarsely chopped walnuts

½ cup slivered almonds

2 to 3 tablespoons honey or sugar (optional)

2 to 3 tablespoons sweet sherry, or sweet white or red wine (optional)

Combine all the ingredients in a large serving bowl and stir until evenly mixed. Refrigerate, covered, for several hours to allow the flavors to blend.

Makes 8 to 10 servings.

SPRING SALAD (D)

(Cottage Cheese and Vegetable Salad)

For many Ashkenazic Jews, this easy salad has long been a favorite way to enjoy some of the special culinary delights of spring. In fact, it is often considered a must for the Shavuot holiday table.

For as long as I can remember, the following version of *spring salad* has been one of my mother's favorite dairy dishes. Though she eats it all year round, Mom insists, and I agree, that it tastes the very best at Shavuot time, when the first luscious, vine-ripened tomatoes of the season are just becoming available.

A very similar salad is often served in Israel, where wonderful ripe produce is almost always "in season." Israelis usually make the salad with *leben* or the richer *lebeniya,* cultured milk products which are similar to yogurt.

Feel free to adjust all the amounts in this salad to taste.

1 1-pound carton cream-style cottage
   cheese (about 2 cups)
1 8-ounce container commercial sour
   cream (about 1 cup)
1 bunch scallions (4 to 5 medium-
   sized ones), including green tops,
   cut into ¼-inch slices
1 medium-to-large-sized tomato,
   preferably vine-ripened, cut into
   ¾- to 1-inch pieces

1 medium-sized cucumber, peeled
   and cut into small pieces
   (optional)
3 to 4 radishes, thinly sliced
   (optional)
Salt and freshly ground black pepper
   to taste

TO SERVE
Lettuce leaves

In a large bowl, combine the cottage cheese and sour cream; then mix in
the remaining salad ingredients. If desired, serve the salad on a bed of
lettuce leaves.

Makes 5 to 6 servings.

HAR GEVEENAH   (D)

(Mount Sinai Fruit-and-Cheese "Ball")

King David's psalms are read on Shavuot, because it is traditionally considered to be the anniversary of both his birth and death. In one of his
psalms, Mount Sinai is described as, among other things, *har gavnunim*
or "a mountain of peaks."

Scholars have interpreted the similarity between the Hebrew word for
"peaks" and that for "cheese" (*geveenah*) as another of the many reasons
why dairy foods should be eaten on Shavuot.

Desserts that are *shaped* like the "mountain of peaks"—that is, cone-
like cakes, cookies, and confections—are also often served on Shavuot.
Sometimes, they are topped with jam or chopped nuts to represent the
dark cloud that is said to have hovered over Mount Sinai at the time
when the Tablets of the Law were given. Or, a perfect walnut half may
be put on top instead, to symbolize the stone Tablets themselves.

The following appetizer/snack combines the custom of eating cheese
with that of eating foods shaped like Mount Sinai. The whimsical Hebrew name translates literally as "mountain of cheese," and is a play on
the words of David's psalm. The cheese "ball" is molded to resemble a

mountain, and its peak is topped with either a prune (for the dark cloud) or a walnut half (for the Tablets). In addition, the cheese mixture includes fruits and nuts indigenous to Israel, which may have been among those offered as *bikurim* during the ancient Shavuot pilgrimage.

1 3-ounce package cream cheese, softened
2 tablespoons commercial sour cream
About 2 tablespoons sweet or dry red wine
8 ounces Cheddar cheese, finely grated (2 cups packed)
½ cup slivered almonds
⅓ cup finely chopped dates
⅓ cup finely chopped dried figs
⅓ cup dark raisins

COATING AND GARNISH
(OPTIONAL)
Finely chopped blanched or unblanched almonds
1 prune or 1 perfect walnut half

TO SERVE
Crackers or small cocktail bread slices

In a large bowl, beat the cream cheese with the sour cream until light and fluffy; then beat in the 2 tablespoons of wine. Add the remaining cheese mixture ingredients and mix very well. Use the back of a spoon to press the mixture against the sides of the bowl to help it form a cohesive mass. If the cheese mixture seems to be very dry, add more wine.

Form the cheese mixture into a mountain-like cone shape and coat it with the chopped almonds (if used). To represent the dark cloud over Mount Sinai, horizontally set the prune on top of the mountain peak. Or, for the Two Tablets of the Law, stand the perfect walnut half upright in the peak.

Wrap the "cheese mountain" in plastic wrap and chill it for several hours or overnight to allow the flavors to blend and the cheese mixture to firm up. Serve it with crackers or bread.

Makes 1 large cheese "ball."

CHILI CON QUESO (D)

(Cheese, Tomato, and Chili Pepper Dip)

This Tex-Mex dip makes a perfect snack, buffet, or party dish, and it takes only a few minutes to prepare. It looks like a chunky cheese fondue.

*1 pound Cheddar, Longhorn, or
  Monterey Jack cheese, shredded*
*2 tablespoons all-purpose white flour,
  preferably unbleached*
2 tablespoons olive or vegetable oil
1 large onion, finely chopped
2 garlic cloves, minced
*1 16-ounce can tomatoes, including
  juice, finely chopped*

*1 3- to 4-ounce can chopped green
  chilies*
*¼ cup chopped ripe (black) olives
  (optional)*

TO SERVE
*Corn chips, nacho chips, or broken
  taco pieces*

Toss the cheese with the flour and set it aside momentarily.

In a large saucepan, over medium-high heat, heat the oil; then cook the onion and garlic, stirring, until they are very tender but not browned. Add the tomatoes with their juice and the chilies. Heat, while stirring, until the sauce comes to a boil. Gradually add the shredded cheese, stirring constantly. Continue to stir over medium to medium-high heat for 5 to 10 minutes, or until the cheese is completely melted and smooth, and the mixture just comes to a boil. Stir in the olives (if used). Remove the mixture from the heat and let it cool, stirring occasionally, about 5 minutes, so it can thicken slightly. Serve the warm chili con queso in a chafing dish, fondue pot, or deep bowl, with your choice of accompaniments for dipping.

Makes about 4½ cups; about 8 servings.

BRANDIED MUSHROOM-WALNUT PÂTÉ (D) or (P)

Tired of chopped liver? Here's a different spread, which may even be served at dairy buffets or as a first course with dairy dinners. The flavor can be subtly changed by varying the herbs and spices.

3 tablespoons butter or margarine
1 tablespoon vegetable oil
1 large onion, finely chopped
1 pound fresh mushrooms, cleaned,
   dried, and very finely chopped
2 garlic cloves, minced
½ teaspoon dried tarragon leaves
½ teaspoon dried thyme leaves
2 teaspoons lemon juice
2 to 3 tablespoons brandy

1½ cups finely chopped walnuts
¼ cup commercial sour cream
   (optional)
Salt and ground black pepper to taste
Walnut halves or toasted sesame
   seeds for garnish

TO SERVE
Crackers or small cocktail bread slices

In a large skillet, over medium-high heat, heat the butter with the oil; then sauté the onion until it is lightly browned. Add the mushrooms, garlic, tarragon, thyme, and lemon juice. Cook, stirring constantly, until almost all the moisture has evaporated.

Stir in the brandy and chopped walnuts. Remove from the heat and cool slightly. If a smoother pâté is preferred, purée the mixture in a food processor or food mill. Stir in the sour cream (if used). Adjust any seasonings, if necessary. Spoon the pâté into a small serving bowl. Garnish the top with walnut halves or sesame seeds. Refrigerate, covered, until chilled. Serve chilled, with crackers or bread slices.

Makes about 2 cups; about 6 servings.

LIGHT AND EASY STRAWBERRY SOUP (D)

Strawberries are usually at the peak of their season during Shavuot, and this chilled soup makes a delicious use of them. If fresh strawberries are not available, frozen ones may be substituted.

⅔ cup cold water
1 cup orange juice
¼ cup sugar
⅛ teaspoon ground allspice
⅛ teaspoon ground cinnamon
4 cups hulled fresh strawberries or
   unsweetened, "dry-pack," frozen
   strawberries (thawing is not
   necessary)

1 tablespoon cornstarch
½ cup sweet red wine, such as a
   fruit-flavored wine, cream sherry,
   Madeira, Marsala, etc. (Or use
   dry wine and add more sugar to
   taste.)
1¼ cups very fresh commercial
   buttermilk

In a large saucepan, combine the water, juice, sugar, allspice, and cinnamon. Bring to a boil over high heat. Add the strawberries and cover the pan. Lower the heat and simmer the strawberries for about 5 minutes, or just until they are tender. Transfer the contents of the pan to a blender or a food processor fitted with the steel blade, and process until the strawberries are completely puréed.

Return the strawberry purée to the saucepan. Dissolve the cornstarch in the wine and stir the wine mixture into the strawberry purée. Stir over medium-high heat until the soup thickens slightly and comes to a boil. Simmer for about 1 minute. Remove it from the heat and let it cool to tepid. Stir in the buttermilk.

Refrigerate the soup, covered, for several hours or overnight, or until it is completely chilled. Serve the soup chilled.

Makes about 4½ cups; 4 to 5 servings.

HUNGARIAN-STYLE CHERRY SOUP (D)

This delicious chilled soup, a favorite of Jews from Hungary and Czechoslovakia, makes an elegant beginning for a Shavuot meal. Or it may even be served as a light dessert.

2 16-ounce cans tart red cherries in
  water
Cold water
⅓ to ½ cup sugar, or to taste
Pinch of ground allspice
Pinch of ground cloves
1 tablespoon cornstarch
½ cup sweet red wine, such as cherry-
  flavored wine, cream sherry,
  Madeira, Marsala, etc. (Or use
  dry wine and add more sugar to
  taste.)

⅓ cup commercial sour cream

GARNISH (OPTIONAL)
Commercial sour cream

Drain the liquid from the cherries and reserve it. Add enough water to the liquid to make a total of 2⅔ cups. Put this into a large saucepan with the cherries, sugar, allspice, and cloves. Cover and bring to a boil over high heat. Lower the heat and simmer the cherry mixture for 5 minutes.

Meanwhile, dissolve the cornstarch in the wine. Add the wine mixture to the cherries and cook, stirring, until the cherry soup thickens slightly and comes to a boil. Simmer for about 1 minute. Remove it from the heat and cool it to tepid. Stir about ¼ cup of the liquid part of the soup into the ⅓ cup sour cream to soften it. Add this back to the rest of the soup and stir well until it is completely mixed in.

Refrigerate the soup, covered, for several hours or overnight, or until it is completely chilled. Serve the soup chilled. If desired, garnish each serving with a dollop of sour cream.

Makes about 6 cups; 6 to 8 servings.

CHILLED SPICED APPLE SOUP (D)

This creamy soup is wonderfully rich and satisfying and makes a nice addition to a company meal.

¾ cup cold water
½ cup apple juice or cider
1 tablespoon lemon juice
¼ cup honey
½ teaspoon ground cinnamon
¼ teaspoon ground cloves
¼ teaspoon ground nutmeg

4 cups peeled and coarsely chopped
  apples
1½ tablespoons cornstarch
½ cup dry sherry or dry white wine
1 cup milk
¾ cup whipping cream (or table
  cream)

In a large saucepan, combine the water, apple juice, lemon juice, honey, cinnamon, cloves, and nutmeg. Bring to a boil over high heat. Add the apples and cover the pan. Lower the heat and simmer the apples for about 10 minutes, or just until they are tender. Transfer the contents of the pan to a blender or a food processor fitted with the steel blade, and process until the apples are completely puréed.

Return the apple purée to the saucepan. Dissolve the cornstarch in the wine, and stir the wine mixture into the strawberry purée. Stir over medium-high heat until the soup thickens slightly and comes to a boil. Simmer for about 1 minute. Remove it from the heat and let it cool to tepid. Stir in the milk and cream.

Refrigerate the soup, covered, for several hours or overnight, or until it is completely chilled. Serve the soup chilled.

Makes about 4½ cups; 4 to 5 servings.

BOREKAS (D)

(Pastries Filled with Cheese and Vegetables)

Also spelled *burekas,* these are probably the most well known of the wonderful, savory pastries favored by Sephardim with Turkish, Greek, and similar backgrounds. The Judeo-Spanish name was likely adapted from the Turkish word for a similar filled pastry, *borek.* Jews from Syria and other Middle Eastern and North African countries make almost identical pastries called *sanboosak* or *sembussak.*

The same rich dough is also used for miniature pot-shaped "tarts" called *pasteles* or *pastelicos,* which are usually filled with meat.

In Israel, very large triangular *borekas* made with flaky, multi-layered puff pastry or, possibly, with filo dough are popular street food, and can even be purchased as a convenience food from the freezer section of some large supermarkets.

Borekas are made with a variety of fillings, each usually including a vegetable and cheese. The favorite vegetables are potato, spinach, and eggplant. And, the cheeses most often used are kaskaval, Parmesan, Romano, and feta. Other choices of cheese include Swiss, Muenster, Monterey Jack, Cheddar, and a dry-type farmer's cheese. Kaskaval, or "katzkaval" as it may be called, has become commonplace in Israel though it is still considered a specialty cheese in the United States. Similar cheeses, which are sometimes substituted, are kasseri and caciocavallo.

When cheese is added to the dough as well as to the filling, the pastries are often called *borekitas* (see the Variation below).

Most Sephardim serve *borekas,* and other delectable cheese-filled pastries, such as *ojaldres* and *bulemas* (pages 350 and 352), on Shavuot as well as on many other festive occasions, particularly for *Desayuno.* Though this Judeo-Spanish word literally translates as "breakfast," the Sephardim usually use it to specifically mean a special dairy brunch that they often enjoy after morning synagogue services on Shabbat and holidays.

In addition to pastries, *Desayuno* customarily includes a selection of cheeses, yogurt, the long-cooked eggs known as *huevos haminados* (page 248), vegetable-cheese casseroles such as *fritada de espinaca* (page 269), olives, homemade preserves, seasonal fresh fruits, and, possibly, the rice pudding called *soutlach* (page 373).

DOUGH
½ cup butter or margarine, melted
   and cooled to lukewarm
½ cup vegetable oil
½ cup lukewarm water
½ teaspoon salt
3½ cups all-purpose white flour,
   preferably unbleached

1 cup finely shredded kaskaval or
   kasseri or grated Parmesan or
   Romano cheese
2 large eggs
¼ teaspoon salt
Matzo meal (optional; use a small
   amount only if the filling is very
   wet)

POTATO-CHEESE FILLING
1¼ cups plain mashed potatoes
4 ounces kaskaval, kasseri, Monterey
   Jack, Muenster, Swiss, or Cheddar
   cheese, finely shredded (1 cup
   packed)
½ cup grated Parmesan or Romano
   cheese
2 large eggs
Pinch of freshly ground black pepper

SPINACH-FETA FILLING
Use the same filling as for the
   Spanakopetes *(page 350)*

GLAZE AND TOPPING
1 large egg beaten with 1 teaspoon
   water
Sesame seeds (optional)
Grated cheese (optional)

EGGPLANT-CHEESE FILLING
1½ cups eggplant pulp from
   approximately 2 large broiled
   eggplants (for directions, see the
   recipe for Salat Hatzilim, *page
   297*), drained of excess moisture in
   a colander or large sieve.

For the dough, combine the melted butter, oil, water, and salt in a medium-sized bowl and mix well. Gradually stir in the flour to make a soft, slightly greasy dough. Mix only until the dough comes away from the sides of the bowl; do not overmix. Gather the dough into a ball and cover it with plastic wrap. Let it rest for 15 to 30 minutes while the filling is prepared. Each filling recipe is sufficient to fill 1 batch of dough.

For the potato-cheese filling or the eggplant-cheese filling, combine all the designated ingredients to make a soft, stiff paste. For the spinach-feta filling, follow the directions with the recipe for *Spanakopetes*.

To make the borekas, shape the dough into about 36 balls, each approximately the size of a small walnut. For each boreka, use your fingertips to flatten one of the balls on a board or other flat surface until it forms a thin oval approximately 3 by 4 inches. Put 1 tablespoon of the filling on one side of the oval (Fig. 23A); then fold it in half crosswise to cover the filling and form a half-moon shape.

Pinch the edges tightly together and secure them with the tines of a fork. Or, to form a decorative, rope-like ("festoon") edge—as most Sephardim do—hold the pastry in one hand and use the thumb and index finger of the opposite hand to squeeze a bit of the edge and then fold it up toward the pastry on a slight angle. Begin at one side of the pastry and move continuously around to the other.

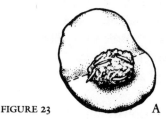 

FIGURE 23   A   B

Put the borekas about 1 inch apart on ungreased baking sheets. Brush the top of each one with the egg glaze. If desired, sprinkle the tops lightly with sesame seeds or grated cheese. (When making borekas with more than one type of filling, use a different topping for each type to make identification easy.) Prick each boreka once with a fork to allow steam to escape.

Bake the borekas in a preheated 375-degree oven for 35 to 40 minutes, or until they are golden brown and crisp (Fig. 23B). (Borekas may be frozen after baking. Reheat them, unthawed, in a 375-degree oven until hot throughout.) Serve the borekas hot or at room temperature.

Makes about 36 3-inch borekas.

VARIATION

To make *borekitas,* use the same fillings as for *borekas* with a slightly modi-fied dough. *Omit* the melted butter and *add ½ cup vegetable oil* and *½ cup grated kaskaval, kasseri, Parmesan, or Romano cheese* to the dough. Proceed as above.

SPANAKOPETES OR OJALDRES (D)

(Spinach and Cheese in Flaky Pastry)

Sephardic Jews, particularly those from Greece and Turkey, make a vari-ety of savory pastries that are wrapped in an ultra-thin dough known as *filo.* (See the recipe for *baklava,* page 218, for details on purchasing and using filo.)

Spanakopetes is the Greek name for filo pastries that are filled with spin-ach and cheese, and typically folded into triangular shapes or rolled into narrow, cigar-like cylinders. (Occasionally, all the filling is baked be-tween layers of filo to form a sort of "pie.") When the filling contains cheese, but no spinach, the same pastry is called *tiropetes.*

Ojaldres (or, possibly, *rojaldes*) is the Sephardic name for the triangular form of the above pastries.

Bulemas or *bolemas* (see Variation) are Sephardic pastries, which are also often made with filo dough, and contain fillings similar to *ojaldres.* For *bulemas,* though, the filling is rolled inside a large filo tube, which is then twisted into a coil. (More traditional *bulemas* may be made with a stretched yeast dough instead of filo.)

All these pastries are often included among those served at the Sephar-dic holiday dairy brunch known as *Desayuno.* They also make excellent hors d'oeuvres for entertaining at any time.

SPINACH-FETA FILLING
2 tablespoons olive or vegetable oil
1 medium-sized onion, finely chopped
1 10-ounce package frozen chopped
 spinach, thawed and very well-
 drained
8 ounces feta cheese, crumbled

1 cup part-skim or regular ricotta
 cheese
2 large eggs, lightly beaten
2 tablespoons plain or seasoned dry
 bread crumbs
1 teaspoon dried dillweed
⅛ teaspoon ground nutmeg

Generous pinch of black pepper,
preferably freshly ground

FILO WRAPPERS
About ½ pound (10 or 11 sheets) filo
dough at room temperature
About ½ cup butter (preferably
unsalted), melted

For the spinach-feta filling, heat the oil in a skillet; then sauté the onion until soft. Add the spinach and cook, stirring, until most of the moisture evaporates. Remove from the heat; cool. Stir in feta, ricotta, eggs, bread crumbs, dillweed, nutmeg, and pepper.

There are two basic ways to shape spanakopetes. For either one, use scissors or a sharp knife to cut each large sheet of filo crosswise into thirds, to make 3 strips. (If desired, cut the stack of sheets together and collect the strips into one pile.) Keep the filo covered with a damp, but not wet, dish towel, so it does not dry out.

For rolls, or *sigaras,* as they are sometimes called, brush 1 strip of filo *very lightly* with melted butter. Place 1 tablespoon of filling along one *narrow* edge of the strip (Fig. 24A). Fold over the edge to cover the filling; then fold in each *long* edge of the strip ½ inch (Fig. 24B). Roll up the strip, beginning at the end with the filling to form a tight cylinder (Fig. 24C). Repeat with the remaining dough strips and filling.

FIGURE 24

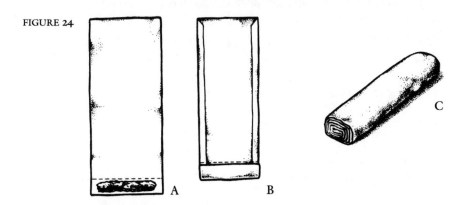

For triangles (or *ojaldres*), brush 1 strip *very lightly* with butter; then fold it in half lengthwise and brush the top surface with butter (Fig. 25A). Put 1 tablespoon of filling about 1 inch from a *narrow* edge (Fig. 25B). Diagonally fold the end of the strip over the filling so that the narrow edge meets the side of the strip and forms a right-angle triangle (Fig. 25C). Fold the triangle forward, and then on the diagonal, just as when folding an American flag (Fig. 25D). Continue to the end of the strip (Fig. 25E). Repeat with the remaining strips and filling.

FIGURE 25

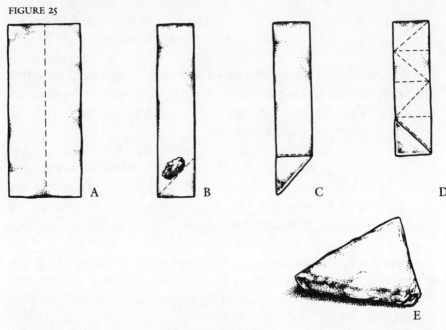

Put all the pastries on greased baking sheets and brush the tops well with butter. Bake them in a preheated 400-degree oven for 20 to 25 minutes, or until golden brown. Serve warm. (Freeze, if desired, in a single layer; then pack into airtight bags or containers when frozen. To serve, reheat the frozen rolls at 400 degrees until warmed through.)

Makes 30 to 33 hors d'oeuvres.

Variation

BULEMAS   (D)
(Coiled Filled Flaky Pastry)

Fold 1 large *lightly* buttered sheet of filo in half lengthwise; then brush the top surface *lightly* with melted butter. Put 3 to 4 tablespoons of filling in a thin line along one of the long edges. Fold each of the shorter sides in 1 inch. Then fold over the long edge to enclose the filling and continue rolling up the filo like a jelly roll. Brush the roll with butter; then gently curl it into a snake-like coil. Repeat with the remaining dough and filling. Place the rolls on greased baking sheets and bake in a preheated 375-degree oven for about 30 to 40 minutes, or until they are golden brown.

Makes about 10 large pastries.

MINIATURE CHEESE TURNOVERS (D)

These delectable American-style hors d'oeuvres are similar to Sephardic *borekas* (page 347). Both make fantastic Shavuot fare, and are also perfect for year-round entertaining.

DOUGH
1 8-ounce package cream cheese, cut into small pieces
½ cup butter, cut into small pieces
1½ cups all-purpose unbleached white flour (may be half whole wheat flour, if desired)

FILLING
8 ounces Cheddar or Muenster cheese, finely grated (2 cups packed)

2 large eggs, beaten
1 teaspoon instant minced onions
½ teaspoon prepared mustard
¼ teaspoon hot red pepper sauce
⅛ teaspoon salt

GLAZE AND TOPPING
1 large egg, beaten with 1 teaspoon water
Sesame seeds

For the dough, put all the ingredients into a medium-sized mixing bowl or a food processor fitted with the steel blade. Blend just until combined; to keep the pastry flaky, do not overmix the ingredients. Gather the dough together into a solid mass and shape it into a thick circle. Wrap the dough well in plastic wrap and chill it for several hours, or until it is firm enough to roll.

When the dough has chilled, prepare the filling. In a medium-sized bowl, combine all the ingredients and mix well.

Roll out the dough on a floured surface until it is about ⅛ inch thick. Cut out 2¾- to 3-inch-diameter circles. Reroll the scraps and cut them out until all the dough has been used.

To form each turnover, put 1 teaspoon of filling on a circle. Brush or dab the perimeter of the dough with a bit of the egg glaze; then fold the circle in half to form a half-moon, enclosing the filling. Pinch the edges of the dough closed; then press them with the tines a fork to seal them tightly together. Repeat until all the turnovers have been formed. Brush the top of each turnover with the egg glaze; then immediately dip it in sesame seeds to coat it. Prick the top of each turnover once with a fork to allow steam to escape.

Put the turnovers on ungreased baking sheets, about 1 inch apart. Bake them in a preheated 400-degree oven for 15 to 20 minutes, or until they are lightly browned. Cool them slightly on wire racks and serve warm.

To freeze the turnovers, cool them completely; then freeze them in airtight containers or bags. To serve, reheat them in a 350-degree oven until they are warmed through.

Makes 40 to 44 tiny turnovers.

CHEESE KREPLAH (D)

(Triangular Noodle Dumplings)

Three-cornered, cheese-filled *kreplah* are eaten by many Ashkenazic Jews on Shavuot because the number "three" has several connections with the holiday. The Law is *three*-fold, comprising Torah, Prophets, and Writing. It was given to Moses, the *third* child born of his parents, on the sixth day (two times *three* equals six) of the *third* month of the Hebrew calendar. Moses brought it to the Jewish people, who were made up of *three* groups: Kohan, Levite, and Israelite.

Cheese varenikes are almost identical to *cheese kreplah,* the only difference being that the dough is cut into circles, not squares, and folded into half-moons.

DOUGH
2 cups all-purpose white flour,
  preferably unbleached
½ teaspoon salt (or ¼ teaspoon, if a
  sweet filling is used)
2 large eggs
2 to 4 tablespoons cold water

SAVORY FILLING
2 7½- to 8-ounce packages (about 1
  pound) farmer cheese
2 tablespoons commercial sour cream
1 large egg
1 tablespoon instant minced onions
Salt and ground black pepper to taste

SWEET FILLING
2 7½- to 8-ounce packages (about 1
  pound) farmer cheese
1 large egg
¼ cup sugar
¼ teaspoon vanilla extract
¼ teaspoon ground cinnamon
  (optional)

TO SERVE
Butter or margarine, melted
Grated cheese to taste, with savory
  kreplah (optional)
Cinnamon-sugar to taste, with sweet
  kreplah (optional)

For the dough, combine the flour and salt in a medium-sized bowl. Make a well in the center of the flour. Add the eggs and water to the well and beat them with a fork. Gradually beat the flour into the egg mixture to form a stiff dough. If the dough is dry and crumbly, add a bit more water; if it is too wet, add more flour. Knead the dough on a lightly floured surface for about 5 minutes, or until it is smooth and silky. Wrap it well in plastic wrap and let it rest at room temperature for 20 minutes to 1 hour.

(Note: The dough can be made in a food processor. Process the flour, salt, and eggs until crumbly. Then, with the machine running, add the water. The mixture should form a ball. If it is too dry, add water; if too wet, add flour. After the ball is formed, process 30 seconds longer to knead it.)

For the savory or sweet filling, combine all the designated ingredients until well mixed. Each filling recipe is sufficient to fill one batch of dough.

Divide the dough into 2 pieces and keep the second one wrapped so it does not dry out. On a lightly floured surface, roll out the first piece of dough to a very thin rectangle about 9 by 15 inches. Cut the dough into about 15 3-inch squares. Put 1 scant tablespoon of filling on each square and dab a little water along 2 perpendicular edges. Fold over the dough on the diagonal to form a triangle. Press the top and bottom edges together; then press on the edges with the tines of a fork to tightly seal them closed. Repeat with the second piece of dough, to make about 15 more kreplah.

(Note: If desired, the kreplah may be frozen at this point. Freeze them in a single layer, uncovered, on a baking sheet; then place them into a sealed plastic bag for storage. Do not thaw them before cooking; just cook them for 5 to 10 minutes longer, or until they are tender.)

To cook the kreplah, gently drop them into a large pot of boiling water, and simmer them for 15 to 20 minutes, or until they are just tender but not mushy. (They will increase greatly in size as they cook.) Remove them from the water with a slotted spoon and drain them very well.

Toss the hot kreplah with melted butter, and, if desired, sprinkle the savory ones with some grated cheese or the sweet ones with some cinnamon-sugar.

Or heat some butter in a large skillet, over medium-high heat, and fry the kreplah until they are golden brown on both sides. Serve hot as a side dish or appetizer.

Makes about 30 kreplah; 6 to 8 servings.

CALSONES (D)

(Sephardic-Style Noodle Dumplings with Pasta)

On Shavuot, some Sephardim eat square or round cheese-filled dumplings called *calsones* or *kelsonnes* (pronounced "kal-soh-nehs"), which use the same noodle dough as *kreplah,* but employ the rolling and filling technique used for Italian *ravioli.* (Interestingly, the Italians have a cheese-filled turnover called *calzone;* however, it is usually made with pizza dough and baked.)

Often, the boiled *calsones* are put into a baking pan with spaghetti or noodles, butter, and grated cheese, and then baked into a rich casserole. This last step may be omitted, though, and the *calsones* simply tossed with melted butter and cheese, or served with sour cream or yogurt.

DOUGH
1 *recipe* dough *for* Cheese Kreplah
  (page 354)

FILLING
1 *recipe* potato-cheese filling *for*
  Borekas *(page 348)*

TO SERVE (OPTIONAL)
Melted butter to taste
*Grated cheese (such as the same kind
  used in the filling) to taste*

*Commercial sour cream or plain
  yogurt to taste*

FOR THE CASSEROLE
(OPTIONAL)
*8 ounces spaghetti or wide egg
  noodles, cooked according to
  package directions*
¼ cup butter or margarine, melted
*¼ to ½ cup grated Parmesan or
  similar cheese (or the same kind
  used in the filling)*

Make the dough and set it aside to rest while you prepare the filling.

Divide the dough into 2 pieces, and keep the second one wrapped so it does not dry out. On a lightly floured surface, roll out the first piece to a very thin rectangle about 9 by 15 inches. Spoon all the filling in small dollops on the dough, spacing them about 2½ inches apart (Fig. 26A). Brush the spaces between the mounds lightly with water to moisten the dough. Roll out the reserved piece of dough to the same size as the first. Then lay it on top of the first, and press down firmly *between* the mounds so that the two sheets of dough make contact (Fig. 26B). For square calsones, cut the mounds apart with a pastry wheel or sharp knife. For round ones, cut out the mounds with a circular cookie cutter or a drinking glass. Press the edges of the calsones tightly together with the tines of a fork (Fig. 26C).

FIGURE 26

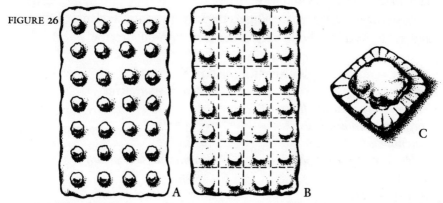

To cook the calsones, drop them carefully into a large pot of lightly salted boiling water and simmer them for 15 to 20 minutes, or until they are just tender but not mushy. (They will increase greatly in size as they cook.) Remove them from the water with a slotted spoon and drain them very well.

Serve them with melted butter, grated cheese and/or sour cream or yogurt. Or, if you prefer, bake them into a casserole with the spaghetti: Toss the cooked spaghetti with the butter and cheese. Gently stir the boiled calsones into the spaghetti mixture, and transfer it to a greased or non-stick spray-coated 9- by 13-inch baking dish. Bake in a preheated 325-degree oven, covered, for 20 minutes; then uncover and bake for 10 to 15 minutes longer, or until the top is crisp and lightly browned.

Makes 25 to 30 calsones; about 6 servings alone, or about 8 servings as a casserole.

MOM'S BEST CHEESE BLINTZES   (D)

It is very traditional for Ashkenazic Jews to eat dairy blintzes on Shavuot. Not only are they filled with the customary cheese, but two of them, placed next to each other, look like the two tablets of the Ten Commandments that were given to Moses on Mount Sinai.

Cheese *blintzes* have always been a favorite of mine, and they were one of the first "Jewish" dishes I learned to cook. When I was a teen, I loved to watch (and occasionally help) my mother prepare the delicate, crêpe-like, blintz wrappers that never seemed to tear. (And, oh how I sometimes wished they would, because then I'd be allowed to nosh on the delectable fragments.) Mom also taught me how to neatly fill and fold the *blintzes,* so they would look as wonderful as they tasted.

To this day, I still prepare *blintzes* the way my mom, Helene ("Hindy") Kaufer, showed me. Following is her easy, "no-fail" recipe.

BATTER FOR BLINTZ WRAPPERS
4 large eggs
1 cup all-purpose white flour, preferably unbleached
1 cup milk
1 tablespoon sugar (optional)

CHEESE FILLING
4 7½- to 8-ounce packages (about 2 pounds) farmer cheese
3 large eggs
1 to 3 tablespoons sugar, or to taste

FOR FRYING
Butter or margarine

TO SERVE
Applesauce
Commercial sour cream or plain yogurt
Fruit preserves or jam

For the blintz wrappers, put all the batter ingredients into a blender or a food processor (fitted with the steel blade), and process until very well combined. Scrape down the sides of the container once or twice during the processing. The batter will be very thin, similar to the consistency of cream. Let it rest for about 30 minutes.

Meanwhile, prepare the filling. Combine all the ingredients and mix very well. Set aside.

To make the blintz wrappers, preheat a shallow 8-inch skillet with sloping sides (and, preferably, a non-stick surface) over medium-high heat. Very lightly grease the hot pan with butter, margarine, or non-stick cooking spray. Give the batter a brief stir to re-suspend the ingredients. Then pour enough batter into the hot pan to completely cover the bottom about ¼ inch deep. Let the pan sit on the heat for only about 5 seconds; then *immediately* lift the pan by the handle and pour all the excess batter out of the pan and back into the original container. The small amount of batter that remains in the pan will make a very thin, perfectly smooth blintz wrapper, about 6½ inches in diameter.

Cook the blintz wrapper for about 30 seconds, or until it is dry on top and cooked through. The bottom does not have to brown very much. Do not flip it over in the pan; it is cooked only on one side.

Use a knife or spatula to loosen the edge of the blintz wrapper. Turn it out of the pan onto a table or countertop covered with paper towels. The cooked side should face upward. (If the wrapper does not come right out of the pan, pull on it gently to release it.) Repeat with the remaining batter, arranging the cooked blintz wrappers next to each other, but not overlapping. (If space is very limited, they may be stacked in one pile; however, it is easier to evenly divide the filling when all the wrappers are spread out.)

Spoon about 3 tablespoons of the filling onto the center of each blintz wrapper (Fig. 27A), dividing the filling evenly among them. To form each blintz, fold two opposite sides of a wrapper over the filling so that they almost meet in the center (Fig. 27B). Then fold up the two remaining sides so that they overlap (Fig. 27C), completely enclosing the filling and forming a rectangle about 2½ by 3 inches. Turn all the formed blintzes over so that the seams are on the bottom (Fig. 27D). The uncooked side of the shell will be on the outside. (Note: The blintzes may be made ahead to this point, and refrigerated or frozen. Arrange them next to each other on a platter or in a freezer container. If the blintzes need to be stacked, place a sheet of wax paper between each layer.)

FIGURE 27

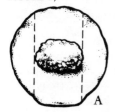

To cook the blintzes, melt a generous amount of butter or margarine in a large skillet over medium to medium-high heat. Beginning with their seamed sides down, fry the blintzes in batches, until they are golden brown on both sides. (If the blintzes have been frozen, do not thaw them before cooking; simply fry them at a lower temperature for a longer time to make sure the cheese filling is cooked through.)

(If desired, uncooked blintzes may be baked instead of fried; however, they are not as rich-tasting as the fried ones. To bake the blintzes, melt a few tablespoons of butter in a casserole dish; then put in the blintzes and turn them so they are lightly coated with butter. Bake them, seam side down in a single layer, in a preheated 400-degree oven for about 20 minutes, or until they are cooked through and hot. Bake *frozen* blintzes in a 350-degree oven for 35 to 40 minutes.)

Serve the blintzes with your choice of accompaniments.

Makes about 20 blintzes; about 5 servings.

QUICK-AND-EASY CHEESE BLINTZ CASSEROLE (D)

Though cheese blintzes rate as an all-time favorite in my family, I don't always have the time to prepare them in the customary fashion. Therefore, I created the following casserole, which has a fantastic flavor very similar to blintzes (some say it's even better!); yet, it takes only a few minutes to prepare. A layer of cheese filling is baked between two layers of a special blintz-type batter. The casserole is then cut into squares for serving, making it a perfect choice for a dairy buffet, and great for Shavuot.

BATTER
4 large eggs
1¼ cups milk
2 tablespoons commercial sour cream
  (or plain yogurt)
¼ cup butter, melted
¾ teaspoon vanilla extract
1⅓ cups all-purpose white flour,
  preferably unbleached

1 to 2 tablespoons sugar
1¼ teaspoons baking powder

FILLING
2 7½- to 8-ounce packages (about 1
  pound) farmer cheese
1 15- to 16-ounce container part-
  skim or regular ricotta cheese
2 large eggs

2 to 3 tablespoons sugar
1½ to 2 tablespoons lemon juice

TO SERVE
Commercial sour cream
Plain or vanilla yogurt
Applesauce

Preheat the oven to 350 degrees. In a blender or a food processor (fitted with the steel blade), combine all the batter ingredients. Process until very smooth, scraping down the sides of the container once or twice. Measure out 1½ cups of the batter, and pour it into the bottom of a buttered or non-stick spray-coated 9- by 13-inch baking dish. Bake in the preheated oven for about 10 minutes, or until it is set.

Meanwhile, combine all the filling ingredients in a large bowl and mix well. When the bottom layer has set, remove it from the oven and spread the filling over it, smoothing the top. Give the remaining batter a brief stir to re-suspend the ingredients; then very slowly pour it over the cheese filling so the filling is completely covered. Carefully return the casserole to the hot oven and bake it 35 to 40 minutes, or until the top is puffed and set.

Let the casserole rest for 10 to 15 minutes before cutting it into squares. Serve with your choice of accompaniments.

Makes about 8 servings as a main course, more as a side dish or buffet dish.

LASAGNE VERDE (D)

(Lasagne with Spinach and Three Cheeses)

This Italian-Jewish favorite was adapted from classic Italian cuisine to follow the rules of *kashrut*. Though it lacks meat, it certainly is not lacking in looks or taste. In fact, the lasagne is especially colorful, because spinach is added to the filling (*verde* is Italian for "green").

The lasagne makes a great company dish, particularly since it can be assembled ahead of time and baked shortly before serving.

SAUCE

2 tablespoons olive or vegetable oil

1 medium-sized onion, finely chopped

2 garlic cloves, finely minced

½ of a medium-sized sweet green pepper, diced (optional)

2 16-ounce cans tomatoes, including juice, chopped

1 6-ounce can tomato paste

1 to 2 teaspoons dried oregano leaves

1 teaspoon dried basil leaves

½ teaspoon dried thyme leaves (optional)

1 bay leaf, crumbled (optional)

⅛ teaspoon black pepper, preferably freshly ground

Salt to taste

PASTA, CHEESES, ETC.

1 8-ounce package lasagne noodles (about 12)

1 10-ounce package frozen chopped spinach, thawed and well drained

1 15- to 16-ounce container part-skim or regular ricotta cheese

1 large egg

¼ teaspoon black pepper, preferably freshly ground

¾ cup grated Parmesan cheese, divided

8 ounces mozzarella cheese, shredded (about 2 cups packed)

For the sauce, heat the oil in a large skillet over medium-high heat; then sauté the onion, garlic, and green pepper (if used) until tender but not browned. Stir in the remaining sauce ingredients and mix until well combined. Bring to a boil; then lower the heat and simmer the sauce, uncovered, stirring occasionally, for 30 minutes, or until the sauce has thickened slightly and the flavors have blended. Remove it from the heat and set it aside.

Meanwhile, cook the noodles according to the package directions and drain them well.

In a medium-sized bowl, combine the spinach, ricotta, egg, pepper, and ¼ cup of the Parmesan cheese.

In a small bowl, mix together the remaining Parmesan cheese and the mozzarella.

To assemble the lasagne, spoon about 3 tablespoons of the sauce into the bottom of a greased or non-stick spray-coated 9- by 13-inch or equivalent baking dish. Cover it with one third of the noodles. Spread half the ricotta-spinach mixture over the noodles; then top with one third of the mixed grated cheeses and one third of the remaining sauce. Beginning with noodles, make a second layer in the same manner, using up the ricotta mixture. Top with the remaining noodles, cheese, and sauce. (The lasagne may be assembled ahead to this point and refrigerated, covered, for several hours or up to overnight. Remove the cover before baking.)

Bake the lasagne in a preheated 350-degree oven for 45 to 55 minutes, or until it is hot and bubbly and very lightly browned on top. Let it rest for 5 to 10 minutes before cutting. Cut it into large squares to serve.

Makes 6 to 8 servings.

TURBAN OF SOLE WITH SOLE MOUSSE (D)

This magnificent turban presents an attractive ring of whole fish fillets wrapped around luscious, spinach-flecked fish mousse. Though it is quite impressive, it is not that difficult to prepare. In fact, the mousse filling is made in just seconds using a food proceessor.

Furthermore, the entire turban may be assembled up to a day ahead of time, and then baked shortly before it is served, making this dish especially convenient for company meals during Shavuot.

2½ pounds thin, skinless sole fillets
3 large eggs
¼ cup butter, melted and cooled to
tepid
⅛ teaspoon ground nutmeg
3 to 4 drops hot red pepper sauce
½ teaspoon salt
½ cup whipping cream

4 ounces fresh, trimmed spinach
leaves, washed, well drained, and
coarsely chopped (about 1 cup
tightly packed)

GARNISH
¼ cup butter or margarine
8 ounces fresh mushrooms, cleaned
and finely chopped

Coat a 6½-cup ring mold well with butter or non-stick vegetable spray. Choose 1½ pounds of the nicest, most evenly sized sole fillets. Line the mold with these fillets (smooth, darker-skinned side up), positioning them so that they go across the ring like the spokes of a wheel. The narrow end of each fillet should point toward the center and possibly overhang the inside rim of the mold; the wider end should overhang the outside rim.

For the mousse, put the remaining 1 pound of sole fillets into a food processor (fitted with the steel blade). Pulse-process until the fillets are puréed. Add the eggs, melted butter, nutmeg, hot pepper sauce, and salt, and process until well mixed. With the machine running, slowly add the cream through the chute. Turn off the machine, add the spinach, and pulse-process only until the spinach is finely minced and flecked through-out the mousse.

Turn out the mousse mixture into the fillet-lined mold. Fold the over-hanging ends of the fillets over the mousse. Chill very well, covered, at least 3 hours or up to overnight.

To bake the turban, remove the cover. Put the ring mold into a larger pan and add boiling water to the pan so that it comes two thirds up the outside of the ring mold. Bake in a preheated 350-degree oven for about 40 minutes, or until the turban is firm. (If dinner is delayed, the turban can stay in the warm, turned-off oven for up to 15 minutes.)

When the turban is almost finished baking, melt the butter for the garnish in a large skillet and quickly sauté the mushrooms just until they are cooked through, but not until they become rubbery and exude juices.

To unmold the turban, run a rubber spatula around the edge of the ring mold to loosen the fish fillets. Carefully tilt the mold over the sink to drain off any excess liquid accumulated during baking. Cover the mold with an inverted serving platter; then invert the two together. Leave the metal mold in place for a minute; then hold it against the plate as you drain off any liquid collected on the plate. Carefully lift the mold off the turban. Sprinkle the sautéed mushrooms and any of their pan juices over the turban; then serve it immediately.

Makes 6 to 8 servings.

SOUTHERN-STYLE SOLE AND CORN BREAD CASSEROLE (D)

Fish fillets and corn bread are baked together for this easy dish, which is especially appealing to children. Based, as it is, on the regional cuisine of the American South, one might say it has "soul" as well as sole.

Some of the earliest Jewish settlements in North America were in the colonial South. Jews have lived in Charleston, South Carolina, for exam-ple, almost since its establishment in the latter part of the seventeenth century. And, the first American Reform congregation was founded there in the mid-1820s.

There are also long-established Jewish communities in Atlanta and New Orleans, as well as several other Southern cities.

As with Jews elsewhere, Southern American Jews have adapted their local cuisine to follow the rules of *kashrut*. Following is just one dish that shows how well they have succeeded.

1½ cups yellow cornmeal, preferably stone ground
1 cup commercial buttermilk
2 large eggs
3 tablespoons vegetable oil
2 scallions, including green tops, thinly sliced
1 tablespoon sugar (optional)
½ teaspoon chili powder
¼ teaspoon salt
1 teaspoon baking soda

1 pound thin skinless sole or flounder fillets, coarsely cut into pieces about 2-inch square
1 16-ounce can tomatoes, well drained and chopped
2 tablespoons chopped fresh parsley leaves
2 teaspoons dried basil leaves
⅛ teaspoon salt
⅛ teaspoon black pepper, preferably freshly ground

For the corn bread batter, stir together the cornmeal, buttermilk, eggs, oil, scallions, sugar (if used), chili powder, and salt. (This may be done up to 1 hour ahead of time, and refrigerated.)

Just before baking, stir in the baking soda until completely mixed. Pour the batter into a greased or non-stick spray-coated 9- by 13-inch or equivalent baking dish or casserole, and spread it evenly over the bottom.

Arrange the fillet pieces on top of the batter so that none of them overlap. Spread the chopped tomato over the fish; then sprinkle the fish and batter with the parsley, basil, salt, and pepper. Bake the casserole in a preheated 425-degree oven for 18 to 23 minutes, or until the fish is tender and the corn bread is done. Cut into large squares to serve.

Makes about 5 servings.

SIMPLE SALMON MOUSSE (D)

This appetizer makes a very tasty addition to the Shavuot table. It takes only minutes to prepare and it can be made way ahead of time. In fact, it's just the thing to keep in the refrigerator in case any unexpected company drops in for a holiday visit.

1 packet unflavored gelatin
2 tablespoons lemon juice, preferably
  fresh
1 small onion, chopped
½ cup boiling water
⅓ cup mayonnaise (or similar
  "spread")
½ teaspoon paprika
1 teaspoon dried dillweed (or 2
  teaspoons chopped fresh dillweed)
½ teaspoon hot red pepper sauce

1 15½-ounce can salmon, drained
⅔ cup whipping cream

TO SERVE
Lettuce leaves
Raw vegetables, such as slices of sweet
  green pepper, carrot, and
  cucumber, and whole cherry
  tomatoes, for garnish
Crackers or small "cocktail" bread
  slices

Put the gelatin, lemon juice, onion, and boiling water into a blender or a food processor (fitted with the steel blade), and process until well combined and the gelatin is dissolved. Add the mayonnaise, paprika, dillweed, hot pepper sauce, and salmon and process until smooth. With the machine running, slowly add the cream, and process until it is completely incorporated. Pour the mousse mixture into a non-stick spray-coated or very lightly oiled 3- to 3½-cup mold, fish-shaped if desired. Refrigerate for several hours, or until set. (The mousse may be refrigerated for up to 2 days, if necessary. Cover it, if it will be stored more than a few hours.)

Up to 2 hours before serving the mousse, unmold it. Run the tip of a knife around the top edge of the mousse to loosen it from the mold; then cover the mold with an inverted plate and invert the two together. Lift off the mold. Garnish the mousse with the suggested vegetables, as desired, and refrigerate it until serving time. Serve with crackers and/or bread slices.

Makes about 3 cups; 6 to 8 servings as an appetizer.

MAMALIGA (D) or (P)

(Romanian-Style Cooked Cornmeal)

One of the staples of Romanian-Jewish cuisine is *mamaliga*—cornmeal mush that is cooked until it is so thick it can be molded into a "cake." It is then sliced with a heavy white thread (never a knife!). For dairy meals, the slices are usually fried or baked with cheese.

Most Romanians prefer to use *brinza* cheese with their *mamaliga*.

However, almost any kind of cheese, Muenster, mozzarella, kaskaval, Parmesan, feta, Monterey Jack, mild Cheddar, etc., works well. It is simply a matter of taste.

Mamaliga is virtually identical to the Italian dish called *polenta,* which Italian Jews make on Shavuot using *white* cornmeal, rather than the customary yellow, because white symbolizes the purity of the Torah.

I adapted the following recipe and that for another Romanian cornmeal dish called *malai* (page 177) from those given me by a "Romanian Jewish friend," who asked that I not identify her by name. Though Romanian Jews love these dishes, and serve them often to their own families, it seems they consider them to be such common, unrefined "peasant" fare that they would rather not publicly admit to making them.

BASIC MAMALIGA
2 cups yellow cornmeal (or white
cornmeal, if preferred), preferably
stone ground
4 cups cold water, divided
1 teaspoon salt
3 tablespoons butter or margarine

FOR BAKED MAMALIGA
About 2 cups grated or thinly sliced
cheese (see comment above for
suggestions)
Butter or margarine to taste, cut
into small pieces

FOR FRIED MAMALIGA
1 to 2 large eggs, beaten
1 to 2 cups very finely grated
Parmesan or similar cheese
Butter or margarine for the pan
Commercial sour cream or plain
yogurt to serve (optional)

For the basic mamaliga, combine the cornmeal and 1½ cups of the water in a medium-sized bowl. (This softens the cornmeal and helps to prevent lumps in the mamaliga.) In a large saucepan, over high heat, bring the remaining 2½ cups of water to a boil. Lower the heat to medium, and add the moistened cornmeal, while stirring constantly with a wooden spoon. (Romanians prefer to use a 1-inch-thick wooden dowel that they keep on hand for just this purpose.) Adjust the heat so that the mixture just simmers and stir it constantly. It will become very thick and stiff. Stir in the salt and butter. Continue stirring constantly for about 10 minutes. Then cook the mamaliga over very low heat, stirring frequently, for 10 to 15 minutes longer, or until it is very stiff and seems to pull away from the sides and bottom of the pan. Use a spoon or a spatula, which has first been dipped in water, to push all the cornmeal mixture from the sides of the pan, forming a mound in the center. Let the mixture sit on the heat for about 1 minute, undisturbed, so that steam can loosen it from the bottom of the pan. Lift up the pan by the handle and immediately invert it onto a wooden board or platter in one quick movement. The mamaliga should fall out into a sort of "cake." If it does not, use a spoon or spatula to remove it from the pan. Smooth out the surface of the "cake" with the back of a wet spoon or a wet knife, and, if necessary, shape it into a neat mound. If plain mamaliga is desired, let it cool only slightly, and serve it as is. Cut it in the Romanian style, with a long thread held taut between your hands, or use a knife.

For baked or fried mamaliga, let it cool completely. (It may be refrigerated overnight, if desired.) Then use a knife or thread to cut it into ¼- to ½-inch-thick slices.

To bake, alternate the slices with the grated cheese and butter in a greased or non-stick spray-coated casserole, ending with cheese on top. Bake, uncovered, in a preheated 375-degree oven for about 20 minutes, or until the cheese is melted and bubbly and the top is lightly browned.

To fry, dip each slice into the beaten egg(s) and then into the finely grated Parmesan. Heat a large skillet over medium-high heat; then melt a generous amount of butter in it. Fry the slices until they are browned on both sides and heated through. If desired, serve the fried mamaliga with sour cream or yogurt.

Makes 6 to 8 servings.

RICH-AND-FRUITY LOKSHEN KUGEL (D)

(Sweet Noodle Pudding)

Dairy *lokshen kugel* is traditional for Ashkenazic Jews on Shavuot. This one is especially appropriate because it contains honey (the Land of Israel and the Torah are both often compared to "milk and honey") and fruits (Shavuot is the time of the "first fruits"), as well as cheese.

The *kugel* is so rich and luscious that it could even be served as dessert. It can be baked ahead and rewarmed just before serving, making it convenient for entertaining.

8 ounces medium-wide egg noodles

1 10½-ounce (or similar) can mandarin orange segments, drained

1 16-ounce can pitted dark, sweet cherries, drained

1 8-ounce can crushed pineapple, including juice

1 cup commercial sour cream

⅓ cup butter, softened and cut into small pieces

1 8-ounce package cream cheese, softened and cut into small pieces

⅓ cup sugar

2 tablespoons honey

1 teaspoon vanilla extract

5 large eggs

TOPPING (OPTIONAL)

2 tablespoons sugar

1 teaspoon ground cinnamon

Cook the noodles according to the package directions and drain them well. Combine them with all the canned fruit, and spread the mixture in a well-buttered or non-stick spray-coated baking dish.

In a blender or a food processor (fitted with the steel blade), combine the sour cream, butter, cream cheese, sugar, honey, vanilla, and eggs. Process until completely smooth, about 1 minute or longer, scraping down the sides of the container once or twice. Pour the mixture over the noodles and fruit; then stir gently with a spoon so that all the ingredients are evenly distributed. Combine the topping ingredients (if used) and sprinkle over the top of the casserole.

Bake the kugel in a preheated 350-degree oven for 1 hour, or until it is set. Let it rest for 10 to 15 minutes before cutting. Serve warm or at room temperature, cut into squares. (If made ahead, let it cool to room temperature, and refrigerate it uncut. Shortly before serving, reheat it, covered, in a 350-degree oven until warmed through.)

Makes about 12 servings.

BRANDIED CHERRY-RICE MOLD WITH CHERRY SAUCE (D)

White foods, particularly rice and milk products, are served by many Sephardim on Shavuot, because the white stands for purity, just as the Torah is pure. This tasty dairy dessert turns ordinary rice pudding into an elegant masterpiece.

(Note: Regular, not "converted"-type, rice is called for in this recipe, because it disintegrates more easily, and thus makes a thicker, creamier custard.)

3 *cups* cooked regular *white rice (see Note above)*
3 *cups milk, any type*
½ *cup sugar, divided*
1 *to 2 tablespoons grated orange rind (colored part only)*
2 *packets unflavored gelatin*
3 *tablespoons cherry-flavored brandy or sweet wine*
2 *large eggs, separated*

1 *teaspoon vanilla extract*
1 *16-ounce can dark, sweet cherries, drained (syrup reserved for sauce)*

SAUCE
1 *tablespoon cornstarch*
1 *to 2 tablespoons sugar*
Reserved syrup from cherries
2 *tablespoons cherry-flavored brandy or sweet wine*

In a large saucepan, combine the cooked rice, milk, ¼ cup of the sugar, and the orange rind. Put the saucepan over medium heat and bring the rice mixture to a simmer, stirring. Simmer, stirring often, for 20 to 25 minutes, or until it becomes thick and creamy.

Meanwhile, soften the gelatin by sprinkling it over the 3 tablespoons of brandy. Put the egg yolks into a small bowl.

When the hot rice mixture is thick, mix the softened gelatin into it until the gelatin is completely dissolved. Stir about ½ cup of the rice mixture into the yolks; then stir the yolk mixture back into remaining rice mixture in the saucepan. (This procedure keeps the eggs from curdling.) Remove the pan from the heat and stir in the vanilla. Let the rice mixture cool to lukewarm, stirring occasionally to prevent the formation of a "skin" on the surface.

In a clean bowl, beat the egg whites until frothy. Gradually add the remaining ¼ cup of sugar and continue beating the whites until they form stiff peaks. Fold the beaten whites into the rice mixture. Then fold in the drained cherries. Transfer the mixture to a non-stick spray-coated or very lightly oiled 2-quart mold. Refrigerate, covered, until completely set, at least 4 hours or up to overnight.

Just before serving the dessert, unmold it and make the sauce. To unmold, run a small knife around the edge of the dessert and invert it onto a serving platter.

For the sauce, combine the cornstarch and sugar in a small saucepan. Measure the reserved cherry syrup; there should be ¾ cup liquid; if not, add water to make this amount. Slowly stir the cherry liquid into the cornstarch mixture so lumps do not form. Stir the sauce over medium heat until it thickens and simmers. Mix in the cherry-flavored brandy.

To serve, cut the chilled rice mold with a cake server. Spoon some of the warm cherry sauce over each serving.

Makes about 8 servings.

COEUR À LA CRÈME (D)

("Heart of Cream" with Strawberries)

This very lovely, perfectly white French dessert is in keeping with the Shavuot custom of eating white foods to symbolize the purity of the Torah. The heart shape can also represent a love for the Law. Strawberries add striking color and a flavorful contrast to the *crème*.

A special heart-shaped porcelain dish, made just for *coeur à la crème*, is the ultimate in elegance for preparing it. However, I've always used an inexpensive aluminum heart mold that I adapted by drilling a few holes in the bottom. The holes allow excess moisture to drain from the cheese, as it chills overnight. An ordinary colander or large sieve can be used instead of a mold, to produce a somewhat "rounded" dessert. (See the Note below for another alternative.)

CRÈME
1⅓ cups cream-style cottage cheese
1 8-ounce package cream cheese,
*   softened*
⅔ cup confectioner's sugar
½ teaspoon vanilla extract
⅔ cup whipping cream, beaten until
*   stiff*

ACCOMPANIMENTS
2 cups sliced fresh strawberries
1 tablespoon granulated sugar
1 tablespoon orange juice or liqueur
*   of your choice*
About 2 cups whole fresh strawberries
Strawberry preserves, heated in a
*   small saucepan until thinned*
*   (optional)*

Line a 3½- to 4-cup heart-shaped mold, which has holes in the bottom (see Note), (or a small colander or large sieve) with 4 thicknesses of rinsed cheesecloth, so that there is a 2-inch overhang of cheesecloth on all sides.

Put the cottage cheese into a food processor (fitted with the steel blade) or a blender, and process until completely smooth (or press it through a sieve). If a food processor is used, add the cream cheese, confectioner's sugar, and vanilla and process until perfectly smooth. Otherwise, use an electric mixer to beat the cream cheese and confectioner's sugar until very smooth; then beat in the puréed cottage cheese and the vanilla until completely combined and smooth.

By hand, fold the cheese mixture and the whipped cream together. Turn out the mixture into the prepared mold. Fold the overhanging cheesecloth on top of the cheese mixture. Set the mold on a rack over a shallow pan or bowl to catch drips and refrigerate it, letting it drain, for at least 8 hours (or overnight). (Some brands of cheese do not release as much liquid as others. The amount is not important.) If the crème is not to be served soon, cover the top with plastic wrap, and refrigerate it, in the mold, for up to 2 days. Do not unmold the crème until just before serving it.

About 2 to 3 hours before serving the crème, mix the sliced strawberries with the sugar and juice, and refrigerate.

To unmold the coeur à la crème, peel back the cheesecloth folded over the top. Then put an inverted platter over the mold and invert the two together. Lift off the mold, and carefully peel all the cheesecloth from the crème. Surround it with the whole strawberries. (If desired, first glaze the strawberries by dipping each one into the heated preserves.)

To serve the crème, cut it with a cake server or use a large spoon; it will be soft and creamy. Spoon some of the sliced strawberries next to each serving, and also include several whole strawberries.

Makes about 6 servings.

NOTE: If necessary, a mold without holes in the bottom can be used; however, the unmolded crème will be a bit softer, and will not hold its shape as well. Line the mold with cheesecloth and chill the crème, as directed above. Obviously, it will not drain at all. Unmold and serve as directed.

SOUTLACH (D)

(Creamy Rice Pudding)

This delicate, tasty pudding is a favorite of those Sephardic Jews who hail from Turkey and nearby areas. It is served on Shavuot and other festive occasions, and is often accompanied with other dairy foods such as cheese-filled pastries. Sometimes, it is eaten as Shabbat breakfast.

In some households, a family member's initial or first name is inscribed on top of each dishful using drizzled ground cinnamon. Those Sephardim who consider Shavuot to be a "Feast of Roses" flavor a similar pudding with rose water, and serve it with rose petal jam.

I first tasted *soutlach* in Istanbul, where it is served in small square bowls at just about every restaurant and cafeteria. Sometimes, the cooked pudding is baked in a low oven for several hours until the top caramelizes and forms a brown skin.

The following version of *soutlach* is simplified and "modernized" by the substitution of Cream of Rice cereal for the customary ground rice or combination of cooked rice and rice flour. Unlike custard-type rice puddings, it does not contain eggs, but relies instead on the starch in the rice to congeal it.

A similar Sephardic pudding is called *arroz con leche*, or "rice with milk."

6 tablespoons Cream of Rice cereal
⅓ cup sugar
4 cups milk (or 1⅓ cups instant nonfat dry milk powder and 3¾ cups water)
½ teaspoon vanilla extract or rose water
Ground cinnamon to taste, for sprinkling

In a large saucepan, combine the Cream of Rice cereal and sugar (and dry milk powder, if used). Slowly add the milk (or water, if used), stirring constantly so that no lumps form. Set the saucepan over medium-high heat and cook, stirring constantly for 5 to 10 minutes, or until the pudding begins to thicken and comes to a boil.

Lower the heat, so the pudding just simmers, and cook, stirring often, for 15 to 20 minutes longer, or until the pudding thickens considerably and heavily coats the spoon. The rice granules should be very soft and mostly disintegrated.

Remove the pudding from the heat and stir in the vanilla. Pour the pudding into small individual bowls or one large, shallow serving bowl. Sprinkle some cinnamon on top. Serve the pudding warm, or refrigerate it and serve it chilled.

Makes about 6 servings.

BANANA-NUT CHEESECAKE SQUARES (D)

Most Ashkenazic Jews enjoy cheesecake on Shavuot. Here's an unusually tasty way to prepare it. Unlike most cheesecakes, this one is cut into squares, making it particularly easy to serve.

CRUST
½ cup butter or margarine
¼ cup packed dark or light brown sugar
¾ cup whole wheat flour or unbleached white flour
½ cup finely chopped walnuts or pecans

FILLING
1 8-ounce package cream cheese, softened

½ cup granulated sugar
1 large egg
1 large egg yolk
1 teaspoon lemon juice
1 tablespoon all-purpose white flour, preferably unbleached
⅔ cup mashed ripe banana pulp (from about 1 large or 2 small bananas)

For the crust, use an electric mixer or a food processor (fitted with the steel blade), to cream the butter and brown sugar. Add the flour and nuts and mix or process just until crumbly. Remove ½ cup of the crumbs and set aside. Press the remainder evenly into the bottom of an ungreased 8-inch-square baking pan. Bake in a preheated 350-degree oven for 15 minutes.

Meanwhile, prepare the filling. Put the cream cheese in the same bowl as above (washing is not necessary), and mix or process with the sugar until light and fluffy. Add the egg, egg yolk, lemon juice, flour, and banana and mix or process until very smooth. Pour the filling over the partially baked crust. Sprinkle the reserved crumbs evenly on top and use your fingertips to lightly press them into the filling.

Return the pan to the oven and bake 25 minutes longer. Cool the cheesecake in the pan on a wire rack; then refrigerate it in the pan until completely chilled. Cut into squares to serve.

Makes 16 squares.

INDEX

In order to make this book especially useful for year-round use, this index includes all the recipes and major variations, arranged according to the type of dish: Appetizers; Breads; Dairy Main Dishes; Desserts; Drinks; Fish; Meats; Muffins; Pancakes; Poultry; Salads; Side Dishes; and Soups.

Within these categories, for the convenience of those who observe the Jewish dietary laws, the recipes are marked (M) for *meat,* (D) for *dairy,* and (P) for *pareve* ("neutral," neither meat nor dairy). (Where "(D) or (P)" is indicated, it depends on the exact choice of ingredients.)

Also, all those recipes that are *suitable for serving during Pesach* have been identified with an asterisk (*). These particular recipes have been chosen in keeping with the more stringent Ashkenazic custom of avoiding *kitniyot* (see the Pesach chapter). Those who follow less stringent Sephardic customs may find many additional recipes that are also suitable.

Abraham, 82, 215
Adar, 204, 206
Ad'lo'yada, 205
Afghans, during Days of Awe, 62
Afikoman, 239–40
Agriculture
    and Pesach, 237
    and Shavuot, 336–38
    and Sukkot, 105, 106–7, 140
Agristada, 249
Ahasuerus, King, 204, 206, 212, 213, 221
Akiva, Rabbi, 316
Aleichem, Sholom, 195
Aliyah, 35
Almendrada, 226
Almond(s), 11
    cardamom cookies, 100–101
    and chicken pie in filo, spicy, 119–21
    cookies, chewy, 285–86
    drinks, variations of, 102–3
    -flavored oat balls, 231–32
    grinding, 285
    honey macaroons, 283
    Israeli orange chicken, 45
    macaroons, Italian-style, 284–85
    "milk," Iraqi-style, 102–3
    paste confections, 226–28
    rice stuffing for dates, 73
    rusks, 135–36
    spicy ground beef with fruit and, 188
    tagine of chicken with prunes and,
        262–63

    on Tu B'Shevat, 187
    see also Haroset
Amaretti, 284–85
American dishes, 8, 308
    during Hanukkah, 148–49
    on Shavuot, 353–54, 364–65
    during Sukkot, 121–23, 125–29, 138
American Jews
    ancestry of, 4
    Hanukkah celebration of, 149
    Sukkot celebration of, 106, 121
    Tu B'Shevat celebration of, 185, 186
Animals, kosher, 6–7
Anise seed(s), 14
    sesame rings, savory, 67–69
Antiochus IV, 147, 174
Apio, 264
Apocrypha, 148
Appetizers
    chicken livers in sauce, Kaved en
        shooma* (M), 28
    canned chick-pea croquettes, Falafel II
        (P), 291–93
    dried chick-pea croquettes, Falafel I
        (P), 289–91
    grape leaves filled with rice pilaf,
        Yalanji dolmas (P), 322–24
    long-cooked eggs, Sephardic-style,
        Huevos haminados (P), 248–49
    pita triangles, toasted (D) or (P), 310–
        11

Appetizers *(cont'd)*
  sesame chicken tidbits with
    honeydipping sauce, Oaf
    soomsoom b'dvash (M), 306
  Welsh rabbit (D), 160–61
  dips
    cheese, tomato, and chili pepper,
      Chili con queso (D), 343
    eggplant-sesame, Baba ganoush
      (P), 318–19
    lemony sesame, Tahina (P), 293–94
  pastries
    cheese and vegetable filled, Borekas
      (D), 347–50
    cheese turnovers, miniature (D),
      353–54
    chicken (or meat) turnovers, Iraqi-
      style, Sambusik (M), 209–12
    coiled, filled, Bulemas (D), 352–53
    spinach and cheese, Spanakopetes
      (D), 350–53
  spreads
    Ashkenazic-style haroset—my
      way* (P), 243
    chicken liver pâté* (M), 75–76
    chick-pea and sesame, Humus (P),
      294–95
    eggplant, provincial* (P), 320–21
    fruit and cheese ball, Har
      geveenah* (D), 341–42
    Israeli-style haroset* (P), 245
    mushroom-walnut pâté, brandied
      (P) or (D), 243–44
    Sephardic-style date haroset* (P),
      246–47
    Turkish-style haroset* (P), 245–46
    Yemenite-style haroset* (P), 247
Apple(s)
  coffee cake, spicy, 58–59
  haroset—my way, Ashkenazic-style,
    243
  and kasha muffins, 179
  lamb and brown rice pilaf, 82–83
  nut strudel, easy Viennese, 132–33
  soup, chilled spiced, 346–47
  squash soup, puréed, 110
  and sweet potato tzimmes, 263
  on Tu B'Shevat, 187
Apple cider, in mulled cran-apple-cot
    swizzle, 139
Apricot(s)
  chicken with, Israeli-style, 190–91
  -fig bars, 200–201

okra with prunes and, Syrian-style,
    92–93
Apricot nectar, in mulled cran-apple-cot
    swizzle, 139
Arabic dishes
  during Days of Awe, 72–73
  on Lag B'Omer, 318–19
  on Purim, 218–20
Arabs, 6
Arak, 205
Ark, 108
Arrope, 254
Artichoke and white bean salad, herbed,
    317–18
Ashkenazic dishes, xiii, 4–5, 8
  during Days of Awe, 61–63, 65–67,
    69–72, 78, 81–82, 91, 94–96, 99–
    100
  during Hanukkah, 148, 159, 178
  on Lag B'Omer, 331–33
  during Pesach, 243, 257–58, 263, 270–
    71, 276–77
  on Purim, 206, 214–16, 221–22
  on Shabbat, 16, 29, 55–56
  on Shavuot, 337–41, 354–56, 358–60,
    368–69, 374–75
  during Sukkot, 111–12, 135–36
  on Tu B'Shevat, 189
Ashkenazic-style haroset—my way, 243
Ashkenazim, 4–5, 8, 241
  during Days of Awe, 63
  kitniyot during Pesach for, 241, 242,
    284
  and Seder ceremony, 238, 240, 252
  Seder dinner of, 257–58, 263
  Tu B'Shevat celebration of, 185
Assyrians, 3
Austro-Hungarian dish, on Shabbat, 59–
    60
Austro-Hungarian Empire, 4
Autumn casserole, 125
Avgolemono (sauce), 249, 260–61
Avgolemono (soup), 76
Avocado, tangerine chicken with, 305–6

Baba ganoush, 318–19
Babylonians, 3
Baklava or baklawa, 218–20
Balkan dishes
  during Days of Awe, 82–83, 103
  on Lag B'Omer, 322–24
  during Sukkot, 113–14
Balkans, 5

Baltimore Jewish Times, xiii, 4
Bamia, 50
Banana
  chicken sate, 329–30
  nut cheesecake squares, 374–75
Barba, 90
Bar-David, Molly, 190
Bar Kochba, Shimon, 315–16
Barley
  omer of, 315
  soup, meaty split pea, bean and, 108–
    10
  yogurt soup, Russian-style, 158
Baytzah, 239
Bean(s)
  black beans, Cuban-style, 51–53
  black-eyed peas in tomato sauce, 93–
    94
  chicken (or meat) turnovers, Iraqi-
    style, 209–12
  canned chick-pea croquettes, 291–93
  chick-pea and sesame spread, 294–95
  chick-peas and rice, spicy, 213–14
  dried chick-pea croquettes, 289–91
  meat stew, long-cooked, 38–39
    North African-style, 40–42
  spiced lentils and rice, 152–53
Bean soup, meaty split pea, barley and,
  108–10
Beating, symbolism of, 78, 90
Beef, *see* Meats
Beer
  cake, spicy, 334–35
  Maccabee, 161
  vs. milk in baked goods, 334
  Welsh rabbit, 160–61
Beet(s)
  during Days of Awe, 62, 90
  fermented, 241
  Pesach candy from, 241
  salad, Moroccan-style, 90
Beet greens salad, Moroccan-style, 91
Beignets, 170–71
Bene-Israel, 123, 174
Ben Yohai, Rabbi Shimon, 316, 317, 333
Besamim, 58
Bestila, 119–21
Beverages, *see* Drinks
Bikurim, 336, 338, 339, 342
Bimuelos
  Hanukkah, 164–66
  de massa, 254–55
  de massa y queso, 255

Biscochos de huevo, 55, 56–57
Black beans, Cuban-style, 51–53
Black-eyed peas in tomato sauce, 93–94
Blini
  even-quicker, 155–56
  quick, 154–55
Blintzes, Mom's best cheese, 358–60
Bohemia, 4
"Book of Splendor," 316
Booths, Sukkot, 105–6, 140
Borekas, 347–50
Borekitas, 350
Borscht, 241
Bow ties, 55–56
Brandied cherry-rice mold with cherry
  sauce, 369–71
Brandied cherry sauce, 47
Brandied mushroom-walnut pâté, 343–
  44
Bread(s)
  challah, Grandpa's (P), 17–19
  cornbread
    double (P), 131
    Romanian-style, Malai (D), 177–78
  flat, round pocket, Whole wheat pita
    (P), 308–10
  holiday egg, Yom-tov round challah
    (P), 64–67
  kneaded one-rise rye (P), 333
  no-knead caraway rye (P), 331–33
  pretzels, soft
    caraway-rye (P), 183
    whole wheat (P) or (D), 179–83
  on Shavuot, 315, 336, 338
  unleavened, on Pesach, 237, 238
  Yemenite Shabbat, Kubaneh (D) or
    (P), 26–27
"Bread of affliction," 238, 239
"Bread of Mordecai," 226
"Bread of Spain," 276–77
Brine-preserved vine leaves, 322
Brisket, easy wine-marinated, 151
British dishes
  during Days of Awe, 69–71
  during Hanukkah, 159–61
  during Pesach, 282–85
British-style cinnamon balls, 285
British-style fried gefilte fish, 69–71
Brit Milah, 57, 67
Broiling, 7
Broth, vegetable, 29
Brownies, fudgiest-ever carob, 195–96
Bubby Rose's farfel-potato dairy soup,
  157

Buckwheat groats, 13, 51
  and apple muffins, 179
  muffins with, 178–79
  see also Kasha
Buckwheat pancakes, thin, 154–55
Bulemas, 350, 352–53
Bulgur wheat, 11–12
  meat loaf stuffed with spiced meat
    and pine nuts, 116–18
  pudding, Sephardic-style, 194
  and vegetable salad, 319–20

Cabbage
  coleslaw for a crowd, 321–22
  stuffed, variations of, 111
  sweet-and-sour stuffed, 111–12
Cakes, *see* Desserts
Calabassah, 107
Calsones, 356–57
Canada, Jewish community in, xiii, 8,
  244
Candelabrum, 147, 184
Candelabrum pretzel, 181
Candies, *see* Desserts
Candle, shamash, 181
Cantor, Freda Michaelson Greene, 34
Caramel-coated orange flan, 273–74
Caraway seed(s), 14
  rye bread, no-knead, 331–33
  rye pretzels, 183
Cardamom, 12
  almond cookies, 100–101
  syrup, fried pastry balls soaked in,
    174–75
Carnatzlah, 327–28
Carob
  brownies, fudgiest-ever, 195–96
  description of, 195
  drop cookies, 201
  on Lag B'Omer, 317, 333–34
  layer cake with carob icing, 199–200
  peanut fudge, easy, 333–34
  sesame halvah, 202–3
  on Tu B'Shevat, 187, 195
Carrot(s)
  and celeriac, 264
  citrus salad, 297
  coins, sunshine, 91–92
  coleslaw for a crowd, 321–22
  during Days of Awe, 62
  gefilte fish loaf with horseradish sauce,
    251–54

  green beans with leeks and, Turkish-
    style, 89
  Pesach candy from, 241
  symbolism of, 91–92
  on Yom Ha'Atzmaut, 297
Casseroles
  autumn, 125
  noodle dumplings with pasta,
    Sephardic-style, 356–57
  quick-and-easy cheese blintz, 360–61
  sole and corn bread, Southern-style,
    364–65
  spinach-cheese, 269
  during Sukkot, 106, 107
  sweet potato-pineapple, 94–95
  vegetable-fruit, 263
Celeriac and carrots, 264
Central Europe, 4, 111–12
Challah
  braiding of, 20–23
  ceremonial, 19, 61, 63, 64–67, 77
  Grandpa's, 17–19
  rolls, miniature filled, 24–25
  symbolism and shaping of, 19–23, 64,
    77
  Yom-Tov round, 64–67
Cheese, 12, 13
  blintz casserole, quick-and-easy, 360–
    61
  blintzes, Mom's best, 358–60
  for borekas, 347
  coins, 159
  cornmeal with, Romanian-style, 366–
    68
  dumplings, tiny, 161–62
  eggplant filling, 348–49
  fluffy pancakes, 156
  and fruit ball, Mount Sinai, 341–42
  during Hanukkah, 148, 180
  kreplah, 354–56
  leek matzo pie, 266–67
  for mamaliga, 366–67
  matzo meal pancakes with, 255
  melted, over toast, 160–61
  meringues, savory, 160
  mock spaghetti and meatballs, 212–13
  pancakes, light and thin, 153–54
  pastries filled with vegetables and,
    347–50
  potato filling, 348–49
  puffs, 160
  rice latkes, 156
  on Shavuot, 337, 347, 366–67, 368

soft pretzels with, for Hanukkah, 179–83

spinach casserole, 269

and spinach in flaky pastry, 350–53

three, lasagne with spinach and, 361–63

tomato and chili pepper dip, 343

turnovers, miniature, 353–54

varenikes, 354–56

wafers, savory, 159

Cheesecake squares, banana-nut, 374–75

Cherry

rice mold, brandied, with cherry sauce, 369–71

sauce, brandied, 47

soup, Hungarian-style, 345–46

Chicken, *see* Poultry

Chicken livers, *see* Liver

Chick-pea(s), 12

canned, tiny croquettes made with, 291–93

chicken turnovers, Iraqi-style, 209–12

dried, tiny croquettes made with, 289–91

and rice, spicy, 213–14

and sesame spread, 294–95

Chiffon cake, honey-spice, 96–97

Children, 8

during Days of Awe, 77

during Hanukkah, 159, 166, 179, 180

on Lag B'Omer, 316

during Pesach, 240

on Purim, 204–6, 221, 226–28

and Shabbat projects, 24, 25

on Simhat Torah, 108

during Sukkot, 125

on Tu B'Shevat, 186, 187, 195

on Yom Ha'Atzmaut, 293–94

young, celebrations for, 83, 194

Chili con queso, 343

Chili pepper, cheese, and tomato dip, 343

Chocolate

curls, 281

drink, Mexican-style hot, 184

-hazelnut Viennese torte, 279–81

mousse, instant, 281–82

Cholent, 38–39

Cinnamon balls, British-style, 284, 285

Cloves, in mulled cran-apple-cot swizzle, 139

"Cock of India," 206

Coconut

honey macaroons, 282–83

orange pudding, 313

pyramids, 282–83

Coeur à la crème, 371–72

Coffee, in instant chocolate mousse, 281–82

Coffee cake, spicy apple, 58–59

Coleslaw for a crowd, 321–22

Columbus, 121, 122

"Come and sit," 288, 317

Confections, *see* Desserts

Cookies, *see* Desserts

Coriander seeds, 12

Corn, word origin of, 138

Corn bread

casserole, Southern-style sole and, 364–65

double, 131

Romanian-style, 177–78

Cornmeal

with cheese, Romanian-style, 366–68

and molasses pudding, thick, 138

Cottage cheese and vegetable salad, 340–41

Counting of the Omer, 315, 316

Couscous

aux sept légumes, 83–85

sweet, with dried fruit and nuts, 163–64

Crackers, poppy seed-onion, 235–36

Cranberry juice, in mulled cran-apple-cot swizzle, 139

Cranberry relish, harvest-time, 125–26

Cranberry sauce, zippy pot roast in, 35

Croquettes

meat-stuffed mashed potato, 114–16

salmon, in tomato sauce, 250–51

tiny, made with canned chick-peas, 291–93

tiny, made with dried chick-peas, 289–91

Cuban dishes

on Shabbat, 51–53

during Sukkot, 114–16

on Tu B'Shevat, 188

Cuban-style black beans, 51–53

Cumberland glaze, Rock Cornish hens with, 47–48

Cumin, 12

Cupcakes, miniature, 232–33

Curaçao, 55, 57–58, 64

Curry, meat, fruit, and peanut, 189

Custard

baked, 273–74

foamy wine, Italian-style, 272

Czechoslovakian dishes
    on Shavuot, 345–46
    during Sukkot, 126–29

Dafina, 40–42
Dairy foods, 7, 10
    during Days of Awe, 64
    during Hanukkah, 148, 180
    at Meemounah, 242
    on Shavuot, 337–38, 339, 341
Dairy main dishes
    cheese blintz casserole, quick-and-easy
      (D), 360–61
    cheese blintzes, Mom's best (D), 358–
      61
    lasagne with spinach and three
      cheeses, Lasagne verde (D), 361–
      63
    leek-cheese matzo pie, Mina de prassa
      con queso* (D), 266–67
    spaghetti and meatballs, mock (P) or
      (D), 212–13
    spinach-tomato pie, Mina de espinaca
      y tomat* (D), 265–66
Dana, Ida and family, 248, 249, 256
Date(s)
    during Days of Awe, 62
    filled cookies, 223–26
    haroset, Sephardic-style, 246–47
    orange-nut torte, Sephardic-style,
      274–76
    pudding with walnuts, creamy, 202
    stuffed, Moroccan-style fish baked
      with, 72–73
David, King, 341
Day of Atonement, 61, 78
Days of Awe, 61–104, 107, 218
Deal Delights, 67, 92–93
Desayuno, 248, 347–48, 350
Desserts
    cakes
      banana-nut cheesecake squares (D),
        374–75
      carob brownies, fudgiest-ever (D)
        or (P), 195–96
      carob layer, with carob icing (D),
        199–200
      chiffon vs. sponge, 96
      diamonds soaked with syrup,
        Tishpishti para Pesach* (P), 277–
        78
      hazelnut-chocolate Viennese torte*
        (P), 279–81

holiday orange-honey (P), 95–96
honeyed sesame, Oogat soomsoom
    b'dvash (D) or (P), 98
honey-spice chiffon (P), 96–97
jam-filled tart, Linzertorte (D) or
    (P), 59–60
orange-nut-date torte, Sephardic-
    style* (P), 274–76
Pesach sponge* (P), 276–77
poppy seed pound (D), 233–34
raised dough (D), 133–35
spicy apple coffee (D) or (P), 58–59
spicy beer (D) or (P), 334–35
streusel-topped gingerbread gems
    (D) or (P), 232–33
sweet crowns for the shabbat queen
    (P) or (D), 24–25
cookies
    almond-cardamom, Hadgi badam
      (P), 100–101
    almond-honey macaroons* (P), 283
    almond macaroons, Italian-style,
      Amaretti* (P), 284–85
    almond rusks, Mandelbrot (P), 135–
      36
    apricot-fig bars (D) or (P), 200–201
    carob drop (D), 201
    chewy almond, Marunchinos* (P),
      285–86
    cinnamon balls, British-style* (P),
      285
    coconut-honey macaroons* (P),
      282–83
    crisp egg, Panlevi (P), 57–58
    date-filled, Minenas (D) or (P),
      223–26
    egg, Eir kichlah (P), 55–56
    filled triangular, Hamantaschen (D)
      or (P) 214–16
    fried Haman's Ears, Sephardic-
      style, Orejas de Haman (P), 216–
      18
    gingerbread sukkah (P), 140–46
    macaroon bar (D) or (P), 230–31
    poppy seed-meringue triangles (D)
      or (P), 229–30
    Queen Esther's, Mohn kichlah (D)
      or (P), 221–22
    rice-flour shortbread, Nan-e berenji
      (D) or (P), 228–29
    sesame ring, Biscochos de huevo
      (P), 56–57
    sesame tahini-oat, Oogiyot tahina
      (P), 314

spicy star, Zimsterne (D) or (P), 101–2
walnut-filled crescent, Travados (P), 222–23
walnut macaroons, Mustachados* (P), 286
confections
almond-flavored oat balls, Mock marzipan (D), 231–32
almond paste, Moroccan-style marzipan "petit fours"* (P), 226–28
balls, fruit-nut* (P), 203
carob-sesame halvah (P), 202–3
crunchy dough nuggets in honey, Taygleh (P), 99–100
crunchy sesame seed candies, Sukariyot soomsoom (P), 176–77
easy carob-peanut fudge (D), 333–34
haroset, Moroccan-style* (P), 244
kumquats, whole preserved* (P), 191–92
fruits
couscous with dried fruit and nuts, sweet (D) or (P), 163–64
pears poached in red wine, Poires bourguignonne* (P), 271
pastries
apple-nut strudel, easy Viennese (D) or (P), 132–33
balls, fried, soaked in cardamom syrup, Gulab jamun (D), 174–75
braided, fried, dipped in syrup, Koeksisters (D) or (P), 172–173
fritters, fried, in honey syrup, Zvingous (D) or (P), 170–71
doughnuts, jelly filled, Soofganiyot (D), 166–67
dried-fruit strudel (D) or (P), 196–99
honey puffs, fried, Bimuelos (P), 164–66
many-layered, with nuts and honey, Baklava (D) or (P), 218–20
rosettes, fried, in honey syrup, Zelebi (P), 168–69
puddings
baked custard, Caramel-coated orange flan* (P), 273–75
bulgur wheat, Sephardic-style (P), 194
cherry-rice mold, brandied, with cherry sauce (D), 369–71

cornmeal and molasses, Indian pudding (D), 138
creamy date, with walnuts (D), 202
creamy rice, Soutlach (D), 373–74
farina, Greek-style, Pyota (D), 234–35
"heart of cream," with strawberries, Coeur à la crème (D), 371–72
mousse, instant chocolate* (P), 281–82
orange-coconut, Raf'refet tapoozim v-cocus (P), 313
orange fluff, Raf-refet tapoozim (P), 312–13
wheat berry, Sephardic-style, Kofyas (P), 193–94
wine custard, Italian-style, Zabaglione* (P), 272
Deuteronomy, 7
Diaspora, 3, 19, 114, 185, 287, 288, 317
Dipping sauce, honey, 306
Dips, *see* Appetizers
Djadja zetoon, 85–87
Dla'at, 107
Dolmas, 113–14
yalanji, 322–24
Dough nuggets in honey, crunchy, 99–100
Doughnuts, jelly-filled, 166–67
Dreidel, 159, 166, 182
dreidel pretzel, 182
Drinks
almond milk, Iraqi-style, Hariri* (P), 102–3
hot chocolate, Mexican-style* (D), 184
melon seed milk, Sephardic-style, Papitada* (P), 104
mulled cran-apple-cot swizzle (P), 139
Dulce, 191
Dumplings, *see* Side dishes
Dutch dishes
on Purim, 206
on Shabbat, 30, 47
Dutch-style fish and potato cakes, 30
Dutch-style sweet matzo fritters, 270–71

Eastern Europe, 4, 19
Eastern European dishes
during Hanukkah, 149–50, 178–79
on Shabbat, 34, 38–39
on Shavuot, 339
during Sukkot, 111–12, 133–35
on Tu B'Shevat, 195–96

East Indian-style sole with onions and
    dill, 123–24
Egg(s), 7
    almond macaroons, Italian-style, 284–
        85
    baked custard, 273–74
    barley, 77
    bread, holiday, 64–67
    cookies, 55–56
    cookies, crisp, 57–58
    foamy wine custard, Italian-style, 272
    lemon sauce, fish in, 249–50
    lemon soup, 76
    long-cooked, Sephardic-style, 248–49
    long-cooked meat stew, North
        African-style, 40
    Pesach sponge cake, 276–77
    on Purim, 206
    roasted, at Seder meal, 239
    rolled parsley-stuffed veal breast, 258–
        60
    soup garnishes, 255–56
    spinach-cheese casserole, 269
    sweet matzo fritters, Dutch-style,
        270–71
    whole hard-boiled, meat loaf with,
        328–29
Eggplant
    cheese filling, 348–49
    preparing of, 297–98
    salad, 297–99
    -sesame dip, 318–19
    spread, provincial, 320–21
    stuffed, Libyan-style, 35–37
Egyptian Jews, 67, 237–38, 241
Eir kichlah, 55–56
Elijah, 240
Enjadara, 152–53
Ensalada de avicas y enginaras, 317–18
Erev Shabbat, 31
Erger, Judith, 127, 129
Erste-steren, 101–2
Esther, Queen, 204, 210, 212, 213, 215,
    217, 221
Esther, Scroll of, 204
Etrog, 106, 107, 108
Europe, 5
Exodus, Book of, 7, 15, 19, 337
Exodus, from Egypt, 106, 237–38, 240

Falafel I, 289–91
Falafel II, 291–93

Farfel
    homemade noodle, 77
    -potato dairy soup, Bubby Rose's, 157
Farina pudding, Greek-style, 234–35
Farmer cheese, 12
Fat, rendered goose, 7, 148, 149, 177
Feast of Fruits, 185
Feast of Roses, 338, 373
Festival, The, 105
Festival of Lights, 148
Festival of the First Fruits, 336
Festival of the Harvest, 336
Festival of the Ingathering, 105
Festival of the Paschal Lamb, 237
Festival of the Tabernacles, 105
Festival of the Unleavened Bread, 237
Feta cheese, 12
    spinach filling, 350–53
Fez, 242
Fig-apricot bars, 200–201
Fijones frescos, 93–94
Filberts, 279
Filo, 12–13
    coiled filled, 352–53
    dried-fruit strudel, 196–99
    easy Viennese apple-nut strudel, 132–
        33
    filled with cheese and vegetables, 347–
        50
    with nuts and honey, 218–20
    purchasing and preparing, 218–19
    spicy chicken and almond pie in, 119–
        21
    spinach and cheese in, 350–53
"First fruits," 336, 338, 339, 368
First fruits rainbow salad, 339–40
Fish
    baked with stuffed dates, Moroccan-
        style (D) or (P), 72–73
    cakes, 250
    during Days of Awe, 62, 63–64
    in egg-lemon sauce, Pescado con
        agristada* (P), 249–250
    gefilte fish
        British-style, fried* (P), 69–71
        easy "nouvelle"* (P), 28–30
        loaf with horseradish sauce* (P),
            251–54
    herring, quick chopped (P), 71–72
    kosher, 6–7
    and potato cakes, Dutch-style,
        Vischkoekjes* (P) or (D), 30
    on Shabbat, 16
    salmon
        croquettes in tomato sauce, Keftes
            de pescado* (P), 250–51

simple mousse* (D), 365–66
and vegetables in sweet-sour sauce,
    Saloona (P), 208–9
in spicy tomato sauce, Libyan-style,
    Heraimeh* (P), 27–28
sole
    and corn bread casserole, Southern-
        style (D), 364–65
    with onions and dill, East Indian-
        style* (D) or (P), 123–24
    turban, with sole mousse* (D),
        363–64
sweet-and-sour, Italian-style, Pesce
    all'ebraica (P), 74–75
symbolism of, 16, 62, 72, 206, 242
in tarragon-tomato sauce* (P) or
    (D), 31
Five Books of Moses, *see* Torah
Flan, caramel-coated orange, 273–74
Flowers
    at Meemounah, 242
    on Shavuot, 338, 339
    on Tu B'Shevat, 186
French dishes
    during Pesach, 255–56, 271
    on Shavuot, 371–72
Frijoles negros, 51–53
Fritada de espinaca, 269
Fritters
    fluffy pancakes, 156
    fried, in honey syrup, 170–71
    sweet matzo, Dutch-style, 270–71
Fruit(s), 7
    and cheese ball, Mount Sinai, 341–42
    during Days of Awe, 90
    filled noodle dumplings, 136–37
    filled potato dumplings, 126–29
    fresh, on Shavuot, 338, 339
    harvest-time cranberry relish, 125–26
    meat and peanut curry, 189
    mixed nuts and, 54–55
    nut confection balls, 203
    nut stuffing, orange-glazed turkey
        with, 121–23
    and rich lokshen kugel, 368–69
    at Seder meal, 239
    soup, chilled mixed, 299–300
    spicy ground beef with almonds, and,
        188
    during Sukkot, 106–7, 108
    sunshine carrot coins with, 91–92
    sweet holiday stew, 81–82
    tiny cheese dumplings, 161–62
    tofu lokshen kugel, 54

on Tu B'Shevat, 185, 186–87
vegetable casserole, 263
see also Haroset
Fruit, dried
    during Days of Awe, 61
    haroset, Moroccan-style, 244
    lokshen kugel, 192–93
    strudel, 196–99
    sweet couscous with nuts and, 163–
        64
    for Tu B'Shevat, 185, 187, 189, 193, 196–
        99, 200, 203
    and vegetable tzimmes, 125
Fruit trees, in Israel, 185
Frutas, Las, 185
Fudge, easy carob-peanut, 333–34
Fudgiest-ever carob brownies, 195–96

Gabes, Rachel Muallem, 43, 102–3, 209–
    10
Galushka, 34
Garbanzo beans, *see* Chick-peas
Gastrointestinal problems, 55
Gebroks, 241
Geese, 148
Gefilte fish, *see* Fish
Gelt, 92, 159
Genesis, 108
German dishes
    during Days of Awe, 101–2
    on Lag B'Omer, 328–29
    during Sukkot, 107
Germany, 4
Gershgorn, David, 52
Geveenah, 341
Gezer hai, 297
Gingerbread
    gems, streusel-topped, 232–33
    sukkah, 140–46
Goose fat, 7, 148, 149, 177
Gordon, Michael, 114–16
Gordon, Regina, 51–52
Gordon, Sharon Cantor, 52
Grains, 7
Grandpa's challah, 17–19
Grape leaves, filled with rice pilaf, 322–
    24
Grapes, 62
Greek dishes
    during Days of Awe, 62, 64, 76, 104
    during Hanukkah, 164–66, 170–71
    on Lag B'Omer, 322–24

Greek dishes *(cont'd)*
  during Pesach, 249–51, 260–61,
    264-67, 277–78
  on Purim, 218–20, 234–35
  on Shabbat, 55, 56–57
  on Shavuot, 347, 350
  on Tu B'Shevat, 193–94
Greek Jews, 186
Greek-style farina pudding, 234–35
Green beans with leeks and carrots,
  Turkish-style, 89
Gremshelish, 270–71
Gribeness, 148
Gulab jamun, 174–75

Hadgi badam, 100–101, 284, 285–86
Hafetz, Hannah Kaufer, 17
Hag, 7
Haggadah, 238
Hag Ha'Asif, 105
Hag Ha'Bikurim, 336
Hag Ha'Katzir, 336
Hag Ha'Matzot, 237
Hag Ha'Pesach, 237
Hag Ha'Sukkot, 105
Hai pretzel, 183
Halvah, carob-sesame, 202–3
Haman, 78, 204, 205, 206, 208, 215, 216
Haman's Ears cookies, Sephardic-style,
  fried, 215, 216–18
Hamantaschen, with poppy-seed filling,
  214–16
Hametz, 240, 241
Hamim, 38, 294
Hamisha-Asar B'Shevat, 185
Hanukkah, 147–84, 206
  bimuelos or loukoumades, 164–66
  celebration of, 148–49
  fried foods during, 147, 148
  history of, 147
  honoring Judith during, 148
  menorah, 147, 184
  menorah pretzel, 181
  soft pretzels for, 179–83
Har gavnunim, 341
Har geveenah, 341–42
Harirah, 64
Hariri, 102–3
Haroset, 239
  date, Sephardic-style, 246–47
  Israeli-style, 245
  Moroccan-style, 244

my way, Ashkenazic-style, 243
  Turkish-style, 245–46
  Yemenite-style, 247
Hasidim, 17, 58, 77, 240, 307, 337
Hasmonean family, 147
Hassan II, 41
Hatikvah, 288
Havadalah, 17, 58
Hazelnut-chocolate Viennese torte, 279–81
Hazeret, 238–39
Heart disease, 55
Heart of cream with strawberries, 371–72
Hebrew, 4, 5–6, 10
Hebrews, ancient, 6
Heraimeh, 27–28
Herring, quick chopped, 71–72
High Holy Days, 61
Hillel, Rabbi, 185
Holishkes, 111–12
Holland, 5
Honey
  almond macaroons, 283
  coconut macaroons, 282–83
  crunchy dough nuggets in, 99–100
  dipping sauce, 306
  glaze, sesame cake, 98
  orange cake, holiday, 95–96
  orange glaze, 122–123
  sesame cake, 98
  on Shavuot, 337, 368
  spice chiffon cake, 96–97
  symbolism of, 61–62, 63, 65, 193, 218
  wine fermented from, 241
Honey syrup, 219, 220
  cake diamonds soaked with, 277–78
  crunchy dough nuggets in, 99–100
  farina pudding, Greek-style, 234–35
  fried braided pastries dipped in, 172–73
  fried fritters in, 170–71
  fried rosettes dipped in, 168–70
  many-layered pastry with nuts and,
    218–20
  puffs, fried, 164–66
  walnut-filled crescent cookies, 222–23
Hors d'oeuvres, *see* Appetizers
Horseradish, 70
  sauce, gefilte fish loaf with, 251–54
  at Seder meal, 238
Hoshanah Rabbah, 78, 107, 136, 205
Hot chocolate drink, Mexican-style, 184
Hrain, 70, 252

Huevos haminados, 248–49
Humus, 294–95
Hungarian dishes
    on Shavuot, 345–46
    during Sukkot, 126–29

Iberian Peninsula, 5
Icing, carob, 199, 200
Independence Day (Israel), 176, 287–314
India, 6
Indian dishes
    during Hanukkah, 168–70, 174–75
    during Sukkot, 123–24
Indian Jews, 123–24
Indian pudding, 138
Indonesian-style kebabs, 329–30
Ingredients, 11–14
Ini, Bellah, 102–3, 208
Iran, 43, 113–14, 217, 228
Iranian dishes, on Purim, 218–20
Iraqi dishes
    during Days of Awe, 64, 67–69, 100–103
    during Hanukkah, 152–53, 168–70
    during Pesach, 284–85
    on Purim, 206, 208–12, 218–20
    on Shabbat, 43–44
    during Sukkot, 115
Iraqi-style almond milk, 102–3
Iraqi-style chicken and rice, 43–44
Iraqi-style chicken or meat turnovers, 209–12
Isaac, 82, 215
Israeli dishes, xiii, 8
    during Days of Awe, 98
    fruit for, 191, 339
    during Hanukkah, 148, 166–67, 168–70, 176–77
    on Lag B'Omer, 317–21, 325–28
    during Pesach, 245
    on Purim, 206–7, 223–26, 231–32
    on Shabbat, 26–28, 38–39, 45
    on Shavuot, 347–50
    during Sukkot, 107
    on Tu B'Shevat, 190–92, 196–99
    on Yom Ha'Atzmaut, 287–314
Israeli Jews
    kosher meat and, 7
    Lag B'Omer and, 316–17
    Purim celebrations of, 206
    Shavuot and, 336–39, 342, 347, 368
    Shemini Atzeret and Simhat Torah celebrations of, 108
    Sukkot celebration of, 106
    Tu B'Shevat celebration of, 185, 186
    Yom Ha'Atzmaut celebrations of, 287–88
    Yom Yerushalaym celebrations of, 288
Israeli-style chicken with kumquats (or apricots), 190–91
Israeli-style haroset, 245
Israeli-style kebabs of lamb or beef chunks, 325–26
Israeli-style meatballs in tomato sauce, 302–3
Israeli-style orange chicken, 45
Israeli-style turkey schnitzel, 206–7
Israelite, house of, 239, 354
Israel Museum, 206
Israel's Independence Day, 287–314
Italian dishes
    during Days of Awe, 62, 64, 65, 74, 99–100
    during Pesach, 272, 284–85
    on Shavuot, 361–63, 367
Italian-style almond macaroons, 284–85
Italian-style foamy wine custard, 272
Italian-style sweet-and-sour fish, 74–75
Italy, 5
Iyar, 287, 288, 315

Ja'alah, 54–55
Jacob, 215
Jam-filled tart, 59–60
Japanese-style marinade, 326
Jelly-filled doughnuts, 166–67
Jerusalem Day, 287–314
Jerusalem noodle pudding, 307
Jewish cuisine, 3–9
    Ashkenazic, 4–5, 8
    Diaspora adaptation and, 3, 8–9
    kashrut, 6–7
    Oriental, 6
    Sephardic, 4–6, 8
Jewish National Fund's reforestation program, 186
"Jews and Romans," 316
Job, 338
Jonah, 72
Judah the Maccabee, 147, 148, 174
Judezmo, 5
Judith, 148, 180

Ka'ak, 67–69
Kabbalah, 316
Kaplan, Lillian Levine, 71
Karpas, 238

Kasha, 13
  and apple muffins, 179
  dishes, 178
  muffins, 178–79
  -mushroom pilaf, herbed, 51
  varnishkes, 178
Kashering, 7
Kashrut, 6–7, 10, 96, 103, 212, 213, 337,
    361, 365
Kaskaval cheese, 13
Kassin, Ginger, 67
Kaufer, Gussie Bransdorf, 133–35
Kaufer, Helene (Hindy) Kaplan, 31, 358
Kaufer, Joseph, 17
Kaved en shooma, 28
Kebab, 325, 327
  grilled ground-meat, 327–28
  of lamb or beef chunks, Israeli-style,
    325–26
Keftes
  de pescado, 250–51
  de prassa y carne, 256–57
Ketchri, 152, 153
Kibbeh, baked, 116–18
Kibbutzim, 295–96
Kibbutz-style fresh vegetable salad, 295–
  96
Kiddush, 15, 19–20, 31
Kislev, 147
Kitniyot, 241
Klops, 328–29
Knedliky or knaidlah, plum, 126–29
Koeksisters, 172–73
Kofyas, 193–94
Kohanim, 20, 239, 354
Kohl mit wasser, 107
Kosher food, 6–7, 242, 284
Kreplah
  cheese, 354–56
  meat, 78–79
  sweet plum, 136–37
K'tzitzot basar b'agvaniyot, 302–3
Kubaneh, 26–27
Kubbah, 116–18
Kubbah sineeya, 304
Kugel, lokshen, *see* Side dishes
Kugel Yerushalayim, 307
Kumquats
  chicken with, Israeli-style, 190–91
  preserved whole, 191–92
  uses for, 191
Kumzitz, 288, 317
Kurdistani dish, on Shavuot, 337

Ladino, 5–6, 10, 186
Lag B'Omer, 288, 315-35
  agriculture and, 315
  carob on, 317, 333–34
  celebration of, 316–17
  history of, 315–16
Lamb, *see* Meats
Latkes
  cheese-rice, 156
  potato, 149–50
  ricotta, 153–54
Lasagne with spinach and three cheeses,
  361–63
Lasagne verde, 361–63
Latin American dishes
  during Sukkot, 115
  on Tu B'Shevat, 188
Law, 6–7, 337, 338, 341, 354, 371
Leben, 340
Leek(s)
  -cheese matzo pie, 266–67
  green beans with carrots and,
    Turkish-style, 89
  for luck, 62, 89
  and meat patties, 256–57
Lemon(s)
  chicken with olives, Moroccan-style,
    85–87
  egg sauce, fish in, 249–50
  egg soup, 76
  pickled, 86–87
  sesame dip or dressing, 293–94
Lentil(s)
  mock spaghetti and meatballs, 212–13
  soup, red, 33
  spiced rice and, 152–53
Levine, Harry, 108
Levine, Rose Dublin, 108, 157
Levites, 239, 354
Leviticus, 6, 105–6
Libyan-style fish in spicy tomato sauce,
  27–28
Libyan-style stuffed vegetables, 35–37
Linzertorte, 59–60
Lithuania, 4
Liver, broiling, 7
  chicken
    fancy chopped, 75–76
    in garlic-tomato sauce, 28
    pâté, 75–76
Livne, Lily, 223
Lokshen kugel, *see* Side dishes
Loukoumades, Hanukkah, 164–66

Lubiya, 93–94
Lulav, 106, 107

Macaroons
  almond, Italian-style, 284–85
  almond-honey, 283
  bar cookies, 230–31
  coconut-honey, 282–83
  walnut, 286
Maccabee, 147
Maccabee brand beer, 161
Mafroum, 35–37
Magen David pretzel, 182
Mahshi, 113–14
Maimonides, Moses, 242
Malai, 177–78
Mamaliga, 366–68
Mandarinah, 305
Mandelbrot, 135–36
Mandlen, 80–81
Manna, 19
Marak payrot, 299–300
Marak taymahni, 300–301
Marinade
  soy-peanut, 330
  teriyaki, 326
Maror, 238
Marunchinos, 284–86
Marzipan, mock, 231–32
Marzipan petit fours, Moroccan-style,
    226–28
Mattathias, 147
Matzo
  fritters, Dutch-style sweet, 270–71
  for Seder, 238, 239–41
Matzo meal
  pancakes, 254
  pancakes with cheese, 255
"Matzo of hope," 239–40
Matzo pie
  leek-cheese, 266–67
  meat-potato, 268
  spinach-tomato, 265–66
Mead or med, 241
Mea Shearim, 307
Meats, 7, 10
  leftover, 78
  roasted, at Seder meal, 239
  on Shabbat, 16
  beef
    chunks, Israel-style kebabs of,
      Shashlik* (M), 325–26

brisket, easy wine-marinated (M),
    151
  fruit and peanut curry (M), 189
  liver, broiling, 7
  -potato matzo pie, Mina de carne*
    (M), 268
  pot roast, zippy cranberry (M), 35
  stew, long-cooked, Cholent (M),
    38–39
  stew, long-cooked, North African-
    style, Dafina, 40–42
  stew, with seven vegetables,
    Couscous aux sept légumes (M),
    83–85
  sweet holiday stew, Yom-tov
    tzimmes* (M), 81–82
  teriyaki marinade (M), 236
  tongue in sweet and sour sauce*
    (M), 257–58
beef, ground
  bulgur loaf stuffed with spiced meat
    and pine nuts, Baked kibbeh
    (M), 116–18
  kebabs, grilled, Mititei* (M), 327–
    28
  and leek patties, Keftes de prassa y
    carne* (M), 256–57
  meatballs in tomato sauce, Israeli-
    style, K'tsitsat basar b'agvaniyot*
    (M), 302–03
  meatloaf with hard-boiled eggs,
    Klops* (M), 328–29
  meatloaf with sesame topping,
    spicy, Kubbah sineeya (M), 304
  spiced, in pita bread (M), 302
  spicy, with fruit and almonds,
    Picadillo* (M), 188–89
  -stuffed mashed potato croquettes,
    Papas rellenas* (M), 114–16
  stuffed cabbage, sweet and sour,
    Holishkes* (M), 111–12
  stuffed vegetables, Mahshi* (M),
    113–14
  stuffed vegetables, Mafroum (M),
    35–37
lamb
  and brown rice pilaf (M), 82–83
  chunks, Israeli-style kebabs of,
    Shashlik* (M), 325–26
  cubed vs. ground, 325, 326
  on Pesach, 237, 238, 239
  stew with seven vegetables,
    Couscous aux sept légumes (M),
    83–85
  teriyaki marinade (M), 236

Meats, lamb *(cont'd)*
lamb, ground
vs. cubed, 325, 327
bulgur loaf stuffed with spiced meat
and pine nuts, Baked kibbeh
(M), 116–118
stuffed vegetables, Mahshi* (M),
113–14
stuffed vegetables, Mafroum (M),
35–37
veal
rolled breast, parsley-stuffed (M),
258–60
Meatballs, in tomato sauce, Israeli-style,
302–3
Meatballs and spaghetti, mock, 212–13
Mediterranean dishes
during Days of Awe, 65
on Lag B'Omer, 320–21
on Yom Ha'Atzmaut, 297–99
Meemounah, 226, 242–43
Megillah, 78, 204, 205, 210, 221
Melavah Malkah, 17, 58
Melon seed milk, Sephardic-style, 104
Memorial Day (Israel), 287
Menenas, 223–26
Menorah, 147, 149, 180, 184
Merenda, 148
Meringues, savory cheese, 160
Meringue triangles, poppy seed, 229–30
Meron, 316–17
Mexican dishes
during Hanukkah, 184
during Pesach, 273–74
on Tu B'Shevat, 188
Mexican-style hot chocolate drink, 184
Mezzeh, 317
Middle East, 5, 6, 19
Middle Eastern dishes
during Days of Awe, 67–69, 82–83,
103
during Hanukkah, 152–53, 168–70,
176–77
as kitniyot during Pesach, 241
on Lag B'Omer, 317–21, 325–28
on Purim, 210, 213, 218–20
on Shabbat, 33, 35–37, 49
on Shavuot, 338, 347
during Sukkot, 113–14, 116–18
on Yom Ha'Atzmaut, 297–99, 302,
304, 308
see also specific countries
Mikvah, 92

Milk
almond milk vs., 103
beer vs., in baked goods, 334
melon seed milk vs., 104
on Shavuot, 337, 368
see also Dairy foods
Mina
de carne, 268
de espinaca y tomat, 265–66
de prassa con queso, 266–67
tuna-vegetable, 266
Miniature cheese turnovers, 353–54
Mishloah manot, 205–6
Mititei, 327–28
Mitzapuny, 108–10
Mitzvah, 15, 38, 63, 140
Mock marzipan, 231–32
Mock spaghetti and meatballs, 212–13
Mohn kichlah, 221–22
Molasses and cornmeal pudding, thick,
138
Mold, brandied cherry-rice, with cherry
sauce, 369–71
Mom's best cheese blintzes, 358–60
Mordecai, 204, 205
Moroccan dishes
during Days of Awe, 62–64, 72–73,
83–88, 90, 91
during Hanukkah, 163–64
during Pesach, 244, 258–60, 262–63
on Purim, 226–28
on Shabbat, 40–42, 49
during Sukkot, 119–21
Moroccan Jews, 163, 242–44, 258–59
Moroccan-style beet greens salad, 91
Moroccan-style beet salad, 90
Moroccan-style fish baked with stuffed
dates, 72–73
Moroccan-style haroset, 244
Moroccan-style lemon chicken with
olives, 85–87
Moroccan-style marzipan petit fours,
226–28
Morocco, 5
Moses, 15, 106, 108, 140, 337, 338, 354, 358
Mothers
haroset symbolism of, 234
postpartum, 55
pregnant and lactating, 103
Mountain of peaks, 341
Mount Sinai, Revelation at, 336, 337, 338,
339, 341, 358
Mount Sinai fruit-and-cheese ball, 341–
42

Mousse
    instant chocolate, 281–82
    simple salmon, 365–66
    sole, turban of sole with, 363–64
Muffins
    with buckwheat groats, kasha (D)
        178–79
    kasha-and-apple (P), 179
    see also Bread
Muflita, 242
Mulled cran-apple-cot swizzle, 139
Mushroom
    kasha pilaf, herbed, 51
    walnut pâté, brandied, 343–44
Mustachados, 286
My mother's chicken soup, 31–33

Nan-e berenji, 228–29
National students' day, 316
Near Eastern dishes
    during Hanukkah, 152–53, 168–70
    as kitniyot during Pesach, 241
    on Shavuot, 338
New Moon, 163
New Year, *see* Rosh Hashanah
New Year of the Trees, 185–203
Nine Days, 152
Nisan, 237, 336
Nockerl, 34
Noodle dumplings
    fruit-filled, 136–37
    homemade farfel, 77
    with pasta, Sephardic-style, 356–57
    tiny, 34
    triangular cheese, 354–56
    triangular meat, 78–79
Noodle pudding, 54, 192–93, 368–69
    Jerusalem, 307
North Africa, 5
North African dishes
    during Days of Awe, 64, 83–87
    during Hanukkah, 168–71, 176–77
    on Lag B'Omer, 327–28
    during Pesach, 274–76
    on Purim, 210
    on Shabbat, 40–42
    on Shavuot, 347
    during Sukkot, 113–14
    on Tu B'Shevat, 194
    on Yom Ha'Atzmaut, 297–99
North African-style long-cooked meat
        stew, 40–42
North America, 5

Nut(s)
    apple strudel, easy Viennese, 132–33
    banana cheesecake squares, 374–75
    chocolate Viennese torte, 279–81
    crunchy dough nuggets in honey, 99–
        100
    fruit confection balls, 203
    fruit stuffing, orange-glazed turkey
        with, 121–23
    haroset—my way, Ashkenazic-style,
        243
    many-layered pastry with honey and,
        218–20
    mixed fruit and, 54–55
    orange-date torte, Sephardic-style,
        274–76
    sweet couscous with dried fruit and,
        163–64
    on Tu B'Shevat, 187, 196–99, 200
    see also specific nuts

Oaf mandarinot in avocado, 305–6
Oaf soomsoom b'rotev dvash, 306
Oaf tapoozim, 45
Oat
    balls, almond-flavored, 231–32
    sesame tahini cookies, 314
Ohayon, Ralph, Suzanne, and Yves, 244
Oil-fried foods, during Hanukkah, 148,
        149, 180
Ojaldres, 350–53
Okra
    with prunes and apricots, Syrian-style,
        92–93
    in tomato sauce, 50
Olive oil, 13
Olives, 85–87, 321
Omer, 287–88, 315, 336, 338
Oneg Shabbat, 67
Onion(s)
    poppy seed crackers, 235–36
    sole with dill and, East Indian-style,
        123–24
Oogat soomsoom v'dvash, 98
Oogiyot soomsoom, 311–12
Oogiyot tahina, 314
Orange
    baked custard, 273–74
    -carrot salad, 297
    chicken, Israeli-style, 45
    -coconut pudding, 313
    flan, caramel-coated, 273–74
    fluff pudding, 312–13

Orange *(cont'd)*
  glazed turkey with fruit-nut stuffing,
    121–23
  honey cake, holiday, 95–96
  -nut-date torte, Sephardic-style, 274–
    76
Orejas de haman, 215, 216–18
Oriental Jews, 6
Ottoman Turkish Empire, 5, 113
Oven-barbecued chicken, 331
Oznai haman, 215, 216–17

Pancakes
  crisp fried, Potato latkes* (P) or (D),
    149–50
  fish and potato, Dutch-style, 30
  fluffy, Cheese-rice latkes (D), 156
  light, thin cheese, Ricotta latkes (D),
    153–54
  matzo meal, Bimuelos de masa* (P),
    254
  matzo meal, with cheese, Bimuelos de
    masa y queso* (D), 255
  sweet matzo fritters, Gremshelish*
    (P), 270–71
  thin buckwheat, Quick blini (D), 154–
    55
  even quicker blini (D), 155–56
  see also Breads
Pan de Espagne, 276–77
Panlevi, 57–58
Papas rellenas, 114–16
Paradesi Synagogue, 124
Pareve (P), 7, 10
Passover, 237–86
Pasta, Sephardic-style noodle dumplings
    with, 356–57
Pasteles, 347
Pastella, 259
Pastry(ies), *see* Desserts
Pâté
  brandied mushroom-walnut, 343–44
  chicken liver, 75–76
Peanut butter
  carob fudge, easy, 333–34
  -soy marinade/sauce, 330
Peanuts, in meat and fruit curry, 189
Pears poached in red wine, 271
Peas, black-eyed, in tomato sauce, 93–94
Pentecost, 336
Pepitada, 104
Pepper, sweet green
  roasted, and tomato salad, 49

Persian Jews, 204, 217
Pesach, 237–86
  and agriculture, 237
  hadgi badam, 285–86
  history of, 237–38
  Meemounah as conclusion of, 242
  other holiday references to, 15, 19, 67,
    105, 148, 226, 288, 315, 336
  Seder, 237, 238–41
  sponge cake, 276–77
Pescado con agristada, 249–50
Pesce all'ebraica, 74–75
Petit fours, Moroccan-style marzipan,
    226–28
Picadillo, 188
Pie, spicy chicken and almond, in filo,
    119–21
Pignoli, 13–14
Pilaf
  brown rice, 53
  herbed kasha-mushroom, 51
  lamb and brown rice, 82–83
  rice, grape leaves filled with, 322–24
Pineapple
  kebabs, Israeli-style, 325–26
  sweet potato casserole, 94–95
Pine nuts, 13–14
  bulgur-meat loaf stuffed with spiced
    meat and, 116–18
Pinyonati, 99–100
Pita bread
  with chick-pea and sesame spread, 294
  dips, 293–95, 297–98
  with meat and vegetable soup,
    Yemenite-style, 300–301
  preparing and baking, 308
  spiced ground beef in, 302
  spicy chick-peas and rice in, 213–14
  spicy ground beef with fruit and
    almonds in, 188
  triangles, 310–11
  whole wheat, 308–10
Plum
  knedliky or knaidlah, 126–29
  kreplah or varenikes, sweet, 136–37
Pocket bread, flat, round, 308–10
Poires bourguignonne, 271
Polish Jews, 178, 331
Pomegranates, 62–63
Poppy seed(s), 14
  cookies, Queen Esther's, 221–22
  filling, hamantaschen with, 214–16
  -meringue triangles, 229–30
  -onion crackers, 235–36
  pound cake, 233–34

Portugal, 5
Potato(es)
  cheese filling, 348–49
  croquettes, meat-stuffed mashed, 114–16
  dumplings, finger-sized, 129–30
  dumplings, fruit-filled, 126–29
  farfel dairy soup, Bubby Rose's, 157
  and fish cakes, Dutch-style, 30
  latkes, 149–50
  meat matzo pie, 268
  shredding, 149
  stuffed, Libyan-style, 35–37
Pot roast, zippy cranberry, 35
Poultry
  relish for, 125–26
  on Shabbat, 16
  chicken
    and almond pie in filo, spicy, Bestilia (M), 119–21
    and banana sate (M), 329–30
    and brandied cherry sauce (M), 47
    with kumquats (or apricots), Israeli-style (M), 190–91
  lemon, with olives, Moroccan-style, Djada zetoon* (M), 85–87
  orange, Israeli-style, Oaf tapoozim (M), 45
  oven-barbecued (M), 331
  and rice, Iraqi-style, Tabeet (M), 43–44
  scaloppine with zucchini in avgolemono sauce* (M), 260–61
  spaghetti and, Syrian-style (M), 46
  spicy, with tomatoes and sesame seeds (M), 88
  stew with seven vegetables, Couscous aux sept legumes (M), 83–85
  stuffing, *see* Stuffing
  tagine of, with prunes and almonds* (M), 262–63
  tangerine, with avocado, Oaf mandarinot b'avocado (M), 305–6
  tidbits, sesame, with honey dipping sauce, Oaf soomsoom b'dvash (M), 306
  before Yom Kippur fast, 63
Rock Cornish hens
  with Cumberland glaze (M), 47–48
turkey
  orange-glazed, with fruit-nut stuffing* (M), 121–23

scaloppine with zucchini in avolemono sauce* (M), 260–61
  schnitzel, Israel-style (M), 206–7
  stuffing, *see* Stuffing
Pound cake, poppy seed, 233–34
Praakes, 111–12
Preserved whole kumquats, 191–92
Pretzels
  caraway-rye, 183
  soft, for Hanukkah, 179–83
  whole wheat (with cheese), 179
P'ri Etz Hadar, 186
Prunes
  okra with apricots and, Syrian-style, 92–93
  tagine of chicken with almonds and, 262–63
Pudding, *see* Desserts
Puréed apple-squash soup, 110
Purim, 204–36
  celebration of, 204–6
  history of, 204
  other holiday dishes on, 78, 99, 100, 165, 241
Purim Se'udah, 205, 206, 212, 230
Purimspiels, 205
Pyota, 234–35

Queen Esther's cookies, 221–22
Queen Esther's Toast, 205

Raf'refet tapoozim, 312–13
Raf'refet tapoozim v'cocus, 313
Raised dough cake, 133–35
Raki, 205
Ram's horn, 61
"Rejoicing in the Law," 108
Relish, harvest-time cranberry, 125–26
Rhodes, 104
Rice
  almond stuffing for dates, 73
  black beans, Cuban-style, 51–53
  brown, mock spaghetti and meatballs, 212–13
  brown, spiced lentils and, 152–53
  cheese latkes, 156
  cherry mold, brandied, with cherry sauce, 369–71
  and chicken, Iraqi-style, 43–44
  fluffy pancakes, 156
  during Pesach, 241, 262
  pudding, creamy, 373–74
  on Shavuot, 337–38
  spicy chick-peas and, 213–14

Rice-flour shortbread cookies, 228–29
Rice pilaf, brown, 53
  grape leaves filled with, 322–24
  lamb and, 82–83
Ricotta latkes, 153–54
Rock Cornish hens with Cumberland
  glaze, 47–48
Romanian dishes
  during Hanukkah, 177–78
  on Lag B'Omer, 327–28
  on Shavuot, 366–68
Romanian-style corn bread, 177–78
Romanian-style cornmeal with cheese,
  366–68
Romans, 3, 315–16
Rosettes dipped in honey syrup, fried,
  168–70
Rose water, 14
Rosh Hashanah, 61–104
  culinary traditions of, 61–63
  dishes, 61–67, 72–76, 81–85, 90–100
  foods avoided on, 63
  other holiday dishes on, 106, 125, 176,
    193, 206, 257
  sweet foods on, 61–62, 64
Rosh Hashanah Le'Ilanot, 185–203
Rosh Hodesh, 163
Rossel, 241
Russia, 4
Russian dishes
  during Hanukkah, 154–55, 158, 178–79
  on Lag B'Omer, 325–26, 331–33
  on Shabbat, 51
  on Shavuot, 338
  during Sukkot, 108–10
Russian-style yogurt-barley soup, 158
Ruth, Book of, 339
Rye flour
  bread, kneaded one-rise, 333
  caraway bread, no-knead, 331–33
  caraway seed pretzels, 183

Sabayon, 272
Sabras, 245
Salads
  beet, Moroccan-style, Barba* (P), 90
  beet greens, Moroccan-style, Selka*
    (P), 91
  bulgur wheat and vegetable, Tabouleh
    (P), 319–20
  carrot-citrus, Gezer hai* (P), 297
  coleslaw for a crowd* (P), 321–22

cottage cheese and vegetable, Spring
    salad* (P), 340–41
  cranberry relish, harvest-time* (P),
    125–26
  eggplant, Salat hatzilim* (P), 297–99
  first fruits rainbow* (P), 339–40
  green beans with leeks and carrots,
    Turkish-style (P), 89
  herbed white bean and artichoke,
    Ensalada de avicas y enginaras
    (P), 317–18
  kibbutz-style fresh vegetable, Salat
    b'nusah kibbutz* (P), 295–96
  okra in tomato sauce, 50
  roasted pepper and tomato* (P), 49
  on Shabbat, 49
  spring, 340–41
  vegetable, 317
  on Yom Ha'Atzmaut, 296
Salat
  b'nusah kibbutz, 295–96
  hatzilim, 297–99
Salmon, *see* Fish
Saloona, 208–9
Salt, 16
  kashering, 7
Sambusik, 209–12
Sate, chicken-banana, 329–30
Sauce
  avgolemono, 249, 260–61
  brandied cherry, 47
  cherry, 370–71
  egg-lemon, 249–50
  garlic-tomato, 28
  honey dipping, 306
  horseradish, 251–54
  onion-tomato, 36, 37
  spicy tomato, 27–28
  sweet-sour, 208, 209, 257–58
  tarragon-tomato, 31
  tomato, 50, 94, 114, 251, 303
Saville, Pauline Rubens, 69–70
Scandinavian dish, on Purim, 206
Schav, 338
Schmaltz, 5, 148, 149, 177
Schnitzel, Israeli-style turkey, 206–7
Sciatic nerve, 7
Seafood, kosher, 6
Seder, Pesach, 237
  ceremony, 238–41
  dinner, 243–86
  no leavened grain at, 240–41
  plate, 238–39, 252
Seder, Tu B'Shevat, 186–87

Seeds, 14
  symbolism of, 63, 98
  on Tu B'Shevat, 199
  see also specific seeds
Sefirah, 315, 316
Sefirat Ha'Omer, 315
Selka, 91
Semolina pellets, steamed, 83–85, 163–64
Sephardic dishes, xiii, 4–6, 8
  during Days of Awe, 61–62, 65–67,
    76, 89, 90, 92–94, 99–100
  during Hanukkah, 148, 149, 152–53,
    164–66, 176–77
  on Lag B'Omer, 317–18
  during Pesach, 243, 246–51, 254–60,
    262–71, 274–78, 284–86
  on Purim, 205, 206, 216–20, 222–23,
    226–28, 234–35
  on Shabbat, 16, 27–28, 33, 40–42, 50,
    55–58
  on Shavuot, 337, 338, 347–53, 356–57,
    369–71, 373–74
  on Tu B'Shevat, 191–94
Sephardic-style date haroset, 246–47
Sephardic-style fried Haman's Ears
  cookies, 216–18
Sephardic-style long-cooked eggs, 248–
  49
Sephardic-style melon seed milk, 104
Sephardic-style noodle dumplings with
  pasta, 356–57
Sephardic-style orange-nut-date torte,
  274–76
Sephardic-style wheat berry pudding,
  193–94
Sephardim, 4–6, 8, 121, 124
  kitniyot during Pesach for, 241
  modern Hebrew and, 10
  and Seder ceremony, 240
  and Seder dinner, 242, 248, 265, 268
  sorting rice during Pesach by, 241
  Tu B'Shevat celebration of, 185, 186
Sesame paste
  and chick-pea spread, 294–95
  dip or dressing, lemony, 293–94
  eggplant dip, 318–19
  tahini-oat cookies, 314
  topping, spicy meat loaf with, 304
Sesame seed(s), 14
  anise rings, savory, 67–69
  candies, crunchy, 176–77
  carob halvah, 202–3
  chicken tidbits with honey dipping
    sauce, 306

honeyed cake, 98
ring cookies, 56–57
spicy chicken with tomatoes and, 88
sticks or rings, 311–12
Se'udah Shelisheet, 15, 16–17
Seven, symbolism of, 16, 84
Seven heavens, 338
Seven Species, 336, 337
Shabbat, 15–60, 65, 84, 287*n*, 337
  bread, Yemenite, 26–27
  explanation of, 15–16
  meals for, 15–17
  other holiday dishes on, 83, 115, 135–36,
    177, 208, 248–50
  no fire on, 16, 38
Shabbat Queen, 24–25, 58
Shabbat queen, sweet crowns for the,
    24–25
Shalah manot, 205–6, 209, 226, 228, 230,
    232, 233
Shamash candle, 181
Shashlik, 325–26
Shavuot, 336–75
  and agriculture, 336–38
  bread on, 315, 336, 338
  dairy foods on, 337–38, 339, 341
  fresh fruits on, 338, 339
  other holiday references to, 64, 105,
    288, 315
  rice on, 337–38
  wheat on, 315, 336
Sheheheyanu prayer, 62
Shemini Atzeret, 107–8
Shevat, 185
Shewbread, 20
Shish kebab, 325
Shortbread cookies
  date-filled, 223–26
  rice-flour, 228–29
Shtetls, 4, 108, 111, 178, 195
Shushan Purim, 205
Side dishes
  beans
    black beans, Cuban-style, Frijoles
      negros (P), 51–53
    black-eyed peas in tomato sauce,
      Lubiya (P), 93–94
    chick-peas and rice, spicy (P), 213–
      14
    lentils and rice, spiced, Enjadara
      (P), 152–53
  dumplings
    finger-sized potato, Slishkas (D) or
      (P), 129–30

Side dishes, dumplings *(cont'd)*
fruit-filled noodle, Sweet plum
kreplah (D) or (P), 136–37
fruit-filled potato, Plum knedliky
(D) or (P), 126–29
homemade noodle farfel (P), 77
in meat stew, 40
noodle, triangular, Cheese kreplah
(D), 354–56
noodle, triangular, Meat kreplah
(M), 78–79
noodle, with pasta, Sephardic-style,
Calsones (D), 356–57
tiny cheese, Topfenknodel (D),
161–62
tiny noodle, Galushka (P), 34
grains
brown rice pilaf (M), 53
cornmeal with cheese, Romanian-
style, Mamaliga (D), 366–68
herbed kasha-mushroom pilaf (M),
51
herbed walnut stuffing balls (M),
130–31
kugels, lokshen
dried fruit (P), 192–93
fruity tofu (P), 54
Jerusalem noodle pudding, Kugel
Yerushalayim (P), 307
sweet noodle pudding, Rich and
Fruity (D), 368–69
vegetables
celeriac and carrots, Apio* (P), 264
fruit-and-vegetable tzimmes* (P),
125
green beans with leeks and carrots,
Turkish style (P), 89
okra in tomato sauce, Bamia* (P),
50
okra with prunes and apricots,
Syrian-style* (P), 92–93
spinach-cheese casserole, Fritada de
espinaca* (D), 269
sunshine carrot coins* (P), 91–92
sweet potato and apple tzimmes*
(P), 263
sweet potato-pineapple casserole*
(D) or (P), 94–95
Siete cielos, 338
Simhat Torah, 108, 140
Sinai desert, 19
Singing Kettle, The, 172
Sisterhood of the Deal Synagogue, 67,
93

Six Day War (1967), 288
Slaughtering animals, 7
Slishkas, 129–30
Snack(s)
fruit and nuts, mixed, Ja'alah (P), 54–
55
poppy seed-onion crackers (P), 235–36
savory cheese meringues, Cheese puffs
(D), 160
savory cheese wafers, Cheese "coins"
(D), 159
savory sesame-anise rings, Ka'ak (P),
67–69
sesame sticks or rings, Oogiyot
soomsoom (P), 311–12
soft pretzels for Hanukkah (P) or
(D), 179–83
Sole, *see* Fish
Song of Songs, 337
Soofganiyot, 166–67
Soomsoom, 311
Sopa de huevo y limon, 76
Sopa de lentijas, 33
Soufflé, spinach, 269
Soup
Bubby Rose's farfel-potato dairy (D),
157
cherry, Hungarian-style (D), 345–46
chicken, my mother's* (M), 31–33
chilled mixed-fruit, Marak payrot*
(P) or (D), 299–300
chilled spiced apple (D), 346–47
diamonds royale* (M), 255–56
egg-lemon, Avgolemono (M), 76
garnishes, 34, 77–81, 255–56
light and easy strawberry (D), 344–45
meat and vegetable, Yemenite-style,
Marak taymahni* (M), 300–301
meaty split pea, bean, and barley,
Mitzapuny (M), 108–10
nuts, Mandlen (P), 80–81
puréed apple-squash* (M), 110
red lentil (M), 33
yogurt-barley, Russian-style, Spas
(D), 158
South African dishes
during Hanukkah, 172–73
on Lag B'Omer, 329–30
during Pesach, 250
on Tu B'Shevat, 189
South American dishes, during Sukkot,
115
Southern-style sole and corn bread
casserole, 364–65

Soutlach, 373–74
Soviet Jews, 240
Soy-peanut marinade/sauce, 330
Spaghetti, Syrian-style chicken and, 46
Spaghetti and meatballs, mock, 212–13
Spain, 5
Spanakopetes, 350–53
Spanish, Castilian, 5–6
Spanish dishes, during Pesach, 273–74
Spanish Inquisition, 5, 41, 57, 124
Spatzle, 34
Spas, 158
Spier, Gerald, 258
Spier, Ginette, 226, 258–59
Spinach
    -cheese casserole, 269
    and cheese in flaky pastry, 350–53
    feta filling, 350–53
    lasagne with three cheeses and, 361–63
    soufflé, 269
    -tomato matzo pie, 265–66
    turban of sole with sole mousse, 363–64
Spinning top, 159
"Spin the Dreidel," 166
Split pea soup, meaty bean, barley and, 108–10
Sponge cake, Pesach, 276–77
Spring salad, 340–41
Squash, 62
    apple soup, puréed, 110
    mock spaghetti and meatballs, 212–13
Star of David pretzel, 182
Stew(s)
    long-cooked meat, 38–39
    long-cooked meat, North African-style, 40–42
    meat, with seven vegetables, 83–85
    Sabbath, 38–42
    sweet holiday, 81–82
Strawberry(ies)
    heart of cream with, 371–72
    soup, light and easy, 344–45
Streusel-topped gingerbread gems, 232–33
Strudel
    dried-fruit, 196–99
    easy Viennese apple-nut, 132–33
Strudel leaves, *see* Filo
Stuffing
    double corn bread, 131
    fruit-nut, 121–23
    herbed kasha-mushroom pilaf, 51
    herbed walnut-bread, balls, 130–31.
    parsley, 259–60

Sugar, caramelized, 273–74
Sukariyot soomsoom, 176–77
Sukkah, 106, 139, 140
Sukkah, gingerbread, 140–46
    baking lattice roof, 143
    baking walls for, 142–43
    cutting dough for, 142
    decorating and assembling, 144–46
    patterns for, 140–42
    storing baked pieces, 143
Sukkot, 78, 81, 105–46, 336
    and agriculture, 105, 106–7, 140
    booths during, 105–6, 140
    festival of, 106–8
    Hoshanah Rabbah in, 107, 205
    stuffed foods during, 107, 111
Sunflower seed(s)
    carob-sesame halvah, 202–3
    sesame tahini-oat cookies, 314
Sweet-and-sour fish, Italian-style, 74–75
Sweet-and-sour stuffed cabbage, 111–12
Sweet crowns for the Shabbat queen, 24–25
Sweet potato(es)
    and apple tzimmes, 263
    -pineapple casserole, 94–95
    symbolism of, 94
Sweet-sour sauce, 208, 209, 257–58
Swizzle, mulled cran-apple-cot, 139
Syrian dishes
    during Days of Awe, 64, 67–69, 92–93
    on Shabbat, 46
    on Shavuot, 347
    during Sukkot, 116–18
    on Tu B'Shevat, 194
Syrian-style chicken and spaghetti, 46
Syrian-style okra with prunes and apricots, 92–93
Syrup
    cardamom, fried pastry balls soaked in, 174–75
    see also Honey syrup

Tabeet, 43–44
Tabouleh, 319–20
Tagine of chicken with prunes and almonds, 262–63
Tahina, 14, 290, 292, 293–94
Tahini, 14, 202, 293
    carob-sesame halvah, 202–3
    sesame, oat cookies, 314
    spicy meat loaf with, 304

"Taking challah," 20
Talmud, 15, 16, 17, 186
Tangerine chicken with avocado, 305–6
Tarnegol hodu, 206
Tart, jam-filled, 59–60
Taygleh, 99–100
Temple, First Holy, 5, 16, 20, 105, 147,
     180, 238, 239, 315, 336, 338, 339
Temple, Second Holy, 20, 238, 239, 315
Temple, Third Holy, 316
Ten Commandments, Two Tablets of,
     338, 341, 342, 358
Teriyaki marinade, 326
Tex-Mex dip, 343
Tikun Leil Shavuot, 339
Time of Our Gladness, The, 105
Time of the Giving of Our Law, The,
     336
Tisha B'Av, 152
Tishpishti para Pesach, 277–78
Tishri, 61, 106
Toast, melted cheese over, 160–61
Tofu, lokshen kugel, fruity, 54
Toledano, Rabbi Joshua, 40–41, 242
Tomato(es)
     cheese and chili pepper dip, 343
     and roasted pepper salad, 49
     spicy chicken with sesame seeds and,
          88
     -spinach matzo pie, 265–66
Tomato sauce, 50, 94, 114, 251, 303
     garlic, 28
     onion, 36, 37
     spicy, 27–28
     tarragon, 31
Tongue, in sweet-and-sour sauce, 257–58
Topfenknodel, 161–62
Torah, 17, 20, 108, 316, 336–39, 354, 367–
     69, 371
Torte
     hazelnut-chocolate Viennese, 279–81
     orange-nut-date, Sephardic-style,
          274–76
Transliterations, 10
Travados, 222–23
Trifleh, 34
Tscholent, 38
Tu B'shevat, 185–203
     customs and traditions of, 185–86
     history of, 185
     Seder, 186–87
Tulkoff, Harry and Lena, 252
Tulkoff, Martin, 251–52
Tulkoff's horseradish, 251–52
Tuna-vegetable mina, 266

Turban of sole with sole mousse, 363–64
Turkey, *see* Poultry
Turkish, 6
Turkish delight, 108
Turkish dishes
     during Days of Awe, 64, 76, 89, 93–
          94, 104
     during Hanukkah, 148, 164–66, 170–
          71
     on Lag B'Omer, 317–18, 322–24
     during Pesach, 245, 249–51, 256–57,
          260–61, 264–67, 277–78, 286
     on Purim, 218–20
     on Shabbat, 55, 56–57
     on Shavuot, 347, 350, 373
     during Sukkot, 113–14
     on Tu B'Shevat, 193–94
Turkish Jews, on Tu B'Shevat, 186
Turkish-style green beans with leeks and
     carrots, 89
Turkish-style haroset, 245–46
Turnovers
     chicken or meat, Iraqi-style, 209–12
     miniature cheese, 353–54
Tzimmes
     fruit-and-vegetable, 125
     sweet potato and apple, 263
     Yom-Tov, 81–82

Union of Jewish Women, 172

Varenikes
     cheese, 354–56
     sweet plum, 136–37
Veal breast, rolled parsley-stuffed, 258–
     60
Vegetable(s), 7
     broth, 29
     and bulgur wheat salad, 319–20
     and cottage cheese salad, 340–41
     during Days of Awe, 61, 62, 90
     fruit casserole, 263
     and fruit tzimmes, 125
     at kibbutzim, 295–96
     and meat soup, Yemenite-style, 300–
          301
     meat-stuffed, 113–134
     my mother's chicken soup, 31–33
     pastries filled with cheese and, 347–50
     salad, kibbutz-style fresh, 295–96
     salads, 317
     and salmon in sweet-sour sauce, 208–
          9
     in Seder dinner, 242

at Seder meal, 238
seven, meat stew with, 83–85
spread, 320–21
stuffed, Libyan-style, 35–37
during Sukkot, 106–7, 108
sweet holiday stew, 81–82
tuna mina, 266
Viennese apple-nut strudel, easy, 132–33
Viennese dishes
during Hanukkah, 161–62
during Pesach, 279–81
during Sukkot, 132–33
Viennese torte, hazelnut-chocolate, 279–81
Vischkoekjes, 30

Wafers, savory cheese, 159
Walnut(s)
creamy date pudding with, 202
filled crescent cookies, 222–23
haroset, Moroccan-style, 244
haroset—my way, Ashkenazic-style, 243
haroset, Turkish-style, 245–46
macaroons, 286
mushroom pâté, brandied, 343–44
stuffing balls, herbed, 130–31
Weeks, 336
Welsh rabbit, 160–61
Wheat
pudding, cracked, 194
on Shavuot, 315, 336
symbolism of, 193
Wheat berry pudding, Sephardic-style, 193–94
Wheat cereal pudding, Greek-style, 234–35
White bean and artichoke salad, herbed, 317–18
White foods, symbolism of, 20, 69, 72, 103, 241, 337, 367, 369, 371
Whole wheat
pita, 308–10
poppy seed-onion crackers, 235–36
soft pretzels for Hanukkah, 179–83
Wine
chicken liver pâté, 75–76
custard, Italian-style foamy, 272
haroset, Moroccan-style, 244
haroset—my way, Ashkenazic-style, 243
marinated brisket, easy, 151
on Purim, 205

red, pears poached in, 271
for Seder ceremony, 240
at Tu B'Shevat Seder, 186–87

Yalanji dolmas, 322–24
Yamim Nora'im, 61
Yeast cake, filled and rolled, 133–35
Yemenite dishes
during Days of Awe, 62, 63
during Hanukkah, 168–70
on Lag B'Omer, 325–26
during Pesach, 247
on Shabbat, 26–27, 54–55
on Yom Ha'Atzmaut, 300–301
Yemenite Shabbat bread, 26–27
Yemenite-style haroset, 247
Yemenite-style meat and vegetable soup, 300–301
Yiddish, 4, 5, 10
Yogurt-barley soup, Russian-style, 158
Yom Ha'Atzmaut, 287–314
celebrations of, 287–89
history of, 288
other holiday dishes on, 176, 288
Yom Ha'Zikaron, 287
Yom Kippur, 61–104, 107, 140, 205
beating symbolized during, 78
break-the-fast dishes, 61, 63–71, 74–76, 85–87, 95–96, 100–104
culinary traditions of, 63–64
fast, 61, 63
pre-fast meal, 63, 78
sweet foods before and after fast of, 61–62, 64
Yom tov, 7
Yom-Tov round challah, 64–67
Yom-Tov tzimmes, 81–82
Yom Yerushalayim, 287–314
history and celebration of, 288, 289

Zabaglione, 272
Zandman, Denise Saville and Dov, 27–28
Zandman, Liora Ben-Chaim, 35
Zelebi, 168–70
Zemen Matan Torahtenu, 336
Zeman Simhatenu, 106
Zeroah, 239
Zimsterne, 101–2
Zlabia, 168–70
Zohar, 316
Zucchini in avgolemono sauce, chicken scaloppine with, 260–61
Zvingous, 170–71